State Politics and Redistricting

Part I

Congressional Quarterly Inc.

Congressional Quarterly Inc., an editorial research service and publishing company, serves clients in the fields of news, education, business and government. It combines specific coverage of Congress, government and politics by Congressional Quarterly with the more general subject range of an affiliated service, Editorial Research Reports.

Congressional Quarterly was founded in 1945 by Henrietta and Nelson Poynter. Its basic periodical publication was and still is the CQ *Weekly Report,* mailed to clients every Saturday. A cumulative index is published quarterly.

CQ also publishes a variety of books. The CQ *Almanac,* a compendium of legislation for one session of Congress, is published every spring. *Congress and the Nation* is published every four years as a record of government for one presidential term. Other books include paperbacks on public affairs and text-books for college political science classes.

The public affairs books are designed as timely reports to keep journalists, scholars and the public abreast of developing issues, events and trends.

They include such recent titles as *The Soviet Union, Elections '82, Dollar Politics and Budgeting for America.* College textbooks, prepared by outside scholars and published under the CQ Press imprint, include such recent titles as *Regulation and Its Alternatives, Change and Continuity in the 1980 Elections, Invitation to Struggle: Congress, the President and Foreign Policy; The Politics of Shared Power: Congress and the Executive; and Congress and Its Members.*

In addition, CQ publishes *The Congressional Monitor,* a daily report on present and future activities of congressional committees. This service is supplemented by *The Congressional Record Scanner,* an abstract of each day's *Congressional Record,* and *Congress in Print,* a weekly listing of committee publications.

CQ Direct Research is a consulting service that performs contract research and maintains a reference library and query desk for clients.

Editorial Research Reports covers subjects beyond the specialized scope of Congressional Quarterly. It publishes reference material on foreign affairs, business, education, cultural affairs, national security, science and other topics of news interest. Service to clients includes a 6,000-word report published four times a month, bound and indexed semi-annually. Editorial Research Reports publishes paperback books in its field of coverage. Founded in 1923, the service merged with Congressional Quarterly in 1956.

Library of Congress Cataloging in Publication Data

Main entry under title:

State Politics and Redistricting

Includes index.
1. The United States. Congress. House--Election districts. 2. Election districts--United States. I. Congressional Quarterly, Inc.
JK1341.S73 1982   328.73'07345   82-7261
ISBN 0-87187-233-1 (set)   AACR2

Editor: Lynda McNeil
Supervisory Editor: Alan Ehrenhalt
Contributors: Martha Angle, Christopher Buchanan, Robert Benenson, Christopher Colford, Rhodes Cook, Phil Duncan, Shirley Elder, Michael Glennon, Diane Granat, Rob Gurwitt, Robert E. Healy, Norman Kurz, Larry Light, Mary McNeil, Albert Menendez, Warden Moxley, Ann Pelham, Stuart Rothenberg
Design: Mary McNeil
Cover: Richard Pottern
Graphics: Cheryl Rowe
Production Manager: I. D. Fuller
Assistant Production Manager: Maceo Mayo

Book Department

David R. Tarr   *Director*
Joanne D. Daniels   *Director, CQ Press*
John L. Moore   *Associate Editor*
Michael D. Wormser   *Associate Editor*
Martha V. Gottron   *Senior Editor*
Barbara R. de Boinville   *Senior Editor, CQ Press*
Lynda McNeil   *Assistant Editor*
Margaret C. Thompson   *Assistant Editor*
Susan Sullivan   *Developmental Editor, CQ Press*
Diane C. Hill   *Editor/Writer*
Sari Horwitz   *Editor/Writer*
Nancy Lammers   *Editor/Writer*
Mary McNeil   *Editor/Writer*
Janet Hoffman   *Indexer*
Carolyn Goldinger   *Researcher/Editorial Assistant*
Patricia Rusotto   *Researcher*
Esther Wyss   *Researcher*
Patricia Ann O'Connor   *Contributing Editor*
Elder Witt   *Contributing Editor*

Congressional Quarterly Inc.

Eugene Patterson   *Editor and President*
Wayne P. Kelley   *Publisher*
Peter A. Harkness   *Executive Editor*
Robert E. Cuthriell   *Director, Research and Development*
Robert C. Hur   *General Manager*
I.D. Fuller   *Production Manager*
Maceo Mayo   *Assistant Production Manager*
Sydney E. Garriss   *Computer Services*

Contents

Editors note: In 1964 the Supreme Court mandated that populations of congressional districts within states must be made as equal as possible. District lines were drawn to reflect the "one-man, one-vote" principle for the first time in 1972. But the 1980 Census revealed that major shifts in population had occurred in the United States during the past ten years and that some legislators were representing districts nearly twice the size of their neighboring districts. In 1982, after a year of slow progress and bitter argument over new congressional districting, Republicans and Democrats alike were still struggling to come up with district lines that ensured safe seats for members of their own party and weak seats for members of the opposition. Meanwhile, other interests at stake in redistricting — such as the preservation of community boundaries and the grouping of constituencies with similar concerns — were being brushed aside. By April 26, 1982, district maps had been completed in 31 states, but 5 of those maps remained under legal challenge or were subject to Justice Department review. In 13 states, final action had not been taken. *State Politics and Redistricting* examines the 20 states that had successfully redrawn their congressional district boundaries by that time. Within each state the districts are discussed individually, and include descriptions of geography, population composition, major employers, concerns in the district and the election outlook for incumbents. The book also contains a name index of incumbents and their opponents. *State Politics and Redistricting* is one of CQ's public affairs books, which are designed as timely reports to keep journalists, scholars and the public abreast of issues, events and trends.

A Recipe for Gerrymandering

The nobly aimed "one-man, one-vote" principle is coming into increasing use as a weapon for state legislators bent on partisan gerrymandering.

From California to New Jersey and points in between, Republicans and Democrats alike are justifying highly partisan remaps by demonstrating respect for the 1964 Supreme Court mandate that populations of congressional districts within states must be made as equal as possible.

Meanwhile, other interests at stake in redistricting — such as the preservation of community boundaries and the grouping of constituencies with similar concerns — are being brushed aside. The people drawing the lines recognize that courts worship at the altar of population equality.

Those conclusions are emerging after a year of slow progress and bitter argument about the new congressional districts required by the 1980 census. By April 23, 1982, district maps had been completed in 31 states, but 5 of those maps remained under legal challenge or were subject to Justice Department review. In 13 states, final action had not been taken. Six states elect one House member at-large and do not have to draw districts. *(Box, p. 3)*

The work so far shows that redistricting will not be the GOP windfall once talked about; Democratic cartographers are proving more than the equal of their Republican counterparts. The ultimate partisan impact is hard to assess, because few of the large states have completed their work.

Equal and Political

But what is strikingly clear is the new relationship between population equality and raw politics.

When the Supreme Court handed down its *Wesberry v. Sanders* ruling in 1964, congressional districts in many states were malapportioned to favor rural interests over urban dwellers, or to make nearly impossible the election of a black candidate to the House. In Georgia, one district had more than three times as many people as another, and the state Legislature had not redrawn district lines in more than 30 years.

Responding to court pressure, 39 states realigned district boundaries between 1964 and 1970. But since legislators were working from outdated 1960 census figures, significant population inequalities among districts persisted.

Meaningful implementation of the one-man, one-vote standard had to wait until publication of the 1970 census figures. In 1972, voters elected representatives to the House from districts of nearly equal population for the first time in history.

A decade ago, there still was lingering suspicion in many legislatures of the relatively new notion that one vote should have the same weight as another. Making district populations equal was seen by many legislators as a chore.

That has changed. Legislators who were then uncomfortable with one-man, one-vote are now eager to use it to the advantage of their party. More than ever before, the dominant theme of redistricting has been partisanship.

In California, candidates will run this year in districts carefully crafted to meet the strictures of one-man, one-vote. In a state of nearly 24 million people, the average population variance among the districts is only 67 people.

But while approaching mathematical precision in its population standards, the map blithely disregards traditional community boundaries as it winds through the state throwing GOP incumbents together and creating territories where Democratic candidates should enjoy an edge. It was drawn as a partisan document by Democratic Rep. Phillip Burton, and the Legislature approved it without even seeing a copy. One of its new constituencies, designed to protect Rep. John L. Burton, D-Calif., Phillip Burton's brother, links together two disparate Democratic communities north of San Francisco whose only geographical link is a body of water. Ironically, once the remap was in place, John Burton announced he would not seek re-election.

Meanwhile, Indiana Republicans were taking advantage of their hold on the governorship and the Legislature to draw a plan that concentrates most Democratic voters in three districts and gives each of the remaining seven a good-sized Republican base. As in California, the lines weave in and out of counties, disregarding traditional community boundaries. The lines of Indiana's 8th District run down Third Street in the city of Bloomington, in an effort to protect a Republican incumbent.

But as in California, the population variance among districts was low enough to make a court challenge on that basis impossible.

A three-judge federal panel in Missouri accepted a Democratic remap proposal that dismantles a district in the south-central part of the state, where population is growing, and saves a district in inner-city St. Louis, where population declined markedly in the 1970s. The plan places two Republican incumbents at a distinct disadvantage for 1982. The judges said population equality was their most

1

important criterion in selecting a plan, and they chose the Democratic map because it "achieves population equality better than any plan submitted to this court. . . . "

Redistricting in New Jersey and Arizona offers further proof that political, economic and social communities are increasingly vulnerable to fragmentation by partisan legislators whose computers can redraw districts nearly equal in population.

The emphasis on one-man, one-vote not only permits gerrymandering, it encourages it. In many states, it is impossible to approach population equality without crossing city, county and township lines. Once the legislature recognizes that move must be made, it is only a short step further to the drawing of a line that dances jaggedly through every region of the state. Local interests, informed that it is no longer legally permissible to draw a whole-county congressional map in most states, are far less likely to object than they were in the past.

It is difficult to tell whether or not the average voter cares that a party computer is drawing serpentine congressional boundaries through the community. One indication of popular sentiment will come in June 1982, when California holds a referendum on the Democratic-passed remap. Republicans gathered more than 900,000 signatures to force the ballot question. And in Oklahoma, Republicans have submitted a petition that calls for a vote to overturn a Democratic remap that gathers several previously separated GOP areas into one district. The state Supreme Court is reviewing the petition.

The residents of Hot Springs, Ark., and surrounding Garland County, have demonstrated that sometimes people do care where redistricting puts them. Disturbed that the Legislature's remap transferred them out of the constituency they had been in since 1966, the Hot Springs group filed suit in federal court to block the move.

The real complaint was that Hot Springs wanted to keep its Republican U.S. representative, John Paul Hammerschmidt. But rather than relying on a community interest argument, the Hot Springs group pointed out that the remap they preferred came closer to population equality than the Legislature's map.

Even though the Legislature's plan left a population variance among the districts of less than 2 percent — smaller than numerous maps routinely approved elsewhere in the country — the federal panel imposed a plan with less than a 1 percent population variance. The court's decision to reject a tiny deviation in favor of an even smaller one may further encourage the hairsplitting numbers game that has given rise to partisan gerrymanders all over the country. But it will not help those who oppose the political fragmentation of communities, since the case was not argued on that basis.

Divide and Dilute

While courts have been concentrating on population, the Reagan administration has been doing something for which it has received little attention — assuming a role as the protector of black political interests. The department has already struck down two congressional maps approved in 1981 on the grounds that they unfairly divided the influence of black voters through two districts rather than concentrating it in one.

The Justice Department found North Carolina's remap in violation of the Voting Rights Act because it took undue care to leave urban Durham County, which has a politically active one-third black population, out of the mostly rural 2nd District, where blacks compose nearly 40 percent of the population. Democratic Rep. L. H. Fountain had successfully lobbied the state Legislature to keep Durham out of his 2nd District because he feared that its inclusion would open him to a primary challenge from a black candidate.

After the Justice Department ruling, North Carolina legislators put Durham in the 2nd District despite Fountain's objections. Fountain subsequently decided to retire rather than endure the expense of a heated re-election battle in a considerably reshaped district.

In Georgia, the Justice Department ruled that the state Legislature improperly divided a "cohesive black community" in the Atlanta area between the 4th and 5th districts, reducing the chances that either would elect a black candidate to the House.

In North Carolina, Georgia and across the South, black political power has increased markedly since the mid-1960s, and blacks are applying stepped-up pressure for self-representation. In some instances, their demands bring them in direct conflict with white moderates and liberals who share the same outlook on many issues.

The ruling of the Justice Department may prompt the Georgia Legislature to create an Atlanta district that is two-thirds black and would probably elect a black to the House of Representatives. The second Atlanta-area constituency would likely be Republican. The area is currently represented by two white Democrats, both moderate in their political outlook.

The end result of the Justice Department action thus could be that blacks would give up two relatively sympathetic votes in exchange for one personal symbol of racial equality and one voice for conservative social policies.

A similar situation has arisen in Dallas, where blacks have in the past enjoyed considerable influence with two moderate-to-liberal, white, House members, Democrats Martin Frost and Jim Mattox.

During debate over Texas' remap, a group of Dallas blacks and Hispanics called the Coalition for Minority Representation agitated for creation of a 24th District with a minority population large enough to elect one of their own to Congress.

But other blacks and many white Democrats tried to block the coalition's efforts because packing minorities into the 24th sacrificed Democratic control to Republicans in the 5th. The state Legislature nonetheless drew a 24th District with a minority population of 64 percent, and the Justice Department approved that step. But a panel of federal judges undid the Legislature's work, fashioning a 24th with a minority population of 46 percent and protecting Democratic control in the 5th.

The creation of minority districts is the subject of ongoing disagreement within the Democratic Party. Some white moderates and liberals think it is unwise to decrease their overall strength in Congress simply to elect more black members. They think Republicans who join with blacks to draw minority districts are interested primarily in packing urban districts with minority voters so that GOP districts can be created nearby.

Black state legislators from cities such as Dallas and Atlanta, however, feel the symbolism of another black representative in Congress is important. They suspect a strong instinct for self-preservation motivates the thinking of white liberals who stand to lose when minority districts are created.

Congressional Redistricting Status*

State	Number of Districts in 1982		Control of: Legislature	Governor	Status or Schedule for Action
Alabama	7		D	D	Completed.
Arizona	5	(+1)	R	D	Compromise plan agreed to March 22, 1982.
Arkansas	4		D	R	Completed.
California	45	(+2)	D	D	Completed. Republicans are seeking referendum to overturn remap; Supreme Court refused to block plan for 1982 elections.
Colorado	6	(+1)	R	D	Completed.
Connecticut	6		D	D	Completed.
Florida	19	(+4)	D	D	Spring 1982.
Georgia	10		D	D	Overturned by Justice Dept. Feb. 11, 1982; Case in U.S. District Court.
Hawaii	2		D	D	Overturned by court March 24, 1982; court appointed masters drawing new plan.
Idaho	2		R	D	Completed.
Illinois	22	(-2)	Split	R	Completed.
Indiana	10	(-1)	R	R	Completed.
Iowa	6		R	R	Completed.
Kansas	5		R	D	Governor vetoed plan April 22, 1982.
Kentucky	7		D	D	Completed.
Louisiana	8		D	R	Completed. Justice Dept. ruling date not set.
Maine	2		Split	D	Only minor changes necessary. 1983.
Maryland	8		D	D	Completed.
Massachusetts	11	(-1)	D	D	Completed.
Michigan	18	(-1)	D	R	Plan passed Legislature April 7, 1982. Governor's veto likely.
Minnesota	8		D	R	Court plan handed down March 11, 1982. Republicans appealing to Supreme Court.
Mississippi	5		D	D	Voided by Justice Dept. March 30, 1982.
Missouri	9	(-1)	D	R	Completed. Court imposed remap Dec. 28.
Montana	2		R	D	1983
Nebraska	3		Non-partisan	R	Completed.
Nevada	2	(+1)	D	R	Completed.
New Hampshire	2		R	D	Completed.
New Jersey	14	(-1)	D	R	Supreme Court allowed Democratic plan to remain in effect for 1982.
New Mexico	3	(+1)	D	D	Completed.
New York	34	(-5)	Split	D	Map must be drawn by June 7, 1982.
North Carolina	11		D	D	Justice Dept. approved new plan March 11.
Ohio	21	(-2)	Split	R	Completed March 25, 1982. Court suit filed.
Oklahoma	6		D	D	Completed. Republicans seeking ballot initiative to repeal remap and call for special election on GOP plan.
Oregon	5	(+1)	D	R	Completed.
Pennsylvania	23	(-2)	R	R	Completed March 3, 1982. Court suit filed.
Rhode Island	2		D	D	Completed.
South Carolina	6		D	D	Court drawing lines.
Tennessee	9	(+1)	D	R	Court approved plan March 8, 1982.
Texas	27	(+3)	D	R	Completed. Lines must be redrawn after 1982 elections.
Utah	3	(+1)	R	D	Completed.
Virginia	10		D	D	Completed.
Washington	8	(+1)	R	R	Completed.
West Virginia	4		D	D	Completed.
Wisconsin	9		D	R	Completed March 25, 1982.

* *Data represented in this chart is as of April 23, 1982.*

Note: No redistricting is necessary in Alaska, Delaware, North Dakota, South Dakota, Vermont and Wyoming, which have at-large districts.

By resisting the diffusion of black strength in North Carolina and Georgia and voicing no objection to the district arrangement in Dallas, the Justice Department has sided so far with the opinion that blacks benefit most when their numbers are concentrated.

Upcoming Justice Department rulings on Louisiana and Mississippi redistricting plans will give a clearer picture of the department's philosophy on how black voting rights are best protected.

In Louisiana, blacks demand creation of a black-majority district in New Orleans, a concept endorsed by both the state House and the state Senate. Republican Gov. David C. Treen opposed the black-majority district because the resulting boundaries would have endangered the seat of incumbent Republican Rep. Bob Livingston, who represents the New Orleans suburbs. The governor prevailed upon state legislators to approve a remap protecting incumbents.

Mississippi blacks object that their state's new map perpetuates the practice of dividing the heavy black population along the Mississippi River among three congressional districts. The Justice Department agreed March 30, 1982, voiding the plan under the Voting Rights Act because the remap "dismembers" the Delta's black population.

Beyond the Scorecard

Much of this year's reporting has focused on the scorecard outlook of redistricting. When a plan clears a state legislature, the emphasis is on short-term partisan gains and losses. The outcome in Missouri, for example, has been projected as a loss of one Republican seat, from four GOP members to three. But this kind of assessment does not reflect the ultimate impact of a congressional map that will be in place for a decade.

The new Missouri districts may well be a boon for the Democrats in 1982: First-term Republican Reps. Bill Emerson and Wendell Bailey are forced to run in territories that favor Democrats, and dwindling St. Louis keeps two Democratic House seats even though Missouri drops from 10 to nine in reapportionment. The current 6-4 Democratic delegation could shift to 7-2 Democratic after the 1982 election.

But the redistricting map preserves several of the existing Democratic districts only by adding to them considerable amounts of Republican territory. To dismantle Bailey's 8th District, the mapmakers had to distribute its Republican counties among the Democratic 2nd, 3rd, and 9th districts, increasing the Republican vote in each. The Democratic incumbents in those districts may face problems later in the decade in strong Republican years. And if any of them decide to leave office, the map could eventually be a net Republican advantage. A similar situation could happen in Illinois, where mapmakers saved several Democratic incumbents in the Chicago area by giving them suburban Republican territory that could cause trouble in the future.

The prophets of redistricting should be cautioned by the example of Iowa. After a new map was drawn there in 1971, The Democratic Party was said to hold an edge in the two more industrialized eastern districts of the state. Republicans were favored to hold the two mostly agricultural western districts. Today, the situation is reversed. The eastern seats are held by moderate Republicans and the western seats by Democrats with strong rural and small-town followings.

GOP EXPECTATIONS FOR 1982 ELECTIONS

This is not the election year the Republican Party looked forward to in the bright budget-cutting spring of 1981.

Instead of campaigning in unison to consolidate their gains of 1980 into a long-term congressional majority, GOP candidates are maneuvering separately to defend themselves against the political consequences of severe unemployment and a $100-billion federal deficit.

To watch these candidates in different areas of the country is to look at a party meeting itself coming and going. While some Republicans are continuing to use the "outsider" rhetoric of 1980, citing the accumulated misdeeds of past Democratic administrations, others are simply pleading with the voters to give Reaganomics a chance. Still others are talking about their own budget alternatives. The one thing none of them do is criticize the president personally. It has not come to that.

It does not have to be fatal for a political party to be saying a variety of different things as it contests nearly 500 separate elections for the House and Senate in 50 states. Democrats have been doing that successfully for more than a generation.

But a campaign of many voices represents a radical departure from Republican strategy in 1980, which was based on a direct, national message communicated to congressional candidates by the party in Washington and passed on to voters in simple terms.

Virtually every Republican candidate for Congress two years ago was for a massive tax cut, a balanced budget and an increase in military spending, as was Reagan. Nearly every one reminded voters that Democrats had controlled both chambers of Congress for a quarter-century. Television commercials financed by the Republican National Committee and the GOP congressional campaign committees pounded away at that theme.

When the GOP took control of the Senate in 1980 and gained 33 seats in the House, it seemed to refute the common wisdom that congressional campaigns could not be run successfully on a national basis.

Now, of course, much of the 1980 agenda is law. It is no longer possible to base a campaign on demands for its enactment. But beyond that, Republicans are discovering that national unity is one of the luxuries of the party out of power. Once there are policies to defend, regional and interest-group loyalties divide. And if those policies seem to be leading to massive deficits and high unemployment, it is likely to be every candidate for his or her self.

Fortunately for Republicans, this is a year in which they have relatively little at risk. Democrats are defending 21 of the 33 Senate seats at stake, a legacy of the results of 1976, when these same seats were last contested. The big Republican classes of 1978 and 1980 do not have to start defending themselves for two more years.

To reclaim the Senate, Democrats would have to win virtually every Republican seat they seem to have any chance of winning and hold nearly every one they now possess. It is not difficult to find Republican seats in jeopardy as the campaign year begins, notably those of Lowell P. Weicker Jr. in Connecticut, Orrin G. Hatch in Utah, and

Congressional Departures

Retiring

	Date Announced	Began Service	Age
Sen. S. I. Hayakawa, R-Cal.	1/30/82	1977	75
Sen. Harry F. Byrd Jr., Ind-Va.	11/30/81	1965	67
Rep. John J. Rhodes, R-Ariz. (1)	1/21/82	1953	65
Rep. John L. Burton, R-Cal. (43)	3/6/82	1975	55
Rep. George E. Danielson, D-Cal. (30)[1]	2/4/82	1971	67
Rep. Clair W. Burgener, R-Cal. (43)	9/21/81	1973	60
Rep. Jack Brinkley, D-Ga. (3)	1/13/82	1967	51
Rep. Robert McClory, R-Ill. (13)	1/13/82	1963	74
Rep. Richard Bolling, D-Mo. (5)	8/14/81	1949	65
Rep. L. H. Fountain, D-N.C. (2)	3/27/82	1952	71
Rep. Shirley Chisholm, D-N.Y. (12)	2/10/82	1952	57
Rep. Donald J. Mitchell, R-N.Y. (31)	2/2/82	1973	58
Rep. J. William Stanton, R-Ohio (11)	4/2/82	1952	50
Rep. Marc L. Marks, R-Pa. (24)	1/27/82	1977	54
Rep. Richard C. White, D-Texas (16)	10/2/81	1965	58
Rep. M. Caldwell Butler, R-Va. (6)	11/24/81	1973	56
Rep. Robert H. Mollohan, D-W.Va. (1)	2/16/82	1969	72
Rep. Henry S. Reuss, D-Wis. (5)	11/18/80	1955	69

Seeking Other Office

	Date Announced	Began Service	Age	Office Sought
Rep. Paul N. McCloskey Jr., R-Cal. (12)	9/28/81	1967	54	Senate
Rep Barry M. Goldwater Jr., R-Cal. (20)	4/21/81	1969	43	Senate
Rep. Robert K. Dornan, R-Calif. (27)	9/30/81	1977	48	Senate
Rep. Toby Moffett, D-Conn. (6)	12/1/81	1975	37	Senate
Rep. L. A. Bafalis, R-Fla. (10)	1/5/82	1973	52	Governor
Rep. Bo Ginn, D-Ga. (1)	7/20/81	1973	47	Governor
Rep. Floyd Fithian, D-Ind. (2)	7/13/81	1975	53	Senate
Rep. David F. Emery, R-Maine (1)	1/20/82	1975	33	Senate
Rep. James J. Blanchard, D-Mich. (18)		1975	39	Governor
Rep. James D. Santini, D-Nev. (AL)	9/8/81	1975	44	Senate
Rep. Millicent Fenwick, R-N.J. (5)	1/20/82	1975	71	Senate
Rep. Clarence J. Brown, R-Ohio (7)	11/9/81	1965	54	Governor
Rep. John M. Ashbrook, R-Ohio (17)	1/20/81	1961	53	Senate
Rep. Robin L. Beard Jr., R-Tenn. (6)		1973	42	Senate
Rep. James M. Collins, R-Texas (3)	10/24/81	1968	65	Senate
Rep. Paul S. Trible Jr., R-Va. (1)	1/25/82	1977	35	Senate
Rep. Cleve Benedict, R-W.Va. (2)	11/4/81	1981	46	Senate

Defeated in Primary

	Date Defeated	Began Service	Age
Rep. Edward J. Derwinski, R-Ill. (4)	3/16/82	1959	55
Rep. John G. Fary, D-Ill. (5)	3/16/82	1975	71
Rep. Tom Railsback, R-Ill. (19)[2]	3/16/82	1967	50

[1] Danielson was named to the California Court of Appeals by Gov. Edmund G. Brown Jr. Feb. 4, 1982. He still must undergo confirmation hearings.
[2] Railsback was defeated in the new 17th District.

the retiring S. I. Hayakawa in California. But Democrats are starting out behind to retain control of an open seat in Virginia and will have serious problems holding seats in New Jersey and Maine.

It would take a net gain of four seats to create a Democratic majority in the Senate of the 98th Congress, and right now it is hard to come up with any plausible scenario that would bring Democrats that many additional seats.

The early indication is that this year's Senate contests will be a sort of standoff, with a higher percentage of incumbents re-elected in both parties than in recent years. Democrats running for re-election have the economic conditions in their favor; most of the 11 Republicans seeking new terms have a personal following or financial advantages to draw on.

There have been only two retirements to date, the smallest number at a comparable stage in more than 10 years, so the massive Senate turnover that marked the late 1970s may come to at least a temporary end in November 1982.

The current disappointment about the year in Senate Republican ranks has more to do with what might have been. Many of the Democrats seeking re-election this year are potentially vulnerable, and a year ago it seemed that Democratic incumbents such as Donald W. Riegle Jr. of Michigan, Howard M. Metzenbaum of Ohio and Jim Sasser of Tennessee were ripe for picking. Republicans need those seats as insurance for 1984 and 1986, when most of their majority wll be up for review.

Senate GOP leader Howard H. Baker Jr. has conceded that if the party is still at 53 seats in 1983, it may be below 50 by 1987. It is in this context that recent changes in the year's Senate odds have to be disheartening to Republicans.

The recession in the industrial Midwest and local political circumstances have made Riegle and Metzenbaum clear favorites eight months before the 1982 election. With the announced retirement of Michigan Gov. William G. Milliken, Riegle has no Republican challenger of statewide reputation. Metzenbaum had one in Rep. John M. Ashbrook, but Ashbrook's death in April 1982 has left Ohio's political situation in doubt.

The recession is having a similar effect on efforts elsewhere in the country. In Montana, where residents of the wheat-and-cattle region are furious about the low prices in the 1981 farm bill, the only current Senate campaign is between incumbent Democrat John Melcher and the National Conservative Political Action Committee. Republicans so far have no candidate and are playing no conspicuous role.

One of the most startling Republican successes of 1980 was a Senate victory in North Carolina over Democrat Robert Morgan. During his one term in Washington, Morgan had done little to associate himself with liberalism or national Democratic policy, but Republican nominee John P. East managed to tie him to the Carter administration nevertheless.

This time, Southern Democrats will not provide an easy target. In Tennessee, Sasser is being challenged by GOP Rep. Robin L. Beard as a free-spending "Kennedy liberal." But Sasser's votes for the Reagan economic package in 1981 allow him considerable room to maneuver. He seems insulated from some of the most punishing criticism.

Among the other more conservative Democratic candidates, Dennis DeConcini of Arizona and Lawton Chiles of Florida appear to have frightened off first-line Republican opposition. DeConcini has done it largely through fundraising; by the end of 1981 he had raised slightly more than the entire cost of his 1976 campaign. His one announced GOP opponent had spent virtually his entire pre-primary budget.

Chiles is a harder case to figure out. He is not a fundraising wizard and is not widely known to most of the three million people who have moved to his state since 1970. But the only announced candidate against him is the Broward County property appraiser. Republican leaders have been unable so far to persuade anyone more established to make the effort.

Republicans can take some comfort in the early season standing of their own Senate incumbents; most of them are doing well. It is hard to imagine John C. Danforth losing in Missouri or John Heinz being defeated in Pennsylvania. And Robert T. Stafford seems to have ensured the Vermont Senate seat for his party with his decision to postpone retirement.

There are signs of increased competition, though, even against some of the strongest Republican senators. The $1.3 million that Richard G. Lugar of Indiana raised in 1981 for his re-election campaign seemed unnecessary at the time; the only Democratic aspirants were an obscure state legislator and an obscure county prosecutor. In mid-February 1982, though, Lugar picked up a credible opponent in U.S. Rep. Floyd Fithian. Redistricted out of his House seat, Fithian had planned to run for secretary of state in Indiana. Nearly at the last minute, he decided instead that a campaign against Lugar, stressing the Reaganomics issue in a recession-plagued state, was worth a try after all.

Lugar remains a heavy favorite, but decisions such as Fithian's are ones that Democrats are making early in 1982; Republicans are generally deciding the other way.

House Prospects

Republicans have a cushion against massive defeat in the House — youth and aggressiveness.

Although the tradition is that a House sweep by one of the parties in a given election brings in shaky candidates vulnerable the next time, that is not the way it works any more. Few House members seeking second and third terms have been beaten in recent years, regardless of the circumstances of their original elections. The losers are veteran incumbents who have grown complacent and out of touch. Incumbency offers nearly any newcomer in either party the financial and public relations tools he or she needs to lock up the district in one term.

When Democrats elected 77 new members of the House in 1974, Republicans had high hopes of ousting dozens of them two years later. They defeated only two. The others protected themselves with the combination of newsletters, mobile offices and town meetings that have become a staple of House politics since then.

And the current contingent of House Republicans is much more like the Democrats of 1974 than like the old-time groups that used to be swept in and quickly swept out. Half the GOP members seeking re-election in 1982 first arrived in 1979 or later. Many ran ahead of Reagan in 1980.

If Democrats make massive gains in the House this year, it will not be at the expense of Republican deadwood. It will have to be over the well-organized and well-financed resistance of some very determined young GOP incumbents.

So while Democrats are optimistic that the current Reagan recession will mean a strong year for them in many parts of the country, few are talking about gaining back all of what they lost in 1980. Not many of the party's strategists go along with House Speaker Thomas P. O'Neill Jr.'s prediction of 25 to 30 new Democratic seats. Rep. Tony Coelho of California, chairman of the Democratic Congressional Campaign Committee, predicts about 15 to 20.

The significance of the election as a pure test of political strength will be blurred, of course, by the effects of redistricting. At least 10 current members will be gone next year who would have won again had their district lines not changed.

It is possible to make a list of Republican House members who seem to be in serious jeopardy. But unless one includes those hurt primarily by redistricting, it is hard to find more than a dozen names that clearly belong on it.

Still, there is a considerable amount of worry in the House Republican Conference. When times are hard, being a messenger of the "in" party is a dangerous role to play. In the urban Northeast, the Great Plains and the recession-hit mid-South, voters will have an opportunity this year to send President Reagan a message without actually casting a ballot against him.

It is in the Midwest that the signs of trouble are clearest. Republicans will have to work hard to defend incumbents such as Jim Jeffries in Kansas and Arlan Stangeland in Minnesota, both of whom were shaky last time in an outstanding Republican year. Their current situations reflect the Democratic recruitment advantage in a year of recession.

For most of 1981, Democrat Gene Wenstrom pondered a third campaign against Stangeland, whom he had held to 52 percent in 1980. In the fall of 1981, as the farm economy worsened, he decided to try again.

In Iowa, two House candidates did surprisingly well in 1980 — Republican Donald Young, who held incumbent Democrat Neal Smith to 54 percent of the vote, and Democrat Lynn Cutler, loser by barely 6,000 votes in a district that had not gone Democratic since 1932. In 1981 Young planned to run again, while Cutler said she was too busy as a member of the Black Hawk County board of supervisors. But in December of 1981 Smith announced he had to spend 1982 working at his new medical clinic. Cutler decided she could spare the time after all.

Members such as Jeffries and Stangeland are the first row of Republican vulnerability. If the political climate grows worse for Republicans in the Midwest, it could threaten strong young GOP members who would otherwise be easy second-term winners.

Republican Rep. Vin Weber of Minnesota employs all the weapons incumbents use to get themselves re-elected. Over the 1981 Christmas recess alone, the 29-year-old Weber held 30 town meetings in his rural district. But that has not been enough to discourage Jim Nichols, a Democrat who won two terms in the state Senate in a Republican district.

Gypsy Moths. Much has been written of the danger faced by the so-called "Gypsy Moths," the moderate House Republicans from the industrial Northeast who reluctantly voted with President Reagan on the major economic initiatives of 1981. Their troubles may prove to be the most overrated political issue of the year.

Except for those who have redistricting problems, such as Carl D. Pursell of Michigan and Bill Green of New York, it is hard to find a Gypsy Moth under serious challenge.

Most of these members have long-established reputations for independence, and there is little visible uproar about their budget and tax votes.

There is no strong Democratic opponent in Connecticut for freshman Republican Rep. Lawrence J. DeNardis, who first applied the term "Gypsy Moth" to the moderate group. First-term GOP Rep. Claudine Schneider, the only Republican to represent Rhode Island in the House in the last 40 years, is a clear favorite to win again.

Boll Weevils. Equally strong, because of or in spite of their 1981 pro-Reagan votes, are the conservative "Boll Weevil" Democrats of the South. Regardless of the ultimate fate of Reaganomics, they have risked little by supporting it. If it works, they can point to their votes with pride; if it fails, they can say they wanted to give it a chance but now feel another approach is needed.

In Louisiana, for example, the GOP has found no one to take on Buddy Roemer, the brash young Democrat who won his first term in 1980 while Reagan was carrying his district by 18,000 votes. Roemer came to Washington threatening to withhold support of Tip O'Neill for Speaker; he did not carry through on that threat but did manage to back Reagan on two-thirds of the House votes in 1981.

At this point, it is hard to see where a serious challenge to Democrats such as Roemer will come from. Any Republican challenging them is likely to be more conservative than they are. Southerners, angry about unemployment and high interest rates, are not going to express their frustrations by changing their votes from Boll Weevil to Republican. In districts all over the South these days, a conservative Democrat is a good thing to be.

Ironically, the one Boll Weevil who may be in some trouble is Phil Gramm of Texas, who not only voted for the president's budget but sponsored it.

Gramm, who is now offering his own budget alternative with massive new spending cuts and a lower deficit, faces a likely challenge from Jack Teague, son of the late and revered Democrat who represented his district for 32 years before 1978. Gramm's critics plan to describe Teague as a conservative and Gramm as an ideologue. Even in this case, however, the threat seems to be based more on local than national politics.

Missed Opportunities

Republicans might choose to be relatively satisfied with the prospect of holding their Senate majority — which they failed to do the last two times they attained one — and keeping a majority of their 1980 gains in the House. The fact that the GOP members of Congress are almost universally gloomy about the coming year reflects the feeling that 1982 will be an election of missed opportunity.

Although Republicans point out that the party in power has lost an average of 36 seats in midterm elections, they probably know that this is misleading. The election that turns out to be disastrous for the party in power is the one six years into its administration. In the first midterm vote, two years after a change in power, voters normally give the administration the benefit of the doubt.

Republicans actually gained two Senate seats in 1970, in the first election of the Nixon era, and held their House losses to nine. Democrats under Kennedy gained two in the Senate in 1962 and lost only five in the House. Even in 1978, when the decline in President Carter's popularity was evident throughout the country, the Democratic loss was three in the Senate and 12 in the House. If the GOP loses

36 House seats this year, it would not be part of some historic pattern. It would be a repudiation.

If the Republican goal is a long-term congressional majority, then the party probably did *too* well in 1980. Strong GOP congressional gains that year, had they been combined with the re-election of Jimmy Carter, would have set up a classic midterm sweep for the Republican Party. Republican candidates would have been in a position to rail against six frustrating years of Democratic rule. A Democratic majority of 26 seats in the House would have seemed fragile indeed. As it is, with Republican candidates on the defensive about the administration's economic policy, 26 seats seem like a fortress.

There are few Republican strategists, of course, who would have preferred to lose the presidency in 1980 so that they could take Congress more decisively in 1982. But this scenario does point up a lesson of partisan skirmishing in hard times: Once a party takes the White House, it loses much of the momentum for its congressional campaigns.

I

The North

Connecticut

It takes barely two hours to drive east across Connecticut from the affluent New York City suburb of Greenwich to the Portuguese fishing town of Stonington, but that drive is a demographic odyssey. On the edge of Long Island sound are the ethnic factory towns, picturesque Yankee villages, and shipbuilding communities heavily reliant on defense contracts. Inland, the ethnic and political mix is almost as great.

For its small geographic size — only Rhode Island and Delaware are smaller — Connecticut covers an enormous social and political spectrum. Through the early part of this century it was dominated by village Yankees, Republican by conviction and conservative by association with the Congregationalist church.

But the massive influx of immigrants from Ireland, Italy and Poland gave a heavy Democratic flavor to towns such as Hartford, New Haven, Bridgeport and Waterbury. As in other states, it nourished a political system that relied heavily on party bosses. By 1920, 70 percent of the people were first or second generation immigrants, and Connecticut was on its way to becoming one of the nation's most urbanized states. Today, less than a quarter of its people still live in rural areas, compared with two-thirds in Vermont and half in New Hampshire.

From the Depression until the mid-1950s, rural Republicans and urban Democrats fought to a virtual standoff as the governorship and the congressional delegation switched back and forth between parties every few years. The 1954 election of Abraham Ribicoff as governor marked a clear swing to the Democrats. Ever since, the Democratic Party has dominated state politics, and Republicans have held the governor's office for only four of the last 26 years. With the beginning of the 97th Congress in 1981 the Democrats held one Senate seat and four of the state's six House seats.

Nearly all that Democratic success occurred under state party chairman John M. Bailey, who controlled nominations to Congress and all major state offices, awarding them at well-orchestrated conventions that provided balanced candidate slates without the inconvenience of the primary process. The machine began to lose its hold in the last few years before Bailey's death in 1975, and since then the Democratic Party has been as wide-open and unmanageable in Connecticut as it had become in most other states many years earlier.

Urban Industrial Crescent

More than half of Connecticut's votes come from Hartford and New Haven counties, located in mid-state. The two areas form the core of a crescent that includes the state's major industrial cities and most of its Democratic votes. Within it are Hartford, the nation's leading insurance city, and New Haven, home of Yale University, but also less-heralded places such as Waterbury, New Britain, Bristol, Meridan, Middletown and the state's most populous city, Bridgeport.

Danbury, once the hat center of the nation, and New London, where all U.S. submarines are built, are the only largely industrialized towns outside the crescent. The economy in nearly all the cities inside it is centered on manufacturing — usually metal parts. Connecticut has specialized in making precision equipment, such as aircraft engines, weapons, helicopters, office machines and typewriters. From the Revolutionary War through World War II its Colt and Winchester factories were the county's arsenal. Today the crescent areas suffer from the economic stagnation common to much of the northeast.

The people who work in the factories come from a variety of ethnic backgrounds. Since 1928, when Alfred E. Smith carried most of the state's major cities, Democrats have been able to count on the allegiance of nearly all the urban Catholic groups, although Italians have strayed occasionally.

Hartford, New Haven and New Britain are the three most solidly Democratic cities, the only major ones in Connecticut to support George McGovern's presidential bid in 1972. In 1980 Jimmy Carter received his largest margins from those towns. Waterbury, Bridgeport and Danbury are still firmly Democratic in local and statewide elections, but show signs of moving away from the Democrats at the presidential level. Waterbury, known for the brass manufacturing skills of its many Italian and Irish immigrants, favored Ronald Reagan in 1980. Danbury, the only large town to gain population in the last decade, has given small majorities to the last three GOP presidential candidates.

In general, the northern half of the crescent is the most solidly Democratic part of the state. Closer to Long Island Sound, voters are more likely to register as independents and split their tickets.

'The Gold Coast'

The comfortable Fairfield County towns nearest New York City bear little resemblance to the rest of the state. They are centers of moderate Republican strength.

The "Gold Coast" towns of Greenwich, Darien, New Canaan, Weston and Westport are among the wealthiest in the country. New York executives, lured by the absence of a state income tax in Connecticut, have lived in these towns for most of the century. More recently, corporations also have started moving out of the city to large park-like headquarters in suburban Connecticut. Fairfield was the only county carried by former New York Sen. James L. Buckley in his 1980 Republican campaign. That is testimony not only to the area's conservatism but to the fact that it faces Manhattan.

The 4th Congressional District, which includes most of the fancier parts of Fairfield County, has stayed firmly in Republican control in all but three House elections since World War II.

Ribicoff and Ella T. Grasso, who was governor from 1975 to 1980, were the only major statewide candidates in the 1970s to carry Fairfield County. But because the county casts only a quarter of the state's vote, it is difficult for a large Republican tide there alone to swing an election to the GOP. To win, a GOP candidate also needs either an overwhelming vote in rural Connecticut or unusual support in the cities, where ethnic voters have begun to break away from their traditional Democratic loyalties.

Berkshire Highlands

After Fairfield County, the next most Republican area is immediately to the north, in Litchfield County. Located in the northwestern corner of Connecticut, this is the state's last outpost of old-fashioned Yankee civilization: town greens, white clapboard houses, church spires and wooded Berkshire hills.

Although usually favoring Republican candidates in statewide contests, Litchfield County has been represented by Democrats in the House for most of the past 20 years, thanks mostly to the presence of New Britain and other industrial areas in the eastern corner of the 6th Congressional District.

Eastern Connecticut

The eastern third of the state is as poor and Democratic as the western third is rich and Republican. Unlike the elite at the other end of the state, the people here are hard-scrabble farmers working marginal land, mill workers in aging industrial towns, and craftsmen whose lives are focused on the sea.

New London and Groton, which together form the region's only significant metropolitan area, are predominantly shipbuilding towns. Their livelihood is largely dependent on orders from the Navy and Coast Guard. Democrats carry these cities unless, like George McGovern in 1972, they are perceived to be weak on defense issues. McGovern won 36 percent in the New London/Groton area. In 1980 Democrat Christopher J. Dodd, running for the Senate as a liberal but avoiding anti-military rhetoric, won 66 percent.

The only sizable pocket of Republican strength in the east is at the mouth of the Connecticut River, where the Yankee domination in towns such as Old Lyme and Essex has lasted for over two centuries.

In the northeast are Tolland and Windham counties, both Democratic but sparsely populated. The University of Connecticut campus at Storrs provides a boost for liberal candidates. In the 1980 Republican presidential primary, John B. Anderson won the Storrs area easily. He captured 20 percent in the general election, far above his statewide average. This was also the only part of the state McGovern carried in 1972.

NEW MAP SATISFIES BOTH PARTIES

With a population that remained stable during the last decade, Connecticut had to make only minor adjustments to its six congressional district boundaries. Not much was gained or lost politically in redistricting, but there was something to please both parties in the compromise that preceded the final ruling of the state's Reapportionment Commission.

The new district lines should maintain the Democrats' modest statewide advantage in congressional contests, strengthening one shaky Democratic incumbent, William R. Ratchford in the 5th District. The GOP tightened its grip on Stewart B. McKinney's 4th District, already the state's most dependably Republican area.

The Democrats, controlling the governorship and solid majorities in both houses of the state Legislature, had the leverage to resist more ambitious GOP claims. The redistricting was to have been decided by an evenly balanced General Assembly committee, but the panel deadlocked over the parties' competing plans in midsummer. That forced the appointment of a special commission, with four Republicans, four Democrats and one non-partisan member who would cast tie-breaking votes when necessary. The commission issued its new map on Oct. 28, 1981. Under rules established for the procedure, the decision was final.

Republicans did not fulfill their original hopes of weakening Ratchford by adding more Republican towns to his district, in which he survived by fewer than 2,000 votes in 1980. Instead, the commission gave Ratchford some closely contested towns near his native Danbury, where his hometown popularity may spill over, and removed his weakest areas from the district.

The non-partisan ninth member of the commission was needed only to settle a dispute over the boundaries of the 6th District. Republicans had hoped to use the remapping of the 6th to improve their chances there in November 1982: Democrat Toby Moffett has given up his safe House seat to challenge Republican Sen. Lowell P. Weicker Jr. But when the Republicans tried to tailor the 6th District's lines to aid an expected GOP House candidate, a state senator, the Democrats balked at a "blatant, though limited, gerrymander." The non-partisan commissioner endorsed a less controversial alternative likely to preserve the thin Democratic edge in the 6th without threatening the solid Democratic lead in the neighboring 1st District.

The new congressional lines leave the constituencies very closely balanced. No district deviates from the ideal population of 517,929 by more than 1,700 people.

New Connecticut Districts

U. S. Congress: 6 districts
  Senate (1D,1R)
  House (4D, 2R)
Governor:
  William A. O'Neill (D)
Population: 3,107,576
Area: 4,862 sq. miles
1980 Presidential Vote:
  Carter (39%)
  Reagan (48%)
  Anderson (12%)

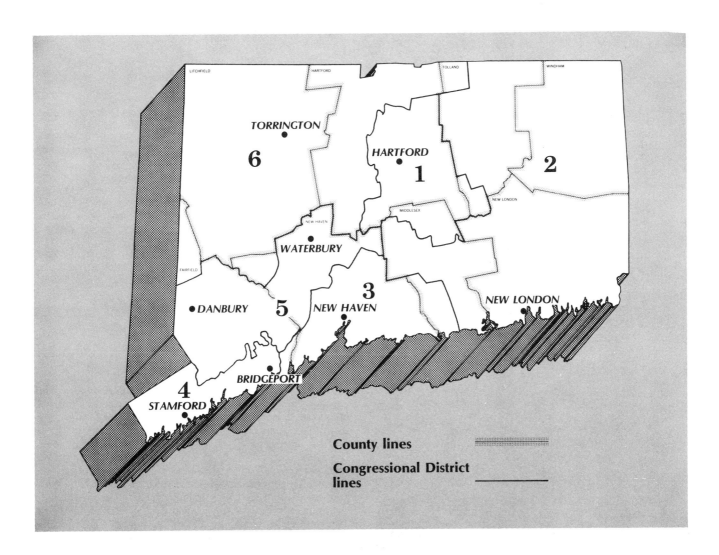

County lines

Congressional District lines

District 1

Central — Hartford

Incumbent: Barbara B. Kennelly (D)

Centered around Hartford and its small-city neighbors, the 1st is primarily urban territory, and it has sent a Democrat to Congress in every election but one since 1948. Once the fiefdom of state party boss John Bailey, who died

in 1975, the district in January 1982 elected his daughter, Barbara Bailey Kennelly, as its member of the House.

Following the statewide pattern, the small cities in the district have gained population since the 1970 census at the expense of the inner city. Hartford lost 13.7 percent of its population, pacing the decline of Hartford County, the state's only county to lose population in the decade. Cities close to the capital also lost population, but several of the district's outlying towns grew, particularly in the Republican areas to the southeast.

The district has a two-to-one Democratic advantage in voter registration, although Hartford itself accounts for only one-sixth of the district vote. Fifty years ago, Hartford had proportionally the third-largest Jewish population of any city in the nation; a variety of ethnic groups have traditionally shared power, and now the city has significant black and Hispanic communities. In the January 1982 special election, the Italian-American wards in the South End voted for Democrat Kennelly rather than the Italian-American Republican, Ann P. Uccello.

As headquarters city for many of the nation's insurance firms, Hartford's economy still boasts a substantial white-collar sector. United Aircraft's Pratt & Whitney headquarters in East Hartford employs 27,000 people, and other aerospace and high-technology firms have attracted a skilled work force, and despite its population decline, Hartford entered the 1980s with more economic resources than some of the other Northeastern industrial cities.

The remapping of the 1st adds three new areas: East Windsor, north of the city, is shifted from the 6th, and East Hampton and the remainder of Portland, to the south, are moved from the 2nd. All three towns usually vote Democratic. The 1st loses Bolton, which moves into the 2nd.

District 2

East — New London

Incumbent: Sam Gejdenson (D)

Stretching from the shores of Long Island Sound to the state's upland hills, the 2nd District is the largest and least urbanized part of Connecticut, and its vote varies with its geography. Along the coast, dependably Democratic shipbuilding cities and fishing villages border wealthy WASPish towns that provide Republican votes. Inland, small manufacturing centers and bustling college towns deliver Democratic margins, while rural Yankee hill towns maintain their GOP tradition.

The fine balance among the areas helps give the 2nd District the state's most volatile congressional voting pattern, although Democratic trends now seem to predominate. When Democrats retained control of the seat in 1980 — Gejdenson succeeding Christopher J. Dodd, who was elected to the Senate — it was the first time in nearly 50

years that the district had changed hands without changing parties. Between 1934 and 1950, it switched parties every two years.

Historically a center for seafaring, the southern coast is the home of the General Dynamics shipbuilding installation, located in Groton. Home of the Trident nuclear submarine program, this is the district's largest industrial concern, employing over 12,000 people. Like Connecticut as a whole, the coastal area's economy is heavily dependent on military spending. The Groton area's maritime complex also features the Naval Underseas Research and Development Center, a Navy submarine port and a submarine-training base. Across the Thames River, in New London, is the U.S. Coast Guard Academy, which coexists peacefully with Connecticut College and several small plastics and hardware plants.

Further inland, college towns and mill towns are neighbors on the hilly landscape. In Willimantic, Eastern Connecticut State College adjoins needle-and-thread and wire-cable firms. The town of Storrs is dominated by the 16,000 students at its University of Connecticut campus.

The latest remap adds to the 2nd District the small but fast-growing town of Bolton, which Dodd carried in 1980 over Republican James L. Buckley despite Ronald Reagan's local plurality. The towns of Portland and East Hampton move into the 1st, and all of Somers will be in the 6th District.

District 3

South — New Haven

Incumbent: Lawrence J. DeNardis (R)

Although New Haven is the 3rd District's anchor and economic center, only one-fifth of the votes come from within that declining old manufacturing city. The district's overall electorate is a mixture of blue-collar ethnics, who are the core of the city's shrinking population, and white-collar suburbanites, many of whom commute into the downtown business district from the fast-growing small- and medium-sized cities on the urban rim.

Once the state's largest city and a New England industrial powerhouse, New Haven was dominated in the 19th century by Yankee Republicans, and for most of the 20th century divided its power among Italian, Polish and Irish communities. Today New Haven itself is almost one-third black, but the black population makes up less than 10 percent districtwide.

Italian-Americans, 10 percent of the district's population, wield powerful political influence. Since 1952, the area's congressional seat has always been held by someone of Italian extraction — regardless of partisan label.

Running to succeed 11-term Democrat Robert N. Giaimo in 1980, moderate Republican DeNardis stressed his ethnic background. He ran well in New Haven's Italian wards, but he lost the traditionally Democratic city by a two-to-one margin. He won the race in the suburbs — which have come to be almost as heavily Italian as the city.

Registered Republicans are outweighed two-to-one by Democrats in the 3rd, but independents outnumber both parties. In 1980, Reagan carried the district by 26,000

Barbara B. Kennelly   **Sam Gejdenson**

New Connecticut Districts

New District	Incumbent	Population	1980 Pres. Winner
1	Barbara B. Kennelly (D)	516,232	Carter
2	Sam Gejdenson (D)	518,244	Reagan
3	Lawrence J. DeNardis (R)	518,677	Reagan
4	Stewart B. McKinney (R)	518,577	Reagan
5	William R. Ratchford (D)	518,700	Reagan
6	Toby Moffett (D)	517,146	Reagan

votes, twice as many as DeNardis, but ticket-splitters gave Dodd a comfortable 24,000-vote Senate margin.

Yale University is New Haven's best-known institution, and the foremost educational establishment in the state, but the town vs. gown division remains a fact of New Haven's political life. The university does not take an active role in city politics, and the Yale student body — at least since the Black Panther trials that inflamed campus sentiment in the late 1960s — has been largely indifferent to the surrounding city's political affairs.

The town of Clinton, with a brisk 9 percent population growth since the 1970 census, was added to the 3rd in this year's remap. Clinton, which had been divided between the 2nd and 3rd districts, is usually Republican territory, although Dodd carried it in 1980.

District 4

Southwest — Stamford, Bridgeport

Incumbent: Stewart B. McKinney (R)

Home to some of the wealthiest towns in the nation, the 4th is the best Republican territory in Connecticut. Both Reagan and Buckley won their biggest majorities here, where towns such as Darien and Westport are symbols of upper-class New York City suburbia. Many of the voters are daily commuters to and from Wall Street and midtown Manhattan. Fairfield County is blanketed by newspapers and broadcasts that report the news of New York, not Connecticut.

But the brand of Republicanism that usually holds sway in the area is liberal: six-term incumbent McKinney often votes with the Democrats, and his predecessor in the House was Lowell P. Weicker Jr. — whose Senate liberalism has become anathema to GOP traditionalists.

The suburbs here retained their high-income status in the 1970s, but they grew very little — in part because of restrictive zoning laws, and in part because children were growing up and moving away. The district as a whole has lost 5.4 percent of its population since the 1970 census.

Despite the area's reputation as an enclave of white-collar Republican wealth, there remain several dependably Democratic areas, including Bridgeport, now the largest city in the state. Industrial Bridgeport actually lost 8.9 percent of its population between 1970 and 1980, but it surpassed Hartford in population because the decline in Hartford was far worse. Bridgeport's aging, heavy industries — which include automobile parts, electrical components and steel products — have been particularly sensitive to recent economic downturns.

While Stamford lost 5.8 percent of its residents in the decade, a more important trend may be the city's gradual change of character: what had once been a small-business center has become a haven for corporate headquarters fleeing New York's high tax rates. The largest single employer in the district is Pitney Bowes' office equipment headquarters in Stamford, employing 4,500.

This year's redistricting returned the town of New Canaan to the 4th, where it had been until the 1970 remap. Also shifted from the 5th District were part of Westport and most of Trumbull, giving the 4th still more GOP areas.

District 5

West — Waterbury, Danbury

Incumbent: William R. Ratchford (D)

Once a Democratic stronghold, the 5th has in recent years been slipping toward the Republican column. The last Democratic presidential candidate to carry the district was Hubert Humphrey in 1968, and his plurality was narrow. The zeal of the Democratic faithful in red-brick mill towns such as Waterbury — whose fervent election-eve campaign rally for John F. Kennedy in 1960 has become a political legend — has given way to split-ticket voting, with some GOP pockets.

In 1980, Ronald Reagan rolled up a 50,000-vote majority here and won all but one community in the district, and his coattails helped Buckley carry the area narrowly against Dodd. Ratchford won re-election only because his 6,000-vote margin in Waterbury offset his suburban and rural losses.

Lawrence J. DeNardis   **Stewart B. McKinney**

William R. Ratchford   **Toby Moffett**

Incorporating medium-sized manufacturing cities and bucolic villages, the 5th stretches through the central Connecticut hills from the New York line toward the well-populated New Haven-Hartford corridor. The economic core is the aging manufacturing area of the Naugatuck Valley, where the decline of small factories has made unemployment a chronic problem. But the district also includes several wealthy suburban towns, such as Wilton and Weston, within the orbit of New York City — staunchly Republican constituencies that help account for the recent GOP advances.

Democrats have depended on the 5th's urban areas to provide their winning margins, but the cities' recent growth has been uneven, despite the district's overall population increase of 7.3 percent between 1970 and 1980. Waterbury, once a shirt-making center, lost 4.4 percent of its population in the last decade as some of its oldest firms closed their doors or moved away. Danbury, whose hat-makers once topped the nation, grew by 19.1 percent, paced by the arrival of corporate headquarters and sophisticated industries.

In this year's redistricting, the 5th District gained the town of Brookfield and the remainder of Newtown. Ratchford will not pick up any solid bases of support by adding these closely fought towns, but he is sure to benefit from the shift of three solidly Republican areas — New Canaan, part of Westport and most of Trumbull — into the 4th District.

District 6

Northwest — Bristol, Torrington

Incumbent: Toby Moffett (D)

The 6th is diverse both geographically and politically. Any constituency that is home to both Ralph Nader and William F. Buckley Jr. is a challenging place in which to fashion a winning coalition.

Extending from quiet villages in the pastoral Litchfield Hills to the Hartford-Springfield metropolitan area, the 6th is closely contested territory in most elections. Reflecting its usual tilt toward the Democrats, it gave Dodd, a 36,000-vote edge in 1980; meanwhile, Ronald Reagan carried the district over President Carter by 23,000 votes.

The "Nutmeggers" of rural Litchfield County, reflecting generations of small-town Yankee control, provide dependable Republican majorities. That pattern is offset by mill towns such as Torrington and Winsted, which usually deliver Democratic margins. To the east, the industrial cities of Bristol and New Britain are bedrock Democratic territory.

New Britain lost 11.5 percent of its population between 1970 and 1980, while Bristol grew by 3.4 percent during the same period.

Extending through some upper-crust Hartford suburbs that vote Republican, the northern arm of the 6th reaches toward the industrial axis along the Connecticut River. Windsor Locks and Enfield are centers of large-scale industry, and the Democrats roll up their vote totals among the blue-collar, heavily Italian-American population.

The district's largest employer, United Aircraft's Hamilton-Standard aerospace division in Windsor Locks, provides 9,000 jobs. The headquarters of the Stanley Works hardware company has 4,500 employees in New Britain, while Textron's ball-bearing plant there employs 2,500 more.

The new map unites the town of Somers, with a population that has grown 22.9 percent since the 1970 census, within the 6th District. East Windsor shifts to the 1st District, and Brookfield and part of Newtown go to the 5th. Incumbent Democrat Toby Moffett is running for the Senate this year, leaving the 6th as the only open district in Connecticut.

Massachusetts

"Don't blame me, I'm from Massachusetts," bumper stickers said in 1973, after things began to go wrong in the second Nixon term that all 49 other states had voted for the previous November. It was a satisfying collective smirk. But if things should go wrong in any sense in the current Republican administration, Massachusetts will have to share the blame with 43 other states. The only state to support McGovern in 1972 went for Reagan in 1980.

Reagan's victory does not signal any pendulum swing to the right in Massachusetts. The Republican won by only 6,000 votes out of 2.5 million cast, with 42 percent of the total vote. Independent candidate John Anderson's 15 percent — his highest in the nation — greatly hurt Carter.

Yet there is an indication of growing dissatisfaction with high taxes and liberal "big government" programs. The 1978 election of conservative Gov. Edward King, who had unseated liberal incumbent Michael Dukakis in the Democratic primary, was a warning. Passage in 1980 of "Proposition 2 1/2," placing a ceiling on local property taxes and leading to reduced services in communities all over the state, was an even more dramatic symbol that Massachusetts is more complicated than the liberal state of the Kennedys.

If the Kennedys have been the source of modern Massachusetts liberalism, they have also been the beneficiaries of broader change in the state's politics. In 1947, when John Kennedy first took a seat in Congress, Massachusetts had a Republican governor, two Republican senators, and the GOP held nine of the state's 14 House seats. In 1981, with Edward Kennedy nearing the end of his third full term in the Senate, his party holds the governorship, both Senate seats, and 10 of 12 House seats.

What the Kennedys did was give leadership to issue-oriented liberals and legitimacy to a party previously associated with machine politics and corruption. They helped tame the fierce rivalry between the Yankee Protestant Republicans and Catholic Democrats.

Irish Democrats were running Boston by the turn of the century, and beginning in the 1920s, the party was competitive statewide in good national Democratic years. The Depression created a stable majority for Franklin D. Roosevelt and the New Deal. But Yankee Republicans continued to win most congressional and gubernatorial elections, helped by their increased willingness to nominate candidates from the "progressive" side of the spectrum, such as Leverett Saltonstall and Henry Cabot Lodge.

When John F. Kennedy first ran for Congress in 1946, the state was nearly ready for a political upheaval, with or without him. It soon had one, symbolized not only by Kennedy's Senate victory over Lodge in 1952 but by the Democratic takeover of the legislature in 1948, which installed Thomas P. O'Neill Jr. as Speaker of the state House. The legislature has not been dominated by Republicans since.

Over the following decades, Massachusetts became a national leader in state spending for welfare, unemployment insurance and other social programs. Democrats did not win every election — internecine party warfare, particularly between Irish and Italian Americans, plagued them into the 1970s — but Republican winners, such as Edward Brooke, the only black senator since Reconstruction, were progressives.

Problems developed, though. Recessions and the decline of the textile and shoe industries left many cities in a state of near-depression. Irish South Boston exploded in violence in 1975 over busing plans involving blacks from Roxbury. Catholic opposition to Massachusetts' liberal abortion laws grew. Taxes to pay for expensive social programs soared, angering millions and sending thousands packing for low-tax New Hampshire.

In 1978, angry Democrats gave a jolt to the liberal "welfare state" policies by dumping Dukakis for Edward King. That same year, Democrat Paul Tsongas unseated two-term Sen. Brooke. By 1980, Tsongas had adapted to current realities by calling for a "new liberalism" to replace what he saw as the dogma of huge spending programs and high taxes.

Boston

The city of Boston was beginning to grow shabby during the post-World War II years. But urban renewal instituted by mayors John Collins (1960-68) and Kevin White (1968-   ) has transformed the city into one of the most amenable (and expensive) places in the nation to live.

The city's population, which peaked just above 800,000 in 1950, had by 1980 fallen back to where it was at the turn of the century — slightly more than 560,000. But the population slide shows signs of abating and new urban shopping precincts, such as the glittery Faneuil Hall market and the revitalization of the harbor area, have given new life to the center city.

17

Boston is unquestionably a Democratic city. Only three Republicans have carried it over the last two decades, all from the liberal wing of the party — John Volpe in 1966, Francis Sargent in 1970, and Brooke in 1972. But each of them also lost the city at some other time to Democrats more liberal than they. Kennedy regularly wins seven of every ten votes in the city, and in 1972, George McGovern took a healthy 66 percent — better than either of Jimmy Carter's victories there.

Boston is best defined by its various ethnic neighborhoods. South Boston is the heart of the Irish Catholic vote in the city. Although historically Democratic, South Boston supported Reagan in 1980 over Jimmy Carter. In the wake of violent anti-busing demonstrations in the 1970s, South Boston's political debate now centers on social rather than economic questions, and that favors conservative candidates. George Wallace swept South Boston in the 1976 Democratic presidential primary.

Blacks make up about one-fifth of the city's population. Concentrated in Roxbury and the South End, Boston's blacks regularly give as much as 90 percent of their vote to Democratic candidates. The North End and East Boston are heavily Italian.

Thousands of college students attending Boston University, Northeastern University, and numerous smaller institutions have also had a profound effect on politics within the city. Activated by opposition to the Vietnam war and permitted to vote on campus by liberal registration laws, the student community has provided the volunteer force and votes for many liberal candidates at both the state and local level.

Suburban Boston

Boston has several sets of suburbs that form concentric circles around the city's north, west and south sides.

Just north of Boston are Cambridge, Watertown and Somerville, three communities that are essentially urban extensions of Boston. All have strong ethnic, blue-collar populations and are Democratic. Harvard and the Massachusetts Institute of Technology give Cambridge a more liberal flavor than the others. House Speaker O'Neill has represented Cambridge for 29 years; his early stand against the Vietnam war was popular at home even when it was controversial in national politics.

Brookline and Newton immediately to the west of Boston have large enclaves of wealthy, liberal, Jewish residents. Just south of Boston are Dedham, Milton and Quincy, where shipbuilding and other industries exist near ethnic, blue-collar neighborhoods.

The next ring of towns farther out from the Hub, as Boston is called, have been traditionally dependent on small-scale industries that have suffered in the second third of the 20th century. As shoe-making and textile work died out, the Democratic workers moved into machine factories. In turn, the machines have given way to high technology. Route 128, a ring road around Boston, has served as a magnet for numerous electronics, defense and space-related firms. With a highly-educated work force, these clean, white-collar industries have brought a new measure of economic prosperity to the area.

Route 128 is a rough dividing line between the "urban" suburbs close to Boston and those that are more countrified. The strong Democratic vote found inside Route 128 wavers in the suburban towns further from Boston, particularly when Republicans nominate liberal candidates such as Brooke and Sargent. Residential communities such

as Belmont, Lexington, and Winchester support a strong GOP tradition. Further from the city, on the North Shore, Marblehead is heavily Republican but the fishing town of Gloucester and industrial Beverly are more divided between the parties. Salem, famous for its witch trials, is a Democratic industrial town. Residents of these communities read Boston's newspapers and watch its television stations, but many of them have little day-to-day contact with the city.

Northern Industrial

Lowell, Lawrence and Haverhill are aging Massachusetts factory towns. Lowell and Lawrence were great cities of textile manufacturing; Haverhill was a leader in shoe-making. The decline of these industries set the cities back drastically but they are beginning to re-emerge as viable economic entities, bolstered by the arrival of new high-technology industry.

Large enough to qualify as a metropolitan area in its own right, the industrial region of Lawrence and Lowell is strongly Democratic. In 1978, King and Tsongas both won more than 70 percent in Lowell and Lawrence. Two years later, Carter carried both cities over Ronald Reagan, but by a less impressive margin.

Heading towards the ocean, northeast Massachusetts is dotted with small towns and fishing villages that often vote Republican.

Southern Industrial

Bordering on Rhode Island is Bristol County, site of two of Massachusetts' larger cities: New Bedford and Fall River. Like the cities at the northern end of the Boston sphere, New Bedford and Fall River suffered blight and high unemployment following the disappearance of major employers.

The economies of both cities were based on textiles, fishing and whaling. With the decline of all three industries, many jobs vanished and there has been little to fill the void.

Seafaring Portuguese-Americans settled in Fall River years ago and have remained an important part of the city's ethnic makeup. New Bedford also has a large Portuguese population. Both cities support Democrats regularly, although the large blue-collar constituency tends to favor moderates, such as Sen. Henry Jackson, over liberals. Jackson was an easy winner in both cities in his 1976 Democratic presidential primary bid.

Cape Cod and Coastal Towns

The old Yankee personality that once dominated the entire state is still alive and well on much of Cape Cod. The area is largely dependent on the thousands of tourists who come to walk on its dunes and beaches every year. It is also one of the nation's major cranberry growing areas, and fishing is still a lively industry.

Running from Cohasset and Scituate in the north to Provincetown at the tip of the Cape, and including the islands of Martha's Vineyard and Nantucket, this region is quite Republican by Massachusetts standards.

The four counties that make up the area — Plymouth, Barnstable, Dukes and Nantucket — all supported Richard Nixon in 1972 when the state went for George McGovern. In the 1980 election, Ronald Reagan carried all but Dukes County (Martha's Vineyard). On the congressional level, however, the area now sends liberal Democrat Gerry

New Massachusetts Districts

U. S. Congress: 11 districts
  Senate (2D)
  House (10D, 2R)

Governor:
  Edward J. King (D)

Population: 5,737,137

Area: 8,257 sq. miles

1980 Presidential Vote:
  Carter (42%)
  Reagan (42%)
  Anderson (15%)

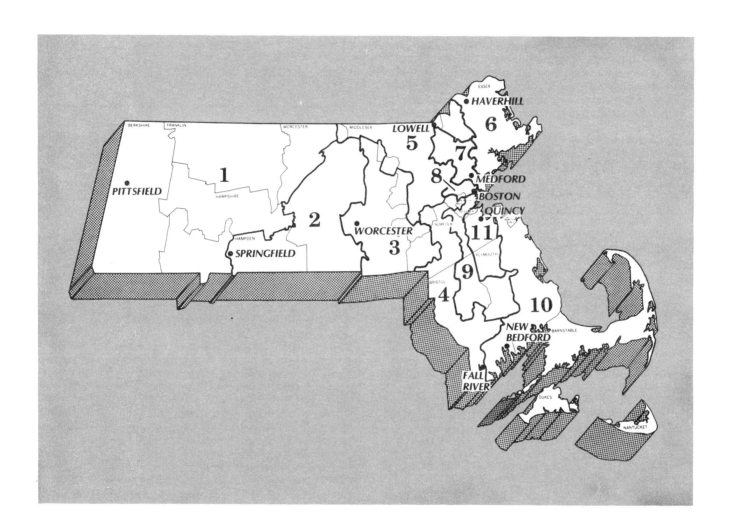

Studds to the House virtually without opposition. During the 1960s, Republican Hastings Keith also won without any opposition.

This is a lightly populated region with slightly more than a half-million people in 1980. But it grew by nearly one-third between 1970 and 1980, more than any other part of the state.

Central and Western Massachusetts

With a few notable exceptions, this is Yankee Massachusetts, where the town meeting and the village green are more reminiscent of Vermont than of Boston.

There are a few industrial centers, but most of central and western Massachusetts is taken up by the Berkshire Hills and small farms which specialize in dairy cattle, chickens, apples and cigar tobacco.

Republicans often do better among the farmers and villagers in this area than with the ethnic working-classes in the eastern part of the state. A moderate Republican, Silvio Conte, has represented western Massachusetts in Congress for 22 years.

The Democratic vote is centered in the major cities. Worcester, in east-central Massachusetts, is the state's second largest city with 162,000 people. Industry is dominant and diversified; the vote is strongly Democratic. Other industrial Democratic cities in Worcester County are Fitchburg and Leominster. The latter supported Reagan in 1980.

Springfield is the third-ranking city in the state. With 152,000 people, it is the Massachusetts focal point of the Connecticut River Valley industrial area, which also includes the cities of Holyoke and Chicopee. All the industrial cities and towns generally vote Democratic, though suburbs such as West Springfield and Westfield sometimes go Republican.

There are numerous French-Canadians in the Springfield metropolitan area. They have been the largest immigrant group in the post-war era, but their numbers and political power do not compare with other ethnic groups.

A few large towns in the remainder of western Massachusetts bring mixed political results. North of Springfield are the college towns of Northampton (Smith College) and Amherst (University of Massachusetts, Amherst College), where Democrats and Republicans are fairly evenly matched. Pittsfield, in Berkshire County, has some industry, but it is neither as "ethnic" nor as Democratic as eastern Massachusetts.

STATE DEMOCRATS VICTIMIZE REP. FRANK

Even though they hold the governorship and control the state Legislature by overwhelming margins, Massachusetts Democrats quarreled with each other rather than the GOP in the state's redistricting process.

With a population that grew by only .8 percent during the 1970s, Massachusetts was forced to drop from 12 House seats to 11. At first, it seemed that the Democrats would pick on Republican Rep. Margaret M. Heckler, sacrificing her 10th District and using the boundary changes to help the one weak Democratic incumbent, first-term Rep. Barney Frank.

But any such plans fell victim to internal Democratic warfare. Heckler's 10th was in fact merged into Frank's old 4th District, but in a way that stood to benefit Heckler, not Frank. The Democrat's iconoclastic style had irked the leadership during his four terms in the state House, and his failure to endorse the full statewide Democratic ticket in 1978 added to the displeasure. When the lines were redrawn, Heckler found that the new district contained more than three times as many of her old constituents as it did of Frank's. Much of the Democrat's old 4th was parceled out among the neighboring 2nd, 3rd and 5th districts.

The Bay State's leading political figures had all kept a wary eye on the remapping process. Gov. Edward J. King, a conservative Democrat who faces a strong intra-party challenge for re-election this year, favored sacrificing Frank — who had endorsed King's liberal Republican opponent in 1978 — to benefit Heckler. His decision may have been influenced by Heckler's threat to run against King for governor if her congressional re-election chances were damaged badly.

U.S. House Speaker Thomas P. O'Neill Jr., whose 8th District is adjacent to Frank's, was not able to persuade the state's legislative leaders to alter the map to help his neighbor. Nor were other safe Democrats who offered to cede dependably Democratic territory to the new 4th to shore

up Frank's chances. Pleas on Frank's behalf from Democratic Sens. Edward M. Kennedy and Paul E. Tsongas were unavailing.

The Special Commission on Congressional Redistricting, led by House Majority Leader George Keverian of Everett and Senate President William M. Bulger of South Boston, unveiled its new map on Dec. 9, 1981. The plan was approved by voice vote in the Senate and by a vote of 122 to 32 in the House. King signed it Dec. 16, 1981. Aside from Frank and Heckler, none of the incumbents' re-election prospects were affected significantly by the new map. No newly drawn district exceeds the statewide average by more than 1,997 or falls short of the target by more than 2,708.

District 1

West — Berkshire Hills, Pioneer Valley

Incumbent: Silvio O. Conte (R)

Extending over parts of five counties, the 1st is the closest thing to a rural district remaining in Massachusetts. It is dominated by small manufacturing centers and placid hill-towns set amid woodland. The only heavily developed patch is a string of small cities along the winding Connecticut River, running through the Pioneer Valley on Interstate 91.

While there are significant Italian, Irish, Polish and French-Canadian enclaves, the 1st as a whole is not as heavily ethnic as eastern Massachusetts. Residents of the area beyond the Connecticut River often feel cut off from Boston's influence, and it is one of the few parts of New England where as many baseball fans cheer for the New York Yankees as for the Boston Red Sox. An area of the state where Republicans often run well, the 1st has been protected from Democrats' redistricting schemes by its isolated western location.

All of the territory's cities, primarily red-brick mill towns with industry based on textiles, electrical equipment and light manufacturing, have lost residents since the 1970 census. Holyoke's shrinkage of 10.8 percent was greater than the loss in Northampton, Pittsfield and North Adams.

The one center of population growth in the 1970s was Hampshire County, which grew by a robust 12 percent. Hampshire includes the youth-oriented "five college" area that is home to the University of Massachusetts, Smith, Mount Holyoke, Amherst and Hampshire colleges. Rustic Franklin County, the smallest on the state's mainland, grew by 8.6 percent, while scenic Berkshire County suffered a 2.9 percent population loss.

The district's largest employer, the sprawling General Electric (GE) installation in Pittsfield, produces electrical transformers, plastics and weapons guidance systems. The plant's reliance on cyclical military contracts and the gradual shift of GE operations to the Sun Belt keep the local economy alternating between periods of stability and decline. The second-oldest commercial nuclear power plant in the nation, the Yankee Atomic plant in isolated Monroe Bridge near the Vermont border, has eased the energy-starved area's dependence on OPEC oil, although it has been the focus of a local controversy over waste disposal.

New Massachusetts Districts

New District	Incumbent	Population	1980 Pres. Winner
1	Silvio O. Conte (R)	522,820	Carter
2	Edward P. Boland (D)	521,669	Carter
3	Joseph D. Early (D)	521,354	Reagan
4	Margaret M. Heckler (R) Barney Frank (D)	521,995	Carter
5	James M. Shannon (D)	519,878	Reagan
6	Nicholas Mavroules (D)	518,841	Reagan
7	Edward J. Markey (D)	522,417	Carter
8	Thomas P. O'Neill Jr. (D)	520,691	Carter
9	Joe Moakley (D)	521,626	Carter
10	Gerry E. Studds (D)	522,200	Reagan
11	Brian J. Donnelly (D)	523,546	Reagan

Outside the cities, dairy farming remains important to the western Massachusetts economy, although the number of farms is comparatively small. There is also some tobacco growing along the Connecticut border.

Pittsfield, the largest city in the 1st, leans Democratic but sometimes splits its ticket to support liberal Republicans. In the closely fought 1978 governor's race, Pittsfield and Berkshire County bucked the statewide trend and supported a liberal Republican, Francis W. Hatch, over the conservative Democrat King. At the same time, the county gave strong margins to liberal Democrat Tsongas over Republican Edward W. Brooke. In that election, Berkshire County's vote was within one-tenth of a percentage point of the statewide outcome; the county is often viewed as a bellwether of Massachusetts political trends.

The remap added to the 1st the town of Orange, unifying all of Franklin County within the district. The new boundaries also extend the 1st into Worcester County, adding the towns of Athol, Royalston, Winchendon, Templeton, Philipston and Petersham.

Although the 1st District is generally as Democratic as the state as a whole, it has never sent a Democrat to the U.S. House. Conte, the son of Italian immigrants, has represented the district in the House since 1959. Conte's base of support is so broad that the 1st is now his political preserve; he frequently runs for re-election unopposed.

District 2

West-central — Springfield

Incumbent: Edward P. Boland (D)

The economic woes of the 1970s badly hurt Springfield and Chicopee, in the center of the industrial corridor that runs along the Connecticut River. The 2nd District as a whole lost 1.3 percent of its population between 1970 and 1980, forcing it to move east to pick up additional territory in northern Worcester County.

Springfield is the population base of the 2nd District as well as the commercial center of the western part of the state. The city has significant French-Canadian and Polish populations, and is 16 percent black and 9 percent Puerto Rican. The largest Springfield employers are the Monsanto chemical plant and the Massachusetts Mutual Life Insurance offices. Springfield has diversified its economy since the mid-70s' recession and was showing signs of renewal when the latest economic downturn began.

Chicopee, the second-largest city in the district, suffered a 17.3 percent loss of population during the past decade. The closure of rubber and metal companies eliminated about 5,600 jobs, and the Strategic Air Command closed its Westover Air Force Base bomber field — once the largest on the East Coast — in 1973. Westover remains a reserve base. In the last few years, however, the city has attracted some new high-technology industries.

The Democratic voters in Springfield and Chicopee usually outvote the Republicans in the territory's smaller towns, but Jimmy Carter carried the district by only 2,000 votes in 1980. Of the cities in the newly drawn 2nd, only suburban Westfield and Leominster voted for Reagan. Boland, a fifteen-term veteran of almost universal popularity, heavily outpolled the rest of the Democratic ticket in 1980 within the old, slightly different district lines.

The addition of the medium-sized cities of Gardner, Fitchburg and Leominster, and the town of Westminster, all of which had been in the old 4th District, preserves the 2nd's character as a center for light industry. The district lost Orange, in Franklin County, and Athol, Royalston, Winchendon, Templeton, Philipston and Petersham to the 1st. It lost Ashburnham to the 5th District and Douglas to the 3rd.

Silvio O. Conte   **Edward P. Boland**

District 3

Central — Worcester

Incumbent: Joseph D. Early (D)

The 3rd District is built around the city of Worcester, the second-largest city in the state of Massachusetts. Worcester's total population declined substantially during the last ten years, however its economy showed signs of health.

Among the nation's first major industrial centers not built on a natural waterway, Worcester started as a center for the manufacturing of textiles and wire. Now it has a broadly based economy, centered around the metals and machine-tool industries, which has given it an unemployment figure below the statewide average and far below the national unemployment rate. The Norton Company, the world's largest maker of grinding wheels, leads the list of Worcester employers.

Computer manufacturers have been attracted in recent years to the Marlborough area and other communities east of Worcester on Interstate 495, the outer highway surrounding Boston. Digital Equipment Company is in Marlborough; Data General has located its facilities in Westborough.

Worcester is also a major educational center. The Public Affairs Research Center affiliated with Clark University has emerged as a major political science institute. Holy Cross College, founded in 1843 as the first Catholic college in New England, towers over the city from a scenic hillside.

The area within the new 3rd District gave a 43-to-40-percent plurality to Jimmy Carter in 1980, but showed little enthusiasm for him; Joseph D. Early carried the same communities overwhelmingly. While the city of Worcester gave Carter a 7,841-vote plurality, Reagan was carrying Worcester County by 2,774 votes. In 1978, the city of Worcester produced almost identical Democratic margins for conservative King for governor and liberal Tsongas for senator.

Redistricting added Douglas from the 2nd; Sherborn, Millis and Norfolk from the old 10th; and Lunenburg, Shirley, Lancaster, Bolton and Stow from the old 4th. The changes should make the district slightly more Republican,

but will probably not pose a significant counterweight to Worcester's usual Democratic turnout or threaten Early's solid hold on the district.

District 4

Boston suburbs, Fall River

Incumbents: Barney Frank (D)

Margaret M. Heckler (R)

The new 4th, built out of portions of the old 4th and 10th districts, has emerged as Massachusetts' electoral battleground this year. On paper, it favors Democrats. The voter registration figures show 115,000 Democrats, 44,000 Republicans and 119,000 Independents. As presently drawn, the 4th favored Carter in 1980 by a 42-to-40-percent margin.

But the new 4th includes 360,000 of Heckler's old constituents, and only about 138,000 of Frank's. Just two of Frank's current towns — Brookline and Newton — are included, but there are 19 towns from Heckler's old 10th District.

Barney Frank had a margin of nearly 13,000 votes in the 1980 election in Brookline, a suburb with a large Jewish population, where he ran 5,500 votes ahead of Jimmy Carter. Frank had more than an 11,000-vote edge in his adopted hometown of Newton, where he ran ahead of the ticket by 6,500. Both towns are longtime Democratic strongholds; both towns gave 60 percent margins to George McGovern in 1972.

Margaret Heckler's hometown of Wellesley, an affluent western suburb with a population of 27,000, usually favors Republicans. Heckler won it by more than 2-to-1 in 1980, running more than 2,300 votes ahead of Reagan. Wellesley voted for Ford in 1976 and Nixon in 1972 by comfortable margins.

The new 4th District extends south from the Boston suburbs all the way to the Rhode Island boundary. The industrial town of Fall River, located on the border of the two states, is traditionally Democratic but has been loyal to Heckler, who is popular among the blue-collar workers in the city's needle trades. The city is trying to diversify beyond its garment industry base. A pilot plant for synthetic fuels development is expected to boost the area's economy.

Heckler won Fall River in 1980 by 3,000 votes. But the city's Democratic leanings have shown up clearly in other contests. In 1978, Fall River gave a 71.1 percent majority to Gov. Edward J. King and a 63.5 percent victory to Sen. Paul E. Tsongas. In 1972, it gave George McGovern 63.0 percent of its vote.

Attleboro, a city of 34,000, is generally good territory for any Republican candidate. Its traditional jewelry trade is now giving way to high-technology industries, symbolized by its Texas Instruments plant. While surrounding Bristol County was giving Jimmy Carter a 6,000-vote victory in the 1980 election, Attleboro gave a plurality to Ronald Reagan. Both Gov. King and Sen. Tsongas carried the city in 1978, but by margins smaller than they enjoyed statewide.

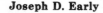
Joseph D. Early   Barney Frank

District 5

North — Lowell, Lawrence

Incumbent: James M. Shannon (D)

A district centered around two gritty mill towns where the American textile industry got its start in the early 19th century, the 5th has seen gradual economic decline and modest recent renewal.

The long-running rivalry of Lowell and Lawrence, the population centers of the district, springs from their different histories as textile centers: Lowell, the model "company town," was carefully watched over by paternal Yankee Protestants, while Lawrence's unsafe work places and substandard living conditions gave rise to immigrant workers' resentment of the city's planners, Boston's State Street financiers. Soon after mill workers won Lawrence's strike of 1912 — in which agitation for wage increases led to one of the sharpest confrontations in labor history — textile companies began leaving the Merrimack Valley, looking for cheaper labor in the South.

A decade ago, both towns were in sad economic shape. Since 1975, however, Lowell has seen its economy revitalized by the arrival of high-technology firms. Wang, a computer company, is the city's largest employer. The nation's first urban historical park has been established in Lowell around the Merrimack River's system of canals.

Lawrence has been slower to profit from the technology boom, but in the late 1970s a paint company and other light manufacturing firms began moving into abandoned mill space downtown. The current recession has slowed that activity somewhat.

Both cities are solidly Democratic. But the rivalry remains. Shannon, a Lawrence product, used votes from his hometown to defeat rivals from Lowell in both 1978 and 1980; Tsongas, his 5th District predecessor, comes from Lowell and had worked to develop Lawrence loyalties early in his congressional career. But by 1978, the year of his Senate campaign, Tsongas had consolidated his strength throughout the district and drew more than 75 percent of the general election vote in both cities.

There is more to the 5th than Lowell and Lawrence. More than 50 percent of the district was suburban in the 1970s, and territory newly added to the district includes the well-to-do suburbs of Weston and Wayland, upper-crust Lincoln and bucolic Sudbury. All four towns gave pluralities to Ronald Reagan in 1980, as did Andover and Concord, which remain in the district. But all these suburbs have strong liberal factions and go Democratic in most contests. Liberal votes in Concord and Andover helped Shannon overcome a Lowell-based primary challenge in 1980. Concord gave 22.5 percent of its ballots to Anderson in 1980, the main reason Reagan came in first there.

Framingham, which blends light manufacturing and middle-class neighborhoods, has been shifted from Frank's old 4th to Shannon's 5th. Frank had hoped to keep the town in his district, and Shannon was willing to cede it to him, but the statehouse cartographers refused. In the 1980 election, Framingham went narrowly for both Carter and Frank. In 1978, it preferred liberal Republican Hatch over conservative Democrat King for governor; in that year's Senate race, the town narrowly favored Tsongas over Brooke.

Republican voters in the smaller towns helped Reagan in 1980 carry the district with just 44 percent, while Carter and Anderson were splitting the majority.

In this year's remap, the 5th gained Maynard, Sudbury, Framingham, Ayer, Weston, Wayland, Lincoln and Harvard from the 4th, and Ashburnham from the 2nd. It lost North Reading to the 6th, and Lexington, Wilmington, Billerica and Tewksbury to the 7th.

District 6

North Shore — Lynn, Peabody

Incumbent: Nicholas Mavroules (D)

An area of geographical variety and economic contrast, the 6th contains chronically depressed mill towns, workaday factory cities, comfortable suburbs, pockets of aristocratic wealth and scenic ocean-front villages. Its vote-heavy areas are at the southern end of Essex County, and are strongly Democratic. But the district's strong 1980 vote for Anderson helped Reagan carry the 6th, and Essex County as a whole, by a plurality.

Lynn, historically a shoe-manufacturing center but now home of a large General Electric aircraft engine plant, has suffered a 13 percent population loss since 1970, but remains the 6th's largest city. Lynn gave Carter only a 3,800-vote margin in 1980, about half the edge it had given conservative Democrat King in the 1978 governor's race. Nearby Peabody, once the largest leather-processing city in the world, gave Carter a 600-vote edge in 1980, also far less than King's margin. Similarly Democratic is Salem, on the northern end of this industrial tier. It gave comfortable margins to Carter, Tsongas and King.

North of Salem are areas of Essex County where the aristocratic tradition of Yankee Protestantism provides GOP votes but now tends to favor liberal Republicans. Prides Crossing, the affluent hometown of 1978 GOP gubernatorial nominee Francis Hatch, was the backdrop for some of King's 1978 campaign advertisements, underscoring the Republicans' lingering elitist image. Beverly and nearby Gloucester provided sizable Republican margins in both 1978 and 1980. Suburban Wenham was one of only

Margaret M. Heckler   **James M. Shannon**

Nicholas Mavroules   **Edward J. Markey**

three towns in the commonwealth where Anderson out-polled Carter.

On the northern coast, maritime interests are central to Gloucester, home of the Fisherman's Memorial landmark, and Rockport, a historic fishing village deluged with tourists and artists in the summer. Newburyport, whose 19th century clipper ship economy gave way to light manufacturing, is the "Yankee City" singled out for study by sociologists in the 1920s. In the past decade it has attracted some emigrants from urban areas and was one of the few Bay State cities to grow, albeit slowly, in the last decade. A major northern coast political issue is the siting of the Seabrook nuclear power plant, just across the New Hampshire line.

Haverhill won the dubious distinction in a 1981 survey of being the nation's metropolitan area with the least desirable "quality of life." The town's economic base in the shoe industry has long since disappeared and there has been no comparable successor.

The district is closely contested in most elections, but Reagan won 29 of the 34 Essex County cities and towns in 1980. Mavroules, who in 1980 lost 18 communities in the old 6th while winning only 11, narrowly won a second term that year on the strength of his margins of 5,600 in Peabody, 9,100 in Lynn and 5,500 in Salem.

In this year's remap, the 6th gained North Reading from the 5th, and Lynnfield and Saugus from the 7th.

District 7

Northern suburbs — Medford, Malden

Incumbent: Edward J. Markey (D)

Primarily a collection of medium-sized cities on the edge of metropolitan Boston, the 7th had to expand north and west through Middlesex County to make up its population deficit. While the newly added areas will give the 7th a slightly more suburban character, the district should remain solidly Democratic for Markey. But it did not prove very friendly to Carter in 1980; while the liberal Markey ran unopposed that year, a strong Anderson vote held Carter's plurality within the district lines to 169 votes.

The communities north of Boston are heavily urbanized and town boundaries are almost invisible. All the blue-collar towns close to the Boston city limits have lost population since 1970, some of them sharply. Chelsea declined by 17.0 percent, Everett by 12.5 percent, Melrose by 9 percent. Energetic urban improvement efforts have slowed the decline of Malden, where Italians are the dominant ethnic group. Carter handily won all these cities in 1980 except Melrose, where Reagan had a 1,900-vote edge. Melrose split its 1978 ticket, backing Republican Hatch for governor and Democrat Tsongas for the Senate.

Woburn, situated along the Route 128 beltway, the core of Massachusetts' high-technology industry, experienced slight growth during the decade 1970-1980. It was one of only nine of the state's 39 cities that underwent any expansion at all. Woburn's residents voted almost 2-to-1 for both Tsongas and King in 1978. In the 1980 presidential race, they gave Carter a 447-vote margin. Independent Anderson was popular in Woburn too, gaining nearly 2,500-votes.

Most of the suburban areas added by the remap have also grown since 1970. Within the orbit of Lowell's rebounding economy, Billerica's 16.0 percent growth paced Tewksbury's 8.3 percent and Wilmington's 2.2 percent. All three towns went narrowly for Reagan in 1980, with the vote for Anderson denying Carter victory in all of them.

The comfortable, upper-middle-class suburb of Lexington, added from the 5th District, went overwhelmingly for liberal Republican Hatch in 1978. However, the one-time stronghold of Yankee Republicanism now can be depended upon to back liberal Democrats against most opponents from the more conservative side of the GOP.

In the recent remap, the 7th yielded Lynnfield and Saugus to the 6th, and gained Billerica, Tewksbury, Wilmington and Lexington from the 5th.

District 8

Boston and suburbs — Cambridge

Incumbent: Thomas P. O'Neill Jr. (D)

Ethnic, working-class Cambridge coexists peacefully, if not always sympathetically, with the Harvard-M.I.T. colossus that surrounds it. There is a political cohesiveness that transcends cultural differences — both segments of the 8th District are Democratic and liberal on economic issues. O'Neill, a product of Irish immigrant parents, Depression poverty and street-corner politics, has had no problems in the academic community since his surprise announcement, in 1967, that he could no longer support the Vietnam War.

The cultural divisions, however, are real. Outside the university precincts exists a crowded, grimy city. The proximity of trendy Harvard Square and seedy Central Square makes Cambridge no stranger to town-vs.-gown tensions. One city councilman has practically made a career of baiting the Ivy League school, suggesting repeatedly that Harvard Yard be paved over to relieve the city's parking problems.

With a straight-ticket Democratic voting history, Cambridge gave 74 percent of its vote to George McGovern in 1972 — his majority statewide was 54 percent — and it gave Carter a 61-to-20-percent victory in 1980. But Cambridge voters sometimes cross party lines to seek out liberals. In the 1978 gubernatorial race, Hatch beat King in the city by 59 to 41 percent.

The 8th extends across the Charles River to include a large segment of Boston. Allston and Brighton, historically centers for Boston's Jewish community, today have a large transient student population. Harvard Business School, Boston University and part of Boston College are within the boundaries of the district in Boston's 21st and 22nd wards. Newly joined to the territory is Boston's 4th Ward, which adds Northeastern University and Harvard Medical School and unifies the Back Bay and the Fenway in the 8th.

The affluent Back Bay has become a symbol of high-income urban "gentrification." Beacon Hill, where the 23-carat gold statehouse dome dominates elegant 18th- and 19th-century homes built by Federalists, is now predominantly liberal and Democratic. Irish working-class Charlestown and heavily Italian East Boston are also in the 8th.

To the west, the district includes the working-class city of Somerville and the middle-class towns of Arlington and Watertown. All three gave large margins to Democrats King and Tsongas in 1978 and distinctly narrower pluralities to Carter in 1980. Suburban Belmont, the home of the John Birch Society's national headquarters, does not have much in common with Birch Society politics; it favored Hatch for the 1978 governorship and Tsongas for the Senate. Anderson's 16.8 percent showing tilted the town to Reagan in 1980.

The remap joins the medium-sized city of Waltham to the 8th, taking it from the dismantled 4th. Waltham has its own town-and-gown problems. It has a blue-collar majority, largely Italian, and is also the home of Brandeis University, with an aggressively liberal student and faculty community.

District 9

Boston and southern suburbs

Incumbent: Joe Moakley (D)

If the 8th District has many of the fashionable and scenic areas that attract tourist guidebook superlatives, it is the 9th that contains most of Boston's workaday precincts. The 9th has suffered a 10.1 percent population loss since the 1970 census — the steepest drop in the state — and its boundaries have had to stretch south from its 12 Boston wards to include several smaller cities and towns.

The population of Boston itself has dipped below the 600,000 mark, and the ethnic character of the city is changing dramatically. While white population has dropped by 24.9 percent since the 1970 count, blacks have increased by 20.6 percent, and now account for 22.4 percent of Boston's population. Blacks and Hispanics together now comprise about 30 percent of the city.

The days of Mayor James Michael Curley may be long gone, but Boston retains one of the country's premier Democratic machines. The deeply rooted operation of four-term Mayor Kevin H. White has easily turned back three re-election challenges. But the city showed some reluctance

to support Jimmy Carter in the 1980 presidential election; it gave the incumbent president only a 53.3-percent showing, far less than the 66.2 percent George McGovern compiled in 1972.

Jimmy Carter's plurality within the boundaries of the new 9th District was less than 5,000 votes. Moakley ran unopposed for a fifth term in 1980; he has had no trouble commanding large majorities since his first general election campaign, which he won as an independent candidate in 1972.

The inner-city part of the 9th includes the heavily Italian North End; the trendy Waterfront area, where young government workers and other professionals are moving; the West End, whose towering high-rises replaced a thriving ethnic community in the 1950s; the Government Center complex; and most of the downtown shopping district. Conversion of the historic Quincy Market into a glittery emporium of upscale merchandise has injected new life into the historic area.

Beyond these areas lies a group of communities that have undergone serious racial tensions in the past decade. South Boston, still 98.5 percent white and overwhelmingly Irish, was the center of bitter opposition to school busing in the 1970s. Substantial support in South Boston allowed George C. Wallace to carry the old 9th when he ran in the 1976 Democratic presidential primary.

Roxbury and Mission Hill, whose census tract is 69.1 percent black, borders on Jamaica Plain, still a predominantly white community but changing rapidly. During the past decade, more than one-third of the white population of this area left, the black population more than doubled in size and Hispanics came to make up 21 percent of the residents. Part of the South End, an area of urban restoration, is also in the 9th District, as is racially mixed Dorchester.

Southern suburbs added by the remapping include Stoughton, Easton, Raynham, Dighton, Taunton, Bridgewater, Halifax, Middleborough and Lakeville. Together they have 148,000 people, and all but one of the towns went for Ronald Reagan in 1980. But the town of Taunton, which has nearly a quarter of the new population, voted for Jimmy Carter and is generally Democratic. The new additions are unlikely to weaken Moakley's hold on the district very much.

The 9th District yields Boston's 4th Ward to the 8th District and the towns of Walpole and Dover to the 4th District.

Thomas P. O'Neill Jr.   **Joe Moakley**

District 10

South Shore, Southeast and Cape Cod

Incumbent: Gerry E. Studds (D)

With a brisk 23.0 percent population increase since the 1970 census, the southeastern district is the only area of the state that has experienced rapid growth during the 1970s. Numbered as the 12th for the past two decades, it was given a new designation as the 10th with the state's reduction to 11 districts.

Paced by the fast-growing South Shore suburbs that send commuters to downtown Boston, Plymouth County grew by 21.6 percent. Further out, the boom that has transformed scenic Cape Cod from a summertime retreat to a year-round residence helped Barnstable County's population to surge by 53.0 percent.

The area is the most Republican in the Democratic-dominated state. Three of the four Bay State counties that Richard M. Nixon carried in 1972 — Barnstable, Nantucket and Dukes (Martha's Vineyard) — are in the new 10th. The district was also Reagan's strongest and Carter's weakest district in 1980, with a 47-to-35-percent Reagan plurality within the new boundaries.

The town of Plymouth has seen its population almost double since 1970. The site of a historic district around Plymouth Rock, the town is also home to the controversial Pilgrim nuclear power plants. In 1980, the town was tilted narrowly to Reagan by Anderson's 2,500-vote showing.

To the southwest, on Bristol County's Buzzards Bay coast, lies New Bedford, which became the world's largest whaling center in the early 19th century and which still retains its orientation toward the fishing industry. The city was a pre-Civil-War way-station along the "Underground Railroad" spiriting runaway slaves to safety, and now is home to a large number of illegal immigrants amid its significant legal migrations from Portugal and the Cape Verde Islands. New Bedford provided 65 percent majorities for King and Tsongas in 1978 and went to Carter in 1980.

Cape Cod is all in Barnstable County, where every town enjoyed at least modest growth during the decade. Environmentalists, fearful of despoiling the area's sandy shores and fragile marine life, have fought to keep oil-drilling exploration in offshore Georges Bank under strict controls. Along the curve of the cape lies the sandy national seashore preserve, a mecca for summer tourists but a lonely winter outpost for seamen in a still vigorous fishing trade. Provincetown, an artists' retreat at the tip of the cape, is the only town in this solidly Republican county where Carter outpolled Reagan in 1980.

The 10th also includes the islands of Nantucket and Martha's Vineyard, where a strong sense of independence reigns. When the recent reorganization of the state Legislature sought to deprive the islands of their own legislative seats, there was considerable discussion of seceding from the Bay State to join Vermont or becoming sovereign states on their own. Nantucket County provided Anderson his highest nationwide showing, 21.7 percent, and Dukes County was his third-highest territory, with 21.0 percent.

In this year's remap, the district lost Rockland and Weymouth to the 11th, and gained Hanson from the 10th.

District 11

South Shore suburbs — Quincy, Brockton

Incumbent: Brian J. Donnelly (D)

The 11th includes the southern wards of Boston and the city's southern suburbs. Its closer-in communities declined slightly in population during the 1970s, but its more distant Boston suburbs gained slightly.

The area is usually Democratic — McGovern won it in 1972 and Carter carried it in 1976 — but the new district gave Reagan a 44-to-41-percent victory in 1980. Anderson pulled only 13.1 percent here, his lowest statewide share.

All four of the Boston wards in the district, which hold about one-third of the 11th's population, lost residents during the decade: Dorchester was down by 26 percent, Hyde Park by 15 percent and Neponset and Mattapan by 18.5 percent. Moreover, all these areas — like Boston and Suffolk County as a whole — showed substantial losses of white residents while the black population soared. The Neponset-Mattapan census tract in Boston, now evenly balanced racially, showed a 50 percent decline among whites as the black population nearly doubled. Hyde Park's black population has multiplied nearly tenfold since 1970.

Quincy, at the end of the MBTA Red Line that brings commuters home to the South Shore from Boston, is the largest community in Norfolk County. It has a heavy concentration of ethnics, with Irish, Italian and French-Canadian pockets. The Quincy shipyards along the Fore River turn out liquefied-natural-gas tankers that bring the highly volatile cargo from the Middle East to energy-starved New England. Quincy gave 60 percent margins to both King and Tsongas in 1978, but Reagan eked out a 61-vote victory in the city in 1980.

Brockton, with 95,000 residents the largest city in Plymouth County, was long the shoe-making center of the nation. Then named North Bridgewater, it shod half the Union Army in the Civil War. But the city's footwear industry has been in decline for a generation. Brockton remains solidly Democratic.

In the remapping process, the 11th District gained the towns of East Bridgewater, West Bridgewater, Rockland and Weymouth.

Gerry E. Studds   **Brian J. Donnelly**

West Virginia

Coal is the symbol of West Virginia — of its decline and fall, and of its current modest reawakening.

The state has other important natural resources, including natural gas, but traditionally it has ranked first in the nation in the production of bituminous coal. It has now slipped to second place behind Kentucky. The coal industry, however, continues to be the largest single employer in the state and the largest contributor to the gross state product.

Even in the strongest coal years, before demand began to decline sharply in the 1950s, West Virginia was one of the poorest states. Most of the mine owners were not West Virginians, and few residents shared in the profits of extraction. In the postwar years, the situation gradually got worse. In 1970, the median family income of $7,414 was lower than that of all but three states, each of them in the deep South. In terms of median school years completed, the state ranked forty-seventh.

Between 1950 and 1970, as the national population was growing by one-third, West Virginia's population was declining by nearly 15 percent, and its six congressional districts were pared down to four.

That is why it is so striking that West Virginia grew by 11.8 percent during the 1970s — slightly more than the national average. Nearly all the growth was in the second half of the decade, generated by the renewed demand for coal that accompanied rising world oil prices. Charleston, the state capital, technically lost population over the ten year period, but by 1980 it had some of the appearance of an energy boom town.

The hopeful economic signs for West Virginia have had their effect on politics as well; in 1980 the state elected two Republicans to the U.S. House of Representatives, the first GOP representatives in more than a decade. Despite those results, however, West Virginia's basic political orientation has not changed very drastically since the state became federally dependent and viscerally Democratic during the New Deal.

Senior Sen. Jennings Randolph survived a strong 1978 challenge and today is the only member of Congress who was serving during Franklin D. Roosevelt's "hundred days" in 1933. Robert C. Byrd, the Senate minority leader, is untouchable at home. Arch A. Moore Jr., who served as governor from 1969 to 1977 and nearly unseated Randolph in 1978, has been the only credible statewide Republican candidate in the last twenty years.

The dominant political figure today is Democratic Gov. John D. (Jay) Rockefeller IV. Defeated in his initial bid for the governorship but subsequently elected in 1976, he won re-election in 1980 after a campaign that advertised his name on television stations in Washington, D.C., a first for any candidate running outside the D.C. metropolitan area. At reports that he was spending almost $12 million in his re-election campaign against Moore, who was seeking a comeback, bumper stickers appeared reading, "Make him spend it all, Arch."

Northern Panhandle

Jutting north from the center of the state, West Virginia's northern panhandle is more like the industrialized Northeast than the rest of West Virginia. Brooke and Hancock counties at the tip of the peninsula identify more with Pittsburgh than with Charleston or Huntington.

In the four counties that make up the panhandle and in the counties just south of it, there is substantially more industrialization and urbanization than is found elsewhere in the state. And there is less poverty. The median family income here is far above the state's average.

The prime industry in the panhandle is steel. Wheeling, often described as a "grimy steel town," is the largest city in the area (population 43,000) and has the same pollution problems found in most of the other steel cities located along the steep banks of the Ohio River.

The counties just south of the panhandle include some rural areas and a number of smaller cities with substantial heavy industry.

The northern panhandle and the adjacent counties make up one of the few areas in the state with significant concentrations of ethnic voters. Wheeling has a large Italian population. The ethnic voters are normally Democratic, although Republicans do well in some areas of the panhandle. A few counties south of the panhandle itself, such as Doddridge and Tyler, are solidly Republican.

Until the New Deal, this region often kept Republican candidates competitive in statewide elections. Moore represented much of the area in Congress from 1957 to 1969.

The Rural East

Relying more on agriculture than on coal, but lacking productive farm land in many places, mountainous eastern West Virginia is traditionally the poorest part of the state.

It has been devoted to farming because there have been few alternatives.

The mountaineers who farm along the broad ridges here grow some corn and wheat and raise broiler chickens. There is a considerable amount of dairy farming as well.

In recent years, the tourist trade has become increasingly important in many of the eastern counties, and has raised the standard of living in some. Among the more popular attractions are the baths at Berkeley Springs, the Monongalia National Forest, and historic Harper's Ferry.

The three easternmost counties, known as the "eastern panhandle," are within long-range commuting distance of Washington, D.C., and have developed a community of white-collar professionals who take the train to the nation's capital every morning.

Eastern West Virginia tends to be Democratic, but there are still traces of mountain Republican tradition, and GOP candidates are competitive in some counties. Berkeley, Morgan and Grant counties are among the more Republican counties in the state.

Democrat Harley O. Staggers represented this area in Congress for sixteen terms, and until his retirement in 1980, he was the dominant political figure in the eastern part of the state. The 1980 election of Cleve Benedict, a conservative Republican, may foretell a shift in the region's political leanings.

The Coal Counties

The southern end of West Virginia is dominated by the coal industry and organized labor. The state as a whole is the second most unionized in the country. Boone County is the leading producer of coal in the state, with McDowell, Mingo and Logan counties not far behind. During the 1920s this area of the state was the scene of mine wars between the coal operators and their hired hands on one side, and miners and union organizers on the other. By the 1940s, thanks to New Deal legislation, the United Mine Workers had become the most powerful political force in the state, and the miners of southern West Virginia had become loyal Democrats. Those counties continue to deliver the largest Democratic margins in the state.

Historically, the coal counties of southern West Virginia have been the scene of some of the most corrupt machine politics in the country. Often with little effort to conceal it, votes have been exchanged for cash or whiskey, and corruption has been tolerated as a part of local life.

Kanahwa Valley

If much of West Virginia seems stagnant, the Kanahwa Valley is today dynamic and vigorous. The area stretches roughly from Charleston to Huntington, the manufacturing center on the Ohio River.

Charleston, in Kanawha County, is the state's financial center and the home of chemical plants belonging to a few major companies, including Union Carbide and Du Pont. In the 1970s, the area began to attract increasing numbers of young people. But Charleston also has a poor black area and considerable pollution.

Most of the voters in the area are traditional Democrats and union members, but like most West Virginians, they are strongly conservative on matters concerning God, country and family. This was demonstrated vividly in the 1974 protest over school textbooks. Fundamentalists in Kanawha County took exception to books that they charged were "un-Christian" and "pornographic." With substantial community support, they burned some offending books and temporarily shut down the schools. One textbook activist, David Michael Staton, was elected to Congress from Charleston as a Republican in 1980.

Kanawha and Cabell counties (Charleston and Huntington) account for about 20 percent of the state vote. A Republican running statewide needs to run well in this area to overcome heavy Democratic pluralities in the surrounding rural area.

FEW CHANGES IN WEST VIRGINIA

After considering proposals designed to unseat at least one of the state's two Republican House members, the Democratic-controlled West Virginia Legislature approved a redistricting plan early in 1982 that made only minor alterations in the existing lines. The plan passed the Legislature Jan. 28 and was signed by Democratic Gov. John D. "Jay" Rockefeller IV on Feb. 8, 1982.

None of the four districts was more than 35,000 out of population balance, so no major surgery was needed. The remap affected only three of West Virginia's 55 counties. All are in the rural north central part of the state and have a combined population of less than 50,000.

The GOP congressional victories in 1980 had tempted legislators to make more drastic changes. Republicans Cleve Benedict and David Michael Staton won House seats, ending a 12-year Democratic monopoly of the congressional delegation.

Intent on regaining at least one of the seats, the Democratic House passed a redistricting bill in 1981 aimed at weakening Staton, who had won the previous year by only 9,603 votes, a margin less than half as large as Benedict's. But state Senate leaders viewed the changes as too drastic. Enthusiasm for the plan evaporated when Benedict announced in November that he would vacate his House seat to run for the U.S. Senate. With the 2nd District suddenly open, Democratic leaders shifted targets and endorsed a redistricting plan that left each district basically intact.

District 1

Northern Panhandle — Wheeling

Incumbent: Robert H. Mollohan (D)

The 1st District's northernmost regions are in the orbit of industrial Pittsburgh. Heavy industry (iron and steel) is concentrated in the Panhandle, a narrow strip of West Virginia crowded between the Pennsylvania border and the Ohio River. To the southeast, coal is mined in Marion and Harrison counties and shipped up the Monongahela River to the western Pennsylvania metropolis.

Both areas of the 1st District are heavily unionized and boast concentrations of Southern and Eastern European ethnics, descendants of immigrants who were

U. S. Congress: 4 districts
  Senate (2D)
  House (2D, 2R)
Governor:
  John D. Rockefeller IV (D)
Population: 1,949,644
Area: 24,181 sq. miles
1980 Presidential Vote:
  Carter (50%)
  Reagan (45%)
  Anderson (4%)

New West Virginia Districts

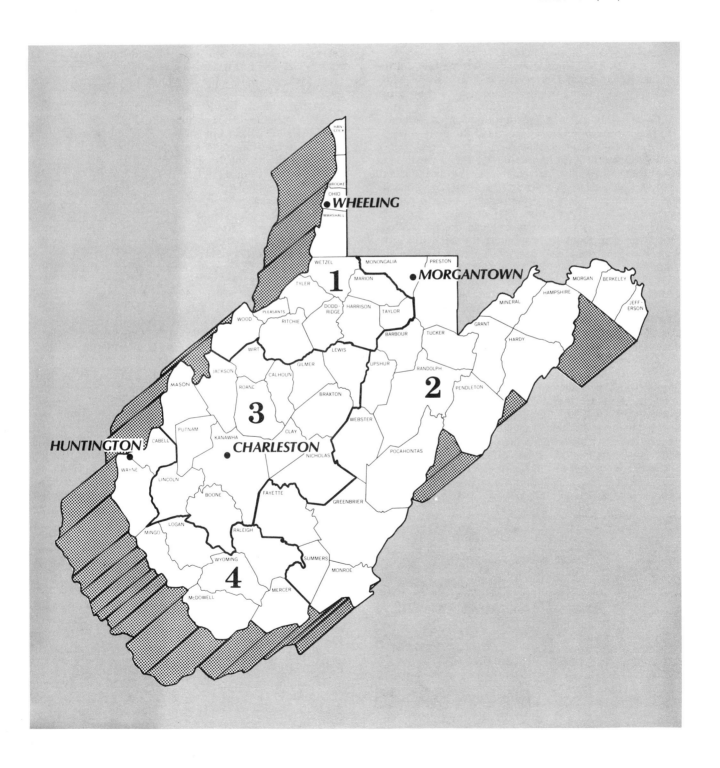

attracted by work in the mines and mills. These areas usually produce Democratic majorities sufficient to carry the district.

Marion and Harrison counties, which also are major glass producers, and Brooke and Hancock counties, at the northern tip of the Panhandle, are the most reliably Democratic counties in the district. All four counties preferred Jimmy Carter by at least 12 percentage points over Ronald Reagan in 1980. Together the four comprise 43 percent of the district population.

Massive layoffs in the steel industry have devastated the economy in Brooke County and Hancock County, where the unemployment rate surpassed 15 percent in late 1981. Ohio County (Wheeling) has fared better. But like the rest of the Panhandle, it lost population during the last 20 years.

In the 1800s Wheeling was the western terminus of the National Road, a major artery between the Eastern seaboard and the growing frontier. Since then, Wheeling has developed into the Panhandle's commercial center, with a significant white-collar population that often produces GOP majorities. Ohio County has voted Republican in the last three presidential elections.

To the south is Marshall County, the home base of former Republican Gov. Arch A. Moore. Ohio and Marshall counties, which together make up 22 percent of the district population, gave Moore a strong enough base to win six terms in the U.S. House, from 1957 to 1969.

The only other population center in the 1st is Wood County, located about midway along the Ohio River between Wheeling and Huntington. The county holds nearly 20 percent of the district voters and anchors the southwestern corner of the 1st. Like the rural counties that separate it from the district's other, more industrialized urban centers, Wood County frequently votes Republican.

Although the 1st District was long the most prosperous district in West Virginia, its population grew by only approximately 6 percent during the 1970s — a lower growth rate than in any other district in the state. Redistricting has added Ritchie County from the 3rd District and Taylor County from the 2nd. Both are rural and Republican oriented, but together they make up only 5 percent of the district population.

Mollohan has decided not to seek re-election. Although the 1st has traditional Democratic loyalties, Mollohan's retirement gives the state's resurgent Republican Party a chance at a third seat in the House delegation.

District 2

East — Morgantown, eastern Panhandle

Incumbent: Cleve Benedict (R)

It does not take long for an incumbent to make his position impregnable in the 2nd District because challengers find it difficult to reach the electorate hidden in its hills and hollows.

One of the largest districts east of the Mississippi River, the 2nd has no major media markets. Democratic Rep. Harley O. Staggers held the congressional seat for 32 years until his retirement in 1980, and many Democratic leaders virtually had conceded a second term to incumbent Cleve Benedict before the Republican announced his bid for a Senate seat.

After several decades of population decline, many counties in the 2nd showed substantial gains in the 1970s. The district's 20 percent growth rate outstripped other districts in the state and forced the 2nd to shed two counties — Taylor to the 1st and Lewis to the 3rd. Both are small, Republican-leaning counties situated along the district's western border.

Population growth was greatest in the eastern Panhandle, where large numbers of retirees and commuters from the Baltimore and Washington, D.C., metropolitan areas have relocated. Jefferson County, located at the tip of the Panhandle, showed a 42 percent population increase during the last decade, the largest increase of any county in the state.

But most of the district is in the Allegheny Mountains, where the standard of living is the lowest in the state. Many mountaineers turn to the large tourist trade to supplement their meager incomes. The luxurious Greenbrier Hotel in White Sulphur Springs is one of the district's major employers.

With mining and industry limited and major agricultural operations restricted to level areas of the Panhandle, neither political party has a large natural constituency in the district. Elections are frequently determined by name recognition.

Democratic strength is greatest in the few mining and industrial areas along the western fringe of the district. Monongalia County, one of the leading coal-producing counties in the state, combines a sizable number of blue-collar voters with the large academic community at West Virginia University in Morgantown. The county holds 15 percent of the district population.

Fayette County, at the southwest corner of the district, is the other major Democratic stronghold. It lies at one end of the industrialized Kanawha Valley and is home for 12 percent of district residents.

Until the New Deal era, Democratic votes in the district were concentrated in the mountain counties along the Virginia border. But these counties often vote Republican now, and virtually all of them supported Cleve Benedict in 1980.

Republican Party candidates usually run best in the Panhandle, which includes the fertile farm land of the northern Shenandoah Valley. Pastoral Grant County regularly turns in the highest Republican voting percentages in the state. It gave Ronald Reagan 75 percent of the vote in 1980. But within this area only Berkeley County, with 10

Robert H. Mollohan   **Cleve Benedict**

New West Virginia Districts

New District	Incumbent	Population	1980 Pres. Winner
1	Robert H. Mollohan (D)	488,568	Carter
2	Cleve Benedict (R)	487,438	Carter
3	David Michael Staton (R)	486,112	Carter
4	Nick J. Rahall II (D)	487,526	Carter

wood have sent the unemployment rate soaring. Three rural counties near the plant registered unemployment rates above 20 percent in December 1981.

The economy is not much healthier in the rolling countryside to the east. There is some coal and natural gas in these central counties, but little industrialization. An area of poor farms, it has been Democratic for generations.

South of Charleston are two counties with coal and natural gas, Lincoln and Boone. These Democratic bastions make up about 10 percent of the 3rd's population.

Redistricting has wrought little change in the complexion of the 3rd. The district exchanges one small, normally Republican county (Ritchie) for another (Lewis). However, Staton has gained a political hot potato — Lewis County is the site of the controversial Stonewall Jackson Dam, a project that has divided county residents.

percent of the district residents, constitutes a major population center.

District 3

Central — Charleston

Incumbent: David Michael Staton (R)

The 3rd District centers on populous Kanawha County (Charleston), which has enjoyed an economic comeback lately as a center for the reviving coal industry. Kanawha contains nearly one-half of the district population.

As the seat of state government and commerce, the Charleston area boasts the most diverse economy in the state. The capital city has a large white-collar work force that frequently produces Republican majorities.

But nearly three out of four voters in Kanawha County live outside Charleston. Many are blue-collar workers employed by the numerous chemical companies that line the Kanawha River. These people vote Democratic.

The result is that Kanawha is a crucial swing county, neither reliably Republican nor reliably Democratic. It went Democratic for president and governor in 1980, but supported Republican Staton for the House.

With more than 230,000 residents, Kanawha is the most populous county in West Virginia. But since 1960 its population has decreased by more than 20,000, due to a decline in the chemical and glass industries and completion of a highway network that encouraged residents to move to bedroom communities outside the county. The recent coal revival has increased population in the surrounding counties, not in Kanawha itself.

Democratic candidates usually run ahead in the portion of the district outside Kanawha. But Staton broke that pattern in 1980 and became the first Republican to capture the Charleston-based seat in more than a half century.

Putnam and nearby counties in the Ohio River Valley long have been centers of rural Republican strength. Together they cast about one-quarter of the district vote. Tobacco, corn and livestock provide an agricultural base. But layoffs at the large Kaiser Aluminum plant in Ravens-

District 4

South and West — Hungtington, Beckley

Incumbent: Nick J. Rahall II (D)

The Appalachian 4th is the most staunchly Democratic district in the state. Carter carried it in 1980 by more than 25,000 votes, even though he failed to take any of the other districts by more than 4,000. Redistricting has made no changes in the district lines.

The 4th is the center of the state's coal-mining industry. The region was loyally Republican early this century when local political bosses were aligned with the mine operators. But the New Deal and the ascendancy of the United Mine Workers shattered old alliances.

Republican strength is now limited to Cabell (Huntington) and Mercer (Bluefield) counties, which are on the fringes of the coal fields at opposite ends of the district. With 22 percent of the district population, Cabell is the largest county in the 4th. Like the other Ohio River counties south of Wheeling, it frequently votes Republican.

Near the junction of the West Virginia, Ohio and Kentucky borders, Huntington grew from a railroad center into the largest city in West Virginia, overtaken in population by Charleston only during the 1970s. Although it has diver-

David Michael Staton   **Nick J. Rahall II**

sified industries, it is not now a boom area. Cabell was one of only three counties in the state to lose population in the past decade. Mercer County, home for 15 percent of the district population, is located in the mountainous southern end of the district along the Virginia border.

Between Huntington and Bluefield is Democratic coal country. The revival of the coal industry has helped to reverse decades of population decline in the region. As the miners returned, all but one of the southern coal counties grew by at least 10 percent in the 1970s.

But even this population surge left some counties below their population levels of a half century ago. Logan County, for instance, had more registered voters in 1928 than in 1980.

Raleigh County's 24 percent population gain in the 1970s was the highest in the coal region. The county seat of Beckley is a prosperous retail center and the home base of Rep. Rahall. About five miles to the southwest is the small town of Sophia, where Rahall's mentor, Senate Democratic Leader Robert C. Byrd, was raised.

Further south along the twists and curves of state Route 16 is McDowell County. One of the poorest of the coal counties, it was the only one in the region to lose population in the 1970s. Most of the mines in McDowell's rugged terrain have been played out.

But West Virginia's small black population has a political impact in McDowell County that it lacks elsewhere in the state. Blacks comprise approximately 15 percent of the county population, a higher share than in any other West Virginia county. As a result, McDowell is the only county that currently has black representation in the state Legislature.

The South

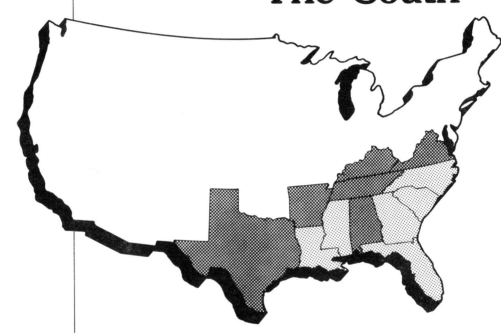

Alabama

For most of the past two decades, George Wallace dominated Alabama elections. Exhibiting a unique ability to combine two of the most popular themes in Alabama politics — race and populism — Wallace won the governorship in 1962, 1970 and 1974, and when he was ineligible to succeed himself in 1966, his wife Lurleen ran as his surrogate and won. Despite the paralysis he suffered as a result of an assassination attempt in 1976, Wallace has not bowed out of Alabama politics; he has hinted that he might run for governor in 1982, despite his infirm health.

But Wallace's last term as governor marked the end of a long era of personality politics in Alabama, in which campaigns were waged under a broad, one-party (Democratic) umbrella, with competing factions forming around dominant individuals.

Historically, Alabama's major rivalries have been sectional, with the large planters of the Black Belt aligned against the small farmers of north Alabama. With a malapportioned Legislature and with blacks effectively disenfranchised from 1901 until the mid-1960s, the Black Belt was usually able to dominate.

But northern Alabama remained a bastion of populism and spawned most of the state's more liberal politicians. Among them was Wallace's early mentor, Gov. James E. Folsom (1947-51, 1955-59), who championed both poor whites and blacks, while railing against the ruling interests of the state's Black Belt and "the big mules" of Birmingham.

For a long time, the base of the small Republican Party was the mountainous north. But that began changing when the GOP veered rightward in the 1960s. In 1962, Republican James D. Martin came within 7,000 votes of upsetting veteran Democratic Sen. Lister Hill with a segregationist appeal. Two years later, in 1964, the GOP rode Goldwater's long coattails to victory in five of eight House races, the party's first congressional triumphs since Reconstruction.

But the Republican groundswell was terminated abruptly. Unable to match Wallace's populism or to compete with him on the racial issue, the GOP lost two House seats in 1966. During the later Wallace years they did not win any major statewide offices nor any more seats in the House.

When the post-Wallace era opened in 1978, the GOP looked no stronger. A member of the state Republican executive committee, Forrest "Fob" James abandoned the GOP to run successfully as a Democrat for governor, handing the Republicans a moral victory and an insult at the same time.

But just two years later, Republican Jeremiah Denton shattered the popular conception that a candidate had to be a Democrat to win major statewide office in Alabama by winning a Senate seat.

Northern Hill Country

This region has had more in common with neighboring Tennessee, where its first settlers came from, than with the planter aristocracy of central Alabama. Northern Alabama never had a widespread plantation economy, so there were fewer blacks. Today they are less than 10 percent of the populace in 13 northern counties.

The dominance of poor whites in this area has made the hill country a haven for populism. For decades politicians railed against the "special interests" of the planters and their Birmingham big business allies. In recent years, utility companies have become a target.

The most heavily populated part of this region and one of the most prosperous areas of Alabama is the industrialized Tennessee River Valley, centered on Huntsville at the extreme northern end of the state. In the 1930s the Tennessee Valley Authority (TVA) provided abundant, cheap electricity that brought more industry into the valley. During World War II, Huntsville landed a chemical warfare plant, which was later taken over by the Army for research in rocketry. Later, the National Aeronautics and Space Administration (NASA) located its major research and development center in Huntsville. As the space program burgeoned during the 1960s, Huntsville's population doubled. With retrenchment in the space program, however, the city has had to diversify its economy in recent years, and now there are fewer high paying, high technology jobs.

The rest of the Valley has prospered from a mixture of agriculture (extensive cotton-growing) and heavy industry, including large aluminum, chemical and textile plants. Industry has been attracted in the 1970s to Decatur and the Quad cities of Florence, Sheffield, Tuscumbia and Muscle Shoals.

One of the most heavily unionized parts of Alabama, the Valley has remained loyally Democratic. In 1980, the Reagan-Denton team carried only one of eight counties along the Tennessee River — Madison (Huntsville) — and that by a narrow margin.

The remainder of northern Alabama is less prosperous, although it contains some of the richest coal deposits in the South. Tuscaloosa is the home of the University of Alabama. Gadsden and Anniston are steel-producing cities.

Like the Tennessee Valley area, most of the rest of northern Alabama is normally Democratic turf. However, Reagan and Denton carried Anniston and most of the counties around Birmingham, including Tuscaloosa. The Democrats held heavily-unionized Etowah County (Gadsden) and most of the rural areas.

Birmingham and Environs

Birmingham is Dixie's steelmaking center, favorably located near iron, coal and limestone deposits. Although it was not founded until after the Civil War, Birmingham outstripped Mobile as the state's major population center by 1900.

Although whites and blacks worked side by side in the steel mills, Birmingham was the scene of much racial violence during the 1960s. And the city's police commissioner, Eugene "Bull" Connor came to epitomize the overt resistance of local government to integration efforts. But resistance began to crack with the development of the black vote. In 1967 the first black was elected to the City Council, and by 1979, when blacks made up more than half the population, Birmingham elected its first black mayor — Richard Arrington.

While blacks account for 56 percent of Birmingham's population, they comprise only 17 percent of the population in the rest of Jefferson County. Suburban communities compose more than half the county population and provide the votes that regularly keep Jefferson County in the Republican column.

Birmingham is facing serious economic troubles, brought about by the decline in heavy industry. It did not attract as much new business as other Southern cities during the Sun Belt boom of the 1970s, and in many ways has inherited the problems of the urban North.

Black Belt

No part of Alabama was more affected by the civil rights movement than the state's Black Belt, a strip of land about 30 miles wide that spans the south central part of the state.

While the term "Black Belt" is said to refer to the color of the rich, sticky soil and not the racial composition, the rural counties of the region are predominantly black. The Black Belt was the centerpiece of Alabama's cotton-based, plantation economy. With a Legislature apportioned to distort their power, the region's wealthy white landowners were able to hold the reins of state government much of this century.

But their world was turned upside-down by the civil rights legislation and court decisions of the 1960s. The enfranchisement of blacks not only stripped the planters of statewide authority, but also relegated them to a back seat in much of their own region. In 1964, when few blacks could vote, Goldwater won the region by a landslide margin. In 1972, the only six Alabama counties that McGovern carried were in the Black Belt.

But new-found black political clout has not stopped the region's long population drain. Not only is the Black Belt an area of extreme poverty, but mechanization and a change in emphasis from cotton to beef and dairy cattle has reduced farm employment. Of the eight Alabama counties that lost population in the 1970s, six were in the Black Belt.

The region's major city and oasis of Republicanism is Montgomery. The state capital and a cotton and cattle market town, Montgomery has been helped economically by a large influx of state and federal government projects. Unlike the surrounding countryside, Montgomery and its suburbs are growing quickly. Two Air Force bases are located in the city, including the Air University at Maxwell Air Force Base.

Mobile and the South

South Alabama is a diverse region stretching from the cosmopolitan port city of Mobile to the poor farming country where George Wallace was raised.

Mobile is a vestige of the Old South. It has a strong Catholic influence and in some ways resembles New Orleans. At the southwest corner of the state, Mobile is a booming international port favorably located 31 miles from the Gulf of Mexico along Mobile Bay.

At the southeast corner is another boom town, Dothan. Since the Army located an airfield nearby in World War II, it has been steadily growing and attracting new industry — most recently Michelin Tire and Sony plants. In the 1970s, Dothan's population increased 33 percent — the largest, except for Montgomery, of any city in the state with a population more than 25,000.

Much of the rest of rural south Alabama is an area of mediocre soil called the Wire Grass. Near the Mississippi border, the land is heavily timbered. In the east are some of the most productive peanut growing counties in the country.

In pre-Wallace politics, rural southeast Alabama — with few blacks — was usually aligned with the northern populists. Mobile and the rest of the region voted with Birmingham and the Black Belt. In recent years, Republican strength in south Alabama has been limited to the major population centers in Mobile and Baldwin counties along the Gulf, and Houston (Dothan). But in 1980, Reagan and Denton expanded the GOP's base by carrying much of rural south Alabama, one-time strongholds of Wallace support.

STATE DISTRICTS STILL LARGELY INTACT

District lines around Birmingham were the main issue as Alabama redrew its congressional map for the 1980s. Once legislators reached agreement on that subject, they finished their work quickly; three of the state's seven districts were left untouched.

The major changes in Jefferson County (Birmingham) took place between the 6th District, represented by freshman Republican Rep. Albert Lee Smith Jr., and the 7th District, held by second-term Democrat Rep. Richard C. Shelby. One faction in the overwhelmingly Democratic state Legislature called for a drastic shift in the Jefferson County lines to ensure Smith's defeat. But the more

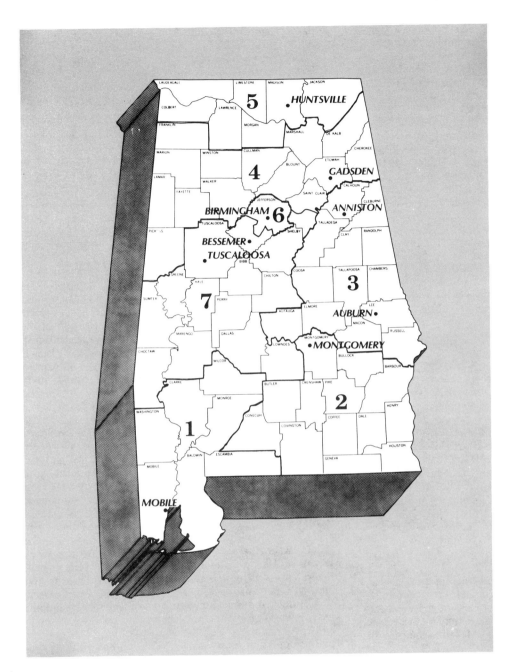

New Alabama Districts

U. S. Congress: 7 districts
  Senate (1D, 1R)
  House (4D, 3R)

Governor:
  Fob James (D)

Population: 3,890,061

Area: 51,609 sq. miles

1980 Presidential Vote:
  Carter (48%)
  Reagan (49%)
  Anderson (1%)

parochial interests of the Birmingham delegation in the Legislature produced an alternative plan much kinder to Smith, who won in November 1980 with 51 percent of the vote after defeating incumbent Republican John Buchanan in a primary.

With the possible exception of Smith, the state's U. S. House delegation should face little difficulty winning re-election. Alabama currently sends four Democrats and three Republicans to the House.

Redistricting was not a dominant issue in the 1981 legislative year. The subject came up in a special session in August. State Rep. Rick Manley, co-chairman of a special redistricting committee, introduced a plan that would have excised from Smith's 6th District the mostly-white, conservative areas that form the basis of his support. Manley's

plan also would have given Smith the Democratic industrial city of Bessemer.

Two Jefferson County legislators, Arthur Payne and Duane Lewis, objected strenuously to Manley's plan and drafted an alternative that won the support of the majority of Birmingham legislators. They said their plan was not designed to help or hurt Smith but was drawn to fit the wishes of their constituents.

Aware that any plan needed Jefferson County support to win, Manley agreed to go along with the Payne-Lewis boundaries, and they were adopted on a 52-11 vote in the House. The House then passed the entire bill Aug. 13, 1981, by a lopsided 93-9 vote. The Senate approved it the same day, 29-2. Democratic Gov. Fob James signed it Aug. 18, 1981.

The opposition to final passage came from black legislators who felt the plan was drawn to make the election of a black congressman nearly impossible. Although more than a fourth of the state population is black, the new redistricting plan follows the long-established pattern of dividing blacks nearly evenly among five districts. As a result, no district is more than 34 percent black.

In order to preserve the existing boundaries of three of the seven districts, legislators were forced to accept a higher population variance than in the past. The largest district, the 1st, is 1.3 percent above the ideal district population of 555,723. The smallest district, the 2nd, is 1.1 percent below the ideal, for a total deviation of 2.3 percent. Neither the 1st nor the 2nd District was changed in this year's action.

District 1

Southwest — Mobile

Incumbent: Jack Edwards (R)

The 1st District, covering seven counties in the southwest corner of the state, is dominated by the port city of Mobile. With a population of 200,000, Mobile is the state's second largest city, and the largest on the Gulf Coast between New Orleans and Tampa, Fla.

Mobile County casts about two-thirds of the district vote. Like the neighboring Mississippi Gulf Coast, this area has been voting Republican in recent national elections.

Mobile's economy revolves around shipbuilding, aluminum, chemicals and lumber, with an important pulp and paper industry. The city has a large Catholic community, one of whose members is Jeremiah Denton, the first Republican U. S. senator popularly elected in Alabama history. In 1980, Denton won 60 percent of the vote in the 1st District, his best showing in the state.

The strong Republican vote in Mobile and coastal Baldwin County easily outweighs the Democratic strength found in the rural, heavily black counties in the northern part of the district. Wilcox County, more than two-thirds of which is black, was one of just six Alabama counties to

support Democrat George McGovern's presidential campaign in 1972. As a whole, the district is 31 percent black.

Only once since his first election in 1964 has Edwards received less than 60 percent of the vote. That was in 1968. In 1978, Democrats put forward a Mobile-based candidate they thought would present a strong challenge to the incumbent. The Democrat was trounced, and in 1980, Edwards faced opposition only from the Libertarian Party.

District 2

Southeast — Montgomery, Dothan

Incumbent: William L. Dickinson (R)

With his district unchanged by the Legislature, Rep. Dickinson should have little trouble winning a 10th term in an area that is growing steadily more Republican.

Most of the 2nd, covering the southeast corner of the state, is rural. But half the population is concentrated in two urban centers found at opposite corners of the district.

At the northwest edge is Montgomery County, with just under 200,000 people. The state capital, Montgomery has long been a national Republican stronghold in Alabama, voting for GOP presidential candidates as far back as 1956. The city has a large white-collar government work force as well as a strong military influence from adjacent Maxwell and Gunter Air Force bases.

At the southeastern corner of the district, near the Florida and Georgia borders, is the Houston County seat of Dothan, an old cotton and peanut market town that grew rapidly in the last decade by attracting new industries. Although fiercely loyal to former Gov. George C. Wallace, it has been voting for conservative Republican candidates in other contests with regularity over the last decade.

Between these two population centers are the Piney Woods of Alabama and a portion of the state's Black Belt. Peanuts and cotton are still major crops. Overall, the new 2nd is 31 percent black.

Bullock and Barbour counties, Wallace's original home base, have large black populations and are loyally Democratic. As one moves south toward the Florida border, the black population drops sharply. The rural counties around Dothan are beginning to join the national trend toward supporting Republicans in statewide elections, although at the local level Democratic loyalties still prevail. In 1980, Reagan won seven of the district's 13 counties, taking 52 percent of the vote, his second highest mark in the state.

District 3

East — Anniston, Auburn

Incumbent: Bill Nichols (D)

Taking in the eastern side of the state from the outskirts of Montgomery to the hilly Piedmont Plateau, the 3rd is a conservative rural stronghold.

Jack Edwards

William L. Dickinson

New Alabama Districts

New District	Incumbent	Population	1980 Pres. Winner
1	Jack Edwards (R)	563,140	Reagan
2	William L. Dickinson (R)	549,505	Reagan
3	Bill Nichols (D)	552,496	Carter
4	Tom Bevill (D)	562,088	Carter
5	Ronnie G. Flippo (D)	549,802	Carter
6	Albert Lee Smith Jr. (R)	554,188	Reagan
7	Richard C. Shelby (D)	558,842	Carter

Textile mills are scattered around the 3rd District, reflecting the traditional prominence of cotton in the area's agricultural economy. There is a heavy concentration of industry in Anniston, the district's largest city with fewer than 30,000 people, and in Opelika, located near the university town of Auburn.

Although most of the voters throughout the district consider themselves Democrats, statewide Republican candidates are beginning to find favor, particularly in the more urbanized areas — Calhoun County (Anniston) in the north and Lee County (Auburn and Opelika) in the south. Reagan and Denton carried both counties in 1980, although both trailed their Democratic opponents districtwide by slim margins.

The central part of the district has always been strong Wallace country and is still partisan toward Democratic candidates. Any national Democrat who stops short of outspoken liberalism can expect to win in these rural counties by a decent margin.

The only change in the district for the 1980s is the removal of predominently black Lowndes County, west of Montgomery. That leaves the 3rd with only one county — Macon — in which blacks are a majority. Blacks comprise 28 percent of the new 3rd.

Nichols, who has not faced a difficult election since turning out Republican Glenn Andrews in 1966, will scarcely be affected by the minor change in the district.

District 4

North central — Gadsden

Incumbent: Tom Bevill (D)

Stretching all the way across the northern part of the state, the 4th is rural, traditionally poor and overwhelmingly white. With just a 7 percent black population, it has a substantially different character from those districts further south.

The 4th has a long populist Democratic heritage. The "common man" rhetoric of former governors Wallace and James E. Folsom Sr. always played well in this area. At the same time, with so few blacks, the area has been generally free of the race-baiting found in other parts of the state.

Gadsden, an iron and steel center of 48,000 people, is the district's only city of substantial size. The remainder of the district is dominated largely by poultry, cotton and livestock farming operations.

Along with the 5th District directly to the north, this is now the most predictably Democratic part of the state. But even here, the political complexion is changing. New residents are moving into this area at a faster pace than in any other district in the state, and many are voting Republican. The four counties with the fastest growth rates in the district during the 1970s — Blount and St. Clair near Birmingham, plus Winston and DeKalb — all voted for Reagan and Denton in 1980. They were the only counties in the district to do so.

Because of its 21 percent growth rate over the last decade, the 4th was forced to give up population in redistricting. The Legislature shifted out about 9,000 people from the eastern side of Jefferson County, most of them Republicans, and 24,000 from southern St. Clair County.

The changes are too slight to have a major impact on politics in the district. If anything, these changes will strengthen the Democratic vote. Bevill, the popular 60-year-old incumbent, should face little opposition. That is the way it has been since his initial victory in 1966.

District 5

North — Huntsville

Incumbent: Ronnie G. Flippo (D)

The Tennessee River connects the seven counties of this district at the northern end of the state. Nearly half a century of natural resource development by the Tennessee Valley Authority (TVA) has contributed to the prosperity of this region, making it an atypical Alabama district.

Bill Nichols

Tom Bevill

Ronnie G. Flippo

Albert Lee Smith Jr.

The 5th has a relatively small black population (only 14 percent), several large federal installations in Huntsville and active labor unions in the metals, automobile and chemical plants along the Tennessee River. It is the state's most reliably Democratic territory in major statewide elections. In 1980 Carter won 54 percent of the vote in this district, his best mark in the state of Alabama.

Huntsville (Madison County) was the only part of the 5th to side with Reagan in 1980, and only by a very slim margin. With 143,000 people, it is the state's fourth largest city and has a large white-collar work force. Boeing, IBM and General Electric all have high-technology plants in Huntsville, and the Army Redstone Arsenal and Marshall Space Flight Center have been economically important.

Located downstream along the Tennessee River are blue-collar towns such as Decatur and the Quad Cities of Florence, Sheffield, Tuscumbia and Muscle Shoals. The Quad Cities are overwhelmingly Democratic. This was the only part of the state where white voters supported the Carter-Mondale ticket in 1980 by margins that approached those in the counties where blacks are the majority.

Since the population of the 5th District grew at the same rate as the entire state in the 1970s, there was no need to alter the district lines. The 5th has comprised the same seven counties since 1964. During that time, Republicans have contested the House seat only twice, in 1966 and 1972.

District 6

Birmingham and suburbs

Incumbent: Albert Lee Smith Jr. (R)

The 6th is split almost evenly between Birmingham and its suburbs. It is fortunate for Smith that the city voters do not turn out in the same numbers as the suburbanites.

Smith's political success has come in the affluent communities in the hills above the steel mills and black neighborhoods of Birmingham. In 1980, Smith defeated moderate GOP incumbent John Buchanan in a primary and won a narrow 51-47 percent victory in the general election.

The largest city in the state, Birmingham is often referred to as the Pittsburgh of the South because of its large steel plants. The city, which is 56 percent black, has an older, industrial flavor that the newer, white-collar Southern cities like Atlanta lack. It also has problems of urban decline more often associated with the North. It usually votes Democratic and has had a black mayor since 1979.

The suburbs of the 6th District are diverse. South of the Red Mountains, which form the southern edge of the city, are Mountain Brook, Homewood and Hoover, all well-to-do areas which vote heavily Republican. The areas north and east of Birmingham in Jefferson County also tend to be Republican but are less densely populated. Smith currently represents most of this territory, and redistricting adds the Leeds area, in the extreme eastern corner of Jefferson County, previously in the 4th. Adding Leeds will help Smith in 1982. It showed its GOP bent in 1980 by supporting both Reagan and Denton by large margins.

However, the Republican Leeds area has only a third the population of the other area Smith is gaining, in what is called the Bessemer Cutoff. The new 6th District stops just short of the labor-oriented steel town of Bessemer, but picks up six other blue-collar communities.

Brighton, Roosevelt City and Brownville are all largely black, Democratic areas where Smith will trail by huge margins. Fairfield, the largest added town, is racially split but Democratic. Midfield, the remaining town, is nearly all-white; Smith hopes its middle-class blue-collar voters will favor his conservative social and economic views.

Smith has been weakened by these additions to the 6th, but he may be able to hold on. Blacks make up about 34 percent of the new district, 2 percent more than before.

District 7

West central — Tuscaloosa, Bessemer

Incumbent: Richard C. Shelby (D)

The 7th has four separate but nearly equal parts. Although Republicans run reasonably well in most of the district elections, the area has been firmly loyal to Democrat Shelby.

Richard C. Shelby

The new 7th will still contain much of the intensely Democratic Black Belt of Alabama. While the term "Black Belt" is said not to refer to the racial composition but to the color of the rich, sticky cotton-growing soil, all but one of the eight rural counties in this portion of the district have black majorities. One, Lowndes County, is newly added by redistricting. These eight counties, which make up a quarter of the district's population, gave Carter 60 percent of the vote in 1980. The black population in this area is 59 percent.

Republicans running in the district would be helped most in the booming area south of Birmingham. Shelby and Chilton counties have been voting increasingly Republican in recent years. Shelby, in particular, is experiencing a rapid population boom, as people continue to move out from Birmingham and Jefferson County.

The Jefferson County part of the 7th District has been leaning Republican in recent statewide contests. Any Republican candidate running in the district will still have to contend with a large black and Democratic vote in the city of Bessemer, which is part of Jefferson County, but Democrats lose strength with the transfer of six towns around Bessemer to Smith's 6th District. Outside Bessemer, Shel-by's Jefferson County constituents will be generally friendly to his conservative politics.

Tuscaloosa and Tuscaloosa County make up the remaining population bloc in the district. About one-quarter black, this county split its vote evenly between Democrats and Republicans in the presidential and senatorial elections of 1980. With 75,000 people, Tuscaloosa is the largest city in the new 7th District. It has an industrial base centered around the manufacture of rubber, chemicals and fertilizer but is more often identified as the home of the University of Alabama. Shelby should do well in this area; he represented it in the state Senate for eight years and as a prosecuting attorney before that.

Arkansas

For most of the 1970s, Arkansas seemed to be living in a different world from most of its Southern neighbors. While other states were flirting with Republicanism and rejecting the views of the national Democratic Party, Arkansas was electing avowed national Democrats to its highest offices. Its Republicans, seemingly on the verge of a breakthrough in 1966, had been virtually wiped out a decade later.

That political situation ended abruptly on Nov. 4, 1980, when the "sacrificial" Republican candidate, Frank White, stunned the state's Democratic gubernatorial prodigy, Bill Clinton, who was seeking a second term at the age of 34.

Clinton's loss can be explained on narrow and personal grounds: the massive influx of Cuban refugees into the state had upset many Arkansans, and Clinton's badly timed increase in automobile license fees had compounded the situation.

But it can also be explained as the political reaction that was bound to come after a decade in which Arkansas had elected only national Democrats to the governorship and the Senate. From 1964, when segregationist Gov. Orval Faubus won his last term, to 1980, when White won, only one conservative Democrat was elected to either office. That was Sen. John L. McClellan, re-elected without serious opposition in 1966 and winning his sixth Senate term in 1972, after being forced into a runoff by David Pryor. All of the other Democrats have been moderate-to-liberal. Dale Bumpers won two terms as governor and then went to the Senate. So did Pryor, following his loss to McClellan. Clinton was an easy winner for governor in 1978.

Meanwhile, the Republican Party was moribund. Winthrop Rockefeller won two terms as governor in the 1960s, but Rockefeller and his money were about all the GOP had, and when he lost to Bumpers in 1970, there was no structure to build on. The one lasting contribution from the GOP era was an end to the race politics that had predominated under Faubus. Rockefeller discredited and all but destroyed the older generation of conservative Democrats in Arkansas, leaving a vacuum for Bumpers, Pryor and Clinton to take advantage of in the following decade.

By 1980, it seemed reasonable to many people that Arkansas simply did not vote like a Southern state. But it is one. It has many of the demographic ingredients that have helped the GOP elsewhere in the South in recent

years: an influx of corporate business and its managers, a growing suburban vote around Little Rock and numerous retirees arriving from other states. After decades of low population growth that cost it two House seats in 1960, the state began to show the results of its in-migration during the 1970s. It grew by 19 percent and in 1978 Little Rock elected its first Republican congressman in the 20th century.

All of that made White's breakthrough in 1980 reasonable, if not exactly predictable. But whether it will continue is hard to tell. While the governorship was going Republican and Reagan was eking out a victory over Carter, Bumpers was winning a second Senate term with nearly 60 percent of the vote. White is certain to have strong Democratic opposition in 1982, and the results of that contest may be a clue to the future of Arkansas politics.

Little Rock

Located in the center of the state on the Arkansas River, Little Rock is the capital, the largest city and the industrial center for Arkansas. It is also the home of the only newspapers with statewide circulation. One of them, The Arkansas Gazette, has a decidedly liberal editorial tone which has influenced politics both on the local and state level.

At close to 160,000 people, Little Rock is more than twice the size of the state's next largest city. With surrounding parts of Pulaski County, it accounts for 15 percent of the state's population.

Now one-third black, Little Rock is remembered as an early battleground in the fight to integrate public education in the South. But the efforts by Faubus in 1957 to keep nine black students from enrolling in Little Rock's Central High School are now dim memories. The city's racial tensions have subsided, thanks in part to governors in the post-Faubus era who have taken an open-minded attitude toward racial questions. And the city's attention has turned to other matters, such as rebuilding the downtown area and eradicating the remaining slum areas.

The voters in Pulaski County recently have shown little partisan consistency. In 1968, the county split its vote evenly in thirds among Humphrey, Nixon and Wallace. Four years later, Nixon won 63 percent, which was the same figure Carter received in 1976.

But by 1980, both Carter and Clinton had lost nearly as much support in Little Rock as they had in the rural areas of the state. Carter's percentage fell 14 points; Clinton, still supported by many blacks and state government workers, dropped nine points from his 1978 mark. While Carter and Clinton barely edged out their GOP opponents in this area, Republican congressman Ed Bethune racked up a whopping 80 percent in Pulaski County.

Republican Ozarks and Ouachita Mountains

Highway 67, which enters Arkansas in the northeast corner and leaves via Texarkana in the southwest, divides the state in two.

To the north and west of that line are the Ozarks, spilling over from southern Missouri, and the Ouachita Mountains, coming from eastern Oklahoma. Bisected by the broad Arkansas River, this is hilly country that is less suited to the large-scale farming found south and east of Route 67. Anti-secessionist during the Civil War, the small-scale farmers of the region blamed the hardships of the war on the plantation east and have been voting Republican ever since.

For decades after the Civil War, Republicans in Arkansas were cloistered in a few counties in the northwest. For the first 60 years of the 20th century, Newton and Searcy counties were the only two that would consistently vote Republican.

But in the last two decades, Republicans have begun to spread their influence. The 3rd District, covering the entire northwestern quarter of the state, has been in GOP hands since 1966. In 1980, White carried virtually every county north and west of U. S. 67.

Fort Smith, with 71,000 people, is the only city of any size in the area. Sitting on the Oklahoma border, it has a Western flavor that comes in part from its large livestock business. The local citizenry rose up in anger in 1980 when thousands of Cuban refugees were housed at nearby Fort Chaffee. Blaming both President Carter and Gov. Clinton for imposing this burden, area voters gave Carter his lowest mark in the state (27 percent) and Clinton his second lowest (33 percent).

The Ozark region is best known for its cattle, poultry and lumbering, but is traditionally a poor area. In the Ouachita Mountains, harvesting pine has been a chief source of income.

Recently, however, an infusion of small industry and the arrival of retirees have brought a population boom to northwest Arkansas. Nearly every county north of the Arkansas River grew by at least 30 percent in the last decade.

It is an overwhelmingly white part of the South. There are no more blacks in this half of Arkansas than in rural parts of Minnesota or Wisconsin. The 1980 census found two counties — Searcy and Madison — where there were no black people at all.

The Mississippi Delta and Southern Plains

While the 1980 election brought out Republican votes in the north and west, it also confirmed that the Mississippi Delta and the Southern Plains are still steadfastly Democratic.

Closer in appearance to Mississippi and Louisiana, this is large-scale farming and oil-drilling country. Although rice and soybeans now enjoy wide popularity with the farmers of the area, the cotton fields still stretch for miles along the Delta.

This was plantation Arkansas in the early 19th century, and secessionist territory prior to and during the Civil War. Since Reconstruction the region has been consistently Democratic, and among white voters, conservative.

Today, the strongest cotton areas are also those with the greatest black population and the largest Democratic vote. Along the Mississippi River from West Memphis to the Louisiana border, every county is at least 40 percent black; three of them — Lee, Phillips and Chicot — have black majorities. The cotton economy, however, is not healthy and the population has declined.

In 1970, many black Delta voters stayed loyal to Republican Gov. Winthrop Rockefeller, in recognition of his many black appointments. Ten years later, while nominal Democrats elsewhere were abandoning the Carter-Clinton ticket, the Delta counties remained firm in their support for both incumbents.

Moving west and south from the Delta, the black population drops to between 20 and 30 percent and the white voters, still ostensibly Democrats, assume a more "redneck" Southern style. George Wallace carried the entire area in his 1968 presidential campaign. Carter did well here even in 1980, but Clinton was too liberal for many Democrats in south Arkansas. He lost every county in the south central part of the state.

This is the oil producing section of Arkansas. El Dorado in Union County, center for oil workers, has become increasingly Republican.

Poultry, cattle and cotton predominate in far southwestern counties, but the land grows more wooded closer to Pine Bluff, the largest city in the southern region. Nearly 50 percent black, Pine Bluff is a solidly Democratic town.

FEW CHANGES
IN ARKANSAS MAP

The first state in the country to draw new congressional district lines for 1982, Arkansas was also the first to have its map thrown out in court. On Feb. 25, however, the three-judge federal panel that had voided the remap early in January handed down a plan only slightly different from the rejected version, leaving the state's four incumbent House members with little to worry about as they gear up for re-election campaigns.

After the first set of lines was enacted in June 1981, citizens from Garland and Grant counties, which had been placed in new districts, filed suit in Little Rock to have the map overturned. Although the real issue was the forced switch in their congressional representation, they based their case on a 1.87 percent variation between the populations of the smallest and largest of the redrawn districts, claiming that this violated the principle of one man, one vote. On Jan. 5, 1982, the court agreed. After Republican Gov. Frank D. White declined to call a special session of the Legislature to revise the map, the court took over the task of picking a redistricting plan itself.

The map the judges eventually chose was one that initially had served as the basis for the rejected plan. Drawn by state Rep. John Miller, it passed the Arkansas Senate in March 1981 before undergoing change in the

New Arkansas Districts

U. S. Congress: 4 districts
  Senate (2D)
  House (2D, 2R)

Governor:
  Frank White (R)

Population: 2,285,513

Area: 53,104 sq. miles

1980 Presidential Vote:
  Carter (48%)
  Reagan (48%)
  Anderson (3%)

state House. In the view of the federal panel, this original Senate-passed version, with only a .78 percent population variance, was more in line with the one-man, one-vote requirement.

Ironically, the court's decision has not left the Garland County residents who brought the case any happier. They will be voting in the 4th District, just as they would have under the first plan. Garland and its chief city of Hot Springs have been in Rep. John Paul Hammerschmidt's 3rd District since 1966, the year the veteran Republican won his first term to the House. With his ranking position on the Veterans' Affairs Committee, Hammerschmidt has developed a faithful constituency in a county with a large population of veterans.

Bill Alexander   **Ed Bethune**

Still, Garland County will find that its interests coincide with those of its new district. The heavily forested 4th long has been a center of the timber industry, and Garland's economic base outside Hot Springs is mostly in lumber.

If Garland County residents gained nothing by their suit against the first redistricting plan, those from Grant County who joined in were more fortunate. The court chose to keep Grant in Democrat Beryl Anthony Jr.'s 4th District, as its residents wanted. The county had been moved to the 2nd in the rejected version. Grant has been in the 4th since Arkansas lost two districts following the 1960 census. Heavily reliant on the lumber industry for jobs, it has been hard hit by the nationwide depression in housing and construction.

District 1

East — Jonesboro

Incumbent: Bill Alexander (D)

Redistricting did little to change the Mississippi Delta character of this district. Covering most of the eastern third of the state and some hilly northern counties, the agricultural 1st is the part of the state with the strongest Deep South tradition. Jonesboro, the home of Arkansas State University, and West Memphis, a suburb of Memphis, Tenn., are the district's only major cities. Most of the area depends on rice, soybeans, and cotton.

The district grew 9 percent in the 1970s, the slowest population increase in the state. So it was required to gain slightly more than 50,000 people. That was accomplished by adding three counties from the 2nd District. Two on the west side — Prairie and Arkansas — have sizable black populations (14 and 20 percent, respectively). Relatively poor farming counties, both are economically and politically similar to the other Delta counties on the eastern side of the district, many of which are nearly half black.

The third county added to the 1st is Cleburne County, 55 miles north of Little Rock. Located at the eastern end of the Boston Mountains, it is nearly all white and has a strong recreational industry centered around the Greers

Ferry Lake, near Heber Springs. Rep. Alexander was happy to gain it; he already represents a part of the lake area and has worked on its development and protection.

All three counties added to the 1st District usually support Democrats, with Prairie and Arkansas somewhat more Democratic. Cleburne narrowly went for Reagan for president and Republican White for governor in 1980. Alexander, who has not had any opposition since 1976, should absorb the new population with little trouble.

District 2

Central — Little Rock

Incumbent: Ed Bethune (R)

Centered around Little Rock, the state capital and largest city, the new 2nd District has been made slightly stronger for its Republican incumbent.

Bethune owed his first election to the House in 1978 to his strength in Little Rock and surrounding Pulaski County. The district grew by 24 percent over the last decade, so the Legislature trimmed its edges and reduced the total population by 31,000. That increased the impact of Little Rock's vote. Fifty-seven percent of the district's voters now are concentrated in Pulaski County.

Three counties — Arkansas, Prairie and Cleburne — were moved from the 2nd District into the 1st. In 1978, when Bethune faced his only serious test, he lost Arkansas and Prairie but scored his highest percentage in Cleburne.

The Legislature's remap would have given Grant County to the 2nd. Under the court's plan, the district instead gains about 4,000 residents with the addition of Yell County, to the west of Little Rock. Named after Arkansas' first U.S. House member, Archibald Yell, the county draws large numbers of tourists with its rivers and forests and the Holla Bend National Wildlife Refuge. The Arkansas River runs through Yell and a hydroelectric power plant at Dardanelle supplies wood mills and the poultry industry concentrated in the northern half of the county. Democrats outnumber Republicans in Yell County.

The 2nd District also gains Perry, a lightly populated county largely devoted to the timber industry.

John Paul Hammerschmidt   **Beryl Anthony Jr.**

New Arkansas Districts

New District	Incumbent	Population	1980 Pres. Winner
1	Bill Alexander (D)	573,128	Carter
2	Ed Bethune (R)	564,818	Carter
3	J. P. Hammerschmidt (R)	575,485	Reagan
4	Beryl Anthony Jr. (D)	572,082	Carter

Outside Little Rock, a politically active labor movement in neighboring Saline County produces a well-organized Democratic vote. Many of the county's workers are employed in the aluminum industry. As the nation's only source of bauxite, Saline County has several large refineries.

District 3

Northwest — Ozark Plateau, Fort Smith

Incumbent: John Paul Hammerschmidt (R)

The hilly 3rd District of northwestern Arkansas is the only strong Republican constituency in the state. It is overwhelmingly white, with a traditionally poor economy that has depended on relatively unproductive farm land. Vast pine forests have provided jobs in the saw mills scattered throughout the rural counties.

In the 1970s, however, the Ozark economy received a boost from a large influx of new residents. Older people from northern states are moving here in large numbers. The 3rd grew by 33 percent in the last decade.

The district's two major cities are Fort Smith, the state's second largest city, and Fayetteville, home of the University of Arkansas. In the past, both have supported Republicans even against popular Democrats. In 1980, when Democratic Gov. Bill Clinton and President Jimmy Carter were sharing the blame for housing Cuban refugees at Fort Chaffee near Fort Smith, Sebastian County (Fort Smith) expressed its opposition to the refugee camps by giving Clinton only 33 percent of the vote and Carter 27 percent.

Before redistricting, the 3rd District had another major city, Hot Springs, which has been transferred to the 4th District, represented by Beryl Anthony Jr. Many of the residents of Hot Springs argued vehemently against the change. But the political impact of losing Hot Springs will be negligible for Hammerschmidt. In the last decade, the Republican incumbent has been seriously threatened only once, in 1974, when he narrowly won re-election over Clinton. Even in that case, it was Fort Smith, not Hot Springs, that saved him.

The 3rd District also lost lightly populated Perry County to the 2nd and gained Sevier County, a Democratic area in the southwestern corner of the state with a large poultry industry. Sevier was marginally Democratic in the two close statewide contests won by Republican candidates in 1980.

District 4

South — Pine Bluff

Incumbent: Beryl Anthony Jr. (D)

Stretching across the southern half of the state, the 4th is so habitually Democratic that Republicans have run a candidate only twice in the last two decades.

Although adding Garland County (Hot Springs) from the 3rd District will reduce the Democratic registration advantage somewhat, it is unlikely to threaten Anthony, who has yet to face a Republican opponent.

With 70,000 people in Garland County now included in his district, Anthony has more new constituents to befriend than any other member of the delegation. About one-eighth of the new district's population lives in the county. But the district's two other urban areas — Jefferson County (Pine Bluff) and Union County (El Dorado) — have twice as many people between them as Garland County. Pine Bluff is solidly Democratic. El Dorado, a center for southern Arkansas' oil industry, voted Republican at the top of the ticket in 1980, but it is Anthony's hometown and has always supported him loyally.

The court remap left Grant County in the 4th; the Legislature would have moved it to the 2nd. Lightly populated, Grant usually votes strongly Democratic, although Democratic Gov. Bill Clinton lost the 3rd District and Grant County to the 2nd as a result of redistricting. The 4th did lose Sevier County to the 3rd District.

Sharing a 165-mile-long border with Louisiana, the 4th is in many ways a Deep South constituency like the 1st. In 1968, all but two counties within the boundaries of the new 4th District supported George C. Wallace for president. The two exceptions were Garland County, which voted Republican, as it has in six of the last eight elections, and Chicot County, a largely black area along the Mississippi River, which voted Democratic.

Democratic Pine Bluff, the state's fourth largest city, is a railroad center with several pulp and paper mills. With a 49 percent black population, it casts the highest minority vote of any major Arkansas city. Altogether, the 4th is 28 percent black, more than any district in the state.

Kentucky

For Republicans, Kentucky is a border state not only in the familiar geographical sense, but in a political sense as well. Despite a statewide preference for conservatism and a traditional party base in the mountain counties, Kentucky Republicans always seem to be bordering on a success they never achieve. They entered the 1970s holding the governorship and both U.S. Senate seats, after years of struggle. But they immediately began losing, and today all three offices are solidly under Democratic control.

Democrats have managed their revival despite continuing GOP strength in national elections. Kentucky has gone Republican for president five of nine times during the postwar era.

While states further south have seen their politics change drastically in recent years with the coming of Sun Belt development, Kentucky, an outer Sun Belt province, is more or less stuck in the political patterns of the past century. This leaves Republicans competitive, but not usually successful at the state level.

The mountainous southeastern corner of the state still furnishes a predictable Republican vote, year after year, but agricultural western Kentucky is still called "the Democratic Gibraltar," and the coal counties along the West Virginia border support Democrats out of residual New Deal loyalties. For a while during the late 1960s, metropolitan Louisville seemed to be a possible source of votes for a statewide Republican breakthrough, but since then it has been moving back in the other direction.

Kentucky grew moderately in the 1970s — slightly more than the national average — but so far it has not attracted the variety of new industries that are changing states such as Arkansas and Mississippi. The old joke that Kentucky specializes in three habit-forming commodities — tobacco, bourbon and horse racing — is still true enough to reinforce political traditions based on old economics.

In addition, Kentucky has not had to endure a racial revolution, with all its turmoil and opportunity for political change. The state is only 7 percent black, and it never had a major voting rights problem. Kentucky did give George C. Wallace 18.3 percent of its vote in 1968, more than the 13.5 percent he got nationally — but that compared to 34 percent in neighboring Tennessee. The most intense racial problem in the state during recent years was an urban problem, the result of mandatory busing in Louisville, which started in 1975.

Jefferson County

Although this metropolitan area has about 20 percent of the state's population, the political differences between Democratic Louisville and the generally Republican suburbs tend to cancel each other out. Jefferson supported Ronald Reagan in 1980, but gave him only about a 2,500-vote plurality.

The county lost population during the 1970s, in part due to white flight caused by the court-ordered busing. This has led to rapid growth in adjacent Bullitt and Oldham counties.

Anti-Louisville sentiment in the state's rural counties ensures that Kentucky seldom elects a governor from Jefferson County. Beyond the borders of the county, the most popular aspect of Louisville is the Churchill Downs racetrack.

Louisville Republicans elected two mayors in a row during the 1960s, partly by appealing to black voters against a decayed Democratic organization. But Democrats swept back into City Hall in 1969 and have held it since then.

Blacks, comprising almost 30 percent of the city's population, occupy most of the West End. Nearby, white liberals cluster around the University of Louisville in a neighborhood of restored Victorian houses. The affluent East End contains the Republicans. Blue-collar whites predominate in the city's southern section and usually go Democratic. Louisville is a strong union town; General Electric, Ford Motor, International Harvester and many other industrial concerns have plants in the city or just outside.

South of the city along Dixie Highway to Fort Knox stretch blue-collar suburbs such as Shively and Pleasure Park Ridge, which normally favor the Democrats. However, most of the Jefferson suburbs, such as St. Regis Park and St. Matthews, are white-collar and Republican. The suburbs, with 56.5 percent of the county's population, usually keep county government in GOP hands.

The Bluegrass and Ohio River Counties

By day, the fabled grass of northern Kentucky appears no less green than any lawn in New Jersey. At dawn with the dew on it, however, the grass takes on a bluish hue.

For livestock, especially racehorses, the local grass has great nutritive value, derived from the limestone beds beneath the soil. The high phosphorous and calcium content of the grass strengthens the bones of the grazing animals.

In addition to the pasture land divided by endless white plank fences, the Bluegrass region has other types of farming. Tobacco is the main crop, with feed grains next in importance.

The Bluegrass farming counties are loyal to the Democratic Party if its candidate is not too liberal. In 1980, Jimmy Carter carried every county in the region. But in 1972, McGovern's only Bluegrass victory came in Carroll County.

Frankfort was chosen as the state capital in a 1792 compromise between competing Lexington and Louisville. But the city where Daniel Boone is buried never grew into a metropolis (1980 population 26,000), and remains a small town with picturesque old buildings. Its state government workers provide a Democratic base.

Lexington, almost eight times the size of Frankfort, is the only major urban center in Bluegrass country and the region's *de facto* capital. The University of Kentucky has attracted a burgeoning high-technology industry here, and the city's rapid growth — it almost doubled in size over the last decade — has been generated by a boom in engineering and other white-collar jobs. That boom has swung Lexington into the Republican column. Republican U.S. Rep. Larry J. Hopkins depends on it to offset the Democratic vote in the neighboring farm counties.

Along the Ohio River, the GOP usually does well in the Cincinnati suburbs, although Democrats have a good grip on local and state legislative offices. Republican strongholds include the wealthy community of Fort Thomas and the new light industrial center of Florence, where plastic bottles are made. Campbell County dropped slightly in population, but Kentucky's other two suburban Cincinnati counties, Boone and Kenton, made up for this. Run-down Newport, a speakeasy mecca in the 1920s, still retains a "sin city" flavor. It is Democratic.

Western Kentucky

A small aromatic mint grows luxuriantly in western Kentucky. Its name is pennyroyal, but the local pronunciation has rendered it pennyrile. It is after that plant that most of the flat and agriculturally abundant western part of the state got its name.

For the most part, Democrats hold sway in the Pennyrile, particularly in the so-called Jackson Purchase, a farm-oriented southwestern piece of the state that Andrew Jackson bought from the Chickasaw Indians. The chief city in the Purchase is Paducah, an old river town that ships tobacco, grain and coal.

In 1980, Carter carried most of the Purchase counties, which perhaps have a more Southern flavor than any other place in Kentucky. Residents of the area look toward Memphis as a major commercial center rather than more distant Louisville. Wallace did well here in 1968.

A smattering of counties in western Kentucky have strong Republican legacies — Crittenden, Butler, Edmonson and Grayson. They supported Barry Goldwater in 1964 and Ronald Reagan in 1980. The Republican affinity of the eastern edge of the Pennyrile seems to have seeped down from the nearby Republican mountains of the 5th District.

North of the Pennyrile, the western coal fields fan out from Owensboro, on the Ohio River, and seldom waver from the Democrats. All the coal counties voted for Carter in 1980.

Eastern Kentucky

The Appalachian counties in the east have traditionally depended on what could be dug out of the rugged ground.

In the 1950s, with coal use declining, times were very hard in east Kentucky. It was a major target for the Johnson administration's War on Poverty. With coal use on the upswing in recent years, the standard of living has improved. Even "up the hollers" — the poorer sections tucked away in the remotest mountain areas — such signs of modern affluence as color televisions and recreation vehicles have appeared in and next to the mobile homes.

During the Civil War, mountain disdain for the flatlanders who backed the Confederacy led many men from Appalachian Kentucky to join the Union forces. When the war ended and the Democrats took hold outside the mountains, the mountaineers embraced the Republican Party.

That Republican affiliation survives today in the core of the 5th Congressional District — the base any Republican statewide candidate must depend upon. Rockcastle, Laurel, Clay and Pulaski counties turned out well for Reagan in 1980.

To the north and east, though, the counties are more Democratic. Seven of the eight Kentucky counties George McGovern carried in 1972 were from this area, which makes up the 7th District. The poverty-stricken mountains suffered a population drain for years. The recent coal boom has reversed that trend. Some mountaineers who left to work in Detroit's auto plants have returned.

The United Mine Workers labor union has considerable influence in the easternmost counties. Harlan County, known as "Bloody Harlan," was the scene of labor violence in the 1930s. During the Evarts Coal Co. strike in 1931, five miners died.

The biggest city in eastern Kentucky is Ashland, an oil refining center and Democratic bastion.

KENTUCKY REMAP WEAKENS TWO CANDIDATES

Working its way around complaints of interference from Washington, Kentucky's Democratic-controlled Legislature approved a congressional map that redrew the lines in the populous northern and central counties while leaving the rest of the state's districts basically intact. Democratic Gov. John Y. Brown signed the bill on March 10, 1982.

The most important alterations provoked little controversy, since each incumbent was able to retain the heart of his old district. There was unexpected legislative turmoil, however, over the fate of small Jessamine County in central Kentucky.

Jessamine's 27,000 residents make up less than 1 percent of the state population. But the county, split between the 5th and 6th districts in the 1970s, was a political hot potato throughout the redistricting process. Legislative leaders finally placed it in the sprawling, poverty-stricken 5th District over the objections of county officials, who contended that Jessamine was economically and culturally tied to nearby Lexington in the Bluegrass 6th.

New Kentucky Districts

U. S. Congress: 7 districts
   Senate (2D)
   House (4D, 3R)
Governor:
   John Y. Brown (D)
Population: 3,661,433
Area: 40,395 sq. miles
1980 Presidential Vote:
   Carter (48%)
   Reagan (49%)
   Anderson (2%)

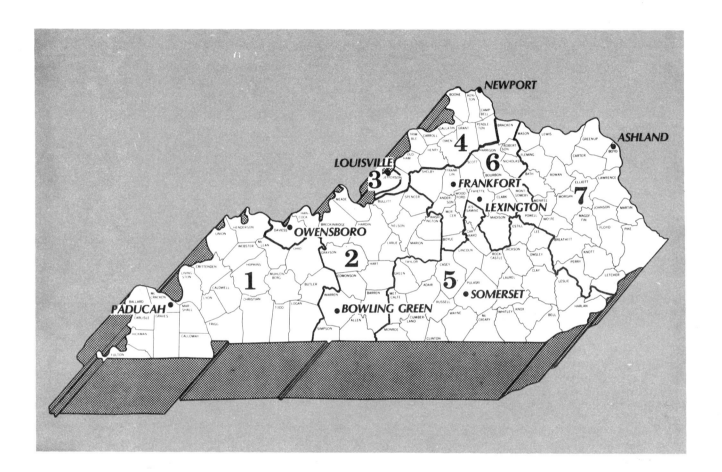

The county drew many legislative allies. But during final floor consideration of the redistricting plan, Democratic Rep. Carl D. Perkins of the 7th District opposed any efforts to take Jessamine out of the 5th. Perkins feared that the shift of Jessamine would force other changes that could cost him part of his base in the southern portion of the mountainous 7th.

As the dean of the congressional delegation, Perkins had considerable clout. With the help of the legislative leadership, his forces defeated amendments that would have placed Jessamine in the 6th. The margin was one vote in both the state House and Senate.

Each chamber subsequently approved the redistricting plan by lopsided margins. The House passed the final plan Jan. 27, 1982, by an 85-9 vote. The Senate approved the remap by a vote of 34 to 3 on Feb. 24, 1982.

The major changes in district lines were forced by population losses in the Louisville area. The predominantly urban 3rd District of Democrat Romano L. Mazzoli was forced to expand into GOP suburbs. In turn, Republican Gene Snyder's neighboring 4th District had to move into rural northern Kentucky to regain the population lost to the 3rd. The adjoining Lexington-based 6th District, represented by Republican Larry J. Hopkins, moved south and east.

Although the Legislature gave Mazzoli his choice of new suburban territory, the changes could hurt him by weakening his district's old urban focus. Hopkins also came away with a less-than-auspicious district, one that adds rural Democratic territory while dropping Ohio River counties favorable to the Republican. Hopkins is a Democratic target for November.

About the only consolation for Hopkins is the fact that the redistricting plan ultimately adopted was kinder to him than the version unveiled by the Democratic state party in 1981. Under that map, Hopkins would have lost half of Republican Fayette County, his home and political base.

That first plan was discarded after Perkins objected. It would have given Perkins a safe Democratic district, but the 34-year House veteran did not want to run in unfamiliar territory.

District 1

West — Paducah

Incumbent: Carroll Hubbard Jr. (D)

The birthplace of Jefferson Davis, Kentucky's 1st District votes more like the Deep South than like other parts of the state.

In contests for governor and for the U.S. Senate, the 1st generally turns in the highest Democratic majorities in Kentucky. Jimmy Carter won it in 1976 with 66 percent of the vote, his highest share in the state. The party has held the House seat throughout the 20th century. A four-term veteran, Hubbard has never drawn less than 78 percent of the vote in a general election.

But the district's tradition is also conservative. The western lowlands near the Mississippi River — known as the Jackson Purchase — were once slaveholding territory. This is the only part of Kentucky where cotton is grown.

The district does not have a massive black population; only one of the 24 counties in the 1st is more than 20 percent black. But the heritage of the district and its relative poverty made it fertile ground for the rural populism of George C. Wallace in 1968.

Four of the five counties Wallace carried in Kentucky are in the 1st. Two were in the Purchase area. The other two —Christian County (Hopkinsville) and Todd County (Elkton) — are located further east along the Tennessee border.

No city in the 1st District has more than 30,000 people. Most of the area is closely tied to agriculture; soybeans and dark-fired (or smokeless) tobacco are major crops. Coal

fields provide employment in the northeastern part of the district. Relatively small factories producing textiles and chemicals are prominent in small cities like Paducah and Hopkinsville.

The Ohio River port of Paducah has long been the population center and political capital of western Kentucky. It was the home of Alben W. Barkley, longtime Democratic senator and vice president under Harry S Truman. Barkley helped provide an economic shot-in-the arm to Paducah by steering an Atomic Energy Commission plant to the area. But the city has lost population since 1950. Recent growth in the Paducah area has been in neighboring Livingston and Marshall counties, which both enjoyed population gains of more than 20 percent in the last decade.

About 60 miles southeast of Paducah and 10 miles north of Clarksville, Tenn., is bustling Hopkinsville, an agricultural market and trade center for the nearby Fort Campbell military base. With its highly mobile population, the Hopkinsville area has developed more independent voting habits than the rest of the district.

Christian was one of only four counties in the 1st that Reagan carried in 1980. The others were traditionally Republican counties in the northern hills. But together these three GOP bastions — Butler, Crittenden and Ohio counties — have less than 10 percent of the district population.

Redistricting has made only one small change in the 1st. Rural Ohio County, formerly split between the 1st and 2nd districts, is now entirely in the 1st. Hubbard gains about 8,700 new constituents.

District 2

West Central — Owensboro

Incumbent: William H. Natcher (D)

Perched between the staunchly Democratic 1st and the reliably Republican 5th, the 2nd is a swing district in state and national elections.

Republicans are consistent winners in only three small counties in the 18-county district. The three — Allen, Edmondson and Grayson — were hotbeds of Union support in west central Kentucky during the Civil War.

But GOP candidates often carry the three major population centers — Daviess County (Owensboro), Hardin County (Elizabethtown) and Warren County (Bowling Green). Together they cast nearly half the district vote. Reagan won all but Daviess in 1980, affording him a narrow plurality in the 2nd.

The T-shaped district is diverse. Primarily agricultural, it has some light industry in small cities like Owensboro and Bowling Green. The 2nd takes in some of the Bluegrass region in the east, touches the Louisville suburbs in the north and includes the rolling hill country of the Pennyrile region in the southwest. The heart of the district is the Knobs area, a region of sinkholes and caves that includes the Mammoth Cave National Park.

Warren County's 24 percent growth rate in the 1970s was the highest of the district's major population centers. Bowling Green is the home of Western Kentucky University, the largest college in the state west of Louisville.

Carroll Hubbard Jr.   **William H. Natcher**

New Kentucky Districts

New District	Incumbent	Population	1980 Pres. Winner
1	Carroll Hubbard Jr. (D)	525,844	Carter
2	William H. Natcher (D)	520,634	Reagan
3	Romano L. Mazzoli (D)	522,636	Carter
4	Gene Snyder (R)	522,706	Reagan
5	Harold Rogers (R)	523,664	Reagan
6	Larry J. Hopkins (R)	519,009	Carter
7	Carl D. Perkins (D)	526,284	Carter

The fastest growth in the last decade outside the district's population centers has been in Bullitt County, a part of the Louisville suburbs. A controversial busing plan in metropolitan Jefferson County helped fuel a 66 percent growth rate in neighboring Bullitt, the second largest population increase in the state. With a sizable blue-collar element that frequently bolts the Democratic ticket, Bullitt was the only Kentucky county outside the 1st to vote for Wallace in 1968. Reagan won it in 1980.

Along the Ohio River in the northwest corner of the district is Owensboro, the largest city in the 2nd and the third largest in the state. Nearby oil and coal fields and a large General Electric plant provide an industrial base.

Between Owensboro and Louisville is Hardin County, the home of Fort Knox. The large military presence makes it the most populous county in the 2nd. But many of the military personnel do not vote, and Hardin regularly has a lower turnout than either Daviess or Warren counties.

The rest of the district is rural. Tobacco and livestock are mainstays of the economy. Republicans are strongest in the poorer farm counties in the center of the district; Democrats run best in the outer Bluegrass counties to the northeast.

Romano L. Mazzoli

Gene Snyder

Because it had about 19,000 more residents in 1980 than the ideal district population, the 2nd shed rural Anderson County in the northeast and half of rural Ohio County in the west. The changes should not alter the political complexion of the district. Ohio County is reliably Republican and Anderson County usually votes Democratic.

District 3

Louisville and Suburbs

Incumbent: Romano L. Mazzoli (D)

Although the 3rd will still be based in Louisville, the district's 15 percent population loss in the 1970s forced Mazzoli to add about 130,000 new suburban constituents.

Even though the Legislature let Mazzoli pick the precincts he wanted, the new territory could create problems for the six-term House veteran. His old district, made up of only Louisville and a few inner suburbs, was reliably Democratic. It gave Carter a 23,438-vote majority in 1980. But Mazzoli's new territory has a Republican tilt. It favored Reagan by about 6,000 votes.

Most of the new voters live south and southeast of the city in such blue-collar communities as Buechel, Fern Creek and Jeffersontown. Many of Mazzoli's new constituents work in suburban Louisville's General Electric, Ford and International Harvester plants. While a large share are registered Democrats, they are swing voters. Their support for Republican candidates frequently puts metropolitan Jefferson County in the GOP column.

The new 3rd takes in very few of the more affluent suburbs east and northeast of the city. A portion of St. Matthews, home to young professionals and retirees, is the only major addition to the 3rd from this part of the metropolitan area.

Even with the expansion, Louisville will contain 57 percent of the district population. Louisville contains large black and Catholic constituencies. Many of the Catholics are descendants of German immigrants who settled in the mid-19th century. But in its social history, Louisville has faced South. Its public places were not fully desegregated until well after World War II. In recent years court-ordered busing has been a major problem, particularly in blue-collar neighborhoods in the South End and in neighboring Shively. The right-to-life movement is strong within the conservative Catholic constituency.

Blacks comprise 28 percent of the city population, a larger share than in any population center in the state. Most blacks live near downtown in the West End, an area that regularly turns in heavy Democratic majorities.

The Republican East End features some remaining mansions on the bluffs overlooking the Ohio River. Slightly inland from the river, though, is the Cherokee triangle, a bastion of liberalism where young professionals live in old houses that have been restored. The South End is predominantly white, blue-collar and Democratic.

The busing furor and a depressed economy spurred a population exodus from both the city and its suburbs in the late 1970s. The countywide busing plan took effect in 1975. On its heels came economic problems that have idled thousands of workers throughout the Louisville area. The work force at the large General Electric Appliance Park is typical. It has declined to about 12,000 from a peak of almost 20,000. Unemployment in the Louisville area stood at 13 percent at the end of 1981.

District 4

Louisville suburbs; Covington, Newport

Incumbent: Gene Snyder (R)

Although the expansion of the 3rd District has forced the neighboring 4th to extend into rural northern Kentucky, Snyder's district will remain predominantly suburban and Republican.

The population is concentrated at each end. Four out of every five district voters live either in the suburbs of Louisville in the west or in those of Cincinnati in the east. Both areas are reliably Republican and have made the district the most consistent GOP bastion outside the mountainous 5th.

But redistricting has shifted the balance of power within the district from Jefferson County to suburban northern Kentucky. Some 55 percent of the population of the old 4th lived in the Louisville suburbs. With the remap, 51 percent live in Boone, Campbell and Kenton counties near Cincinnati. Along the Ohio River between the two population centers are four predominantly rural Democratic counties.

To compensate the 4th for the loss of some Louisville suburbs, four rural Bluegrass counties have been added from the 6th, plus the southern portions of Campbell and Kenton counties.

The new rural terrain gives the Democrats a bigger toehold in the 4th, but probably not enough to threaten Snyder. He represented all but two of the newly added counties — Henry and Owen — before the last redistricting in 1972.

Snyder's home base is suburban Jefferson County. Although he loses about 130,000 constituents to the 3rd, Snyder retains most of the Republican loyalists. The portion of the county remaining in the 4th gave Reagan 61 percent of the vote in 1980. The veteran Republican has a largely blue-collar constituency at the southern end of the county. But in the northeastern sector are some of the wealthiest communities in the United States.

Populous northern Kentucky is not so affluent. But the suburban commuters and factory workers who live there regularly turn in GOP majorities. Reagan carried Boone, Campbell and Kenton counties in 1980 with at least 56 percent of the vote in each.

Covington and Newport are old factory towns directly across the Ohio River from Cincinnati. Like the Louisville area, they have a large Catholic population of German extraction. Anti-abortion candidate Ellen McCormack ran a close second to Carter there in the 1976 Democratic presidential primary.

The major population growth in northern Kentucky has been in Boone County. Attracting suburban spillover from Campbell and Kenton counties, it grew 40 percent in the 1970s.

Oldham County, at the other end of the district, has had an even higher growth rate. Thanks largely to the busing furor in neighboring Jefferson County, it grew 91 percent in the last decade, the largest growth rate in the state. Oldham, however, contains only 5 percent of the district population.

While the rural counties are generally Democratic, most have supported the conservative Snyder. Sometimes that produces political schizophrenia, as in 1972, when pastoral Carroll County gave majorities to both Snyder and George McGovern.

District 5

Southeast

Incumbent: Harold Rogers (R)

Rural and poor, the 5th District is worlds apart from the suburban 4th. But it equals and usually exceeds the 4th in its Republicanism. The mountain counties have been voting the GOP ticket for more than a century.

Since the Civil War — when its small-scale farmers were hostile to slaveholding secessionist Democrats elsewhere in Kentucky — southeast Kentucky has been one of the most loyal GOP strongholds in the nation. Alfred M. Landon carried nearly all its counties in 1936. Barry Goldwater won the 5th in 1964, the only district in Kentucky he carried.

The only significant sources of Democratic votes are Bell and Harlan counties, in the coal-producing southeast corner of the district.

Bell and Harlan were the only counties in the district to back Carter in 1980, but together they have only 15 percent of the district's population. Every place else in the 5th was Reagan territory. In nine counties, the Republican nominee drew more than 70 percent of the vote.

In spite of some of the richest coal deposits in the nation along the district's eastern border, the 5th is the poorest district in Kentucky and one of the poorest in the nation. In 1970 nearly one-quarter of the residents lacked a sixth-grade education. The recent revival in the coal industry has helped end decades of population decline, but none of the counties in the district has a per-capita income that approaches the statewide level.

Tobacco, apples, poultry and livestock are mainstays of the farm economy in the rolling hill country in the central and western parts of the district. Poor transportation and the absence of major population centers have curtailed industrial development. The new 5th is the only district in the state — and may turn out to be the only one in the country in the 1980s — without a city of 15,000 population. Its largest community, Middlesboro, has 12,251 residents.

Madison County (Richmond) was the most populous in the old 5th, but redistricting has moved its 53,000 residents into the 6th. Its loss probably will not be mourned by Rogers. Madison was one of the few counties that he failed to carry in 1980.

Other changes in the district lines were comparatively minor. Jessamine County, which was split between the 5th and 6th districts, is now entirely in Rogers' district. And the 5th District's share of Letcher County along the Virginia border has been expanded to include a few more precincts from the old 7th. Together the two additions give Rogers about 20,000 new constituents.

District 6

North central — Lexington, Frankfort

Incumbent: Larry J. Hopkins (R)

The 6th is Kentucky as the rest of the nation pictures it. Horses, tobacco and whiskey are the mainstays of its culture and economy.

The population of the 6th was fairly evenly divided in the last decade between Republican Fayette County (Lexington) and the Democratic countryside. But the ripple effect from the extensive redistricting in the Louisville area has forced the 6th to move south and east. Although Hopkins retains the heart of the Bluegrass region and more than three-quarters of his old constituents, the new lines will make re-election more difficult for him.

The Democratic Legislature removed from the 6th four rural counties in northern Kentucky and replaced them with five small counties on the district's eastern and western flanks. It also took out areas near Cincinnati (in the southern portions of Campbell and Kenton counties) and near Lexington (the northern portion of Jessamine County) and put in a populous swing county (Madison).

The centerpiece of the 6th remains Fayette County, home for 40 percent of district residents. Lexington is best known for its thoroughbred horse farms that regularly produce Kentucky Derby champions. But a diverse economic base has made it the most prosperous part of the state outside Louisville.

A large white-collar element enables GOP candidates to carry the Lexington area. Fayette, which voted Republican in the last four presidential elections, supported Hopkins in 1980 by a margin of more than 2-to-1.

Still, Fayette is no bastion of conservatism. Reagan's 49 percent share of the 1980 presidential vote in the county was 5 percentage points below Gerald R. Ford's showing four years earlier. Many of the defectors in 1980 went to independent John B. Anderson, who drew 7 percent there, his highest vote in Kentucky.

The attraction of new businesses to the Lexington area produced a postwar population boom. But during the 1970s the county began to curb residential and industrial expansion, spurring population and manufacturing growth in rural Bluegrass counties within commuting distance of Lexington.

The most populous of the adjoining counties is Madison (Richmond), transferred in 1982 from the 5th. Madison voted for Reagan in 1980, while also backing the Democratic congressional candidate.

The northern portion of the county is dotted with bedroom communities whose residents work in the nearby city of Lexington. The southern portion revolves around Richmond, a tobacco market and site of Eastern Kentucky University. Ten percent of the district population lives in Madison, making it the second largest county in the 6th District.

The five Democratic counties added to the district on its eastern and western borders will represent 10 percent of the district vote. Anderson County, on the western end, was moved over from the 2nd District. Bracken, Montgomery, Nicholas and Robertson counties are on the eastern flank and were switched from the fast-growing 7th.

The district's other major population center is Franklin County, which includes the state capital of Frankfort. The long heritage of Democratic governors has produced a loyal pool of state workers who help keep the county in the Democratic column. Carter won it in 1980 with 60 percent of the vote, his top showing in the district.

District 7

East — Ashland

Incumbent: Carl D. Perkins (D)

The 7th District reaches into poverty-stricken Appalachia. Major products in the hill country along its northern boundary include tobacco, cattle and fruit. Natural gas and coal are mined in the mountains of the southeast. Ashland, the district's only population center, is home to petrochemical and steel plants.

The 7th is one of the poorest district's in the United States, yet in the 1970s it grew faster than any other Kentucky district. The population grew by 23 percent in the decade, as many former residents were lured back to their hometowns by a revival of the coal industry and a decline in automobile industry jobs in the urban Midwest.

With the United Mine Workers (UMW) a major force in politics, the 7th is a Democratic bastion. It has supported the party presidential nominee in five of the last six elections, failing only in 1972. Even then, seven of the eight Kentucky counties won by McGovern were in the district. In congressional contests, Perkins has not faced a serious challenge in a quarter century.

Democratic strength is greatest in the southern two-thirds of the district where coal is king. The rugged area is one of the nation's leading producers of bituminous coal. Since the New Deal and the UMW transformed politics in

Harold Rogers   **Larry J. Hopkins**

the region, the coal counties have regularly turned in some of the highest Democratic percentages in the state. Four counties gave Carter more than 70 percent of the vote in 1980.

Carl D. Perkins

Pike County anchors the eastern tip of the 7th District. In land area, Pike is the largest county in Kentucky. In population, it is first in the district — Pike County residents make up about 15 percent of the voters in the 7th. And in recent years, Pike has been the leading county in the country in coal production.

Coal and poverty go hand in hand. Some of the poorest counties in the nation are deep in the Kentucky coal country, which dominates the 7th and stretches over into the neighboring 5th District. Many of the counties in this part of the state have per-capita incomes less than half the national level.

Within the 7th, the standard of living is highest in the area around Ashland. The Ohio River city lies just across the border from Huntington, W. Va., and is headquarters for the Ashland Oil Company. Although layoffs have hurt the local economy, strong unions help keep the Ashland area — industrialized Boyd and Greenup counties — in the Democratic column. Along with oil refineries, there are major railroad maintenance facilities and steel and cement plants that provide employment for a large blue-collar work force. Residents of the Ashland area account for about one-sixth of the district vote.

The northern portion of the 7th District, stretching from the West Virginia boundary northwestward into the Ohio River Valley, is primarily agricultural. But compared to the fertile Bluegrass region, it is mediocre land dominated by small-scale and subsistence farming. This area usually votes for Republican candidates. Three small farm counties gave Reagan at least 60 percent of the vote in the 1980 election.

Perkins was forced to surrender about 40,000 constituents in redistricting, but the political complexion of his district will not change. The veteran Democrat approved the switch of four small counties in the northwest corner into the 6th District, but refused to allow the Legislature to transfer any significant part of his home base in the loyally Democratic coal fields. The only change in the coal country was the move of several more precincts in Letcher County into the 5th District.

Tennessee

Tennessee is three distinct regions, stretching 400 miles from the Appalachian highlands to the Mississippi. The different regions' politics are as varied as their topography.

The farmers in the highland valleys of East Tennessee have traditionally been Republican, doggedly self-reliant and suspicious of outsiders.

Middle Tennessee, where the rolling hills and bluegrass fields are well-suited to livestock and tobacco, has been the part of the state most receptive to populist Democratic candidates. West Tennessee began as a province of "King Cotton" and slavery, and continued into the 20th century as a region of bourbon Democratic control.

More than almost anywhere else in the South, Civil War voting patterns are still the clue to politics in Tennessee. Pro-union sentiment was strong in the east, where the small-scale farmers owned few slaves and resented the planters in the Mississippi valley. Even though the state seceded and joined the confederacy, most of East Tennessee stayed loyal to the Union, and Republican ever after.

After the Civil War, loyalties in Middle and West Tennessee guaranteed one-party Democratic rule, over objections in the east. Memphis political boss Edward H. Crump, first elected mayor in 1909, made Tennessee his political fiefdom until after World War II. Crump controlled state Democratic primaries through a patronage network that delivered about 65,000 votes in Shelby County (Memphis) and a significant share of the outstate vote.

Voter turnout increased in the postwar years, and Crump eventually lost control to a younger breed of progressive Democrats such as Gov. Frank Clement and U. S. senators Estes Kefauver and Albert Gore. Gore, last of those to leave public office, lost in 1970 to Republican Bill Brock.

Brock's victory was part of a GOP resurgence that elected Howard H. Baker Jr. to the Senate in 1966 and Winfield Dunn to the governorship in 1970. Since 1970, two-party competition has flourished as it has in few other parts of the country. Democrats recaptured the governorship in 1974, but lost it in 1978. Carter beat Ford convincingly in 1976, but Reagan won narrowly in 1980. Brock lost his Senate seat in 1976 to Democrat Jim Sasser, but Baker has been re-elected comfortably twice. Republicans surged

to control of the Tennessee House as early as 1968, but failed to hold it. Democrats control both houses of the state Legislature now, and have a 5-3 advantage in U. S House seats.

East Tennessee

The Tennessee Valley Authority's programs for flood control, electrical generation, and soil conservation lifted much of this region from rural poverty. But the TVA has shaken few natives from their historic party ties and instinctive suspicion of big government. East Tennessee is Republican territory, with rare exception.

Sullivan and Washington counties encompass northeast Tennessee's growing Tri-Cities — Kingsport, Johnson City and Bristol, an area with chemical manufacturing, paper milling, book printing and other industry.

Washington County (Johnson City) opposed secession in 1861, like most of the region, and has since regularly voted Republican.

Sullivan County (Kingsport) is one of the few eastern areas with a consistently high Democratic vote, one that goes back to its endorsement of secession in 1861. Sullivan went for Democrats Sasser and Carter in 1976, and chose Reagan over Carter only narrowly in 1980. Coal mining is an economic staple for many of the mountainous eastern counties, and in recent years exploration for oil and natural gas has boosted the economy.

Knoxville, in the center of East Tennessee, is the region's largest city and third largest in the state. TVA headquarters are there, as is the University of Tennessee's main campus. Knoxville grew up on textile and iron production and now has a larger role as regional retail and distribution center. The 1982 World's Fair will be held on a 70-acre site near the downtown area.

Despite the TVA and its association with Democratic administrations, Knoxville and surrounding Knox County remain solidly Republican. One enclave of Democratic support exists near Knoxville — among the scientific intelligentsia in Oak Ridge, the city established by the federal government during World War II to purify uranium for use in the atomic bomb.

In Tennessee's southeastern corner is the heavily industrialized city of Chattanooga, fourth largest city in the state. Steel, iron and chemicals are produced there. Former

Sen. Bill Brock began building the Republican Party in Chattanooga in the early 1960s, and represented it in the U. S. House for eight years before moving to the Senate. Hamilton County, containing Chattanooga, has voted Republican in all but one presidential contest since 1952; in 1968, American Independent George Wallace finished first and Nixon second.

Middle Tennessee

The "capital" of Middle Tennessee is Nashville, which has also been capital of the state since 1843. Today it is a center for banking, insurance, and higher education, but it is known better regionally for religious publishing, and nationally for the country music industry.

Many Middle Tennesseans resented Crump's conservative political machine, which controlled the statehouse in Nashville by pulling strings in Memphis. Anti-Crumpism played a part in making Middle Tennessee the spawning ground for a number of the state's populist and progressive Democrats. One was Frank Clement, a Bible-thumping, evangelical-style orator who as governor (1955-59, 1963-67) enacted educational reforms, improved mental health services and vetoed several segregation bills passed by the state Legislature. Albert Gore Sr., born in north central Tennessee, championed public power and civil rights as a member of Congress.

Clement, Gore and Estes Kefauver, a liberal East Tennessee Democrat, set the political tone in Tennessee's post-Crump era and shared the spotlight at the 1956 Democratic convention: Clement was the keynoter and Gore and Kefauver vied for the vice presidential slot won eventually by Kefauver. Their larger ambitions went unrealized. The Stevenson-Kefauver ticket lost to the Republicans in 1956 and Clement failed in two later bids for the Senate. Gore was twice re-elected to the Senate, but lost in 1970 to Republican Brock. Gore's son currently represents much of Middle Tennessee in the House, and carries on the rural populist-progressive tradition, although he himself is urban in style and background.

Democratic candidates can usually depend on carrying Middle Tennessee (Reagan won only two counties in the region in 1980), but metropolitan Davidson County (Nashville) has been inclined to wander a bit in recent years. It voted for George Wallace in 1968, Richard Nixon in 1972 and Republican gubernatorial candidate Lamar Alexander in 1978.

West Tennessee

More than ever, the west is dominated by Memphis, whose metropolitan area is the South's seventh largest. The city's economy, born out of plantation crops, shifted its emphasis to chemicals and machinery and now attracts corporate headquarters and warehousing and distribution facilities.

Shelby County (Memphis), the bulwark of one-party rule under Crump, became the key to two-party politics in Tennessee when Crump died in 1953 and his organization crumbled. The power vacuum in Shelby County was filled partly by suburban middle-class businessmen and professionals. This group, uneasy about the Democrats' preoccupation with racial equality, found a haven in Goldwater Republicanism and extended their organization beyond Memphis to traditionally conservative rural West Tennessee.

The Shelby County Republican voters elected Dan Kuykendall to the Memphis congressional seat in 1966 and brought strong West Tennessee support to Howard H. Baker Jr. in 1966 as well as Winfield Dunn and Bill Brock in 1970. Kuykendall lost to a black Democrat in 1974, as the district's white population was declining, but upper-income whites in Shelby County continue to vote the Republican ticket in large numbers. In most parts of suburban Shelby County, Reagan won about two-thirds of the vote in 1980. Memphis itself, now heavily black, went for Carter decisively.

West Tennessee has a pocket of Republican strength in the Highland Rim area, where poor hill country farmers in counties such as Hardin, Wayne, Henderson and Carroll owned few slaves in antebellum days and opposed secession. Nearby Madison County (Jackson) is another area that often votes Republican.

STATE DEMOCRATS CREATE TWO OPEN SEATS

The Democratic Party had a classic gerrymander in mind when they drew Tennessee's new congressional districts, but only the 1982 elections will tell whether or not they carried it off.

Endeavoring to bring two more Democrats into the delegation, which will expand from the current eight members to nine, the Democratic state Legislature passed a redistricting bill June 17, 1981, that establishes two open districts.

One is a sprawling rural catchall of 23 counties in eastern and middle Tennessee. This new 4th District is basically the territory that was left over after five overpopulated districts were trimmed down to the ideal population size.

The other open district, the 7th District in west-central Tennessee, contains much of the territory now represented by Republican Rep. Robin L. Beard, although it does leave out Beard's strongly Republican home base, Williamson County.

Tennessee Gov. Lamar Alexander, a Republican, took a close look at the map proposed by the Democrats and decided that Republican candidates had a chance in both open districts. Since the map also did nothing to harm East Tennessee's two Republican incumbents, Reps. James H. Quillen and John J. Duncan, Gov. Alexander decided not to veto the Democrats' attempted gerrymander. He allowed the new redistricting proposal to become law without his signature.

The redistricting map poses problems for one Democratic incumbent, Rep. Harold E. Ford of Memphis. Ford is Tennessee's only black congressman. Because of a population drain from his district during the 1970s, Ford's territory was forced to expand into neighboring suburban areas, which are composed of voters very different from the urban, black-majority constituency he has been representing since 1975.

Tennessee earned its new district by taking in nearly 665,000 new residents during the last decade. But it is merely gaining back a seat it lost in redistricting ten years

New Tennessee Districts

U. S. Congress: 9 districts
  Senate (1D, 1R)
  House (5D, 3R)
Governor:
  Lamar Alexander (R)
Population: 4,590,750
Area: 42,244 sq. miles
1980 Presidential Vote:
  Carter (48%)
  Reagan (49%)
  Anderson (2%)

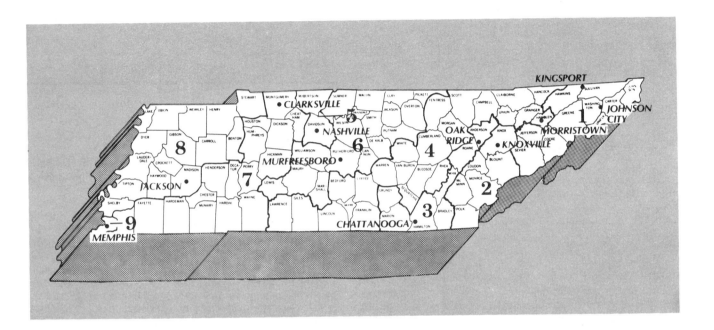

ago, when it fell just short of the population required for nine seats. None of the districts created this year vary from the ideal population of 510,083 by more than 1.3 percentage points.

District 1

Northeast — Tri-cities

Incumbent: James H. Quillen (R)

By removing three western counties, the Legislature pushed Quillen's 1st District further into the northeastern corner of the state. Hamblen, Grainger and Hancock counties are steadfastly Republican, but their transfer to the new 4th District will not affect GOP control in the 1st. The 10 counties that make up the new 1st gave Ronald Reagan 61 percent of their vote in 1980, his highest percentage in any of Tennessee's congressional districts.

The Tennessee Valley Authority (TVA) has freed this district and much of East Tennessee from the pervasive rural poverty of an earlier era. Isolated highland towns, tobacco patches and livestock clearings were once the 1st District norm, but in the past generation, small cities have

grown up around industries drawn to the area by the availability of TVA power.

Forty-five percent of the people in the 1st District live in Sullivan and Washington counties, which encompass northeast Tennessee's Tri-cities — Johnson City, Kingsport and Bristol. These towns make everything from textiles, paper and cement to electronic calculators.

Because of its industrial work force, the Tri-cities area has a respectable Democratic vote. In 1980, Reagan managed only 51 percent in Sullivan County; in 1976, Carter narrowly took Sullivan and Rep. Quillen carried it by only 543 votes. Reagan was much stronger in Washington County in 1980, but Democrats still held him below 60 percent.

Even when Democrats do well in the Tri-cities, however, they are generally swamped districtwide. More than one-half of the people in the 1st District still live in rural and small-town counties where the impact of TVA has not shaken natives from their instinctive suspicion of big government. These counties regularly elect Republican candidates by wide margins.

The rural areas raise tobacco, poultry and livestock. Zinc and limestone are mined, and some people commute to factory jobs in Knoxville or the Tri-cities.

At the southern end of the 1st, Sevier County feeds on tourist dollars. It is the gateway to the Great Smoky Mountains National Park, which draws about 10 million visitors yearly. At the very edge of the park in Sevier County is Gatlinburg, a town of 3,210 people whose motels sleep 40,000.

District 2

East — Knoxville

Incumbent: John J. Duncan (R)

The 2nd has been impeccably Republican for years in nearly every contest for national, congressional and state-wide office. Redistricting alters the appearance of the 2nd, but not its partisan preference.

The remap removes four northern counties and enhances the already-dominant role of Knoxville and Knox County in the district. Sixty-three percent of Duncan's constituents will now be residents of Knox County, compared to 54 percent before redistricting.

With 183,139 residents, Knoxville is the third-largest city in the state. TVA headquarters are there, as is the University of Tennessee's main campus. The city grew up on textiles, tobacco marketing and meatpacking, but now has a larger role as a regional retail and distribution center. Knoxville is undergoing a massive overhaul in preparation for the 1982 World's Fair, to be staged on a 70-acre site adjoining downtown.

Federal employees who work for TVA are generally Democratic, but the labor vote in private industry is a mixed bag; although union leaders are Democratic, many of the rank-and-file are conservative and vote Republican. The state university also has a conservative orientation, and the outlying rural sections of Knox County are strongly Republican. Democratic candidates consider 45 percent a good showing in Knox County, where the Republican tradition has not abated since the Civil War.

Blount County, south of Knoxville, has 15 percent of the district's residents. Located there are the sprawling plants of Alcoa Aluminum, where 4,500 people work. In 1980, Blount was Reagan's best 2nd District county, giving him 64 percent of the vote.

Moving south toward the Georgia line, Democratic strength picks up. McMinn and Monroe counties gave tiny

margins to Carter in 1976, but reversed field last year and cast more than 55 percent of their vote for Reagan. Polk County, added to the 2nd by redistricting, is the eastern-most county in Tennessee carried by Carter in 1980. A massive sulfuric acid plant is located in the Ducktown Copper Basin of Polk County. But the Democratic votes of Polk's 13,602 residents will barely be noticed in the 2nd.

The four northern counties that will switch from the 2nd to the 4th are Campbell, Claiborne, Scott and Union. All usually vote Republican, but their combined 1980 vote was just 12 percent of the district total. Duncan, whose home base is Knoxville, is safe with or without them.

District 3

Southeast — Chattanooga, Oak Ridge

Incumbent: Marilyn Lloyd Bouquard (D)

Though the 3rd usually votes Republican in state and national elections, it should remain safe for Bouquard, a conservative Democrat and staunch ally of nuclear power. Bouquard's pro-nuclear stance is a must in this district: many jobs are tied to the nuclear research and production facilities at Oak Ridge, to the Clinch River breeder reactor, and to the Sequoyah nuclear plant in northern Hamilton County.

The population center of the 3rd is Chattanooga, a heavily industrialized city producing iron, steel and textiles. Chattanooga and surrounding Hamilton County contain 56 percent of the 3rd District's residents. There has been some racial tension between Chattanooga's working class whites, many of whom come from rural backgrounds, and blacks, who make up about one-third of the population — a high percentage by East Tennessee standards.

Hamilton County has voted Republican in all but one presidential contest since 1952; that once was in 1968, when George C. Wallace finished first and Republican Richard M. Nixon second. In 1980, Democrat Bouquard managed to run even with Reagan in Hamilton County, taking 56 percent of the vote.

The district's most loyally Democratic counties are Anderson and Roane, in the northern part of the 3rd. The major city is Oak Ridge. Nearly 18,000 people work at Union Carbide's three Oak Ridge plants, which build weapons components and enrich uranium for use in reactors.

The government workers and scientific intelligentsia at Oak Ridge have traditionally been the most consistent Democratic voting bloc in East Tennessee, but that is changing as the GOP takes the leading role in promoting nuclear energy. In 1976, Carter won 56 percent in both Anderson and Roane counties, but in 1980 he averaged only 38 percent there. His attempt to shut down the Clinch River breeder reactor was widely unpopular. Bouquard resisted the 1980 Republican tide, winning more than 70 percent in both Anderson and Roane.

Redistricting removed three counties along the western edge of the 3rd (Rhea, Bledsoe and Sequatchie), plus one county in its northwest corner (Morgan) and one at its eastern edge (Polk). Altogether, the counties given up cast only about 10 percent of the total vote in the last election.

James H. Quillen

John J. Duncan

New Tennessee Districts

New District	Incumbent	Population	1980 Pres. Winner
1	James H. Quillen (R)	512,686	Reagan
2	John J. Duncan (R)	510,197	Reagan
3	Marilyn Lloyd Bouquard (D)	516,692	Reagan
4	No Incumbent	510,650	Reagan
5	Bill Boner (D)	514,716	Carter
6	Albert Gore Jr. (D) Robin L. Beard (R)	511,716	Carter
7	No Incumbent	504,250	Reagan
8	Ed Jones (D)	504,743	Carter
9	Harold E. Ford (D)	504,846	Carter

Grundy County, a small but strongly Democratic area, is added to the 3rd by redistricting.

District 4

Northeast and South Central

No Incumbent

The all-new 4th slants across the state for approximately 300 miles, from Hamblen County in the northeast to Lawrence County on the Alabama border. It crosses one time zone and dips into four major media markets.

After Democrats tightened the boundaries of the three East Tennessee districts to meet population requirements, they were left with 11 counties that had to be attached elsewhere. They joined those 11 to 10 other counties split off from the mid-state district of Democrat Albert Gore Jr. Then Democrats threw in two counties from the old 6th District, bringing the new 4th to a population of 510,650.

The partisan strains in the 4th District vary from staunch Appalachian Republicanism in the northern counties to plateau Democratic populism at the southern end. Either party could win an election here. In 1980, the 23 counties that make up the new 4th gave Ronald Reagan 49 percent and Jimmy Carter 48 percent of the vote.

One unifying feature of the district is its rural nature. There is no county with a population greater than 50,000; the district's largest population center is Morristown, in Hamblen County, with 19,683 people.

Morristown is a marketing center for area farms, and a nearby American Enka plant keeps 3,200 people busy making synthetic fibers. Reagan won 61 percent in Hamblen County in 1980, a typical showing for this rugged, traditionally Republican area.

Coal has long been an economic staple here. Underground activity has mostly given way to surface mining, and in some places rapacious strip-mining techniques have defaced the landscape. Abandoned coal mines pose a health hazard, since fresh water trickling through them becomes too acidic to drink. In recent years, exploration for oil and natural gas has helped the economy.

Agriculture focuses on tobacco, poultry and dairying. Those looking for a steady wage commute to factories in Knoxville, Morristown, and a few other towns.

Further south, the terrain levels out and voting habits shift from mountain GOP to populist Democratic. Coffee County, where sour mash whiskey is made, gave Carter 57 percent of the vote in 1980. In Bedford County, famous for its Tennessee Walking Horses, Carter won 63 percent.

Democratic strength is less pronounced in Lawrence County, at the extreme southwest end of the district. Reagan won 49 percent there in 1980.

Despite the expense and effort of running for Congress in the wide-ranging 4th, at least three Democrats have already started campaigning. Cissy Baker, 26, daughter of Sen. Howard H. Baker Jr., is seeking the GOP nomination.

District 5

Nashville

Incumbent: Bill Boner (D)

More than 90 percent of the 5th District vote comes from Nashville and surrounding Davidson County, where Democrats are firmly in control. Carter carried the 5th with 60 percent in 1980, and it rarely supports a Republican in statewide elections.

Since Nashville is Tennessee's capital, state government employees are a large part of the work force. Davidson County is home to 17 colleges and universities, and factories in the area manufacture aircraft parts, glass, clothing, and tires. Nashville is also a banking and insurance center and headquarters for the country music industry and several publishers of religious materials.

The Democratic inclinations of government workers, academic communities and labor unions uphold Nashville's traditional position as the focal point of Middle Tennessee Democratic populism. Populist politics took hold in Nashville early in this century as a reaction to the conservative

Marilyn Lloyd Bouquard   **Bill Boner**

Albert Gore Jr.   **Robin L. Beard**

Democratic machine in Memphis that controlled Tennessee politics until after World War II.

Nashville's population is 23 percent black, a relatively low figure for a large Southern city. Nashville politics has not polarized along racial lines to the degree seen in Memphis and Chattanooga, where blacks make up a higher percentage of the population and whites have drifted away from Democratic loyalties. Most white voters in Nashville are still consistent Democrats.

Robertson County, a rural area north of Nashville, is even more Democratic. Carter won 59 percent in Davidson County in 1980, but took two-thirds of the Robertson vote.

The only change in the 5th District brought about by redistricting is a transfer of 21,616 residents of Cheatham County to the neighboring 7th District. Cheatham, strongly Democratic, cast just 3 percent of the 5th District's total 1980 vote.

After a midsummer flirtation with the idea of returning to Nashville to run for a local office, Boner has decided to seek re-election to Congress in 1982. His indecision may have tempted other Democrats to challenge him in next year's primary. If renominated, Boner should have a clear path to victory in the general election.

District 6

North Central — Murfreesboro

Incumbents: Albert Gore Jr. (D)
                      Robin L. Beard (R)

Albert Gore, a Democrat now serving his third term, is so well ensconced here that Democrats threw Republican territory into his district in an effort to help Democratic candidates elsewhere in the state.

On the eastern and southern ends of his constituency, Gore gives up 11 counties — nearly all of them strongly Democratic — to Bouquard's 3rd District and the new 4th. He gains Williamson County, the increasingly Republican home-base of GOP Rep. Robin L. Beard Jr., who is planning to depart to run for the U. S. Senate.

Williamson County, containing Nashville's southern suburbs, is the fastest-growing county in the state; it saw a 68.8 percent population increase in the last decade. Although Carter won Williamson narrowly in 1976, GOP gubernatorial candidate Lamar Alexander carried it with 68 percent in 1978, and Reagan won 55 percent there last year.

In recent House elections, Williamson has teamed with affluent Memphis suburbs to give wide margins to Republican Beard, helping him win comfortably. But the remap makes Williamson an isolated GOP enclave in Gore's otherwise Democratic district.

Most voters on the farms and in the small towns of the 6th heartily endorse Gore's populist positions on issues involving oil companies and other corporate interests. Though the 6th is mostly rural — Murfreesboro, the largest city, has 32,485 people — there are several other small cities where factories produce air conditioners, furniture, pencils, and textiles.

In Smyrna, a Rutherford County town with 8,839 people, Japan's Nissan Motor Company is building a $300 million truck assembly plant. The factory is the largest single industrial-capital investment in Tennessee history and will employ more than 2,000 people. Industrial expansion is increasing the district's blue-collar work force, and the labor vote seems inclined to hold to the Democratic loyalties that are traditional in middle Tennessee.

In addition to Williamson County, the 6th picks up Maury and Lewis counties from Beard's old district. Lewis is a small, strongly Democratic rural county. The Democratic grip is not quite as tight in Maury County, but Carter was able to win 53 percent there in 1980. Phosphates are mined in Maury, and the city of Columbia there is a marketing center for surrounding livestock and dairy farms.

District 7

West Central — Clarksville, part of Shelby County

No Incumbent

Robin Beard, who represents most of this territory, has been campaigning unofficially against Democratic Sen. Jim Sasser for months. His unannounced but active Senate candidacy encouraged Democratic legislators to sever his Williamson County home from his old 6th District and place it in Gore's new 6th. The intention was to make the new 7th a Democratic seat.

However, the move will not necessarily end Republican control of this west-central district. Although the 7th loses GOP-voting Williamson at its eastern end, it also gives up four other eastern counties where Democrats have an edge.

And further west, the new 7th will add thousands of staunch Republicans in bedroom communities northeast of Memphis. They are currently represented by Democrat Ed Jones, who was eager to drop them. Suburbs such as Bartlett, Cordova and Raleigh now join other residential areas such as Germantown, southeast of Memphis, that have voted strongly for Beard since his initial 1972 race. With the remap, more than one-third of the 7th District's people will live in Shelby County, and these areas gave Reagan 72 percent of their vote in 1980.

Without Shelby County, Beard would not have had the easy time he enjoyed all during the 1970s. There are 15 other counties in the 7th, and in 1980 Carter won 10 of them, most with more than 60 percent of the vote.

At the northern end of the 7th, there is a solid Democratic vote in Montgomery County, home of Clarksville, which will be the largest city in the new district. A longtime market for livestock and crops from the surrounding farmland, Clarksville is now more dependent on its factory payroll than its tobacco auction.

About one-half of the district's people live on farms and in small towns that lie between Shelby County and Montgomery County. Beard's popularity has lured some conservative voters in this area to vote Republican, but most remain Democratic.

There is a pocket of Republican strength in the Highland Rim area, where poor hill country farmers opposed secession and have been loyal to the GOP ever since. Five counties in that south-central area voted for Reagan in 1980.

District 8

West — Jackson, part of Shelby County

Incumbent: Ed Jones (D)

Reagan carried Jones' mostly rural and suburban 7th District in 1980, but Jones' new constituency, redrawn and renumbered the 8th, gave Carter a majority. The difference is the removal of 75,000 mostly Republican voters in suburban Memphis. Although Jones has been able to carry those suburbs in past elections, his margins there have never matched his strong rural support.

Jones has been interested primarily in farm issues since he came to Congress, but to lend a cosmopolitan tinge to his image, he likes to point out that he does represent some voters in the city of Memphis. To allow him to continue making that claim, the Legislature kept the Fraser area of Memphis in the district. Jones will also represent a significant part of northern Shelby County, where suburbia and GOP dominance give way to farms and Democratic leanings. The Memphis Naval Air Station is in north Shelby, near Millington, where Jones runs well among blue-collar workers.

Twenty percent of the people in the 8th live in Shelby County; 57 percent of these voters went for Reagan in 1980, but three-quarters supported Jones.

Madison County (Jackson) is home to another 15 percent of the 8th's residents. Republicans are gaining ground there, thanks in part to an influx of managerial people to Jackson's increasingly diversified industries, among them a Rockwell hand tool factory, a Bendix auto parts plant and a Procter & Gamble Co. facility that makes Pringles potato chips. The surrounding farm counties look to Jackson, the district's largest city, as a source of retail goods and services. Reagan won 50 percent of the Madison County vote in 1980, but Madison's drift to the GOP has not affected Jones: he won 81 percent there in the last election.

Thirteen mostly rural counties account for two-thirds of the 8th District population. This is a region of soybeans,

corn, wheat, and cotton. Population grew little in the past decade. Lake County, the only Tennessee County to lose population during the 1970s, is located at the northwest corner of the 8th. The 13 agricultural counties are nearly always Democratic. Carter took all but one of them in 1980, although Reagan's strong appeal among conservative voters brought him close in a few counties.

District 9

Memphis

Incumbent: Harold E. Ford (D)

Redistricting added about 80,000 people to Ford's underpopulated district and changed its number from 8 to 9. Nearly all of Ford's new constituents are suburban Republicans, and they may cause him some trouble in future elections.

Like most heavily-black districts throughout the country, Ford's old 8th District has been reliably Democratic in good years and bad. Carter won 68 percent of the vote there in 1980, considerably more than in any other Tennessee district and an improvement on his 1976 performance.

Blacks are still a majority in Ford's new 9th, but with the new white communities brought in by redistricting, blacks and whites will be about even among registered voters. In the old 8th, blacks have enjoyed a 60-40 advantage among registered voters.

Ford has known for some time that the remap would not be good news for him. While Tennessee's population grew by 16.9 percent during the last decade, an exodus from center-city Memphis cut population in Ford's territory by 16.9 percent.

Since Ed Jones wanted to keep part of Memphis and most of north Shelby, and since suburbia rings Memphis on the east, Ford had no choice but to take in middle- and upper-middle class residential communities.

In partisan terms, the 9th District is still strongly Democratic. Some 63 percent of its voters chose Jimmy Carter in 1980. But because the black population will be lower, Harold Ford will have to rely on white working-class Democrats more than he has in the past. That will be a

Ed Jones   **Harold E. Ford**

challenge in Memphis, where politics often polarizes along racial lines.

The Memphis economy is a mixture of old and new. Cotton marketing, warehousing and processing of cottonseed into oil have been important for more than a century and a half, and still are. But now the emphasis has shifted to manufactured goods such as farm machinery, tires and pharmaceuticals; International Harvester, Firestone and Schering-Plough are the major employers in this area. Memphis is also headquarters for the Holiday Inn empire and for the air fleet of Federal Express, the air freight carrier.

Texas

The spread of prosperity is changing life and politics in Texas at a rapid pace, boosting the development of a strong Republican Party and diminishing the opportunity for liberals to take the reins of state government.

The state's economy now rests on a diverse range of industries, including aerospace, defense and chemicals. Drawn by economic opportunity, newcomers have been flooding in for a generation. Since 1940, Texas' population has more than doubled. In the last decade alone, it increased by 27 percent, a rate faster than that of any other state except Florida.

The population boom — augmented by a large in-state migration from rural to metropolitan areas — has gradually unsettled Texas' traditional Democratic voting patterns. Much of the growth has occurred in the Republican metropolitan areas — Houston and Dallas-Fort Worth. And as Republicans gather additional support in the oil, wheat and grazing country of west Texas, they inch closer to a majority position in state and national elections.

The new GOP coalition was strong enough in 1978 to narrowly elect William Clements, former oil executive and deputy defense secretary, as the first Republican governor since Reconstruction. The party's only post-Reconstruction senator, John Tower, was re-elected the same year, although just barely. In 1980, Ronald Reagan expanded the successful formula to carry Texas with 55 percent of the vote.

For nearly a century after the Civil War, Texas was like the rest of the South, solidly Democratic. There has always been a vocal liberal wing in the Democratic Party, but it was crippled until the 1960s by the poll tax, which restricted participation by blacks and Hispanics.

In recent years, liberals have wielded more power within the Democratic Party. But victories by the left at the primary level have sometimes meant defeat for the party in November. In 1978, liberal and moderate Democrats succeeded in defeating three-term Democratic Gov. Dolph Briscoe in his bid for renomination. That was the prelude to Clements' breakthrough.

Still, Democrats remain dominant at the grass roots level. Republicans have been slow in making inroads into the huge Democratic majorities in Congress and the state Legislature. After the 1980 election, Republicans controlled less than 25 percent of the seats in the state Legislature and only five of 24 U.S. House seats.

East Texas

Geographically and culturally, east Texas is an extension of the Deep South. It was settled prior to the Civil War by Southerners from Georgia, South Carolina and the North Carolina lowlands. They developed a cotton-based, slaveholding economy.

The region extends westward from the Louisiana line to the outskirts of metropolitan Houston, then northward to the Red River, Texas' boundary with southern Oklahoma. It is a rural region with no large cities. Small-scale cotton and dairy farms are common in the northern sector. Further south are the "Piney Woods," a timber belt. Lumber and wood finishing plants are sprinkled throughout east Texas.

But since the 1930s, farming and lumber have taken a back seat to oil. The discovery of major oil deposits in east Texas a half century ago changed the face of the entire state — from rural and agrarian into a land of opportunity and new wealth. But few people in the area profited from the oil. Except for the Hispanic Rio Grande Valley, east Texas is the poorest part of the state. It has the highest concentration of black voters, although their numbers are not as large as in the rural Black Belt areas of Mississippi and Alabama. No Texas county has a black majority.

Capitalizing on the Dixie traditions, George Wallace ran better in east Texas in 1968 than anywhere in the state. He carried virtually every county within 50 miles of the Louisiana border.

But the strong Wallace showing did not presage realignment. Rural east Texans have remained Democratic. Most of them voted against Clements in 1978 and against Reagan in 1980. Republican breakthroughs have been limited to the small population centers of the region, such as Longview and Tyler, centers for the independent oil industry.

In spite of its relative poverty, the region has been growing quickly. Most of the counties of east Texas increased their population by 20 to 40 percent in the last decade.

Greater Houston

Probably no part of Texas has made better use of limited geographical assets than Houston. From a small bayou town 50 miles inland from the Gulf of Mexico, it has grown into the largest city in Texas (nearly 1.6 million in 1980), the fifth-largest in the country, and the commercial center of the Southwest.

Before World War II, Houston's trade centered on the processing of local food products and the production and refining of oil. After the war, the economy diversified. Chemicals, synthetic rubber and steel became major products, and heavy industry lined the long ship channel. Air conditioning made its climate tolerable in the summer.

Although its economy hardly needed a boost, Houston and surrounding Harris County picked up another plum in the early 1960s when the city was selected as the site of the National Aeronautics and Space Administration's Manned Spacecraft Center.

The lure of wealth has attracted not only ambitious businessmen to Houston, but also aspiring politicians. Lloyd Bentsen, George Bush and John B. Connally all moved to Houston to make their fortunes and advance their political careers.

Along with the advantages of the great boom, Houston also has suffered some discomforts. The air and some of the waterways are polluted, rush hour lasts most of the day, and the area suffers from uncontrolled development. There is no zoning in Houston, and the city sprawls for miles into Harris County and beyond.

Harris County has been dabbling with Republicanism for more than a half century — it voted for Herbert Hoover in 1928. But recently, Republican voting patterns have become more pronounced. In 1968, Richard Nixon won Harris County by only four percentage points. Twelve years later, Reagan carried the county by 20 points.

Republicans have benefited from a population boom in the suburbs. While the city of Houston grew by 29 percent in the 1970s, suburban Harris County increased by 61 percent. The growth has been even more dramatic in adjacent counties that have felt the effects of Houston sprawl. Montgomery County to the north grew by 160 percent in the 1970s, while Fort Bend County to the southwest had a population boom of 150 percent. Both counties were turning in large Republican majorities in major statewide races by the end of the decade.

The brand of Republicanism in the middle- and upper-class suburbs has long been staunchly conservative. But in the inner city, the political climate is different. With the help of labor unions, an active core of liberal whites and a large minority population — 28 percent black and 18 percent Hispanic — inner Houston has been a hotbed of Texas liberalism.

Since 1972, the inner city 18th District has sent a black Democrat to Congress — first, Barbara Jordan, then Mickey Leland. The adjoining 8th District elected a white populist Democrat, Bob Eckhardt, from 1966 until 1980, when the city's massive demographic changes caught up with him, and he was beaten by a Republican in a constituency turning more suburban.

Industrial Gulf Coast

One of the few parts of Texas with much ethnic diversity is the industrial Gulf Coast, which extends about 300 miles from the Louisiana border to Corpus Christi.

In the northern coastal area around the major port cities of Galveston, Beaumont and Port Arthur, there is a mixture of blacks, Cajuns and blue-collar whites, many of German, Czech or Polish stock. Moving southward, the concentration of Hispanics increases. In Nueces County

(Corpus Christi), they comprise nearly 50 percent of the population.

The northern coastal area is also one of the few strongholds of organized labor in Texas. Statewide, labor is not very popular; there is a strong right-to-work law. But on the docks and in the oil refineries, organized labor does have clout and has helped keep the industrial Gulf Coast in the Democratic column.

Although there has been little population growth in the industrial areas, the more Republican coastal counties such as Brazoria, south of Houston, have been growing quite rapidly.

Along with oil and related manufacturing and maritime industries, fishing and rice production are important to the Gulf Coast economy. The coastal prairie south of Galveston is the trading center for the state's valuable rice crop.

Dallas-Fort Worth

Few American cities have as controversial a reputation as Dallas. Following the assassination of President Kennedy in downtown Dallas in 1963, the city suffered with an image of frontier violence and extremism that was hard to shake. Just as that perception was fading, the television series "Dallas" came along to popularize the image of a metropolis ruled by an oligarchy of oil interests obsessed with money and power.

But Dallas is more than ostentatious wealth and unbridled conservatism. It has long been a cosmopolitan city and a financial center of the Southwest. Northerners looking for a city that fits their definition are much more likely to find it in Dallas than in newer, sloppier, more chaotic Houston.

Dallas began as a cotton and textile town in the shadow of Fort Worth. But with the opening of the east Texas oil fields, it began to boom. Many of the oil companies placed their headquarters there, and the city went on to attract a diversified array of industries, many of them high-technology electronics firms. With more than 900,000 residents, Dallas is the seventh largest city in the country.

Dallas County — which includes the city and its immediate suburbs — has been a Republican stronghold for several decades. Clements received 58 percent of the Dallas County vote in 1978, while Reagan drew 59 percent in 1980. With a minority population somewhat smaller than in Houston, Dallas is a few shades more Republican.

Thirty-three miles to the west of Dallas is the city of Fort Worth. Once the senior partner of the two, Fort Worth is now less than half the size of Dallas and declining in population.

Fort Worth has always projected more of a blue-collar image than Dallas. During the early years of the oil boom, it was headquarters for west Texas operations before they moved to Midland and Odessa in the heart of the fields. Since World War II, Fort Worth has been a major manufacturer of military and aerospace equipment.

Fort Worth has less wealth than Dallas, and in national elections, Republican majorities in surrounding Tarrant County tend to be smaller than those in Dallas County. Democratic Rep. Jim Wright, the House majority leader, has had little trouble holding his Fort Worth-based district.

Over the past three decades, the fast-growing suburbs between Dallas and Forth Worth have filled the space between the two cities. As in greater Houston, the largest

U. S. Congress: 27 districts
  Senate (1D, 1R)
  House (19D, 5R)

Governor:
  William Clements (R)

Population: 14,228,383

Area: 267,339 sq. miles

1980 Presidential Vote:
  Carter (41%)
  Reagan (55%)
  Anderson (3%)

New
Texas
Districts

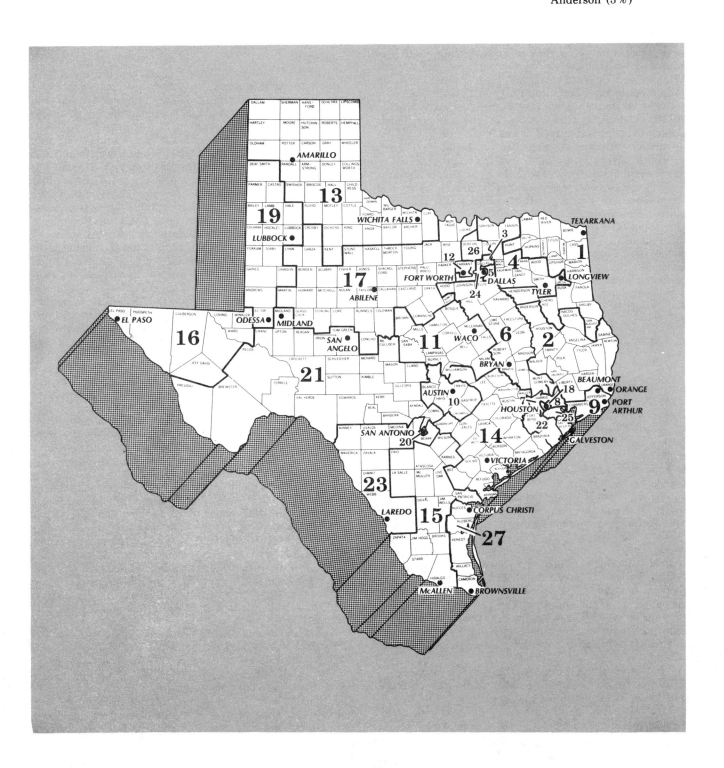

growth in the Dallas-Fort Worth area in the last decade has been in adjacent suburban counties. Dallas and Tarrant counties both had growth rates of 20 percent or less in the 1970s, but Collin and Denton counties to the north both grew by at least 85 percent.

Hill Country

Interstate 35, which runs north-and-south through central Texas from Dallas to San Antonio, is something of a geographical dividing line. To the east is the low country and the concentration of black voters. Immediately to the west is the rolling terrain of the hill country, a rural area best suited for grazing livestock.

This is the area of Johnson City and the LBJ Ranch, as well as communities such as Fredericksburg and New Braunfels, originally settled by German immigrants in the 19th century. Opposed to slavery, these Germans were an early force in the Republican Party in Texas.

The major population center in the region is Austin, the state capital. Of Texas' six largest urban centers, Travis County (Austin) is the smallest but the fastest growing. Its population increased 42 percent in the 1970s.

With a large government work force and sizable academic community affiliated with the University of Texas, it is also the least conservative politically. Travis County was the only one of the large urban counties not carried by either Clements or Reagan.

About 90 miles to the north of Austin is the region's other major city, Waco. Often called the "Baptist Rome," it is the site of numerous Baptist churches and of Baylor University, which is affiliated with the Southern Baptists. Although more conservative than Austin, Waco has not developed Republican voting patterns as strong as those of Dallas-Fort Worth or Houston.

South Texas

South Texas sits like the keel of a sailboat at the bottom of the state. That shape suggests the political significance the area plays in Texas politics — it provides the votes that prevent the state from tipping over into a sea of conservative predictability.

South Texas is home for most of the state's Hispanics. In the Lower Rio Grande Valley, Hispanics make up a large majority of the population. Even as far north as Bexar County (San Antonio), they comprise 47 percent of the population. Jimmy Carter received nearly 80 percent of the vote from Texas Hispanics in 1980, even though much of south Texas had voted for Sen. Edward M. Kennedy in the presidential primary that spring.

Although Hispanics have numerical superiority in the region, they have only recently begun to crack "Anglo" control of local government and commerce. While the Rio Grande Valley has large ranches and irrigated farms that produce bumper crops of cotton, vegetables and fruit, Hispanics have not shared in the prosperity. On a per capita basis, south Texas is among the poorest areas in the country, although some of the Sun Belt growth has begun to affect it, especially in the fast-growing port of Brownsville.

For much of this century, the political influence of Hispanics was curbed by the poll tax. From 1904 until the mid-1960s, Texans between the ages of 21 and 60 had to pay the tax several months before a primary in order to be eligible to vote. Throughout south Texas, Anglo bosses

paid the poll taxes of many Hispanics and controlled their votes as a bloc.

Modern Hispanic political awareness dates from 1960, when Hispanics enthusiastically supported fellow Catholic John F. Kennedy for president. By 1964 the area had two Hispanic congressmen, both Democrats.

Younger, militant Hispanic activists, however, viewed the Democratic Party as an arm of the Anglo establishment and, in the early 1970s, formed a third party, La Raza Unida. The party had some early successes, winning several town elections in south Texas and drawing more than 5 percent of the statewide vote in the 1972 and 1974 gubernatorial elections. But the appeal of the party began to ebb by the end of the decade, and in 1978 Luis A. Diaz DeLeon received less than 1 percent as La Raza Unida's Senate candidate.

As the third-party effort has waned, Hispanics have begun to make inroads in Democratic Party politics in south Texas. In April 1981, 33-year-old Henry Cisneros was elected mayor of San Antonio, becoming the first Hispanic mayor of a major American city.

With nearly 800,000 residents, San Antonio is the 10th largest city in the United States. While it was founded in the early 18th century by the Spanish, San Antonio has long had an economy controlled by Anglos. Once a cattle center, the city now depends on local military bases for its prosperity. The combination of military families and descendants of German settlers have given the Republican Party a strong base, particularly in suburban parts of Bexar County (pronounced "bear"). Reagan managed to carry the county in 1980.

While Bexar grew by 19 percent during the last decade, the greatest growth in south Texas was taking place in the Lower Rio Grande Valley along the Mexican border. Hidalgo County (McAllen) had a population increase of 56 percent, while neighboring Cameron County (Brownsville) along the Gulf grew by 49 percent.

Western Plains

The open plains of west Texas will have to be a cornerstone of any emerging Republican majority.

GOP strength in the region was long limited to the oil boom towns of Midland and Odessa and scattered wheat-growing counties in the panhandle. But in their recent statewide victories, Republicans have carried most of the counties west of Abilene.

The Texas plains are a part of America's legendary Western frontier. Grazing and farming are major sources of income in the panhandle, while ranching and oil and gas production are predominant further south.

Between 1940 and 1960, blue-collar Odessa grew from a town of fewer than 10,000 to more than 80,000 inhabitants. Today, at 90,000, it is mainly a white-collar city and the home for many oil executives. Both Midland and Ector (Odessa) counties gave Clements and Reagan more than 70 percent of the vote, a higher share than any other urban counties in the state.

About 120 miles to the north of Midland is Lubbock. Irrigation has enabled the Lubbock area to replace east Texas as the state's predominant cotton growing area. Although Lubbock is not in the center of any oil fields, several oil companies have established offices in the city.

Farther north is the panhandle. This windy area was devastated by the great Dust Bowl of the 1930s. Discovery of underground water supplies, however, has helped stabi-

New Texas Districts

New District	Incumbent	Population	1980 Pres. Winner
1	Sam B. Hall Jr. (D)	527,016	Carter
2	Charles Wilson (D)	526,772	Carter
3	James M. Collins (R)[1]	526,411	Reagan
4	Ralph M. Hall (D)	526,991	Reagan
5	Jim Mattox (D)[2]	527,580	Reagan
6	Phil Gramm (D)	527,393	Reagan
7	Bill Archer (R)	527,083	Reagan
8	Jack Fields (R)	527,528	Reagan
9	Jack Brooks (D)	526,443	Carter
10	J. J. Pickle (D)	526,943	Carter
11	Marvin Leath (D)	526,871	Reagan
12	Jim Wright (D)	527,074	Reagan
13	Jack Hightower (D)	526,840	Reagan
14	Bill Patman (D)	526,920	Reagan
15	E. "Kika" de la Garza (D)	526,803	Carter
16	Richard C. White (D)[3]	527,401	Reagan
17	Charles W. Stenholm (D)	526,831	Reagan
18	Mickey Leland (D)	527,393	Carter
19	Kent Hance (D)	527,805	Reagan
20	Henry B. Gonzalez (D)	526,333	Carter
21	Tom Loeffler (R)	527,044	Reagan
22	Ron Paul (R)	526,602	Reagan
23	Abraham Kazen Jr. (D)	526,548	Reagan
24	Martin Frost (D)	526,976	Carter
25	No Incumbent	526,801	Reagan
26	No Incumbent	526,640	Reagan
27	No Incumbent	527,341	Carter

[1] *Retiring to run for the U.S. Senate.*
[2] *Retiring to run for Texas Attorney General.*
[3] *Retiring.*

publican. Anglos, however, control the city's economy, which relies on textiles produced with locally grown cotton.

COURT'S REMAP PRODUCES FEW CHANGES

Highly touted as a Republican windfall when it passed in August 1981, Texas' congressional redistricting plan has emerged from the Justice Department and federal court scrutiny with revisions that make it unlikely to alter the partisan balance in the state's congressional delegation in any significant way.

An alliance between Republican Gov. William Clements and state House Speaker Billy Clayton, a conservative Democrat, produced the original plan in 1981. A coalition of GOP and conservative Democratic state legislators pushed the map through the solidly Democratic Texas Legislature Aug. 10, 1981.

But soon after Clements signed the bill on Aug. 14, 1981, a group of blacks and Hispanics filed suit in federal court, claiming that voting rights had been curtailed by the Legislature's reshaping of districts in South Texas, the Dallas-Fort Worth area and metropolitan Houston.

Since election law changes in Texas must comply with the 1965 Voting Rights Act, the federal judges deferred action on the minorities' suit pending Justice Dept. review.

The department ruled Jan. 29, 1982, that the map improperly distributed the Hispanic population in two districts, the 15th and the 27th. The Legislature had made the districts 80 percent and 52 percent Hispanic, respectively; the department said that the plan packed the 15th with Hispanics while diluting their strength in the 27th.

The department's rejection of two districts rendered the redistricting bill legally unenforceable because Texas is wholly covered by the Voting Rights Act. Gov. Clements declined to call the Legislature into special session to redraw boundaries, thus setting the stage for court action.

The ruling of the three-judge panel, handed down Feb. 27, 1982, rearranged the two South Texas districts to give Hispanics a good chance to win both. In addition, it reshaped four districts in the Dallas-Fort Worth area in a way that dashed GOP hopes of creating a new district for itself in Dallas County.

The Legislature had fashioned a strongly Republican 5th District in Dallas County by transferring most of the minority voters in that district to the Democratic 24th, which would have become 64 percent black and Hispanic. The court felt it was fairer to redistribute minority voters more evenly between the 5th and 24th, giving blacks and Hispanics substantial influence in each district but majority control in neither.

Texas Republicans appealed that decision to the Supreme Court, which ruled April 1, 1982, that the panel had acted improperly in drawing the four districts. The justices agreed with GOP arguments that the panel had ignored legislative intent.

But in remanding the case to the federal panel, the Supreme Court left the judges with the option of keeping their plan in place for 1982 because candidates had already filed for the court-drawn districts. The panel chose that option April 5, 1982; the state GOP is appealing that ruling.

lize the livestock industry and farming in wheat, cotton and sorghum grains. Amarillo is the center of the agricultural region. While regularly Republican, neither Amarillo nor Lubbock turn out the huge GOP majorities that are found in Midland and Odessa.

West of the plains is the desert and ranch land of western Texas. The lone population center is El Paso, far removed from the rest of the state. Enjoying steady growth since the 1940s, it is now the fourth largest city in Texas.

With Hispanics comprising nearly two-thirds of the population, El Paso is the only major urban county in the western half of Texas that does not consistently vote Re-

Sam B. Hall Jr.   **Charles Wilson**

Few, if any, seats are likely to change party control as a result of the remap. The boundaries shore up or protect Republican strength in all five of the seats the party currently holds, and Democrats begin with an advantage in each of the 19 districts they control.

During the last decade, population grew by 27.1 percent in Texas. In the 1980 reapportionment, the state qualified for three additional House seats. Republicans are favored in the new 26th, which lies between Dallas and Fort Worth, although a conservative Democratic candidate has a chance to win. The new South Texas 27th will almost certainly elect a Democratic representative, and Democrats seem to have an edge in Houston's 25th District.

District 1

Northeast — Texarkana

Incumbent: Sam B. Hall Jr. (D)

Republicans have broken the barriers of Democratic domination in many parts of Texas, but the GOP still encounters stiff resistance in the rural 1st in the northeastern corner of the state.

Today, blacks make up more than 20 percent of the population in one-half of the rural counties of the 1st District. By running well among blacks and appealing to the Southern sympathies of rural whites, Jimmy Carter won the district comfortably in 1976 and edged Ronald Reagan in 1980.

Republicans have made some inroads in Texarkana (Bowie County) and Marshall (Harrison County), both manufacturing centers providing goods and services to the surrounding farms and towns. Reagan carried Bowie and Harrison counties in 1980, averaging 53 percent of the vote. But those two urbanized counties cast less than a quarter of the district's 1980 vote; the rural counties still dominate politics in the 1st, and nearly all of them are Democratic.

Redistricting does not make substantial changes in the character of the district. At its northwest corner, the 1st moves out of Wood, Rains and Fannin counties and adds territory in the northern half of Hunt County.

District 2

East — Lufkin, Orange

Incumbent: Charles Wilson (D)

Redistricting should make the 2nd better territory for Rep Charles Wilson. He gives to Rep. Phil Gramm's 6th District about 80 percent of the residents of Montgomery County, where politics is dominated by white-collar Houston suburbanites who helped Ronald Reagan win two-thirds of the county's 1980 presidential vote. Wilson carried Montgomery in 1980, but with an uncomfortably low 53 percent of the vote.

Remaining in the 2nd District are 27,000 people in the northeast section of Montgomery County. Although this area is in Houston's sphere of influence, it has much in common with the mostly rural Piney Woods counties of east Texas that will dominate the redrawn 2nd District.

Like all of East Texas, the 2nd is conservative and has strong ties to Dixie; in 1968, this was the only Texas district carried by George C. Wallace. But it has a residual populist streak in the smaller counties and sometimes has been hospitable to moderate Democrats willing to speak its language. Carter carried the old 2nd easily in 1976 and would have done so in 1980 but for the massive GOP majority in Montgomery County.

Wilson, who holds views to the left of his constituents on some issues, has secured his seat by becoming a persistent defender of independent oil producers, an important force in the 2nd. Some voters who once enthusiastically subscribed to rural populist rhetoric now have oil-related jobs in the district's small cities and see the industry as a source of prosperity.

The district's largest cities, Lufkin (Angelina County) and Orange (Orange County), each have fewer than 30,000 people. Besides oil, their businesses deal with timber, chemicals and cattle. Orange has the district's only significant concentration of union members. Carter won both Angelina and Orange counties in 1980.

In addition to removing most of Montgomery County, redistricting takes away four Democratic-majority counties along the western edge of the 2nd District. Each of the counties voted for Carter in 1980, but they cast less than 5,000 votes apiece, so their loss should not harm Wilson.

District 3

North Dallas, northern suburbs

Incumbent: James M. Collins (R)

After serving in the House since 1968, Collins is leaving the 3rd to challenge Democratic incumbent Lloyd Bentsen in the 1982 Senate race. The Republican contest to replace Collins is crowded with candidates who recognize that winning the GOP nomination is tantamount to election in this district, which is home to many of Dallas' high-status moneymakers.

Foremost among the affluent communities of North Dallas are Highland Park and University Park, traditional enclaves of the city's economic establishment. Rapid development of high-rise offices and shopping malls is occurring along the Dallas North Tollway leading into the suburbs. Suburban Richardson and Carrollton are peopled with young newcomers who work for electronics manufacturers, research firms and corporate branch offices.

More than a quarter-million people moved into the 3rd during the 1970s, making it Texas' third fastest-growing district. To bring its population down to ideal district size, the 3rd loses all of its Denton County territory, all except a segment of Plano in Collin County and most of northwest Dallas County, including Irving. It adds voters in northeast Dallas County, taking in upper-middle-class Republican-voting areas in Garland.

Republicans are firmly in control throughout North Dallas and the suburbs. In 1980, Collins' Democratic opponent received only 18 percent of the vote.

District 4

Northeast — Tyler, Longview

Incumbent: Ralph M. Hall (D)

Three distinct areas constitute the 4th District. In the northern end of the district, slow-growing Grayson and Fannin counties raise livestock, sorghum, peanuts and hay. Sherman, the seat of Grayson County, is an old, cotton-processing town now turning out meat products, castings and metal pipe.

The counties in the central part of the district are caught up in the sprawl of metropolitan Dallas; population doubled in both Collin and Rockwall counties during the last decade. Many people in those counties commute to Dallas jobs.

At the eastern end of the district are two cities that serve as supply and distribution hubs for the East Texas oil fields — Tyler (Smith County) and Longview (Gregg County). Fueled by the expansion of the independent oil industry, those two counties also surpassed the state's 27 percent growth rate during the 1970s.

Hall's first-term victory in 1980 came in the face of continued Republican gains in the district, especially in the eastern and central regions. Ronald Reagan won 68 percent in Gregg County and 65 percent in Smith and took both Rockwall and Collin counties by comfortable margins. All those counties voted for Gerald R. Ford in 1976, but not by such wide margins as Reagan enjoyed. In the north, Grayson County swung to Reagan last year after voting for Carter in 1976.

In the remap, the 4th loses voters who live directly north of the Dallas-Fort Worth area: Denton County and western Collin County are incorporated into the newly created 26th District. Still in the 4th is eastern Collin County, and Hall takes in two new counties nearly equal in population, Wood and Fannin. Wood went for Reagan in 1980, but Fannin chose Carter.

Any district that votes solidly Republican in national elections is a temptation to GOP congressional candidates. But Hall's tendency to vote a conservative line in the House of Representatives may help him put down opposition in the 4th.

District 5

Downtown Dallas, eastern and southern suburbs

Incumbent: Jim Mattox (D)

The 5th District was one of the four affected by the court battle. The Legislature had drawn the 5th so that it would likely elect a Republican. Mattox' home was moved to the 24th District and many of the 5th's Democratic black and Hispanic portions also were removed. However, under the plan imposed by the judges, the 5th is changed from a very marginal Democratic district into one that will be more difficult for Republicans to capture.

The 5th is anchored in politically divided southeast Dallas County, but arms of the district reach into Democratic areas of Garland and downtown Dallas. The most conservative parts of Garland have been moved to the 3rd District, leaving in the 5th the parts of central Garland where Democrats are strongest.

The Trinity River is the dividing line in downtown Dallas, with areas immediately north of the river in the 5th and those further south in the 24th. Minorities make up nearly a third of the 5th District's population; most of them live in a concentrated area adjacent to downtown.

Outside of Dallas, the 5th retains white, middle-income suburban communities such as Mesquite, Sunnyvale, Seagoville and Balch Springs. A sizable number of blue-collar workers live in those areas and many of them have shown waning affection for Democratic policies in recent elections.

In suburbs further south and west, working-class dissatisfaction with Democrats is less evident, though the voters prefer candidates in the moderate-to-conservative mold. Fitting that political profile are Hutchins, Wilmer and Lancaster, three towns that move from the 6th into the 5th under the remap.

Facing near-certain defeat in the 5th as the Legislature redrew it last August, Mattox launched a campaign early this year for Texas attorney general. The court-ordered revisions give him a district he probably could win, but Mattox has decided to stay in the attorney general's contest rather than seek re-election to the House. Democrats are holding a competitive House primary, and their nominee probably will be favored in the 1982 election.

James M. Collins   **Ralph M. Hall**

District 6

Dallas-Fort Worth and Houston suburbs; Bryan

Incumbent: Phil Gramm (D)

The redrawn 6th District contains the two fastest-growing counties in the state. In the northwest corner of the district, spillover from metropolitan Fort Worth nearly tripled the population of Hood County. Far to the south, Montgomery County grew approximately 160 percent, filling up with affluent professionals who commute to their jobs in Houston.

Between those population concentrations lies mostly rural territory. The urban exception in this central part of the district is Bryan (Brazos County), a city with a population of 45,000. Near Bryan is College Station, home of Texas A & M University, which has an enrollment of more than 30,000 students.

The rural counties, most of them more than one-fifth black, have remained loyally Democratic — all eight voted for Carter in the 1976 and 1980 presidential elections. But the Democrats' rural strength has to compete with the broadening influence of suburban, white-collar Republicans flooding into the northern and southern ends of the 6th District.

In the Dallas-Fort Worth sphere, Hood, Johnson and Ellis counties each voted for Reagan in 1980, turning away from their 1976 preference for Carter. Montgomery County supported Ford in 1976 and gave Reagan a 2-to-1 majority. Parts of Montgomery will be in the redrawn 2nd and 8th districts, but Gramm will represent the bulk of the county's voters. Brazos County is also good GOP territory; it gave Reagan 60 percent in 1980.

Redistricting brings in Hood County from the 11th District well as four rural counties and most of Montgomery from the 2nd. Gramm gives up all his territory in Tarrant County (Fort Worth) and neighboring Parker County and retains only the southwest corner of Dallas County.

Gramm won easy re-election in 1980 by taking advantage of his Democratic ties in rural areas and his economic conservatism in Republican suburbs. But before he can employ that strategy again in November 1982, Gramm

must get past a primary challenger who faults him for his prominent role in shaping economic policy for the Reagan administration.

District 7

Western Houston and suburbs

Incumbent: Bill Archer (R)

As Houston has grown into America's fifth largest city and the commercial center of the Southwest, the 7th has grown dense with the homes of the prosperous corporate community. More than 400,000 people moved into Archer's territory during the last decade, giving the 7th an 86 percent growth rate, highest of any district in Texas.

The upper-income neighborhoods that make up the 7th are foremost in Texas in terms of affluence, education and Republicanism. In 1976, Ford swept the presidential vote in the district by nearly a 3-to-1 margin. Reagan improved on that in 1980, taking 74 percent of the vote.

Because of the rapid growth in the 7th, redistricting doles out more than 340,000 of Archer's constituents to neighboring districts. The 22nd and 25th take much of the southwest Houston part of the 7th, and the 8th picks up territory all along the northeastern border of the 7th.

The remap leaves Archer with plenty of Republicans to spare. He has won his six House elections with ease.

District 8

Houston suburbs, eastern Harris County

Incumbent: Jack Fields (R)

Redistricting has improved freshman Fields' chances for re-election. A narrow 1980 winner over Democratic Rep. Bob Eckhardt, Fields gives up strong Democratic areas to the underpopulated urban 18th, loses all his blue-collar territory south of the Houston Ship Channel to the 25th and picks up residential and semi-rural areas in northeastern Harris County that are now part of the 7th and 9th districts. Fields also takes in the eastern corner of suburban Montgomery County.

Thousands of middle- and upper-middle-income families have moved into the Harris County part of the redrawn 8th in recent years, dramatically increasing the Republican voting base. Pollsters found some new subdivisions voting Republican 9-to-1 in the 1980 presidential contest.

But the 8th is not as monolithically white-collar and Republican as Archer's 7th. Among Fields' constituents will be blue-collar residents of Baytown, site of a huge Exxon refinery and other petroleum-related industries. The 8th District also keeps a significant amount of territory in minority areas on Houston's perimeter; nearly 30 percent of the people in the 8th are either black or Hispanic.

Jim Mattox   Phil Gramm

Bill Archer   **Jack Fields**

District 9

Southeast — Beaumont, Galveston

Incumbent: Jack Brooks (D)

The 9th is dominated by three industrial cities: Beaumont and Port Arthur, near the Louisiana border in Jefferson County, and Galveston, further south along the Gulf of Mexico in Galveston County.

The central element of the economy is the refining and distribution of petroleum and its products. Several oil companies have their largest refinery facilities in this district; there also is considerable shipbuilding and steelmaking.

This northern coastal area is one of the few strongholds of organized labor in Texas and the unions have helped keep the 9th in the Democratic column. This is also one of the more ethnically diverse parts of Texas. There are Cajuns and blue-collar whites, many of German, Czech or Polish stock, and nearly 30 percent of the people are either black or Hispanic.

Carter carried the 9th easily in 1976, but he won only narrowly in 1980; Reagan tapped the same conservative element in the district that supported W. L. Pate, a conservative political novice, against Brooks in the Democratic primary the same year. Pate charged that Brooks was out of step with his district. Brooks barely avoided a runoff against Pate by winning big in heavily unionized Galveston, but he lost his home county of Jefferson, not an encouraging sign.

As Brooke tries in 1982 for nomination to his 16th term, he again is facing determined primary opposition, including Pate who says his impressive 1980 showing has given him the name recognition and momentum he needs to defeat Brooks. Since that scare in 1980, Brooks' activity in the district has increased dramatically; he has contacted business interests and other groups who have accused him of inattention in the past.

Under the remap, Brooks gives to the 8th District all of his northeastern Harris County territory; that area gave Reagan 61 percent in 1980, casting about 15 percent of the district's vote. In return, Brooks receives a smaller section of southeastern Harris County, including part of Clear Lake City, an enclave of Republican engineers who work at the Johnson Space Center.

District 10

Central — Austin

Incumbent: J. J. Pickle (D)

Though the redrawn 10th takes in five counties and most of a sixth, 80 percent of the district's people live either in the state capital of Austin or in surrounding Travis County.

Since it has a large state government work force and huge academic community affiliated with the University of Texas (with an enrollment of approximately 46,000 students), Austin traditionally has been less conservative than other major cities in the state. Travis County was the only one of the state's large urban counties not carried by either Gov. Clements in the 1978 election or by Ronald Reagan in 1980.

The Austin economy has diversified beyond reliance on state government and the university. Electronics and computer companies flocking to the area in recent years have lured upwardly mobile, middle-class employees, many of whom are sympathetic to the GOP. The influx of these professionals helped Travis County's population jump by 42 percent in the 1970s, the fastest growth rate among the state's six largest urban counties.

But the population boom has also spawned some anti-growth sentiments not usually associated with Republican Party doctrine. In November 1981, the residents of Austin voted to end the city's financial commitment to a nuclear power generating project plagued by construction delays and cost overruns. Anti-nuclear activists urged energy conservation to trim the city's burgeoning appetite for power.

When a flood swept through the city on Memorial Day 1981, killing 13 and causing millions in property damage, anti-growth forces blamed the destruction on pell-mell development of the area's watershed.

Because of Austin's population growth, the remap trims the 10th down to just Travis County and five largely rural counties adjoining it on the south and west. Pickle gives up to the 14th District 10 counties now either completely or partially within his territory. Because the counties Pickle loses have been more likely to vote for Republican candidates than the counties he keeps, redistricting does him no harm.

Jack Brooks   **J. J. Pickle**

District 11

Central — Waco

Incumbent: Marvin Leath (D)

The primarily rural 11th District is evolving from a Democratic stronghold into a competitive two-party district. Recent elections point to a GOP trend in the two more urbanized counties of the district as well as in the rural areas.

In 1976, Jimmy Carter carried every county in the 11th District at that time, taking 57 percent of the vote districtwide. Two years later, Republican Gov. Clements managed to capture 45 percent in Bell County (Killeen and Temple) and 49 percent in McLennan County (Waco). In the 1980 election, Ronald Reagan averaged 54 percent in winning Bell and McLennan counties and carried seven of the 11 rural counties that lie entirely in the redrawn 11th District.

Waco, the district's only city with a population of more than 100,000 people, is often called the "Baptist Rome." It houses numerous Baptist churches and is the home of Baylor University, which is affiliated with the Southern Baptists. Southwest of Waco are the rapidly growing cities of Killeen and Temple, both pushing toward 50,000 in population.

Waco, Killeen and Temple all serve as retail and marketing centers for the farm-lands surrounding them. Among the industrial products available are computer equipment, solar collectors and rocket fuel. Killeen's economy benefits from the military payroll of nearby Fort Hood.

Democratic Rep. Marvin Leath was unopposed in his bid for a second House term in the 1980 election; the key to his success in the district is philosophical rather than political, however. He is a conservative small-town banker who rarely votes in agreement with the national Democratic Party.

The redistricting plan smoothes the 11th District's jagged fringes but makes no substantial change in the politics of the area. McLennan County and Bell County account for more than 60 percent of the new district's population.

District 12

Fort Worth; northwest Tarrant County

Incumbent: Jim Wright (D)

Less than half the size of neighboring Dallas and declining in population, Fort Worth projects a blue-collar and Western roughneck image that contrasts with its more sophisticated neighbor.

But the city's reputation is not entirely accurate. Cattle marketing and agribusiness are still important in the Fort Worth economy, but since World War II the city has been a major manufacturer of military and aerospace equipment and electronics is increasingly prominent. House Majority Leader Wright has cultivated his constituency by helping to steer defense contracts to the district's largest industries, General Dynamics and Bell Helicopter.

Wright, who had to work hard in 1980 to draw 60 percent against an aggressive GOP challenger, has been given a safer seat in redistricting. The 12th, which needed to add nearly 20,000 residents, picks up blue-collar territory in south Fort Worth that is currently part of the 6th District.

The wealthier residential areas of Fort Worth and its suburbs give the 12th a Republican vote of some significance; Reagan narrowly took the 12th in 1980. But Wright has won House elections for nearly 30 years by forging a coalition of organized labor, liberals, minorities and low-income whites. Hispanics and blacks make up more than one-fourth of the redrawn district's population.

District 13

The Panhandle — Amarillo, Wichita Falls

Incumbent: Jack Hightower (D)

The two parties are closely matched in the 13th District; Republicans rule in the Panhandle and Democrats hold sway in the Red River Valley to the south. But the voters are uniformly conservative, and they flocked to Reagan in 1980. Of the 37 counties in the redrawn 13th District, three-fourths voted for Reagan, many by margins exceeding 2-to-1.

Because of its scant rainfall, most of this region long was used only for cattle grazing. Discovery of underground water supplies in the 1940s sparked cultivation of wheat, cotton and sorghum grains on huge, highly mechanized farms. The agricultural revolution has been so extensive that the underground Ogallala aquifer is being rapidly depleted. Some of the wheat and cattle growers went heavily into debt in the 1970s and have fallen on hard times; the 13th was well represented among the members of the American Agriculture Movement who brought their tractors to Washington in the 1979 protest against low farm prices.

Amarillo (Potter and Randall counties) is a city of nearly 150,000 that serves as the focal point of the Panhandle's farm-lands. Its factories pack meat, mill flour and

Marvin Leath   **Jim Wright**

handle oil and natural gas drilled locally. Like the rural areas surrounding it, Amarillo is Republican. In 1980, Reagan took 61 percent in Potter County and 74 percent in Randall County.

To the southeast is Wichita Falls (Wichita County), an area with Democratic affections whose votes usually help Democratic candidates compete districtwide. Carter won 53 percent of the Wichita County vote in 1976, but he fell about 2,000 votes short of carrying the 13th. In 1980, Reagan won 55 percent in Wichita, paving the way for his easy victory in the district.

Wichita Falls' population declined slightly during the 1970s and stood at 94,201 in 1980. The city has a large industrial sector that makes fiberglass products, wearing apparel and mechanical parts. Located north of the city is Sheppard Air Force Base, one of the largest Air Force training facilities.

Hightower has satisfied the 13th by paying close attention to local interests while maintaining limited — though cordial — ties with the Democratic Party. His 1980 reelection margin was a disappointing 18,000 votes; the upcoming election will tell whether the 1980 results were a warning or simply a reflection of Ronald Reagan's enormous strength in this district.

The district's population grew by only 8 percent during the 1970s, so the remap brings the 13th to ideal size by adding just over 21,000 people in four rural counties. The political impact will be slight.

Jack Hightower   **Bill Patman**

With Corpus Christi out of the 14th, the district's largest city is now Victoria, with a population of just over 50,000 people. The economy revolves around petrochemicals, oil-field equipment and steel products. Victoria County gave 63 percent of its 1980 presidential vote to Reagan.

District 15

South — McAllen

Incumbent: E. "Kika" de la Garza (D)

De la Garza loses Cameron County (Brownsville) and two other coastal counties to the new 27th District, pushing his 15th farther north, almost to San Antonio, far from the Rio Grande Valley where the majority of the district's people live.

But as redrawn, the 15th is still the most heavily Hispanic district in Texas — 72 percent — and it is good territory for de la Garza, an 18-year veteran who was the first Hispanic to win a House seat in South Texas.

Although this area is still among the poorest in the country, the economic boom that has transformed much of the Southwest is affecting the Rio Grande Valley. Population in the three southernmost counties of the 15th increased by more than 50 percent during the 1970s. McAllen, on the Mexican border, is a major port of entry into Mexico and an important foreign trade center that grew 78 percent during the last decade, to a 1980 population of 67,042. The city and surrounding Hidalgo County together have more than 283,000 residents.

Many of the newcomers to the district have been lured by jobs in plants that make electronic components, medical equipment and food processing machinery. Tourism is a reliable revenue producer, with visitors drawn by the sun and the chance to shop and go sightseeing in Mexico.

But the economic underpinning of the valley is agriculture. Freezes are rare, so the almost year-round growing season produces an abundance of grapefruit and other citrus, vegetables, cotton and grain. Factories that process, pack and ship the fruits and vegetables are major employers; there is a substantial influx of farm workers during the harvests.

District 14

South Central, Gulf Coast — Victoria

Incumbent: Bill Patman (D)

This district is among those significantly altered by the remap. Patman loses dependably Democratic Nueces County (Corpus Christi), which cast half the 14th District's vote in the 1980 presidential election.

The 14th gains most of Williamson County, an increasingly Republican and fast-growing county north of Austin where Reagan won 56 percent of the vote in 1980. The 14th also takes part or all of several rural conservative counties currently located in the 10th, 15th, 22nd and 23rd districts.

These boundary changes initially prompted speculation that Patman, who is considered a liberal by some Texas Democrats, might draw a serious conservative challenge either in the primary or general election. But Patman actually fits more into the tradition of rural populism exemplified by his father, former Rep. Wright Patman (1929-76). The populist style has seemed to play well in this mostly rural district so far. Patman is a comfortable reelection favorite for 1982, although he faces Republican opposition from Joe Wyatt Jr., who served in the House as a Democrat from 1979 to 1981.

Minorities make up about one-third of the population in the redrawn 14th. Most of the Hispanics are grouped in the district's southwestern counties and account for 20 percent of the residents. Blacks — 12 percent of the population — are concentrated in the northeastern part of the district.

E. "Kika" de la Garza   Richard C. White

North of the valley, the rolling brush is broken by an occasional stream. There is oil and gas development in this region. Beef cattle and other livestock roam the ranches and feed grains grow well there.

The most populous county outside of Hidalgo is San Patricio County, with 58,013 people. San Patricio lies just across the bay from Corpus Christi, is closely linked economically to that city and before the remap was in the same congressional district as Corpus Christi. But to help balance the Hispanic populations in the 15th and 27th districts, the federal judges' remap puts San Patricio and Corpus Christi into separate districts.

Jimmy Carter's 1980 margin in San Patricio was only 301 votes, and five rural counties in the northern part of the 15th voted for Reagan. But further south, in such heavily Hispanic rural counties as Duval, Brooks and Jim Hogg, Carter won huge majorities. This is the area where wealthy Anglo-landlords traditionally have controlled the votes of poor Hispanic farm workers. De la Garza himself has always had consistent support from conservative Anglos. And all-important Hidalgo County is solidly Democratic.

District 16

West — El Paso

Incumbent: Richard C. White (D)

Although the redrawn 16th covers much of far West Texas, 91 percent of its population lives in El Paso and the surrounding county of the same name. El Paso's population increased by nearly one-third during the last decade, making it the fourth-largest city in Texas. El Paso and Ciudad Juarez — its sister city across the Rio Grande — constitute the largest urban concentration on the Mexican-American border.

The El Paso economy relies heavily on textiles produced with locally grown cotton. Also economically important are electronics firms, oil refineries, food processing plants and the government — the U.S. Army's Fort Bliss is located in El Paso and a number of people work across the New Mexico state line at the White Sands Missile Range.

Though White has kept the 16th in Democratic hands since 1965, the district has voted Republican in the last three presidential elections. With the House seat open in 1982, due to White's retirement, Republicans hope to draw conservative voters to their side. Hispanics make up 60 percent of the population in the redrawn 16th, but they have not generally turned out in large numbers or voted as a bloc for Democrats.

Outside El Paso County, the seven counties that fill out the district are loyally Republican, but consist mostly of desert and prairie grass. Their political impact is minimal. In 1980, for example, Loving County went for Reagan over Carter by more than 2-to-1; the vote was 50-22.

In the only notable boundary change, the remap moves the 16th out of western Odessa (Ector County), a Republican oil-producing center. Ector County voters cast 13 percent of the 16th's 1980 presidential vote, and two-thirds of them chose Reagan.

District 17

West Central — Abilene

Incumbent: Charles W. Stenholm (D)

Except for two urban districts that lost population, the 17th was the slowest-growing constituency in Texas during the last decade — its numbers increased by only 8 percent.

Redistricting adds nearly 23,000 people to the 17th to bring it up to ideal size, but the remap does not significantly alter the district's rural, conservative, traditionally Democratic character. While Republicans have made inroads in presidential voting — Reagan swept more than half the district's counties in 1980 — the GOP has made few dents in Democratic voting habits in state and local races. Between 1966 and 1980, Republicans fielded a congressional candidate in the district just once, in 1978, when the seat was open. In 1980, Stenholm was one of only three members of the Texas congressional delegation to run unopposed.

The best Republican territory is the district's largest population center, Taylor County (Abilene), which is home for about one-fifth of the the district's residents. Taylor

Charles W. Stenholm   Mickey Leland

voted for Republican Clements in the 1978 gubernatorial race and Reagan won 62 percent there in 1980. Abilene's highly successful economy is based on agribusiness, diversified small manufacturing and a major military installation, Dyess Air Force Base. For the month of January 1982, Abilene's unemployment rate was the lowest of any major city in the United States.

In the eastern part of the 17th, there has been significant population growth in some counties near metropolitan Fort Worth. Parker County, for instance, added nearly 11,000 people during the 1970s; Reagan won Parker with 52 percent in 1980. But the bulk of the district's vote is still cast by the normally Democratic voters from small towns, ranches and farms.

In the remap, the 17th gives a tier of its northern counties to the 13th, another slow-growth district that needed to gain population. Along its southern border, the 17th gains territory from the overpopulated 21st and 11th districts.

District 18

Central Houston

Incumbent: Mickey Leland (D)

The 18th contains the office towers of downtown Houston, a magnet for corporate executives and the focal point of this booming city's infamously long rush hours. The 18th also serves as a reminder that Houston has suffered some growing pains in its drive to become a world-class cosmopolitan city.

As Houston's population climbed by nearly one-third during the last decade, the 18th lost more than 39,000 residents. The pleasant suburbs of Harris County seem rather distant to many residents of central Houston, where there is controversy over the police department's reputation for rough treatment of minorities.

There are signs of public concern over the gap between the affluent and the poor in Houston. In November 1981, Houstonians elected former city Controller Kathy Whitmire as their mayor. She promised a break with business-dominated politics and an effort to broaden participation in the city's prosperity.

But Whitmire's appointment of a black to lead the Houston Police Department has provoked strong criticism in some quarters, and it is not clear whether her new style of politics will carry the day in Houston.

In redistricting, the 18th catches up with some of those who left it in the 1970s, adding nearly 100,000 people, most of whom live in black and Hispanic areas not too far outside the district's current boundaries. The redrawn 18th, containing nearly half of Houston's black community, is 41 percent black. Hispanics account for another 31 percent of the population.

Although blacks, whites and Hispanics have about the same number of people in the 18th, the district has sent a black Democrat to Congress since it was created in 1971 — Barbara Jordan in 1972 and Mickey Leland in 1978. The 18th is the most staunchly Democratic district in the state; George McGovern in 1972 and Carter in 1976 won a higher percentage here than in any other Texas district.

Kent Hance   **Henry B. Gonzalez**

District 19

Northwest — Lubbock, Odessa

Incumbent: Kent Hance (D)

In state and national elections, Democratic Rep. Kent Hance's 19th has evolved into one of the most Republican districts in Texas. Although the remap deprives it of Midland County, where Reagan won 77 percent in 1980, the redrawn 15th will take in all of heavily Republican Ector County (Odessa). Currently only the eastern section of Ector is in Hance's territory. The Democratic incumbent told the Legislature flatly that he would not be willing to represent both counties in the 1980s.

Odessa, with more than 90,000 residents, refines petroleum and provides equipment and supplies to surrounding oil fields. It has a reputation as the blue-collar stronghold of the Midland-Odessa population center, but it is firmly Republican. Both Clements in 1978 and Reagan in 1980 won more than 70 percent of the Ector County vote. The county's population is about one-fifth of the district's total.

More than 100 miles north of Odessa is the district's other major urbanized area, Lubbock County. Like Ector, Lubbock nearly always falls in the Republican column; Clements took it with 55 percent in 1978 and Reagan fell just short of 70 percent in 1980.

Irrigation has enabled the agricultural region around Lubbock to replace East Texas as the state's predominant cotton-growing area. Lubbock, a city of 174,000 residents, calls itself the world's largest cottonseed processing center. Texas Tech University and Reese Air Force Base are important employers. Lubbock County has 40 percent of the redrawn district's population.

Republicans have also made inroads in the Democratic farming and ranching counties. Carter carried most of them in 1976, but four years later Reagan swept them all, carrying most by a 2-to-1 margin or better.

Besides giving Midland County to the 21st and incorporating into Hance's territory the part of Ector County currently in the 16th, the remap makes boundary changes in two rural counties. Though the redrawn 19th is a good Republican district, the conservative Hance should continue to win re-election.

Tom Loeffler   Ron Paul

District 20

Central San Antonio

Incumbent: Henry B. Gonzalez (D)

A 9 percent population decline during the last decade left the 20th District with 423,610 residents accounted for in the 1980 census, about 100,000 people short of the ideal congressional district size. The remap corrected that disparity by extending the perimeter of Gonzalez' circle-shaped district.

But the extension of the district's boundaries should not endanger Henry B. Gonzalez, who in 1961 became the first person of Mexican-American extraction to be elected to the House of Representatives from Texas. The 20th District will still be firmly anchored in the heart of San Antonio, the only major American city with a Hispanic mayor. Democrat Henry Cisneros made that breakthrough in 1981.

Although Hispanics have numerical superiority in the region, they have only recently begun to crack "Anglo" control of local government and commerce. While the Rio Grande Valley has large ranches and irrigated farms that produce bumper crops of cotton, vegetables and fruit, Hispanics have not shared in the economic prosperity. On a per capita basis, south Texas is among the poorest areas in the country, although some of the Sun Belt growth has begun to affect it, especially in the fast-growing port of Brownville.

The redrawn 20th is 62 percent Hispanic, a percentage exceeded only by the 15th and 27th districts south of San Antonio. Gonzalez' new constituency should be as loyally Democratic as his old one, which gave Carter 69 percent of the vote in 1980.

Despite the decline in the 20th District, growth elsewhere in San Antonio helped the city's population exceed 785,000 in 1980, a figure that ranks it as Texas' third-largest city and the 10th-largest in the country. Although San Antonio was founded in the early 18th century by the Spanish and has a Hispanic majority, its economy has been controlled by Anglos since its early days as a cattle center. Today, federal payrolls are the key economic component. There are seven major military installations in or near San Antonio, including five Air Force bases.

District 21

San Antonio suburbs, San Angelo, Midland

Incumbent: Tom Loeffler (R)

Under the remap, Loeffler loses to the 23rd District many faithful Republican voters in northern Bexar County. But more than 300 miles northwest from those San Antonio suburbs, the 21st picks up from the 19th another GOP bastion, Midland County, which gave Reagan more than three-fourths of its 1980 presidential vote.

A 72 percent population growth rate in the Bexar County portion of the 21st was the major factor that made Loeffler's territory the fourth fastest-growing district in Texas during the 1970s. Although he gives up all but the north-central part of the county in redistricting, he should not suffer at the polls. In the last two presidential contests and in the 1978 gubernatorial election, GOP candidates carried all but two of the 26 counties outside Bexar that make up the redrawn 21st.

Midland votes solidly Republican because it is the white-collar administrative center for the vast oil fields of the Permian Basin in west Texas. Scores of oil companies maintain offices in this city of about 70,000.

Slightly larger and somewhat less Republican than Midland is San Angelo (Tom Green County), also in the northern part of the 21st. That city bills itself "the sheep and wool capital" of the nation and is a center for sheep raising and wool processing and shipping. Reagan took 61 percent of the Tom Green vote in 1980.

There are few other population centers in the sprawling district; the dry range-land of the rural counties is best suited to grazing and oil drilling. Many ranchers also receive royalties from oil drilled on their lands.

Besides the boundary changes in Bexar and Midland, the 21st gives five northern rural counties to the underpopulated 17th and takes in Presidio County on its western edge and McCulloch County in its northeast corner. Both Presidio and McCulloch have consistently voted Democratic, but together they have fewer than 14,000 people.

The district's Hispanic population — nearly 25 percent — is Democratic, but the Hispanic turnout is low and has little impact on the congressional outcome.

District 22

Southwest Houston and suburbs; Fort Bend and Brazoria counties

Incumbent: Ron Paul (R)

The remap takes advantage of rapid growth in the 22nd to give Ron Paul, a narrow winner in his last two House elections, a much more reliably Republican district.

Population in Paul's territory increased 52 percent during the 1970s, making it the second fastest-growing district in Texas. In redistricting, the 22nd loses all its Harris County territory south of the Ship Channel, an area where Republican strength is closely matched by regularly

Democratic labor votes and a significant black population.

Paul takes from the 8th District established residential areas of southwest Houston such as Bellaire, Sharpstown and West University Place, where the people are middle- to high-income Republicans. Also in the redrawn 22nd is Missouri City, which is divided between Harris and Fort Bend counties. It grew phenomenally during the last decade; population in the Fort Bend part of the city jumped from less than 1,000 in 1970 to nearly 25,000 in 1980.

All of Fort Bend County remains in the 22nd. Although parts of the county are still rural and small-town in character and have little to do with Houston, residential subdivisions with high-priced, single-family homes are becoming the norm. The influx of Houston professionals more than doubled Fort Bend's population in the 1970s; Reagan won two-thirds of the county's 1980 presidential vote.

Toward the Gulf, the 22nd loses to the 14th the southwestern half of Brazoria County, including the towns of West Columbia and Sweeny. Conservative Democrats are numerous in northeast Brazoria towns such as Alvin, but closer to the coast, Republicans are stronger in Freeport and in Lake Jackson, Paul's home.

District 23

Southwest — San Antonio suburbs, Laredo

Incumbent: Abraham Kazen Jr. (D)

The 23rd changes substantially under the remap, adding most of San Antonio's northern Bexar County suburbs and losing all its rural eastern territory to the 14th and 15th districts.

Republican strength in the redrawn 23rd is concentrated in Bexar and three other counties also in the northern part of the district — Medina, Uvalde and Kinney. All of those counties voted for Clements in 1978 and Reagan in 1980.

To the south, the overwhelming Hispanic presence ensures that Democratic voting patterns prevail. The population center in this part of the 23rd is Laredo, in Webb County. Nine out of every 10 Webb residents are Hispanic;

the county was the largest in Texas to vote for George McGovern in 1972 and Carter won 67 percent there in 1980.

Laredo, with 91,449 people, is a gateway for trade and tourism with Mexico and has petroleum operations. It is surrounded by vegetable-growing farm-lands irrigated with water from the Rio Grande. Dry areas to the north and east are best suited to cattle ranches and exploration for oil and gas.

Hispanics account for 53 percent of the redrawn district's population, the same as in the current 23rd. Kazen has sometimes been criticized as insufficiently responsive to the needs of that generally impoverished group; except on housing and education bills that directly affect his constituency, he votes a conservative line in the House. But by maintaining good relations with Hispanic political leaders, Kazen has put down feeble uprisings by liberal Anglo and Hispanic elements dissatisfied with his record. He should continue to prevail, since the addition of most of northern Bexar County brings in more conservative voters.

District 24

South Dallas and western suburbs

Incumbent: Martin Frost (D)

The redrawn 24th gives Frost a favorable political situation. The minority population of the district — 46 percent — is large enough to provide electoral support for his moderate-to-liberal philosophy, but not large enough to make him vulnerable to a serious minority challenge in the Democratic primary. As drawn by the Legislature, the new 24th was more than 60 percent black or Hispanic, posing possible renomination problems for Frost. The federal judges nullified any such threat.

The black population of the 24th is concentrated at the district's eastern end, south of the Trinity River in Dallas. The Hispanic population is heavier in the central part of the district. The suburbs of Grand Prairie and Irving on the western edge of the 24th are mostly white.

The South Dallas areas with their heavy minority influence are predictably Democratic. The Democratic Party also plays a dominant role in Grand Prairie and Irving, which contain manufacturing and distribution facilities and the homes of many blue-collar factory workers and laborers in construction-related trades. Part of the sprawling Dallas-Fort Worth Airport is located in the northwestern corner of the district and some of Frost's constituents are employed at the airport or by the airlines that use it.

The 24th also crosses into Tarrant County to pick up a section of Arlington where a General Motors plant is located. Labor delivers a sizable Democratic vote there. The bulk of the Tarrant County territory in the old 24th is incorporated into the newly created 26th District.

Frost has maintained good relations with minority groups since he came to Congress three years ago and he has been more successful at holding white working-class support than Democratic Rep. Jim Mattox in the neighboring 5th District. The district's white precincts gave Reagan solid majorities in 1980, but tend to divide about evenly between the parties in statewide contests.

Abraham Kazen Jr.

Martin Frost

District 25

South Houston and southeast suburbs

No Incumbent

One of three "new" House districts that Texas gained in the 1980 reapportionment, the 25th looks Democratic on paper, although Republicans harbor hopes that it will go their way. The 25th takes in much of the Harris County portion of the current 22nd District, which Republican Ron Paul has held tenuously in recent elections.

The 25th contains all of Harris County south of the Houston Ship Channel, a waterway lined with heavy industry. The cities of Pasadena and Deer Park are filled with blue-collar workers employed at huge refineries run by Shell, Crown and other petroleum giants.

The working-class vote is not faithfully Democratic. Reagan's conservative themes played well enough for him to win the blue-collar precincts here in 1980 and there are pockets of GOP regulars in the more affluent parts of Pasadena, Deer Park and neighboring South Houston.

West of those three communities is a concentration of minority voters. Blacks and Hispanics make up 39 percent of the district's population; among all the Houston-area districts, only central Houston's 18th has a higher minority percentage than the 25th.

Living in the southeastern corner of the 25th are many employees of NASA's Manned Spacecraft Center, which is located across the district boundary in the 9th. Another component is a politically active Jewish population at the district's western end.

District 26

Fort Worth suburbs; Arlington, Denton

No Incumbent

The majority of the population in the newly created 26th lives in conservative portions of Tarrant County unsuitable for inclusion in Democrat Jim Wright's Fort Worth-based 12th District, which was drawn to protect the House majority leader.

The suburbs south of Fort Worth are home to doctors, lawyers and other upper-middle-class professionals who are hard-core conservative voters. Much of this area has been part of the 6th District, represented by New Right Democrat Phil Gramm. In the southeastern part of Tarrant County, towns such as Mansfield are growing and becoming more Republican; they appeal to white-collar city workers who want to live in a more rural setting that is still within a reasonable commuting distance of their jobs.

The dominant city in the 26th is Arlington, which sits astride the "mid-cities" growth corridor between Dallas and Fort Worth. Arlington grew 78 percent during the 1970s, to a 1980 population of about 160,000. Arlington contains a wide array of industries and tourism and the hotel/motel business are critical to the economy. The Texas Rangers baseball team plays there and the Six Flags Over Texas amusement park is located in the city.

A labor-oriented Democratic part of eastern Arlington is included in Rep. Martin Frost's 24th District. The white-collar population that dominates the 26th District portion of Arlington generally prefers Republicans, although a sizable number of people there have voted in House races for Frost, who represented all of Arlington before redistricting.

Also included in the mid-cities category are the closely linked towns of Hurt, Euless and Bedford, just north of Arlington and demographically similar to it. In northeastern Tarrant County are the small but fast-growing communities of Grapevine and Colleyville, which are near the Dallas-Fort Worth Airport.

North of Tarrant County is Denton County, which is wholly within the 26th. Primarily rural and Democratic not too long ago, Denton County grew 89 percent during the last decade and is now solidly Republican. There are some liberal votes in older sections of the city of Denton and some traditional Democrats in the areas of the county that are still devoted to farming and ranching. Also in the 26th are portions of Collin and Cooke counties, both politically conservative.

Although the district has a decided rightward bent, the Republican nominee could face a tough general election contest; conservative Democrats have put forward a strong candidate in former Arlington Mayor Tom Vandergriff.

District 27

Gulf Coast — Corpus Christi, Brownsville

No Incumbent

This new district looks tidy and compact: five counties lined up along the Gulf Coast in far southern Texas with the region's two largest cities at either end.

But when the boundaries of the 27th were released by federal judges, there were grumblings in Brownsville, a Mexican border city in the Rio Grande Valley that has never had a great deal of contact with Corpus Christi, its much larger competitor for tourists and seaport trade. Since about 55 percent of the district's population lives in Nueces County (Corpus Christi), some Brownsville residents worry that their interests will take second place to Corpus Christi's in the new 27th.

These people were more comfortable with the old district arrangement, which paired Cameron County (Brownsville) with McAllen, another Mexican-border city just to its west. But the judges disregarded that traditional Brownsville-McAllen affinity in order to balance the Hispanic populations in the 15th and 27th districts.

Among Texas ports, Corpus Christi is second only to Houston in tonnage handled yearly. The city has large petrochemical and aluminum plants and seafood processing facilities. Manufacturers of clothing and oil drilling equipment are also important employers. Tourists are lured to Corpus Christi by its mild climate and direct access to the Padre Island National Seashore.

By comparison, Brownsville offers more of a south-of-the-border flavor than Corpus Christi; Nueces County is not quite half-Hispanic, but in Cameron County, nearly 80 percent of the residents are Hispanic. Export-import trade with Mexico is vital to the economy, and the bounteous harvests of the Rio Grande Valley keep many workers busy with fruit and vegetable processing.

Nueces and Cameron behave similarly at the polls, as reflected in the 1980 presidential results. Carter carried both counties, although in each case by less than 3,000 votes over Reagan. There are three other counties in the 27th, but these sparsley populated ranch-lands should have scant electoral impact. Since the district overall is nearly two-thirds Hispanic, the Democratic nominee will be favored to win this new House seat in 1982.

Virginia

Few states have undergone as striking a political transformation in recent years as Virginia. From a tightly controlled "oligarchy" under the thumb of Democratic Sen. Harry F. Byrd Sr., the Old Dominion has developed into one of the nation's most fluid and chaotic political cauldrons.

The Byrd era ended in the mid-1960s with the death of the senator and the declining influence of his courthouse alliances in an increasingly urban state. The organization's demise ended nearly a century of one-party Democratic rule and more than three centuries of government by rural aristocracy.

Taking advantage of the loosening party alliances in Virginia, Republicans moved skillfully to capitalize on the upheaval. Combining conservative ideology with computer technology, they emerged as the state's dominant party in the 1970s.

But the political situation is still in flux. Virginia statutes do not favor strong party ties. There is no party registration and the party affiliation of candidates does not appear on the general election ballot.

The system encourages independents. Sen. Harry F. Byrd Jr. bolted the Democratic Party to win election in 1970 as an independent (a status he has maintained), and the following year an independent was elected lieutenant governor.

But the GOP has clearly been the prime beneficiary of the political turmoil. Wracked by some bitter infighting, the Democrats have not won a presidential, gubernatorial or U.S. Senate election in Virginia since 1966. And the U.S. House delegation, which had five Democratic members as recently as 1975, was reduced to one Democrat by 1981. In no other state in recent years have Democrats experienced such a political famine.

In large measure, the historic roles of the two parties in Virginia have been reversed. For a century after the Civil War, the narrow-based GOP was the more liberal of the two — urging racial moderation, election law reforms and more state spending for basic services. Virginia's conservative "Bourbon" Democrats — frequently at odds with the national party — offered balanced budgets, racial status quo and pro-business government.

But in the early 1970s, the two parties swapped roles. The Republicans were taken over by a conservative element led by the late Richard D. Obenshain, while the Democrats moved leftward with the defection of many Byrd Democrats.

The upheaval has enabled the GOP to expand its base eastward — from the Shenandoah Valley and mountainous Southwest into the onetime Byrd strongholds of the rural Piedmont, Southside and Tidewater regions, as well as the fast-growing suburbs of Washington, D. C., and Richmond. That has left the Democrats with a base large enough to be competitive but facing great difficulty in winning major statewide elections.

Northern Virginia Suburbs

The increasing urbanization of Virginia has transferred political power from the rural areas to the population centers — a relocation that has swelled the importance of the fast-growing Virginia suburbs of Washington, D. C.

The suburbs are home for about 20 percent of the state population. Their growth has been spurred in the last generation by the rapid expansion in the federal government and the attraction of a diverse array of white-collar industries.

A large military population, working in the Pentagon and at nearby military installations, has created a more conservative political climate than exists in suburban communities across the river in Montgomery County, Md.

Party roots are shallow in the suburbs. The rapid growth has tended not only to blur community lines but also reduce the effectiveness of local party structures. A large proportion of suburban voters are non-Virginians, and many live in the area only a few years before moving on.

The Democrats have their greatest strength in the older, inner suburbs of Alexandria and Arlington County. Both Alexandria and Arlington are much like urban areas in their settled appearance and substantial minority populations.

On the outskirts of revitalized "Old Town" Alexandria — an affluent competitor to the Georgetown section of Washington — is a large black community which comprises 22 percent of the Alexandria population. While there are fewer blacks in Arlington, the county has become a major melting pot for other nationalities. Together Asians, Hispanics and a variety of other minority groups make up 23 percent of the population. Arlington has one of the highest concentrations of Vietnamese people in the nation.

To the west and south, the suburbs are newer, whiter and more Republican. And unlike Alexandria and Arlington, they are still growing rapidly. While the two inner suburbs lost population in the 1970s, the outer suburban counties grew by more than 30 percent.

In the last 40 years, Fairfax County has grown from a largely pastoral home for 40,000 residents into a sprawling suburban colossus with nearly 600,000.

More than twice as populous as any other jurisdiction in Virginia, the county has come to dominate suburban politics. With majorities in Fairfax County in 1980, the GOP regained the two suburban House seats it lost in 1974.

While Fairfax County grew by 31 percent in the last decade, the more distant suburban counties grew at an even faster pace. Commuters seeking lower housing costs and more countryside settled in Loudoun County, to the west in the Virginia "hunt" country, and Stafford and Spotsylvania counties, which lie astride Interstate 95 to the south. All had growth rates exceeding 50 percent.

Greater Richmond

Most of Virginia's population lives in an "urban" corridor that extends from the northern Virginia suburbs to the industrial Tidewater. At its fulcrum is Richmond and surrounding suburbs, an area that comprises 10 percent of the state population.

Blessed with a favorable location along the James River, Richmond has long been the center of Virginia commerce and government. It has been the state capital since the Revolutionary War and was the capital of the Confederacy for most of the Civil War.

Richmond was also one of the South's early manufacturing centers, originally concentrating on tobacco processing. But over the years, the economy has diversified, enabling the Richmond area to remain vibrant.

Politics in the region reflect racial divisions. Predominantly black Richmond is Democratic. The heavily white suburbs of Chesterfield and Henrico counties are conservative Republican. They have a much higher proportion of native-born Virginians than the more liberal suburbs of Washington, D. C.

The political split between Richmond and its suburbs was obvious in 1980 congressional voting. While the Republican winner, Thomas J. Bliley Jr., carried the suburbs by nearly 50,000 votes, his underfinanced Democratic opponent won the city by 3,000 votes.

And the population figures seem to favor the GOP. While Richmond lost population in the 1970s, both suburban counties gained enough new residents to exceed Richmond's population for the first time in history. Chesterfield County nearly doubled its population, growing by 84 percent in the 1970s.

Tidewater

The Tidewater region extends from the Potomac River on the north to the James River on the south, and from the Chesapeake Bay on the east to the Fall Line on the west, where the coastal plain meets the Piedmont plateau.

Most of the Tidewater is rural, suited for farming and fishing. It was the center of colonial Virginia and the birthplace of the state's plantation economy. But in the 20th century the center of the region's economy has been its industrial southeastern corner.

There, in the Hampton Roads, is one of the nation's finest natural harbors. The U. S. Navy has been the linchpin of the local economy since the 19th century, building the largest constellation of naval installations on the Atlantic coast in the area. The headquarters of the Atlantic fleet is in Norfolk, while across the Hampton Roads in Newport News is one of the Navy's largest shipbuilding contractors. The Hampton Roads area is also a lively port for the shipment of coal, grains and other products from the interior of Virginia.

The heavy blue-collar element, coupled with the large black population, makes the urban Tidewater one of the few remaining bastions of Democratic strength in Virginia. The cities of Hampton, Newport News, Norfolk and Portsmouth are all at least 30 percent black.

In 1978, all four cities supported Democratic Senate nominee Andrew P. Miller in his losing campaign against Republican John W. Warner. And in 1980, all except Newport News loyally backed Carter over Reagan.

The primary Republican base in the area is the military center and coastal resort of Virginia Beach. Through population gains and annexations it is now the second-largest city in Virginia, with 262,000 residents to Norfolk's 267,000. Virginia Beach is the only one of the Tidewater cities still experiencing a population boom, growing 52 percent in the last decade.

Southside

Probably the most conservative region in Virginia is rural Southside, which extends across the southern flank of the state from the Tidewater region to the Blue Ridge Mountains and to the north roughly as far as Richmond.

This area resembles the Deep South. It is relatively poor and has a substantial black population and an agrarian-based economy that in the 20th century has turned increasingly to textiles. The region is the leading tobacco and peanut-growing area of the state, but much of the soil was exhausted earlier this century by overproduction.

Conservatism is deeply imbued in the region's rural white population. Southside was a stronghold of the Byrd organization, the leading bastion of Virginia support for George C. Wallace for president in 1968 and a focal point of "massive resistance," the Byrd-supported attempt to stave off federally mandated school integration during the 1950s.

The heaviest concentration of blacks is in the eastern half of the region, which has remained loyally Democratic. The western half, where whites comprise a large majority of the electorate, has tended to vote Republican in recent years.

Piedmont

Just north of Southside is the Piedmont, a region of small towns, farms, forests and rolling hills. Like the Southside, it supported the Byrd organization and in recent years has been a part of the Republican coalition.

But with fewer blacks here, racial issues have caused less polarization. And the region has a more prosperous agricultural base, producing livestock, dairy products and fruits. A number of affluent country estates are located around Leesburg and Middleburg in the midst of the northern Virginia "hunt" country and around the bustling academic center of Charlottesville — one of the few Democratic footholds in the Piedmont.

Shenandoah Valley

Before Virginia became a two-party state, the Shenandoah Valley was one of the Republican Party's few strong-

New Virginia Districts

U. S. Congress: 10 districts
 Senate (1R, 1IND.)
 House (1D, 9R)
Governor:
 Charles S. Robb (D)
Population: 5,346,279
Area: 40,815 sq. miles
1980 Presidential Vote:
 Carter (40%)
 Reagan (53%)
 Anderson (5%)

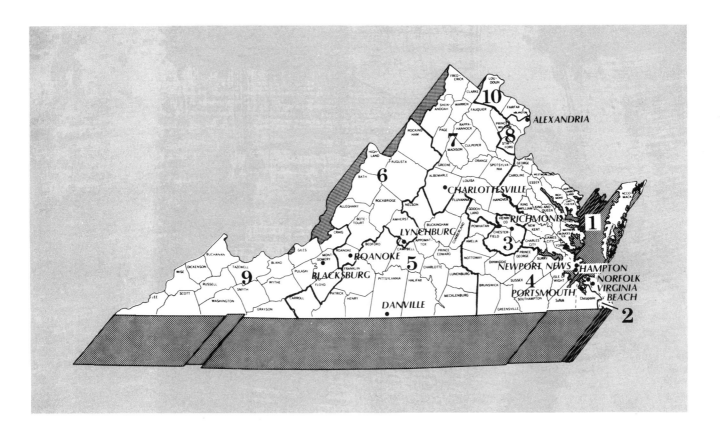

holds in the state. The area was settled from the north during the 18th century by English, German and Scots-Irish settlers.

The German immigrants established roots in the northern end of the region — in Page, Rockingham and Shenandoah counties. Foes of the Tidewater plantation aristocracy, they quickly became the backbone of the Republican Party in the Shenandoah Valley after the Civil War.

The Shenandoah Valley's rural economy is composed of a mixture of farming, light manufacturing and tourism. The prosperous, well-tended farms of this area produce a variety of fruits, livestock and poultry. The small city of Winchester, located at the northern end of the Valley, is the center of a large apple-growing industry and home base for the Byrd family.

Southwest

This region had a rough-and-tumble two-party system well before the development of the Republican Party on a statewide level. Geographically removed from the rest of the state and facing chronic economic doldrums, the mountainous region regularly bucked the Byrd organization and in the century after the Civil War was the GOP's major stronghold in Virginia.

In the party's lean years, heavy support from the poor farming and coal-producing counties of the Southwest region frequently enabled the GOP gubernatorial candidate to draw 35 to 40 percent of the statewide vote. In 1969, mountain votes helped to elect native-son Linwood Holton of Roanoke as Virginia's first Republican governor.

But as the state Republican Party has moved to the right in recent years and developed ties with the Richmond business establishment, it has lost part of its historic base in the Southwest. The coal-mining counties that share a border with West Virginia now regularly vote Democratic, as does the industrial city of Roanoke, the only major urban area in Virginia founded in the aftermath of the Civil War.

PARRIS SEAT THREATENED BY NEW MAP

Displaying just a tinge of partisanship, Virginia's Democratic-controlled Legislature adopted a congressional district map that could help unseat 8th District Republican Rep. Stan Parris.

But the state Legislature's conservative Democratic Party leadership rejected a more ambitiously partisan proposal that might have undermined several other Republican incumbent candidates. So the new redistricting law will not threaten Republican control of Virginia's delegation in the House of Representatives. The GOP now holds a 9-1 advantage.

The 8th District lines have been refashioned to help Democrat Herbert E. Harris II in his 1982 comeback attempt against Stan Parris. Harris, who represented the district for three terms, narrowly lost the 8th to Parris in the 1980 election.

On May 1, 1981, legislators sent a tentative redistricting plan incorporating the 8th District changes to Republican Gov. John Dalton and asked for his comments. Gov. Dalton asked that the 8th District be redrawn to make it more favorable for Rep. Parris, but the state Legislature rejected that suggestion in a special session held in June 1981. Dalton signed the redistricting bill into law June 12, 1981.

Despite the damage done to Parris, the remap is much kinder to him than a redistricting proposal favored by a group of more liberal Democratic lawmakers. They wanted to throw Parris into the same district with fellow Republican Frank R. Wolf and change boundaries elsewhere in the state to the disadvantage of Republican incumbents.

Paul S. Trible Jr.

G. William Whitehurst

District 1

East — Newport News, Hampton

Incumbent: Paul S. Trible Jr. (R)

When Trible won this district in 1976, he was the first Republican in this century to take it. He has worked to broaden his support and had no Democratic opposition in 1980. Now Trible has decided to run for the Senate in 1982; there is no assurance that his successor will be Republican.

Though the district has come loose from its traditional Democratic moorings, it is no GOP stronghold; its significant black and working-class populations make it less than predictable in most contests. In close statewide races, the 1st is a swing district. Carter carried it with 50 percent in 1976. In 1980 Reagan finished 5 points ahead of Carter.

Half the people in the 1st live in two cities at the district's southern end — Hampton and Newport News. These two cities frequently turn in Democratic majorities. In 1980, Carter won Hampton, while Reagan eked out a 357-vote plurality in Newport News.

Both cities are about one-third black, with economies tied to military and shipbuilding facilities; the Newport News Shipbuilding Co. alone employs 25,000 people.

The balance of the district's population is scattered through rural counties along the Chesapeake Bay and inland from it. Colonial Virginia's plantation economy was centered in this area; fishing, oystering, crabbing and the growing of corn, soybeans and wheat are important today.

This conservative rural territory is where the GOP has made its most significant inroads into the traditional Democratic strength. Of the 18 counties outside Hampton and Newport News, Reagan won all but four in 1980, accumulating an 11,000-vote cushion.

In redistricting, the 1st takes in Caroline County from the 7th. An agricultural county that is 43 percent black, Caroline gave 57 percent of its vote to Carter in 1980. But the county's population is just 3 percent of the district's total, so its impact will be minimal.

District 2

Norfolk, Virginia Beach

Incumbent: G. William Whitehurst (R)

The 2nd is composed of adjacent cities: the fast-growing residential and resort municipality of Virginia Beach, and the unionized port city of Norfolk, which lost 13 percent of its population during the last decade.

The two cities present a stark political contrast. Norfolk, which is 35 percent black, gave Carter a 52-41 percent edge in 1980. Virginia Beach, which is 86 percent white, went to Reagan by nearly 2-1.

Like the southern portion of the 1st District, the 2nd is heavily dependent on the massive concentration of naval installations, shipbuilders and shipping firms in the Hampton Roads harbor area, which ranks first in export tonnage among the nation's Atlantic ports and is the biggest coal

New Virginia Districts

New District	Incumbent	Population	1980 Pres. Winner
1	Paul S. Trible Jr. (R)	535,085	Reagan
2	G. William Whitehurst (R)	529,178	Reagan
3	Thomas J. Bliley Jr. (R)	533,720	Reagan
4	Robert W. Daniel Jr. (R)	535,391	Carter
5	Dan Daniel (D)	530,988	Reagan
6	M. Caldwell Butler (R)	538,644	Reagan
7	J. Kenneth Robinson (R)	534,911	Reagan
8	Stan Parris (R)	534,366	Reagan
9	William C. Wampler (R)	538,871	Reagan
10	Frank R. Wolf (R)	535,125	Reagan

shipper in the world. There is a Ford Motor Co. truck assembly plant in Norfolk, and the city also processes seafood and makes fertilizer and farm implements.

During the 1970s, many military families, business people and retirees settled in Virginia Beach, changing its earlier identity as a summertime tourist center. The city's retail and service trade has boomed in response to this influx of affluence. After growing 52 percent in the past 10 years, Virginia Beach now has 263,000 residents and is just 4,000 people short of supplanting Norfolk as Virginia's largest city.

One key to Democrat Charles S. Robb's successful 1981 gubernatorial campaign was his unusually strong showing in the 2nd District. It was Robb's second-best district, giving him 59 percent of the vote.

The 2nd has been slightly expanded by redistricting. It picks up 35,000 people in the southern part of Virginia Beach who are currently in the 4th District. Whitehurst's new territory is a solidly Republican and rural area into which suburbia is encroaching.

G. William Whitehurst was first elected in 1968, when the Democratic Party split after a bitter primary that nominated a liberal. He has not had Democratic opposition since 1976.

District 3

Richmond and suburbs

Incumbent: Thomas J. Bliley Jr. (R)

Like the 2nd District, the 3rd has two distinct parts: the black-majority, traditionally Democratic city of Richmond, and the surrounding suburbs in Chesterfield and Henrico counties, which are overwhelmingly white and predominantly Republican.

Because the population has grown in the suburbs and shrunk in the city, the 3rd in recent years has emerged as a GOP stronghold. With redistricting, Bliley sees his constituency becoming even more of a Republican bastion. To make up for Richmond's 12 percent population decline in the 1970s, the 3rd picks up 33,000 western Chesterfield voters from the 5th.

The political split between Richmond and its suburbs was obvious in 1980 voting. Carter won 55 percent in Richmond, which is home to 41 percent of the people in the redrawn 3rd. But Reagan took more than two-thirds of the vote in both Henrico and Chesterfield. In one Henrico precinct, Reagan's margin was 8-1.

Richmond, the third-largest city in the state, has long been the center of Virginia commerce and government. It was also one of the South's early manufacturing centers, originally concentrating on tobacco processing. Over the years, factories have diversified into chemicals, textiles, paper and processed foods.

Richmond's business elite exercises considerable influence over politics in the district and in the state. Bliley, director of a prominent funeral home and former Democratic mayor, had the endorsement and financial support of the business establishment in his solid 1980 victory. Bliley's win marked the first time the district had switched party control since the 19th century.

Population trends point toward long-term GOP dominance. With the 1980 census, suburban Henrico and Chesterfield counties together gained enough new residents to exceed Richmond's population for the first time in history.

District 4

Southeast — Chesapeake, Portsmouth

Incumbent: Robert W. Daniel Jr. (R)

With Portsmouth's large black population and blue-collar work force joining diehard rural Democrats, the 4th is solidly Democratic on paper. It was the only Virginia district to give Jimmy Carter a majority in 1980. Democrat Robb won 60 percent here en route to election as governor.

Thomas J. Bliley Jr.   **Robert W. Daniel Jr.**

Dan Daniel   M. Caldwell Butler

But Republican Daniel has been winning in the 4th since 1972, and redistricting is not likely to alter the situation very much. Republicans and conservative Democrats will still form a voting majority.

Portsmouth is 45 percent black and home to nearly a quarter of the people in the redrawn 4th. The city is oriented toward the naval and shipbuilding economy of Norfolk, Hampton and Newport News. In 1980, Carter won 58 percent in Portsmouth, his highest percentage in any of Virginia's major cities.

The neighboring city of Chesapeake, slightly larger than Portsmouth, gave Reagan a slim victory in 1980. Chesapeake is less black and less industrial than Portsmouth; many who work in Portsmouth's shipyards and factories have homes in Chesapeake.

There is some industry in the smaller cities of the 4th, which together make up another 20 percent of the district's population. Suffolk processes peanuts, Petersburg makes tobacco products and Hopewell calls itself the chemical capital of the South. Of these towns, Carter lost only Hopewell in 1980. The most reliably Democratic of the smaller cities is black-majority Petersburg, where Daniel's 1980 margin was only 189 votes, far below his 61 percent districtwide average.

Peanuts and tobacco are the important crops in the farm lands of the 4th District, where more than one-third of Daniel's constituents live. Democratic ties are still strong there. Sussex County, for example, gave Carter 57 percent of the total vote there last year. Rural population exodus, a trend that has virtually ended elsewhere in Virginia, still plagues this area; four agricultural counties lost population in the 1970s.

Four counties and part of another will be joining the 4th District because of redistricting. Along its western border, the district gains Brunswick, Nottoway, Powhatan and Amelia counties and a slice of Chesterfield County. But while Rep. Daniel will be taking on more than 50,000 new constituents, he will not be hurt politically. All of the new counties except Brunswick County voted for Ronald Reagan in 1980; Brunswick is 57 percent black and gave Jimmy Carter 58 percent of its vote, however it has only 15,000 people.

Although much of the new territory is rural, the eastern end of Powhatan is an outlying Richmond suburb, and that county had a growth rate of 70 percent in the last decade. Daniel gives up the southern part of Virginia Beach to the 2nd District.

District 5

South — Danville

Incumbent: Dan Daniel (D)

The 5th is in the heart of Virginia's rural "Southside," a largely agricultural region that more closely resembles the Deep South than any other part of the state does. It is relatively poor and has a substantial black population. Tobacco and soybeans are major crops, but this region lacks the rich soil of the Tidewater.

Dan Daniel stands as the lone obstacle to full GOP control of Virginia's U. S. House delegation. He first won in 1968 and has been unopposed for re-election since 1972.

Though the 5th continues to support conservative Democrats like Daniel, it has long refused to vote for more liberal Democratic candidates at the state and national level. It was one of only two districts in Virginia to back George Wallace in 1968 and has not supported a Democrat for president in more than a quarter-century. Even Barry Goldwater in 1964 carried it with 51 percent of the vote.

The district's largest city is Danville, a tobacco market and textile center on the North Carolina border. Reagan received 61 percent in Danville in 1980. The residents of the city and those of surrounding Pittsylvania County, which Reagan took by 2-1, make up about one-fifth of the district's population.

Most of the people in the 5th are scattered through farming areas and a few factory towns. Most of these areas normally vote Republican at the state level. The best area for Democrats is Henry County. Carter won it with 49 percent in 1980 and was beaten by only 96 votes in its county-seat town of Martinsville, a major furniture-producer.

To the north, the district takes in part of Lynchburg. That section of Lynchburg and its southern neighbor, Campbell County, are strongly conservative areas where Reagan won two-thirds of the 1980 vote.

In redistricting, Dan Daniel loses a tier of counties on the eastern end of his district to the 4th — Powhatan, Amelia, Nottoway and Brunswick — and gives to the 3rd the western half of Chesterfield County. On the southwestern edge of the 5th, Floyd County moves over to the 9th and Carroll County comes into Daniel's territory from the 9th. The 5th also picks up Bedford County from the 6th and Fluvanna and Nelson counties from the 7th.

The changes will have no great impact on the political character of the 5th. Of the counties Daniel will lose, all but one chose Reagan in 1980; of the counties he will gain, Carter took only one, Nelson County.

District 6

West — Roanoke, Lynchburg

Incumbent: M. Caldwell Butler (R)

The 6th currently encompasses the lower portion of the Shenandoah Valley. The addition of Rockingham

County in redistricting stretches the district into the northern part of the valley.

Republicans are on a 28-year winning streak in 6th District House elections, but pockets of Democratic strength show up in state and national elections.

Jimmy Carter won 52 percent of the 1980 vote in the city of Roanoke, which has more than 100,000 people and 19 percent of the district's population. An array of industries in Roanoke make textiles, furniture, and metal and electrical products. Carter also carried towns to the north like Covington, Buena Vista and Clifton Forge, and the two counties surrounding them, Bath and Allegheny. There are chemical plants and pulpwood and paper mills in that area.

But Democratic support is surpassed by the Republican vote in Roanoke's suburbs, in Lynchburg and in most of the rural areas. Reagan won 56 percent in Roanoke County, took nearly all the rural counties and defeated Carter 59-33 percent in Lynchburg, the home base of evangelist Jerry Falwell and the Moral Majority. An important Lynchburg employer is the nuclear energy firm Babcock & Wilcox, which conducts nuclear research and works on defense contracts.

Outside of metropolitan Roanoke and Lynchburg, the district is rural and depends primarily on livestock and poultry. Rockingham County, the new addition for 1982, contains the city of Harrisonburg, supplier of turkeys for thousands of Thanksgiving dinners. Rockingham County is more populous and more Republican than Bedford County, which switches from the 6th to the 5th.

Butler has announced plans to retire after the 1982 election. But the district's GOP future seems assured.

District 7

North — Charlottesville, Winchester

Incumbent: J. Kenneth Robinson (R)

The 7th runs from Richmond's northern suburbs across the Shenandoah Mountains to Winchester, the center of the state's apple-growing industry and home of Virginia's political dynasty, the Byrd family.

For generations, the district has been rural and conservative. But like Harry F. Byrd Jr., who took over his father's Democratic Senate seat in 1965 and became an independent four years later, the 7th has abandoned its Democratic roots and emerged as the state's foremost Republican stronghold. In the 1981 gubernatorial election, the 7th was the only district carried by unsuccessful Republican candidate J. Marshall Coleman. Reagan drew 57 percent of the district's 1980 presidential vote.

With expansion of the Richmond suburbs and steady growth in the Upper Shenandoah Valley and most of northern Virginia, population in the 7th increased by 29 percent in the 1970s. This was the fastest growth rate of any district in the state. Because of it, redistricting had to trim the edges of the 7th: Caroline County moves to the 1st District, Fluvanna and Nelson counties to the 5th and Rockingham County to the 6th.

To weaken the Republican incumbent in the neighboring 8th District, Democratic cartographers also shifted about 35,000 mostly-Republican voters in Prince William County out of the 8th into Robinson's 7th. Robinson has not faced a serious challenge since 1974, and redistricting does nothing to undermine his safe position.

Two suburban areas contribute heavily to Republican majorities. Hanover County, which is becoming one of Richmond's outlying residential areas, gave Reagan 70 percent of its 1980 vote. Northwest Prince William County is in the Washington, D. C., suburban sphere, and it favored Reagan by almost 2-1.

In counties along the Blue Ridge Mountains, a well-developed agricultural economy is keyed to dairying, livestock and fruit. There is also some manufacturing. Reagan won more than 64 percent in both the "apple capital" of Winchester and in surrounding Frederick County, at the northern tip of the 7th.

Reagan's margins were somewhat smaller, though still solid, in Spotsylvania and Stafford counties. Those are longtime farming areas recently adopted by people who depend on long-distance commuter buses to get to jobs in Washington, D. C. Spotsylvania was Virginia's fastest-growing county in the 1970s, more than doubling its population.

The few Democratic footholds in the 7th are in the southern part of the district. In Charlottesville, the district's largest city and home of the University of Virginia, the academic community boosted Carter to 47 percent of the vote; John Anderson took 10 percent. Neighboring Louisa and Goochland counties, both about s third black, were almost a dead heat between Carter and Reagan.

District 8

D. C. suburbs, Alexandria

Incumbent: Stan Parris (R)

Parris' 1,094-vote victory in 1980 depended largely on his strength in the cities of Manassas and Manassas Park, outlying suburbs of Washington, D. C., located in Prince William County. By moving those two cities and about one-fourth of the county's population from the 8th into J. Kenneth Robinson's 7th District, the Democratic Legislature has complicated Parris' re-election task.

J. Kenneth Robinson   **Stan Parris**

The redrawn 8th still includes most of the southern portion of Virginia's Washington-area suburbs. Growth there has been spurred by the rapid expansion of the federal government and the attraction of a diverse array of white-collar industries to the area.

The district's close-in suburb is Alexandria, with about one-fifth of the population of the 8th. Alexandria is the district's most reliable Democratic territory. The revitalized "Old Town" part of the city is an affluent competitor to the Georgetown section of Washington, and it has thousands of Democratic-voting young professionals. On the fringe of Old Town is a black community which comprises 22 percent of the Alexandria population and adds to Democratic strength. In 1980, Democratic Rep. Herbert E. Harris II took 55 percent in Alexandria, but that did not enable him to overcome challenger Parris districtwide.

Beyond Alexandria to the south and southwest, the suburbs are newer, whiter and more Republican. Population in these outlying areas is booming: Fairfax, Prince William and Stafford counties each grew by more than 30 percent during the 1970s.

Once-pastoral Fairfax County is now a suburban colossus of 600,000 people; development is spreading so quickly that the county board enacted tax incentives to encourage preservation of the scarce agricultural land that remains.

More than twice as populous as any other jurisdiction in Virginia, Fairfax is divided nearly evenly between the new 8th and 10th districts. Fairfax residents will account for 56 percent of the population in the redrawn 8th.

Party roots in Fairfax County are shallow because rapid growth has blurred community lines and reduced the effectiveness of local party structures. Elections are often close; in 1980, Parris won slightly more than 50 percent of the vote in the 8th District portion of Fairfax County.

Parris' cumulative 1980 advantage in Prince William County and in the cities of Manassas and Manassas Park was 3,171 votes, more than half his districtwide plurality. By taking half the county and both cities from Parris, redistricting eradicates that advantage.

Remaining in the 8th will be southern Prince William County, whose 110,000 residents will make up one-fifth of the district's population. This area was a ticket-splitter in 1980, voting narrowly for Democrat Harris but giving Reagan a comfortable margin.

Rounding out the district is generally Republican Stafford County; its 40,000 people are split between the 8th and the 7th districts.

Harris kept his campaign office open after his 1980 defeat and has been running non-stop since then. It would be the third contest between the two men; Harris defeated incumbent Parris in 1974.

District 9

Southwest — Blacksburg, Bristol

Incumbent: William C. Wampler (R)

This Appalachian district has long been called the "Fighting Ninth" because of its fiercely competitive two-party system and traditional isolation from the Virginia political establishment in Richmond.

Southwestern Virginia was settled by Scots-Irish and German immigrants, who had little in common with the English settlers in the Tidewater and Piedmont. In the years when Democrats routinely dominated Virginia politics, the 9th was the only consistently Republican district.

But as the state GOP has moved rightward in recent years, it has lost part of its historic base in the southwest.

Coal-mining counties along the Kentucky and West Virginia borders now regularly vote Democratic. Nearly half the 9th District's 17 counties went for Carter in 1980; Reagan received only 49 percent overall in the 9th.

The largest city in the district is Blacksburg, which grew from fewer than 10,000 to more than 30,000 people in the last decade. Located there is Virginia Tech University (20,000 students), the largest school in the state. Some residents of northeastern Montgomery County drive to jobs in nearby Roanoke, the commercial center of southwest Virginia. Reagan won this county by less than 800 votes.

Redistricting brings Floyd County into the 9th from Dan Daniel's 5th and moves Carroll County out of the 9th into the 5th. Wampler grumbled about losing Carroll — it has twice as many voters as Floyd and is slightly more Republican — but he should not be damaged by the shift.

District 10

D. C. suburbs, Arlington County

Incumbent: Frank R. Wolf (R)

The 10th is one of the most affluent districts in the South, but it is hardly fair to identify it as southern. It is mainly a set of bedroom communities for civil servants, Pentagon and nearby military installation employees, and others who work for the federal government.

Redistricting does not alter the 10th, which had a population gain of 14.9 percent during the 1970s, precisely the statewide average.

Arlington County, just outside Washington, grew rapidly in the 1950s and 1960s as the federal government expanded. Democrat Fisher held the 10th from 1974 to 1980 by winning big margins there, where about 30 percent of the district's people live. He lost to Wolf in 1980 because

William C. Wampler   **Frank R. Wolf**

he did not carry Arlington by enough to offset losses elsewhere. Reagan won the county in 1980, but his margin was held down by John Anderson's 12 percent showing.

Although suburban sprawl has peaked in Arlington — the county lost 21,685 people in the 1970s — there has been some movement of younger, affluent professionals into the county's condominiums and rental apartments. These people are generally less conservative than the average Virginian, but they are transient and politically unreliable.

There are fewer blacks in Arlington than in neighboring Alexandria, but the county is becoming a melting pot for other minorities. Asians, Hispanics and other minority groups together make up 23 percent of the county's population. Arlington's "Little Saigon" area is a magnet for Vietnamese-owned businesses.

West of Arlington, the 10th takes in nearly 300,000 people living in the northern part of Fairfax County. Like southern Fairfax County, which is part of the 8th District, this part of the county is filling up rapidly with people who commute to work in Washington, D.C. Reagan took 56 percent in the Fairfax County portion of the new 10th last year, and Wolf ran slightly behind him.

Further northwest is Loudoun County, home base of some long-distance commuters, but also a slice of Northern Virginia "hunt" country. Both Wolf and Reagan got nearly 60 percent of the Loudoun vote in 1980.

The Midwest

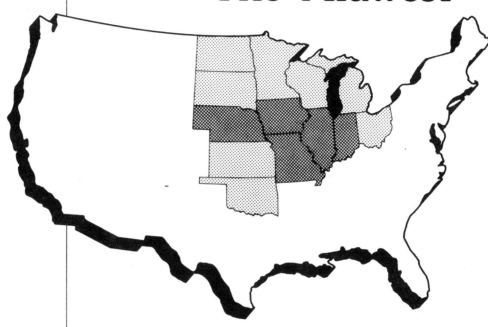

Illinois

Illinois may not be the "core America" that political observers have insisted on calling it for most of this century, but it does have more different demographic pieces than most of the big industrial states: the nation's second largest city; a suburban colossus that has come to be the single most important factor in state politics; a vast, rich, conservative section of the Corn Belt; and coal country more akin to Kentucky than to the Midwest. Other states have three of those four elements; none has all four.

What this has meant politically in recent years is a fairly even partisan split. Republicans have won 6 of the 9 presidential elections in Illinois since 1948, but two of those wins, Nixon over Humphrey in 1968 and Ford over Carter in 1976, were by less than three percentage points.

Of the nine elections for Governor since 1948, Republicans have won five, Democrats four. Republicans have won seven of 13 elections for the Senate. Over more than a quarter century between 1944 and 1972 no one of either party drew as much as 60 percent in any gubernatorial or Senate election.

The standard cliché has been that Illinois politics is a matter of Chicago vs. downstate. And to some extent it has been true. Chicago, with its huge Catholic population of Eastern Europeans and its ever-expanding black community, became a Democratic stronghold in the New Deal era. Party loyalty was inspired, maintained and often bought by Mayor Edward Kelly into the late 1940s and later Richard Daley until his death in 1976.

The big Democratic margins in Chicago were generally offset by the downstate vote, which usually supplied Republicans with healthy majorities, despite concentrations of industry (Peoria, Rock Island and Moline) and poverty (East St. Louis), and a strong Democratic vote in the southern counties.

The rough outlines of that truism still apply. Democrats still carry Chicago in virtually every statewide election, and Republicans win most of downstate. But the equation is now far more complicated. Illinois elections are now won and lost in the Chicago suburbs.

In the 1950 Senate election, Chicago accounted for 80 percent of the Cook County vote, and 72 percent of the vote in its metropolitan area. In the 1978 Senate election, Chicago's vote amounted to 60 percent of the Cook County total, and only 44 percent of the overall Chicago metropolitan vote. Suburban Chicago, including the Cook County suburbs and the five "collar counties" (McHenry, Lake,

Kane, DuPage and Will) totaled 56 percent of the Chicago metro vote and 35 percent of the state vote.

The suburban growth has been generally beneficial to the Republicans. In the newer subdivisions of the collar counties, ethnic Catholics who voted Democratic when they lived in Chicago have changed party affiliation outside the city limits. Republican Senator Charles Percy carried the Cook County suburbs with 67 percent in 1978; Republican Gov. James Thompson won with 75 percent there the same year.

Du Page, the largest of the collar counties, is the most dependable Republican territory in the state. Sometimes it can wipe out a Democratic lead everywhere else in the state all by itself. Without Du Page, Gerald R. Ford would have lost Illinois by 10,000 votes in 1976; with it, he carried the state by 90,000.

But the growth of the suburbs has not made Illinois a Republican state, because the suburban vote in many places is more independent than it is Republican. Sen. Adlai E. Stevenson III cut deeply into Republican suburban strength in his 1970 and 1974 victories, and in 1974 he carried two of the five collar counties (Lake and Will) as well as the Cook County suburbs.

Maverick Democrat Daniel Walker, running for governor in 1972 on a mixed platform of fiscal conservatism and political reform, used a different formula. He drew better than any Democrat in recent memory in the Corn Belt counties downstate. Walker's controversies with the Daley machine and his abrasive personality led to his defeat in a Democratic primary in 1976, but he proved what a Democrat can do downstate with the right issues.

In the 1980 Senate contest, Illinois voters had an unusual choice. The Democrat and the Republican were not only both from downstate, but both from the same small town, Belleville. Dixon was an easy winner, not only taking Chicago and most of the downstate counties but running respectably in most of the suburbs.

Chicago

Chicago slipped dangerously close to losing its "second city" population status to Los Angeles in 1980, but it remains first in the nation in quite a few things. It is still the heart of the nation's leading industrial area, one which is first in the production of iron and steel, electrical equipment and machinery. Chicago is still the nation's leading transportation center, with the busiest airport.

But it also has a reputation for being first in segregation among Northern cities, and its public housing projects, called "vertical ghettoes" as far back as the 1950s, are as blighted and dangerous as anything in the country. It can no longer point proudly to itself as the "city that works," as it did during the fiscally calm years under Daley. Its metropolitan transportation system lives virtually from day to day, and it has the same general money problems as any of the most troubled industrial cities.

The Daley years made permanent the Democratic Party's hold on Chicago's voters. Democrats gained local primacy at the start of the New Deal, replacing the old Republican machine, but for years Republicans managed to put up a fight within the city, and with the addition of the suburban vote, often carried Cook County in state elections. Franklin Roosevelt was held below 60 percent of the vote in Cook County in three of his four runs for president.

Since the late 1950s, the Chicago Democratic vote has been overwhelming, and most statewide Democrats who do even respectably well carry Cook County. Since Daley's first election in 1955, only one major Democratic statewide candidate has lost the city itself: Adlai Stevenson Jr. running for president in 1956. Only one other major Democrat, Senate candidate Roman Pucinski in 1972, has drawn less than 54 percent in Chicago.

Democrats are in the majority almost everywhere in Chicago. Their biggest margins are on the overwhelmingly black West Side, once the center for the city's Italian and Jewish communities. In certain West Side wards, Democrats receive over 90 percent of the vote. Some of these wards continued for years to have white party bosses who had long since moved to the suburbs, but that practice ended in the 1970s.

The South Side contains more than half of the city's population. It too is overwhelmingly black, an older, more stable community that never experienced a serious riot at the height of the racial tension in the 1960s. Dominated politically for more than 30 years by congressman William Dawson, the boss of black patronage politics in the Daley regime, the South Side has traditionally been an organization stronghold. But it has been more independent since Dawson's death in 1970. Some of the black wards broke party ranks to support Percy over Pucinski in 1972, and Democratic Rep. Ralph Metcalfe continued to win re-election to the House even after he broke with Daley in 1975. The current Democratic congressman, Harold Washington, is not a machine loyalist.

Most of the white vote on the South Side is cast by Eastern European ethnics who have remained as homeowners in the neighborhoods near the city's western border; by Irish in the "back of the yards" enclave that produced Daley and other recent political leaders; and by white-collar liberals around the University of Chicago in Hyde Park. All are Democratic in general elections, but the university community usually casts a strong anti-machine vote in primaries.

Most of the white middle class remaining in the city is on the North and Northwest sides, but these areas too are increasingly black and Hispanic. The district represented by the chairman of the Ways and Means Committee, Dan Rostenkowski, was drawn to follow the northwest migration of ethnic whites. Even so, his new district is more than one-third black and Hispanic.

Chicago has lost much of its traditional influence, both in state elections and in the Legislature. Daley's immediate successor, Michael Bilandic, was not a strong party leader, and his perceived ineffectiveness led to his defeat by Byrne in 1979. But Byrne's confrontational style has hindered relations with the state Legislature and alienated much of the machine. Many Daley loyalists are lining up behind Richard Daley Jr. to challenge Byrne in 1983. Daley was elected Cook County states attorney in 1980.

If the machine is getting weaker, Chicago's Democratic slant is getting stronger. The city is now 40 percent black and 14 percent Hispanic; these communities are not fertile recruiting grounds for the GOP. In 1978, the unsuccessful Democratic candidates for governor and senator carried Chicago with 59 and 57 percent, respectively. Both Carter and Dixon took Chicago by wide margins in 1980.

But like other big cities, Chicago has lost influence because it has lost population. The city lost more than 10 percent of its population in the 1970s, and now casts only 27 percent of the state vote, down from 35 percent in 1960.

Chicago Suburbs

Republicans have traditionally won majorities in the Chicago suburbs, and they still do. In 1952, Eisenhower carried the Cook County suburbs of Chicago with 64 percent of the vote. In 1976, Ford carried them with 62 percent. What has changed is the size of the vote.

A generation ago, suburban Chicago for the most part meant established lakefront towns like Evanston and Wilmette, Republican by tradition and moderate in social outlook. Now the "suburbs" extend west for miles, north almost to the Wisconsin border and south into the Corn Belt. As one moves west from Lake Michigan, into the newer developments, one finds increasing numbers of ethnic, Catholic, former Chicago Democrats. But these are prosperous communities for the most part, and strongly Republican.

From 1950 to 1978, only one major statewide Democratic candidate carried the Cook County suburbs: Adlai Stevenson III in 1970 and 1974. No major Democrat carried any of the three most solid Republican collar counties, Du Page, Kane and McHenry. The only two collar counties that sometimes vote for attractive statewide Democrats are Will, with a large blue-collar population, and Lake, which has significant black communities in Waukegan and North Chicago.

Democrats run best now in the Cook County suburbs closest to the city. Some of these, such as Skokie and Glencoe are heavily Jewish, others such as Evanston, have a large black vote. The 10th Congressional District, which includes Evanston and Skokie, was represented in the House of Representatives by liberal Democrat Abner Mikva from 1975 to 1979.

Central Illinois

The agricultural heart of Illinois covers about two-thirds of the territory of the state, from the Wisconsin border almost as far south as St. Louis. There are dairy farms in the north, but mostly it is corn and soybean country. Illinois is the second leading corn-growing state in the country, the leading soybean state, and one of the leading hog states.

They also raise Republicans in central Illinois. In all but a very few counties, Republican Party members are in the clear majority. In many counties, statewide Republicans average better than 60 percent of the vote.

Perhaps the most Republican county in the state is Kendall County, located just southwest of the metropolitan

U. S. Congress: 22 districts
  Senate (1D, 1R)
  House (10D, 14R)

Governor:
  James R. Thompson (R)

Population: 11,418,461

Area: 56,400 sq. miles

1980 Presidential Vote:
  Carter (42%)
  Reagan (50%)
  Anderson (7%)

New Illinois Districts

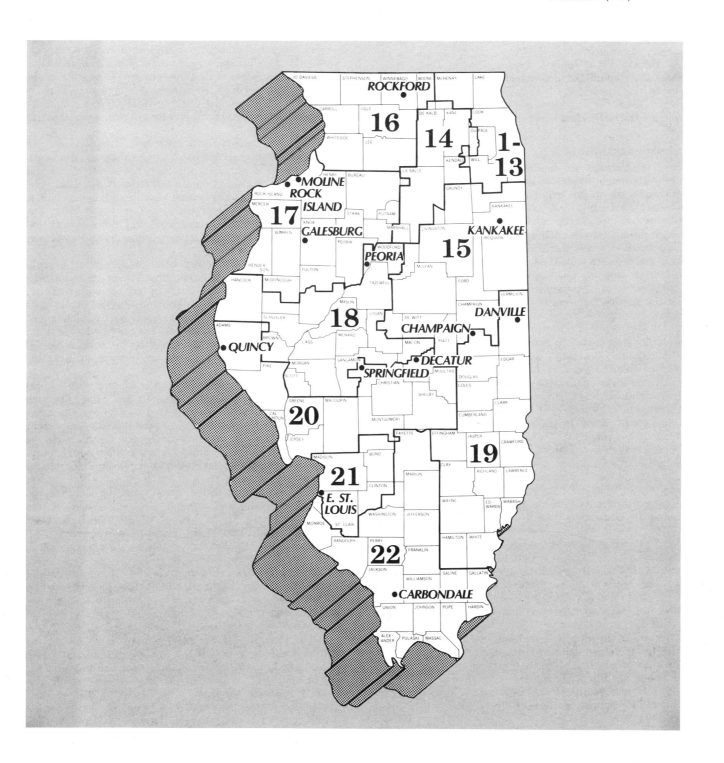

Chicago area, where GOP candidates often draw more than 70 percent of the vote. Even Dave O'Neal, the weak Republican Senate nominee in 1980, exceeded 60 percent of the vote. Ronald Reagan did especially well in north-central Lee County ... he grew up there, in the small town of Dixon.

There are scattered areas of Democratic voting in central Illinois. Most of these are small industrial cities, such as the farm machinery capitals of Moline and Rock Island on the Mississippi River.

Democrats sometimes win in Decatur, a corn and soybean processing center. There is some blue-collar Democratic strength in Peoria and Rockford, the two largest cities in the state outside Chicago, but neither Peoria County nor Winnebago County (Rockford) votes Democratic in most elections.

Rockford sent John B. Anderson to the House for 20 years as a Republican; Peoria sent Everett McKinley Dirksen to the House for 16 years before he went on to the Senate, and the city now is represented by Robert H. Michel, the GOP House leader.

Southern Illinois

The Chicago vs. downstate political equation was never thoroughly correct. Republicans Party candidates did win easily in the farm country of central Illinois. But Chicago Democrats had allies far away — in southern Illinois.

Industrial towns such as East St. Louis and Granite City, situated across the Mississippi River from St. Louis, Mo., have pulled the Democratic lever for most of the twentieth century. The southern end of the state is predominantly coal country, settled by migrants from states further south who brought their conservative Democratic voting habits with them.

Today, southern Illinois has about 9 percent of the state population and 25 percent of the population outside metropolitan Chicago. It has a Democratic majority, but one that is narrower than in years past.

Democratic candidates do best in St. Clair and Madison counties. St. Clair, which includes Belleville and overwhelmingly black East St. Louis, is the most heavily Democratic county in the state. Major Democratic candidates have carried it 25 of 28 times since 1950. Madison County, which has Granite City, is only slightly less consistent.

East St. Louis is southern Illinois' largest city. Once a major industrial and railroad center, it has been in deep decline for decades. Unemployment and poverty are endemic. Its population declined by 21 percent during the 1970s.

The coal country is gradually dropping its partisan predictability as its voters split with the national Democratic Party. There are still strongly Democratic counties in this part of the state, such as Franklin, Gallatin and Alexander. But there are also some heavily Republican counties now, and others where serious competition between parties exists.

Some of the counties have been growing in recent years with the increased demand for coal, and these seem to be the ones where Republicans are getting stronger.

Southern Illinois demonstrated its changing politics in the 1980 congressional election, nearly unseating Paul Simon, its seemingly entrenched liberal Democratic representative.

ILLINOIS MAP SURPRISE FOR GOP

The surprise ending of the Illinois redistricting saga was the approval of a partisan Democratic congressional map despite the presence of a Republican governor, a Republican-controlled state House and a three-judge federal panel with two Nixon appointees. The map eliminates two suburban Republican districts even though most of the state's population decline occurred in Chicago's inner city.

A major realignment was necessary because reapportionment cost Illinois two districts, forcing a reduction from 24 House seats to 22. Since control of the state Legislature is split between the parties, it was obvious early in 1981 that no compromise could be reached. As a result, the federal court took responsibility for selecting a redistricting plan.

Its ruling came Nov. 23, 1981, on a 2-1 vote that chose the redistricting map drawn up by Democrats in the Legislature over a Republican proposal. The decisive vote was cast by U.S. Appeals Court Judge Robert Sprecher, who had been named to the federal bench by President Nixon. Sprecher sided with the court's one Carter appointee. The third judge, also a Nixon selection, said in his dissent that the map was a partisan effort to preserve urban Democratic constituencies in Chicago.

The Democratic victory was due in part to a sophisticated computer program that made possible the creation of congressional districts having almost exactly equal population. The most populous district in the state has only 171 more residents than the least populous one. That accuracy seemed to impress the court, which did not express any concern over the fact that the redrawn district lines divided cities and carved up counties all over the state.

The court did commend the Democratic plan for preserving three black-majority districts in Chicago. Though the Republican plan also appeared to preserve the three districts, at least one would have been less than 65 percent black, and the court felt a 65 percent figure might be necessary to ensure continued black congressional representation. The Democratic plan kept all three districts at least 67 percent black.

Another explicit factor in the court decision was the overall strength of each party in the state. The court said Illinois appeared to be about evenly divided between Democrats and Republicans, based on recent election returns, and that the Democratic map would come closest to that split.

Democrats drew their map for the express purpose of protecting as many of their incumbents as possible. Led by Michael Madigan, the state House minority leader, they concentrated their cartographic ingenuity on the Chicago area.

The adjoining 1st, 5th and 7th districts in Chicago had suffered respective population losses of 20, 14.6 and 19.8 percent, making them obvious targets for consolidation. All but one of the other five city districts had also lost population. In contrast, the surrounding suburban districts had gained population; the old 14th, for example, had grown by 34.8 percent. To retain the eight Democratic seats based in

New Illinois Districts

New District	Incumbent	Population	1980 Pres. Winner
1	Harold Washington (D)	519,045	Carter
2	Gus Savage (D)	518,931	Carter
3	Marty Russo (D)	519,084	Reagan
4	Edward J. Derwinski (R)	519,005	Reagan
5	John G. Fary (D)	518,971	Carter
6	Henry J. Hyde (R)	519,033	Reagan
7	Cardiss Collins (D)	519,034	Carter
8	Dan Rostenkowski (D)	519,034	Carter
9	Sidney R. Yates (D)	519,064	Carter
10	John E. Porter (R)	519,015	Reagan
11	Frank Annunzio (D)	518,995	Reagan
12	Philip M. Crane (R)	519,008	Reagan
13	John N. Erlenborn (R)	519,001	Reagan
14	Tom Corcoran (R)	519,015	Reagan
15	Edward R. Madigan (R)	518,995	Reagan
16	Lynn Martin (R)	519,035	Reagan
17	Tom Railsback (R)	519,102	Reagan
18	Robert H. Michel (R)	519,026	Reagan
19	Daniel B. Crane (R)	519,082	Reagan
20	Paul Findley (R)	519,015	Reagan
21	Melvin Price (D)	518,954	Reagan
22	Paul Simon (D)	519,017	Reagan

*Retiring.

his hometown and the surrounding area shifted to a new 4th District. Unfortunately for him, the new district also includes Joliet, home base of another Republican incumbent, George M. O'Brien. The two faced each other in the March 16, 1982, Republican primary. O'Brien defeated Derwinski by piling up a 5-1 margin in the Will County portions of the district, the political base that has sponsored his long career in politics.

After rearranging the Chicago districts, the mapmakers focused their attention on southern Illinois, where Democrat Paul Simon had barely held his seat in 1980. By borrowing about 40,000 Democratic voters from St. Clair County and shifting a few other counties, they made the new 22nd a more firmly Democratic district.

Once these goals were accomplished, the Democrats worked a little mischief on downstate Republican Rep. Paul Findley, giving him three traditionally Democratic counties he did not want, along with the industrial city of Decatur. They removed from Findley's 20th District suburban Springfield, where he had run well in the past.

Elsewhere in the state, the computer cranked out population equality with little regard for county lines or other government jurisdictions. In Decatur, the district line goes through the middle of a Caterpillar Tractor plant, placing the plant manager in the 18th and the director of employee relations in the 20th. House Minority Leader Robert H. Michel gets a district largely new to him, with his traditional home base of Peoria barely inside the line. The 15th District had to be given an artificial thumb to include GOP Rep. Edward R. Madigan's home of Lincoln.

The Democratic victory provides a form of revenge for the redistricting that took place a decade ago, when a different federal panel accepted a Republican map that cost the Democratic Party two seats.

District 1

Chicago — South Side

Incumbent: Harold Washington (D)

The 1st contains the heart of Chicago's black South Side, an area that has been important in local politics since the 1920s — before most Northern cities even had substantial black populations. Although it is a very poor area, with the decaying buildings common to the inner city everywhere, it also has a stable black middle class. In the 1960s, when blacks on the more transient West Side rioted, this area was quiet.

Before World War II, most of the city's black population was concentrated here, just west of the wealthy residential areas on the shore of Lake Michigan. But in recent years, as color barriers have fallen in other parts of the city and its southern suburbs, people have been leaving the South Side in large numbers. During the 1970s, the 1st lost 20 percent of its population. In order to keep it in existence for the 1980s, mapmakers extended its boundaries in virtually every direction, bringing in voters from other urban districts, which in turn were stretched into the suburbs to gain back the population they gave up.

Like the old 1st, the new district is overwhelmingly Democratic. About 92 percent of its residents are black,

the city, Madigan extended them into the Republican suburbs, adding enough population to reach the ideal district size but leaving the city residents with the voting majority. Several districts reached outside the city limits for the first time. Only one district is now entirely within Chicago.

As a result of the new alignment, two sets of Republican incumbents were thrown into merged constituencies. On the northern edge of the city, the 9th District expanded into the heart of Republican John E. Porter's old suburban 10th. With his home placed now in the 9th District, Porter moved north to the new 10th, where 74-year-old GOP veteran Robert McClory had been planning to seek an 11th term. Confronted with the challenge, McClory chose to retire.

In the southern and western suburbs, Republican Edward J. Derwinski found his district broken apart, with

Harold Washington   Gus Savage

But the new 2nd also takes in some white suburban territory, including Dolton, Riverdale, and part of Calumet City, all blue-collar in orientation and less than 10 percent black. Many of the people here moved out from the far South Side of the city in the past two decades.

The district still includes the vast industrial area around the Calumet River, where the sky, trees and grass have long been blackened with soot, but where factory workers have been able to count on steady work and decent pay. These days the grass is still gray, but the mills are in decline. U.S. Steel, Republic Steel and other companies are working far below capacity; Wisconsin Steelworks, which employed 2,800 people, closed two years ago. Fewer freighters are coming to the Chicago ports, reducing the number of jobs for dockworkers. A Ford Motor Company plant in the district is still operating, although layoffs are frequent.

Outside the city, the economic picture of the district is is also bleak in most places. Harvey has gradually lost its heavy equipment industry in the past decade. The city's decline is reflected in the closing of Dixie Mall, which had been a major shopping center.

For most of the 1970s, the dominant political force in the district was the white ethnic community centered around the steel mills. These people proved loyal to Democratic Rep. Morgan F. Murphy (1971-81), a Daley organization ally. However, the district's black population grew during the decade from 39 percent to 77 percent, eroding the power of the machine and the remaining ethnic voters.

When Murphy retired in 1980, the Democratic organization agreed to endorse a black candidate, Reginald Brown Jr. But Brown lost the nomination to Gus Savage, who for many years had campaigned against the machine through the community newspapers he published on the South Side.

Savage surmounted a serious primary challenge in March 1982 from another anti-machine candidate, state Rep. Monica F. Stewart, and from Chicago Transit Authority Chairman Eugene M. Barnes, who was the choice of Mayor Jane Byrne's organization on the South Side. But Savage, a 30-year activist in South Side politics, lured to his side a number of precinct captains. Some of them had been his friends for years, others were dissatisfied with Barnes' delivery of patronage jobs when he was CTA chairman. A few of the party leaders who backed Savage are pondering a future run for the House seat themselves and opposed Barnes to prevent the mayor's organization from planting its man in the 2nd District seat.

and its small white population, centered around the University of Chicago in Hyde Park, is as Democratic as the black majority.

Some of the district's middle-class professionals live around the Michael Reese Hospital complex, newly added to the district on its northern border. Others live in Chatham, which has been a prosperous black residential neighborhood since the 1950s. Blue-collar workers at the southern end of the 1st work in the steel mills of south Chicago.

Many of the district's poorer black residents live in public housing projects, buildings seen as enlightened urban renewal when built during the 1950s but are now derided as "vertical ghettoes." One of them, the Robert Taylor Homes, is the largest such project in the country. It extends for 25 blocks and houses 75,000 people.

A generation ago, these compact projects made the black vote easier for the city's Democratic organization to control. But the South Side, long the fiefdom of veteran Democratic Rep. William L. Dawson (1943-70), has been rebellious in recent years. Voters here also backed the late Rep. Ralph H. Metcalfe (1971-78) when the veteran Democrat broke with the machine in 1976. In 1980 they turned out Metcalfe's machine-backed successor and replaced him with the independent Washington.

District 2

South Side Chicago, Harvey

Incumbent: Gus Savage (D)

For the first time, the 2nd District has crept beyond the city limits, into the southern suburbs formerly included in the 3rd. The politics of the district will not change dramatically, however.

The new lines of the 2nd were carefully drawn to take in communities with black majorities. As a result, blacks still comprise 70 percent of the population, compared to 77 percent in the old city district. Harvey, an older industrial city, and Dixmoor, a suburb, are about two-thirds black. Phoenix, a village of about 3,000, has only 136 white residents. Phoenix has been nearly all-black for the past 60 years.

Marty Russo   Edward J. Derwinski

District 3

Southwest Chicago and suburbs

Incumbent: Marty Russo (D)

The line between the 2nd and 3rd districts is also the line between black and white Chicago. Russo's district, concentrated on the west side of Western Avenue and in the suburbs just beyond the city, is 91 percent white.

About 40 percent of the population is new to Russo. The new territory comes primarily from the old 4th District, a suburban constituency that Democratic mapmakers divided up and used to fill out underpopulated city-based districts. The 3rd lost some of its eastern portions to the 2nd and picked up suburban communities in exchange.

The remaining city portions of the district are dominated by blue-collar ethnics, many of Polish and Lithuanian origin. But Beverly, traditional home for Chicago's well-to-do Irish Catholics, is also included.

The suburbs in the 3rd include Blue Island, developed for Illinois Central railroad workers, and Oak Lawn, a 19th century suburb that now has a large Greek-American population. Midlothian and Oak Forest, built up in the 1960s, have drawn blue-collar workers from South Chicago. Most of the district's small black population is in Robbins, which has been majority-black for a generation, and Markham, which lost many of its white residents in the 1970s and is now about two-thirds black.

Russo lives in South Holland, which has a significant Dutch population but has also attracted Italians, Poles and others from Chicago's South Side. In many ways he is typical of the district: he grew up in an Italian neighborhood in the city and then lived in an apartment in Calumet Park before buying his South Holland home.

The area's voting patterns have been erratic in the past decade. Many of the people here are ethnics who emerged into prosperity in the 1960s, left the city, and began to vote Republican in some contests. When the old 3rd was drawn in 1972, containing most of the suburban territory in the new district, it was expected to send a Republican to the House. But it turned out GOP Rep. Robert Hanrahan for Democrat Russo in 1974, and returned Russo by comfortable margins for the rest of the decade. Many of these communities swing back and forth between the parties in state and national elections, choosing Republicans in better times and returning to the Democratic fold in years of recession.

District 4

Southern Chicago suburbs, Joliet, Aurora

Incumbents: Edward J. Derwinski (R)
George M. O'Brien (R)

The 4th is a new animal, built from remnants of the old 4th, 15th and 17th districts. It includes the southern end of Cook County, the section of Will County around the city of Joliet, and portions of Kane and Kendall counties

George M. O'Brien   **John G. Fary**

around the city of Aurora. This conglomeration is firmly Republican, although it has pockets of Democratic voters in Aurora, Joliet and Chicago Heights. The primary was the key election, where voters had to choose between fellow-incumbents Derwinski and O'Brien, who are allies and friends on Capitol Hill.

Derwinski's old 4th District, a suburban area that ran along the western edge of the city and then spread out to the southwest, was completely dismantled in the redistricting plan. Only Rich Township, an affluent suburban area that includes Derwinski's home of Flossmoor, was left in the new 4th. The rest of the old district was a casualty of the geographic realignment designed to preserve the Democratic districts in Chicago.

The mapmakers were far more kind to Rep. O'Brien. Although forced to give up Iroquois and Kankakee counties and the southern half of Will County, George M. O'Brien retains in the new 4th District his political base of Joliet, a largely blue-collar city of 78,000 that has several oil refineries.

Amoco, Mobil and Union Oil are major employers in Joliet, as is Caterpillar Tractor. Although once a major steel center, the city has lost most of its steel plants, including a U.S. Steel facility that shut down in late 1979. Joliet is also a center for barge traffic coming through the Chicago Sanitary and Ship Canal and for the Illinois Central railroad. O'Brien has been popular in Joliet, although it is essentially a Democratic city.

Both incumbent Republican candidates had some claim to Bloom Township, which has been in O'Brien's old 17th District but was represented by Derwinski for ten years before 1972. Bloom includes the blue-collar communities around the old industrial city of Chicago Heights, the site of the first steel-making facility in Chicago. Nearby Lansing, a bedroom community shifted from the 3rd District to the new 4th, is also former Derwinski territory.

New to both incumbents is the town of Aurora, about 60 percent of which is in the new 4th, and a section of Kendall County around the small town of Oswego. These areas had been in Republican Tom Corcoran's old 15th district. Aurora, a 19th century industrial city on the Fox River, still has a heavy equipment industry, including a Caterpillar plant.

O'Brien was the victor in the March 1982 GOP primary, garnering 54 percent of the vote to Derwinski's 46 percent.

District 5

South central Chicago and suburbs

Incumbent: John G. Fary (D)

Nearly twice the geographic size of the old 5th District, the new version begins about a mile from Lake Michigan and extends west to the split-levels of suburban Willow Springs, following the route of the Adlai Stevenson Expressway.

The 5th had to expand because it lost 15 percent of its population during the 1970s. But despite the realignment, it remains firmly Democratic territory; it keeps not only the home territory of the late Mayor Richard J. Daley, but also the political organization he dominated. The Daley machine has stayed intact in most of the city parts of the new 5th District, even though it has decayed elsewhere in Chicago.

Daley lived his entire life in Bridgeport, an almost exclusively Irish neighborhood, but Eastern Europeans, especially Poles, dominate the broader territory within the congressional district.

Some of the additions will increase the district's Republican vote. The new 5th picks up the Czech and Bohemian enclaves of Cicero and Berwyn, which have been voting Republican in most contests, and the white-collar suburbs of Bridgeview and Hickory Hills, which lean to the GOP.

But the inner suburban communities of McCook, Countryside, Hodgkins and Summit, all industrial, echo the Democratic tendencies of the Chicago part of the district. Reynolds Aluminum and General Motors have plants in this area, and Argo Cornstarch has an enormous operation in Summit. At the district's eastern end is the old Union Stockyards, a few blocks from the Daley home. Largely abandoned in the 1950s by the meatpacking industry, the huge Stockyards area has in recent years become an industrial park, with two dozen new warehouses and light industrial operations.

The racial makeup of the 5th changes dramatically. By 1980, the old 5th District had become 30 percent black, reflecting the movement of blacks into the southeastern part of the district, despite some white resistance. But the redistricting plan transferred these neighborhoods to the overwhelmingly black 1st District, and the suburbs brought into the 5th are virtually all white. As a result, only 3 percent of the residents of the new 5th District are black.

The new 5th does retain a significant Hispanic population. About a quarter of its people are Hispanic, up from 17 percent in the old 5th.

The defeat of Rep. John G. Fary in the March 1982 Republican primary had little to do with either issues or redrawn district boundaries. Fary lost because the bulk of the party organization that installed him in office and sustained his career scuttled him in favor of a younger man. William O. Lipinski, age 44, received 60.6 percent of the district vote.

District 6

Far West Chicago Suburbs — Wheaton

Incumbent: Henry J. Hyde (R)

Henry J. Hyde trades his old GOP constituency for one equally Republican but almost entirely unfamiliar to him. Fewer than 5 percent of his new constituents were in the district he represented in the 1970s.

Like the neighboring 4th, the old 6th was chopped up and grafted in pieces onto the western ends of inner-city Chicago districts that needed to gain population. Only a small area around Itasca and Wood Dale was carried over to the new 6th.

If Hyde feels disoriented, however, he has little to complain about politically. The old 6th, while it re-elected him comfortably, had pockets of Democratic strength in Maywood and other moderate-income suburbs with significant black populations. There are no such enclaves apparent in the new district, whose suburban territory is nearly all white-collar and Republican. The only political change necessary for Hyde may be a shift in attention from ethnic holidays and festivals to sessions with the Rotary and Jaycees.

The new 6th follows the route of two commuter railroad lines that drew Chicago residents westward as early as the 1930s. The suburbs of Elmhurst, Villa Park, Lombard, Glen Ellyn and Wheaton spread out from the city in the southern part of the district. Further north are Wood Dale, Itasca and Roselle, newer suburbs that are still undergoing expansion. Roselle has more than doubled in size since 1970. Schaumburg, which was still rural in 1960, has tripled in size during the past decade, with condominiums and apartment complexes cropping up around its enormous shopping center.

Less affluent is the area between the rail lines, including Glendale Heights and Addison, which have some light industry. A huge industrial park is located near Elk Grove Village, another fast-growing suburb to the north.

On its northeastern border, the new 6th District hooks into neighboring Cook County to take in the older, prosperous suburbs of Des Plaines and Park Ridge. Des Plaines adjoins O'Hare Airport and is the home of many airline employees.

Henry J. Hyde   **Cardiss Collins**

District 7

Chicago — Downtown, West Side

Incumbent: Cardiss Collins (D)

Only a few blocks west of Chicago's lakefront, with its elegant high-rises and nearby shops, the rank poverty of the West Side begins, with burned-out buildings and abandoned factories that stretch for miles. The West Side has traditionally been a port of entry for migrants to the city: Jews and Italians early in this century, and blacks in the past generation. Roosevelt Road, running west from downtown out to the city limits, was the urban riot corridor in the 1960s.

The old 7th lost one-fifth of its population in the past decade, but both parties wanted to preserve a black-majority district for Collins, the senior black member of the Illinois delegation. So the 7th was redrawn to stretch twice its previous length, from Lake Michigan more than a dozen miles west to suburban Bellwood. Mixed in among the residential areas are industrial zones, with a major A & P warehouse and Sears trucking facilities. The campus of the University of Illinois at Chicago Circle is in the district, along with the West Side medical center complex.

Much of the new territory is made up of areas such as Austin along the city's western border, traditionally Eastern European in ethnic makeup but increasingly black during the 1970s. Collins picks up these communities from Democrat Dan Rostenkowski's 8th District. Because of these moves, the 7th actually increases its black population from 50 percent to nearly 70 percent, despite the suburban additions.

Further west, the 7th does pick up some white-collar suburban territory, including Oak Park, one of the city's oldest suburbs, and Republican River Forest. The suburbs of Maywood and Bellwood are predominantly black and vote Democratic.

District 8

Chicago — North and Northwest Sides

Incumbent: Dan Rostenkowski (D)

Redistricting has given Rostenkowski just the constituency he wanted, and he should be able to hold it with little strain. The 8th District expands northwest along Milwaukee Avenue, Chicago's traditional "Polish corridor," to take in such symbolic places as St. Hyacinth Parish, still a first-stop for Polish immigrants and a spot where a question asked in Polish will draw a ready response.

The changes were probably necessary to preserve Rostenkowski's political control through the 1980s. In the past decade, his old 8th lost much of its ethnic Polish flavor as blacks and Hispanics moved into its southern and eastern portions, nearest to downtown Chicago. By 1980, only 49 percent of Rostenkowski's constituents were white.

The new 8th essentially follows Rostenkowski's old loyalists in their movement northwest from the inner city.

Dan Rostenkowski   **Sidney R. Yates**

It is more than 70 percent white, thanks to the addition not only of Polish neighborhoods within the city but of suburbs to the west, including River Grove and Elmwood Park. The new suburban constituents have voted Republican in the past, but they are largely ethnic, recently transplanted from the city and should respond well to Rostenkowski.

Another important change was the shift of the southern arm of the old 8th to Collins' new 7th. It was in this area, on Chicago's far West Side, that the black population of the old 8th had been concentrated. The new 8th is just 4 percent black.

Rostenkowski will, however, be representing a substantial Hispanic population, increased to more than 30 percent from the 27 percent in the old 8th. Lower Milwaukee Avenue, once the heart of the city's Polish community, is now overwhelmingly Hispanic. The 31st Ward has a strong Hispanic political organization.

District 9

Chicago — North Side lakefront, northern suburbs

Incumbent: Sidney R. Yates (D)

The most striking characteristic of the new 9th is its shape. Narrow at its base along Lake Michigan, it widens and turns westward once it reaches the city's northern limits, ending in a hook around the suburbs of Glenview and Northbrook. The purpose of the elaborate cartography was to create a secure district for Yates by including liberal areas within the city and heavily Jewish suburban communities where he should run well.

The old 9th was confined to the city, but it lost 10 percent of its population in the 1970s, forcing an expansion into the suburbs. The new 9th is still anchored on the North Side of Chicago, but it now runs north along the lake all the way to Evanston, and its western portion takes in Skokie, Wilmette, Morton Grove and a chunk of Northfield township. About 35 percent of the population is new to the district.

The city portion of the new 9th includes a mixture of neighborhoods, from the wealthy lakefront high-rises to the two- and three-story walkups just a few blocks to the west.

John E. Porter

Robert McClory

These apartments house many of the prosperous singles and childless couples who work in professional jobs in downtown Chicago. There is also an urban restoration contingent living in older homes in the area. The city portion of the 9th contains some of Chicago's few remaining GOP wards, but even here voters have been loyal to Yates.

The large Jewish population in the urban lakefront portion of the 9th is predominantly middle-aged, well-to-do and politically active. It has been the basis of Yates' strength in recent years. The 44th and 46th wards, west of the more prosperous neighborhoods, are mostly Hispanic; Hispanics comprise about 10 percent of the overall population of the district. The new 9th is also about 10 percent black. Minorities should also be solid Yates supporters.

The parts of the new 9th that lie beyond Chicago are not typically suburban in their political outlook. Evanston, once a bastion of conservative Republicanism, has a large liberal community around Northwestern University; it has also attracted young professional couples from Chicago in recent years, and they vote Democratic. Aiding the Democrats in Evanston is the racial makeup: the city of 74,000 is about 30 percent black. Morton Grove, west of Evanston, has passed the nation's most stringent gun control law. Morton Grove and neighboring Skokie both are heavily Jewish.

North and west of these communities, in Maine and Northfield townships, are newer suburban developments where voters generally preferred Reagan to Carter in 1980. Their addition to the district has given Republicans some optimism that they can win the 9th in a good Republican year or upon Yates' retirement. But it would take an exceptionally strong campaign.

District 10

North and Northwest Suburbs — Waukegan

Incumbents: John E. Porter (R)
Robert McClory (R)

When Porter's Evanston home was placed in the Democratic 9th by redistricting, he announced he would move north to challenge McClory in the 10th, where Re-

publican loyalties are solid. But the showdown never took place. The 74-year-old McClory, after announcing and filing for an 11th term, said in January 1982 that he was stepping down to make room for his younger colleague.

The communities along Lake Michigan north of Chicago are the city's oldest suburbs, and generally its most affluent. Fully developed long ago, they declined in population in the 1970s as the younger residents grew up and moved away. To erase the resulting population deficit in Porter's old 10th District, centered on these communities, the mapmakers moved it north to merge with portions of Republican Philip M. Crane's 13th District and McClory's old 12th, based in Waukegan. The new 10th extends north to the Wisconsin border, including McClory's old lakefront towns but shedding most of the newer suburban territory further west.

The hybrid district is firmly Republican. The only major Democratic enclave is the old port city of Waukegan, now a manufacturing center producing pharmaceuticals, hospital supplies and outboard motors. About a quarter of Waukegan's population is Hispanic.

Much of the district's vote will be cast in affluent Lake County towns such as Highland Park, Lake Forest and Deerfield, where most voters tend to prefer moderate Republicans but rarely cross over to the Democratic side. Porter fits this area well. Many of the people who live here commute to professional jobs in downtown Chicago, but in recent years corporate outposts have sprung up among the bedroom communities. Allstate and Kemper Insurance, Walgreens' and Household Finance all are major employers in the district.

Also in the 10th is the Great Lakes Naval Training Center, on the lake near North Chicago. The largest such operation in the country, it is the work place for 22,000 military and 3,000 civilian employees.

Almost 80 percent of the population is new to Porter. About half comes from Crane's old 12th and 30 percent from McClory's old 13th. But the 20 percent that Porter keeps generally includes the most loyal Republicans in his old constituency. As a whole, the district gave Reagan 60 percent of its vote in 1980.

District 11

Northwest Chicago and suburbs

Incumbent: Frank Annunzio (D)

Concentrated entirely within Chicago during the past decade, the 11th District takes on new Republican territory in the suburbs but still seems likely to provide a base for Annunzio. The veteran Democrat successfully transplanted himself a decade ago, when his old West Side district was eliminated, and he is already working on a similar effort. Many of his new suburban constituents moved out in the 1970s from the old 7th District; like other Chicago Democrats, Annunzio is simply following them to the suburbs.

"These are my people," Rep. Annunzio said recently. "Lincolnwood? My daughter lives in Lincolnwood. Stone Park? There's a seminary there for Italian priests, and an Italian-American cultural center. Northlake? That's where we have an Italian old folks' home."

The redrawn 11th stretches north to Niles and west to O'Hare Airport, taking in a collection of middle-class suburban developments built in the 1950s and early 1960s. Its residents are largely ethnic in background, but they have moved beyond their blue-collar roots; many of them voted for Republican candidates in statewide elections during the past decade. Suburban Leyden and Norwood Park townships, both located almost entirely within the new 11th, voted for Reagan by comfortable margins in 1980. It remains to be seen whether Annunzio can hold these people; for 1982, at least, he seems secure.

The city part of Annunzio's district was left intact except for a chunk in the southeast section shifted to Rostenkowski's 8th district. Added to the eastern side of the 11th were some city neighborhoods from Yates' 9th District. These should be reliably Democratic.

Like the old 11th, the new district is overwhelmingly white. About 6 percent of the population is Hispanic; less than 1 percent is black. The substantial Jewish community in Rogers Park, within the city limits, will be joined by a large Jewish population in part of Skokie, which has been split between the 11th and the 9th.

District 12

Far Northwest Suburbs — Palatine

Incumbent: Philip M. Crane (R)

Crane's new district contains only 46 percent of the people who lived in his old 12th, but the veteran GOP conservative can take his time getting to know his new constituents. Crane faces no opposition either for renomination or re-election.

The lack of competition is a clue to the political makeup of the district. Crane's new 12th is even more Republican than the old one, which cast 62 percent of its votes for Reagan in 1980.

The population center of the new district will still be the outer suburban area of Chicago, including Palatine and Hoffman Estates, which have grown dramatically during the past 20 years. But the geography of the district has been totally revised. In the past decade, Crane represented the populous southern portion of Lake County, including wealthy lakefront suburbs such as Highland Park and Deerfield. For the 1980s, he has been moved north and west, taking on semi-rural McHenry County and only the western two-thirds of Lake.

Arlington Heights, the largest city Crane now represents, has been shifted to Porter's new 10th District.

The new 12th has both suburban and farm-oriented voting blocs. The western part of McHenry County still has dairy farms and small market towns. The largest city in McHenry is Woodstock, with fewer than 12,000 residents. But suburbia encroached on the county in the 1970s, and may continue to do so. There is good rapid transit from this area to downtown Chicago.

The new alignment all but removes the district from the metropolitan Chicago political orbit. When Crane won his first term in 1969, his district took in most of northern Cook County. But population increases forced that constituency to be split in two, and Crane chose to run in 1972

in the newer suburban area to the northwest, which was more Republican. Now the lines move again, and not an inch of Crane's original territory remains in the new district.

District 13

Southwest Chicago Suburbs — Downers Grove

Incumbent: John N. Erlenborn (R)

The new 13th moves out of Du Page County to concentrate much of its vote in Cook County suburbs nearer to Chicago, but it keeps its political and economic character. It is one of the most affluent districts in the country, and is certain to return Erlenborn to Congress in November 1982. Erlenborn turned back a primary challenge from a conservative state senator.

Because it grew during the 1970s by 34.8 percent — more than any other district in the state — Erlenborn's old 14th had to be redrawn. In the past decade, its lines were virtually identical with those of Du Page County. Now Du Page will cast barely 50 percent of the vote. About 44 percent will be cast within Cook County.

The most densely populated areas of the new district cluster along the old Burlington Northern tracks that extend west from the city to Riverside, Western Springs, Hinsdale, Clarendon and Downers Grove. The cul-de-sacs of Riverside, one of the first planned suburban developments in the area, were copied again and again as suburbia crept along the railroad line, out from Cook County into Du Page. By shifting the district to the east, closer to the city, the remap gives up a set of 1960s suburbs and takes on an older group.

The only blue-collar territory in the new 13th is in Broadview, Lisle and Westmont, prewar industrial suburbs. But any Democratic votes in these areas will be canceled out by the affluent communities surrounding them.

In the geographic center of the new district is the Argonne National Laboratory, a federal energy research center that employs about 5,000 people. At the southern end of Cook County, the district opens up to rolling

Frank Annunzio   **Philip M. Crane**

countryside, with pockets of new residential developments. Much of the Cook County park system is located in this area. The district also includes a corner of Will County, located between Joliet and Chicago, which is largely undeveloped. Only 4 percent of the vote will be cast in Will County.

District 14

North Central — De Kalb, Elgin

Incumbent: Tom Corcoran (R)

The new 14th stretches from Naperville, whose commuters hop the train for Chicago, south to Wenona, a crossroads farm town that serves the surrounding agricultural community in Marshall County. In between, in the valleys of the Illinois and Fox rivers, are a host of light industrial plants, including two large glassworks in Ottawa and Streator.

The semi-industrial character of the district does not interfere with its Republican loyalties; the four counties that will cast most of the vote — Kane, De Kalb, Kendall and La Salle — all went for Reagan easily in 1980. All but La Salle even went for the badly beaten GOP Senate nominee, Dave O'Neal.

Located on the Fox River is Elgin, the largest city in the district. Elgin began as an industrial center; its name is on many of the country's street sweepers. In recent years, however, it has become a suburban outpost for white-collar Chicagoans who have settled on its east side, within Cook County. The 14th also includes the portion of industrial Aurora on the western side of the Fox River, which contains the city's white-collar residential section. Elgin and Aurora together give Kane County about 40 percent of the district's population.

The only other large city in the district is De Kalb, an agricultural research center and site of Northern Illinois University, which has about 20,000 students. Ronald Reagan's 1980 showing was weaker in De Kalb than in any of the district's other counties, not because Jimmy Carter was strong but because John B. Anderson drew nearly 10 percent of the vote.

John N. Erlenborn   **Tom Corcoran**

Unlike Corcoran's old 15th, which was predominantly rural and extended further downstate, the 14th is a mixture of suburban and agricultural interests. Corn and soybeans remain important to the economy in De Kalb and La Salle counties, where the farm land is among the richest in the country. But there is a new orientation toward Chicago with the added territory in Du Page and Kane counties.

Redistricting has complicated the geography of the district. Up to now, Corcoran has represented nine full counties and part of a tenth. But his new 14th has only one complete county and parts of eight others. Cook, McHenry, Boone and Marshall counties each come into the district, but each has less than 1 percent of the overall population. The district line cuts right through Aurora and Elgin; about 2,000 Elgin residents were placed in Crane's 12th.

District 15

Central — Bloomington, Kankakee

Incumbent: Edward R. Madigan (R)

Madigan, whose old 21st District was a compact area in the heart of the state, will find himself campaigning this year in a constituency that sprawls north from his hometown of Lincoln in the center of the state all the way to the edge of Chicago's suburbs.

Redistricting essentially dismantled the old 21st District. After carving away the population centers of Decatur and Champaign/Urbana, the mapmakers combined the remainder of the district with the southern sections of the old 17th and 15th districts, most of them sparsely populated. About 57 percent of the constituents are new to Madigan.

Like the old 15th, however, Madigan's new district is traditional Republican farm country. Corn and soybean counties such as Iroquois and Ford are among the most Republican in the state; both gave Reagan more than two-thirds of their 1980 vote. The Will and Kankakee County portions of the district include numerous truck farms whose products are sold at Chicago area markets.

Madigan's old 21st had a core Democratic vote in the university towns of Champaign and Urbana, and in industrial Decatur. Madigan had a close call in 1972 before settling down to comfortable pluralities. The new 15th should be even safer for him. Even its small cities are Republican.

Bloomington, with about 44,000 residents, and nearby Normal, with about 36,000, comprise the major population centers in the new district. They are linked by Illinois State University and Illinois Wesleyan University; also in Bloomington is the national headquarters of State Farm Insurance, the largest car insurer in the world. In Kankakee, chemical plants are major employers, as is the Roper Appliance Company, which makes stoves for Sears. Rantoul, with about 20,000 residents, is dominated by the Chanute Air Force Base.

Madigan will find it prudent to take an interest in nuclear power. Although the old 21st had no operating nuclear plants and just one under construction, the new 15th includes three operating plants in Grundy County, two under construction in southeast LaSalle County, and a major nuclear-waste storage facility in Morris.

Edward R. Madigan   Lynn Martin

District 16

Northwest — Rockford

Incumbent: Lynn Martin (R)

Even though it includes the industrial city of Rockford, the 16th has not elected a Democrat to the House in this century, and redistricting changes it very little. While districts all around it were undergoing major surgery, the 16th was preserved virtually intact and will nestle compactly in the northwest corner of the state, much as it did in the 1950s.

The district does take in two new counties, Carroll and Whiteside, which border the Mississippi River. They replace Boone and part of McHenry County, which were pared away. But about 90 percent of the population is carried over from the old 16th. The most populous county is Winnebago, where about 50 percent of the district's vote will be cast. Rockford, the seat of Winnebago County, is the second-largest city in Illinois.

There is substantial industry in the district. Rockford has a large blue-collar population that is unionized in plants making machine tools, automotive parts, agricultural implements and defense-related aviation equipment. Nearby Belvidere in Boone County has a Chrysler plant. Freeport, just west of Rockford in Stephenson County, produces computer parts and tires. But all three of these industrial counties vote consistently Republican in most state elections.

The rest of the district is largely rural, settled by Germans, Swedes and Yankees transplanted from New England. It ranks first in the state in dairy farming. The northwest corner of the district is a popular vacation area, with antique stores and state parks scattered throughout hilly Jo Daviess County.

Two small towns in the 16th District were home to Ronald Reagan; he was born in Tampico and grew up in Dixon. John B. Anderson, who is from Rockford, represented the 16th as a Republican in the House of Representatives for two decades until he ran for president in the 1980 election. Anderson's neighbors in Winnebago County gave him approximately 22 percent of their presidential vote — his second-best countywide showing in the country.

District 17

West — Rock Island, Moline, Galesburg

Incumbent: Tom Railsback (R)

Cradled between the Mississippi and Illinois rivers, the 17th is prime farm land where most corn and soybean growers can survive even bad years. In the northern part of the district, in Bureau and Henry counties, billboards proclaim the area the "Hog Capital of the World."

The urban center of the district is at its northwestern edge, in Rock Island County, where Rock Island and Moline make up the Illinois half of the "Quad Cities." (The Iowa cities are Davenport and Bettendorf.) Together, Rock Island and Moline have more than 90,000 residents.

The Rock Island Arsenal employs 8,000 defense workers who produce guns and bullets for the U.S. government, continuing an activity begun in 1862. Also in Rock Island and Moline is one of the country's most intensive concentrations of farm equipment manufacturing. Deere & Company is headquartered at Moline, and, along with International Harvester, has several plants elsewhere in the district. New to the redrawn 17th are a plant and two foundries operated by the Caterpillar Tractor Company outside of Peoria.

Times are bad for the agricultural implement industry, however, and the unemployment rate in the Quad Cities in early 1982 was more than 15 percent. Also in trouble is Galesburg, which was shifted back to Railsback's territory after a 10-year absence. A city of 35,000, Galesburg recently lost its second largest employer, a lawn mower manufacturer who moved south. A machine tool plant there has also closed, helping to push the unemployment rate to 20 percent.

Like Railsback's old 19th District, the new 17th tilts Republican, although it is more competitive between the parties than other downstate districts. Labor in Rock Island County provides a substantial Democratic base, but the rural areas usually outvote the cities of Rock Island, Moline and Galesburg. Railsback's moderate House voting record has allowed him to carry portions of these cities that prefer Democrats in statewide contests.

This year, however, the lines were somewhat less favorable for the incumbent. While the district is no less

Tom Railsback   Robert H. Michel

Daniel B. Crane   **Paul N. Findley**

Republican, about 30 percent of the population is new, nearly all of it in the rural counties at the eastern end. This was the basis of the conservative primary challenge launched against Railsback by livestock farmer Kenneth McMillan. McMillan's agricultural background and conservative views brought him strong support in the rural areas of the new 17th. Besides gaining unfamiliar territory, Railsback lost Carroll, Whiteside and Hancock counties, Mississippi River territory where he had performed well, along with part of McDonough and Fulton counties.

McMillan won the Republican primary with 51.1 percent of the vote.

District 18

Central — Peoria

Incumbent: Robert H. Michel (R)

The 18th zigs and zags from Peoria south to the outskirts of Decatur and Springfield, and west to Hancock County on the Mississippi. A mostly rural area, it is linked by the broad Illinois River basin, ideal for growing corn. The only major urban area is Peoria, with 124,000 residents, and neighboring Pekin, with 34,000.

Michel, the House Republican leader, follows a long line of Republican representatives that includes Everett M. Dirksen, the late Senate GOP leader. The GOP may even be a bit stronger within the new district lines than in the old ones; Reagan's 1980 vote was 60 percent in the old 18th, and 61.2 percent in the new one.

Michel's hometown of Peoria, however, is a troubled industrial city. It is dominated by the international headquarters of the Caterpillar Tractor Company, which employs more than 30,000 people in the district at five different plants. But Peoria has lost much of its other industry in the past decade, including a once-thriving brewery. Pekin is a grain processing and shipping center; it produces ethanol, both for fuel and for drink.

Outside the Peoria environs, the 18th has been drastically rearranged. In the 1960s Peoria anchored the southern end of the district; in the 1970s it was in the center. Now it is perched at the northern tip. Peoria and Tazewell

counties are the only territory remaining from the district that elected Michel in 1970.

As a result, the Republican leader faces a constituency about 45 percent new to him. Michel once represented eight counties and most of a ninth, but now he is responsible not only for eight complete counties but parts of eight more. It is still a Republican district — seven of the eight full counties gave Reagan at least 60 percent of the vote in 1980 — but it will not be an easy one to represent, especially at a time when it is hit hard by recession.

District 19

Southeast — Danville, Champaign-Urbana

Incumbent: Daniel B. Crane (R)

The new 19th is part of the Midwest Corn Belt on the north and strictly southern Illinois on the south. The corn-growing areas are fertile and the farms profitable. The southern counties are less prosperous and devoted more to general farming.

Politically, the district tends to divide along the same lines. Yankee Republicans settled the northern portion of the district, while conservative Democrats migrating from below the Mason-Dixon Line settled the southern part.

Before Crane's emergence in 1978, the old 22nd District, similar to the new 19th, elected Democrat George Shipley by comfortable margins. But Crane has done well even in the southern counties, where his conservative views have appealed to both parties. He outpolled Reagan in 1980 in the old 22nd.

Crane has been given a constituency in which 28 percent of the people are new to him. He loses four counties in the center of the state — Christian, Fayette, Shelby and Moultrie — all traditionally Democratic. Christian, a coal-mining county, has a strong Democratic organization. To make up for the loss of population, Crane picked up Hamilton and White counties in the south and the urban portion of Champaign County around the University of Illinois.

In Crane's old 22nd district, the largest city was Danville, with about 40,000 residents. But Champaign and Urbana together have about 95,000 people, and the univer-

Melvin Price   **Paul Simon**

sity influence leads them into the Democratic column in most contests. They could cause Crane some problems in the long run. Remaining in the district is Danville, an industrial and farm market center. Danville has significant Democratic strength, but it is Crane's home and he has done well there. General Motors is a major employer there.

Hamilton and White counties, on the district's new southern border, are laced with stripper oil wells. White is the major oil-producing county in the state, and Hamilton is not far behind. A huge coal mine is also under construction in White County.

District 20

Central — Springfield, Decatur, Quincy

Incumbent: Paul N. Findley (R)

Redistricting has complicated Paul N. Findley's life and threatens his career in the House. By design, his new 20th District is considerably more Democratic than the one he has been representing.

The new map drawn up by Democrats weakens him by expanding the district east to Christian, Shelby and Moultrie counties — traditional Democratic territory where southern folksiness has traditionally played better than Findley's Yankee politics of issues and moral principle. It also includes Decatur, an industrial city of nearly 100,000 that often votes Democratic.

Meanwhile, the 20th loses the reliably Republican suburbs of Springfield, and nearby Scott and Morgan counties, also good Findley territory. The result is a marginal district that the incumbent will have to work to hold, although he does carry over about 65 percent of the constituents in his old 20th. Findley keeps the town of Quincy, on the Mississippi River, and the inner-city part of Springfield, with the state capitol and a substantial bloc of white-collar workers in state government. Springfield is the district's largest city, and altogether the portion of Sangamon County included in the district will cast more than a quarter of the vote.

Agriculture remains the economic base of the district, thanks to the rich bottom lands of the Illinois and Mississippi rivers. Hogs, corn and soybeans are important; the soybean market in Decatur sets prices for a large area of the Midwest. But coal takes on additional importance in the new 20th, with the addition of the mining counties of Christian, Shelby and Moultrie. Macoupin County had already given the district the third largest coal mine in the world.

District 21

Southwest — East St. Louis, Alton

Incumbent: Melvin Price (D)

Like Price's old 23rd District, the new 21st is dominated by the grimy industrial region located across the river from St. Louis. Steel, petroleum refining and glass are the dominant industries, although they are in serious decline. Southern St. Clair County has an active coal industry, with major strip-mining operations. East of the river are rural areas devoted to dairy farming, wheat, soybeans and corn.

East St. Louis is still the largest city in the district, but it is a shell of its former self. Abandoned by manufacturing firms, the city is also losing most of its remaining retail stores. About 21 percent of its population has left in the past 10 years, leaving the city about the size it was in 1910.

East St. Louis is overwhelmingly black, while neighboring Belleville to the south and Granite City to the north are predominantly white. Of the three blue-collar communities, Belleville is the most viable; many of its residents commute to work in St. Louis. Further north is the old river port of Alton, now an industrial community producing steel.

Previously composed only of St. Clair County and half of neighboring Madison, the 21st had to expand significantly to make up its population deficit. It now includes all of Madison and Bond, all but two townships in St. Clair, and sections of Montgomery and Clinton counties.

This poses no immediate problem for the 77-year-old Price. At some point in his 37-year congressional career, Price has represented most of the area added to the 21st. And thanks largely to St. Clair County, the 21st remains the only rock-solid Democratic district outside the Chicago area. St. Clair was one of only three Illinois counties that voted for Carter in 1980.

District 22

South — Carbondale

Incumbent: Paul Simon (D)

At the southern tip of Illinois the prairies give way to hilly countryside, and coal replaces large-scale farming as a dominant economic activity. About 15,000 miners work in the Illinois Basin, a coal vein that runs under Franklin, Williamson, Saline, Perry and Jefferson counties. The people here are descendants of 19th century settlers from Kentucky, Tennessee and other parts of the South; they are traditional Democrats, although those loyalties are gradually changing.

The new 22nd is similar in outline to the old 24th, but it has been redrawn for the benefit of Simon, its liberal Democratic incumbent, who escaped defeat by fewer than 2,000 votes in 1980. The most important change is the addition of heavily Democratic territory in St. Clair County. Simon takes on Centreville and Sugar Loaf townships, on the southern outskirts of East St. Louis, urbanized blue-collar areas that had been in Price's old 23rd District.

Simon also loses two counties — Hamilton and White — that are historically Democratic but turned against him in 1980. Oil royalty holders there were disappointed in Simon's vote for the oil windfall profits tax, which reduced their income from the area's productive stripper wells. In a separate exchange, marginal Bond County was moved to the 21st, and Fayette, slightly more Democratic, was given to Simon in replacement.

Carbondale and the other small cities of the 22nd lie along the Main Street of the district: state Route 13. Carbondale is dominated by Southern Illinois University, with 23,000 students.

At the southern tip of the district is Alexander County, in the region called "Little Egypt." The depressed river town of Cairo is its county seat. Alexander County gave Jimmy Carter 51 percent of its vote in 1980, making it second only to Cook County in its Democratic presidential showing.

Indiana

Of the nation's major industrial states, Indiana is probably the least typical. It is more conservative and more Republican than its counterparts. Only once since 1936 have the state's voters chosen the Democratic presidential nominee, Lyndon B. Johnson in 1964.

It is less urbanized, with a higher percentage of people living in rural areas. And it has held its own in population better than most other industrial states: its loss of one congressional seat in 1980 was the first since 1940.

Indiana's conservatism pervades both parties, and comes from a variety of factors. There is a Southern influence in the state that goes back to the early 19th century, when southern Indiana was settled by pioneers from Kentucky and Virginia. Until recently, that meant Democratic dominance in the southern part of the state. But the Democratic politics that prevailed were Southern-style. In 1976, when Jimmy Carter ran for president, 24 of the 27 Indiana counties he carried were in the southern half of the state.

Indiana has fewer Eastern and Southern European immigrants and fewer blacks than other industrial states. Ethnic and minority votes that contributed to the strength of New Deal Democrats in Michigan and Illinois were not as much of a factor in Indiana. The state has only one center of major ethnic strength — Lake County, with huge steel and petrochemical industries. The small- to medium-sized industrial centers elsewhere in the state have drawn their work force from the countryside or the South. Germans, the state's most prominent ethnic group in the beginning, have for generations been largely a white-collar and professional group and a conservative political force.

Given all that, Democrats have won more than their share of elections in Indiana in recent years, thanks to a combination of good candidates and good luck.

The 1958 recession brought a Senate victory for Democrat Vance Hartke, and while he never developed much of a personal following in the state, he managed to run for reelection in two more very good years, 1964 and 1970. His luck finally ran out in 1976, when Republican Richard Lugar defeated him.

Meanwhile, Democrat Birch Bayh won a Senate term in 1962 on a combination of hard work and Hoosier folksiness. The same combination allowed him to survive a liberal Senate voting record in 1968 and 1974, giving the state two liberal Democratic senators for a period of 14 years — a situation it remedied fully by defeating Bayh in 1980.

Indiana is traditionally a straight-ticket state. Democrats took advantage of that in 1974 to turn a 7-4 Republican House delegation into a 9-2 Democratic delegation. Many of that year's Democratic winners proved to be good politicians, and even today Democrats have a 6-5 edge.

But those days are probably ending. Indiana Republicans redrew the district lines in early 1981 for the express purpose of unseating three Democratic congressmen, and even if they do not get all three, the 1980s appear to promise that Indiana will be voting as conservatively in Washington as it has been doing at home.

Northern Industrial Tier

Indiana's premier industrial region is its waterfront along Lake Michigan in the northwest corner of the state. It was here that U. S. Steel decided in 1905 to build one of the largest steel plants in the world and thus created the city of Gary, named after the company's president. The three Lake County cities of Hammond, Gary and East Chicago became an industrial strip, more like industrial Chicago, Detroit or Cleveland than like the rest of Indiana. Lake County attracted East European immigrants and a large black community. An often-corrupt county machine regularly delivered Democratic majorities.

A growing black presence in Gary led to racial tensions in the 1960s and to the election of a black mayor, Richard Hatcher, in 1967. That weakened the hold of the Democratic machine, which unsuccessfully fought his election.

Republicans are concentrated in suburban communities in central Lake County. Reagan proved attractive to these voters in 1980, and his suburban strength allowed him to come within 6,000 votes of carrying the county.

Reagan also made inroads into the ethnic Democratic vote in this area. Hurt by troubles in the steel industry and alienated by the Democratic Party's identification with liberal social causes, many steelworkers in Lake County decided to try the GOP at the presidential level, while remaining Democratic for other offices.

Moving eastward from Lake County, the density of industry declines. But there is a series of industrial communities along the railway lines that traverse northern Indiana on their way to and from Chicago. Chief among them are South Bend and Fort Wayne.

South Bend has been heavily dependent on the transportation industry and was badly hurt by the 1980 recession — one reason it threw 22-year veteran Democratic Rep. John Brademas out of office in November 1980. South Bend is essentially Democratic, making St. Joseph County as a whole strongly competitive between the parties.

Fort Wayne, better diversified economically than South Bend, has been better able to maintain its economic health. Despite its industry, it has never been a strong Democratic city, partly because of its conservative German element. Most small rural counties in the area are Republican.

The Corn Belt

Rolling across northern and central Indiana is one of America's most productive agricultural regions, part of the Corn Belt that stretches all the way to the Missouri River. The rich soil and favorable weather conditions of this area have both contributed to produce a prosperous, mostly conservative farm population that is usually a backbone of Republican strength.

The corn and hog economy is the underpinning of the region. In some counties, hogs outnumber people. But the area is studded with a series of small industrial cities such as Lafayette, Kokomo, Anderson and Muncie.

The cities manufacture a variety of products, however automobiles and auto parts have a large share of the employment. The strength of the United Auto Workers labor union among the large blue-collar work force reduces the Republican vote in parts of the area. Nevertheless, the Republican Party plays a predominant role in most of the local governments and usually carries their counties in presidential elections. They have not fared as well in congressional elections, however; much of this region has been represented by Democrats during the 1970s.

Indianapolis

Indianapolis has managed to do something that other Northern cities have longed to do but have not accomplished: expand its boundaries to take in much of the suburban ring surrounding it. This was accomplished in 1969 with the establishment of a unified governmental structure — called Unigov — that combined Indianapolis and Marion County.

The political results of this move were significant. Republican votes in the formerly suburban part of Marion County gave the GOP control of the unified government. Before Unigov, Indianapolis was predominantly Democratic. Since Republican Mayor (now senator) Richard Lugar pushed Unigov through the state Legislature in 1967, the Republican Party has not lost control of City Hall.

In broader elections, Marion County generally reflects the statewide choice. In every election since 1920, it has given the majority of its vote to the candidate who carried the rest of the state. When Democrats do carry the county, it is not by the margins that they receive in the largest cities of other industrial states. Indianapolis has a substantial black population and some labor union strength, but it remains one of the most conservative of all Midwestern cities.

Southern Indiana

From the Civil War to recent times, Indiana was divided politically between a Republican North and a Democratic South.

Southern Indiana was the earliest-settled area of the state, with migrants coming in from neighboring Kentucky or other Southern states. The land is not as flat or fertile as the northern Corn Belt area. There is a substantial amount of coal here, abandoned for years but now being worked because of the energy crunch.

Voters here are conservative, but have retained much of their Democratic political heritage. While the liberalism of the national Democratic Party during the 1960s and early 1970s alienated many southern Indiana Democrats, they continue to support local Democratic candidates. Most of the counties in this section of the state are controlled by Democrats and the bulk of the state's Democratic contingent in the state Legislature usually comes from this area.

Among the urban centers in this region are the old coal and railroad town of Terre Haute and the university city of Bloomington, both Democratic; Columbus, with its large white-collar engineering community; and Evansville, the state's second-largest city, an old Ohio River town trying to revitalize its economy.

Evansville and surrounding Vanderburgh County form an island of Republican strength in the rural Democratic sea. The 19th century German settlers of Evansville established the pro-Union Republican tradition. The area has maintained that flavor, with the county voting Republican in every presidential election but one since 1952.

CLASSIC GERRYMANDER BY INDIANA REPUBLICANS

Gerrymandering was resurrected in Indiana this year when the Republican Party, in complete control of the Legislature and the governor's office, redrew congressional district lines in a way that seriously jeopardizes three of the state's six Democratic incumbents.

Forced to drop one of the state's 11 districts, Indiana Republicans carefully carved through counties and townships to concentrate most of the Democratic vote in three constituencies and spread the Republican vote thickly and evenly across the rest of the state.

The plan is likely to shift the state's House delegation from its current 6-to-5 Democratic majority to at least a 6-to-4 majority for Republicans, and possibly 7-to-3. The uncertainty revolves around the new 2nd District, where Democratic incumbent Philip R. Sharp will try to win a fifth term despite losing much of his old district and having several new Republican areas added.

Democratic Reps. Floyd Fithian and David W. Evans were even more seriously hurt than Sharp. Fithian's district in the northwestern part of the state was cut up four ways, effectively eliminating any hope he had of re-election. He has decided to run for the Senate, challenging Republican incumbent Richard G. Lugar.

Evans' district in and around Indianapolis was also divided among four new districts, leaving him with a series of options, none very attractive. He finally decided on a primary challenge against fellow Democrat Andrew Jacobs Jr. in the new 10th District in Indianapolis, which should be reliably Democratic for whoever wins the nomination.

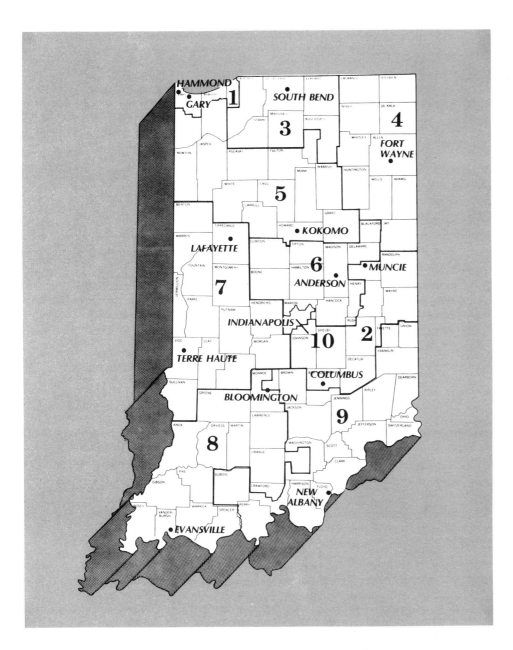

New Indiana Districts

U. S. Congress: 10 districts
  Senate (2R)
  House (6D, 5R)
Governor:
  Robert D. Orr (R)
Population: 5,490,197
Area: 36,291 sq. miles
1980 Presidential Vote:
  Carter (38%)
  Reagan (56%)
  Anderson (5%)

Even though the state lost a district, Republicans were able to carve out a new constituency north of Indianapolis without a resident incumbent. This 6th District has the highest GOP vote of any new district in the state. Winning agreement on the exact location of the new 6th was difficult because several ambitious GOP politicians live in the area and wanted to have the option of running there in 1982.

The partisan map, drawn up by Allan Sutherlin, former executive director of the state Republican Party, was not shown to the legislators until the last day of the legislative session, April 30, 1981. It was attached to an unrelated bill and presented to the Indiana House.

Although the plan had received final approval the night before from the state's Republican congressmen and GOP legislative leaders, many Republican legislators were upset by the last-minute timing. As a result, the plan was initially rejected in the House by a 47-51 vote. The Republican leadership hastily called a caucus, explained the new

map and assured a handful of legislators loyal to Republicans Dan Coats and Joel Deckard that both representatives were happy with their new district lines.

Democrats introduced an alternative plan that had a smaller population deviation than the Republican version and that split only one county. But it was quickly rejected when Republican legislators fell back into line. The House then adopted the Republican plan it had earlier rejected by a 53-42 vote. The bill was sent the same day to the Senate, where it won quick approval on a 32-13 vote. It was signed May 5, 1981 by Gov. Robert D. Orr.

The population difference between the new districts will be 3.1 percent, compared to just over 0.2 percent for the plan that was adopted in 1971. The largest district, the 3rd, is 1.7 percent above the ideal, and the smallest, the newly created 6th District, is 1.4 percent below the ideal.

Democrats, labor leaders and some civic groups talked about filing a suit against the plan charging that the popu-

Adam Benjamin Jr. **Philip R. Sharp**

lation variance was too large and that the lines were drawn with purely political motives. However, in late September the state's Democratic congressional delegation opted against a suit. By then, most of the incumbents were already running in their new districts and did not welcome the added uncertainty of a court case.

District 1

Industrial Belt — Gary, Hammond

Incumbent: Adam Benjamin Jr. (D)

For the first time in half a century, redistricting has pushed the 1st District beyond the borders of Lake County. Stretching from the Illinois border at Hammond to Michigan City, 40 miles to the east, the new district covers the entire Indiana shore line along Lake Michigan. It extends inland only slightly beyond the congested and polluted lakefront industrial area.

The district's industrial base and large black population in Gary make it the state's most Democratic territory. Although Jimmy Carter drew only 50 percent of the vote in 1980 within the new district lines, this was still a higher percentage than he received in any other district in the state.

The Democratic strength in the new district lies principally within Lake County, which will cast more than 80 percent of the vote. Centered on Gary, the state's third largest city with 151,000 people, and Hammond, with a population just under 100,000, the new district carefully avoids the increasingly Republican parts of the county found roughly south of U. S. Route 30.

Incumbent Benjamin also will be receiving the more Democratic parts of LaPorte and Porter counties in his new constituency. Although not as strongly Democratic as the Lake County portion of the district, northern Porter County and Michigan City in LaPorte County are heavily industrial and blue-collar oriented. Porter County contains Burns Harbor, the state's only shipping port. There are also several steel mills and the state prison in the area. Many of the steel and oil refinery workers from Gary and Hammond have moved out to this area.

Of the six Democrats in the Indiana delegation, Benjamin was the only one pleased with what the Legislature did to his district. He is delighted to have the entire Indiana Dunes National Lakeshore in his new district. The area used to be split among three districts, which caused some rivalries among the various members of the delegation who hoped to draw credit for the project's creation.

District 2

East Central — Muncie, Richmond

Incumbents: Philip R. Sharp (D),

Probably more by happenstance than design, Republicans included the homes of half the state's Democratic delegation within the boundaries of the new 2nd District. But the situation soon sorted itself out. Hamilton will give up his home in Columbus, newly placed in the 2nd, and move to the new 9th District, which contains most of his old district and has no incumbent. Evans, whose home was in Johnson County, had a more difficult decision, but eventually decided to move to Indianapolis and run in the new 10th District. That leaves the new 2nd to Sharp, who has represented the eastern side of it since 1974.

But with fewer than half of his old constituents living in the new 2nd District, Sharp faces a tough fight to stay in office. Potential Republican challengers include two prominent local officials. State Sen. Charles Bosma, who had a role in the creation of the new map, considered entering the race but decided against it.

Sharp's new district retains his hometown of Muncie, but loses part of surrounding Delaware County. With the Delaware County portion of the district reduced from one-quarter to less than one-fifth of the total vote, Sharp will be forced to shift his attention more to the Indianapolis end of the new J-shaped 2nd District. There he confronts an additional 86,000 constituents from Indianapolis (Marion County) and another 77,000 from suburban Johnson County.

Sharp's allies point out that the incumbent is already known in the Indianapolis area because he has used the Indianapolis television market in the past to reach the western side of his old district. They also note that since

John Hiler **Dan Coats**

New Indiana Districts

New District	Incumbent	Incumbent's Current District	Population	1980 Presidential Winner
1	Adam Benjamin Jr. (D)	1	550,013	Carter
2	Philip R. Sharp (D)	10	553,425	Reagan
3	John Hiler (R)	3		
4	Dan Coats (R)	4		
5	Elwood Hillis (R)	5	558,348	Reagan
6	No Incumbent		553,698	Reagan
7	John T. Myers (R)	7	555,191	Reagan
8	Joel Deckard (R)	8	541,357	Reagan
9	Lee H. Hamilton (D)	9*	555,191	Reagan
10	Andrew Jacobs Jr. D)	11*	546,744	Reagan
	David W. Evans (D)	6*	544,475	Reagan
			541,832	Carter

Evans and Jacobs plan to run in the new 10th District; Hamilton plans to run in the new 9th District.

1974, this area has consistently voted for Democratic congressional candidates.

But the area votes a solid Republican ticket in statewide contests; incumbent Democratic Sen. Birch Bayh, who was defeated for re-election in November 1980, drew less than 35 percent of the total vote in the Marion and Johnson County parts of the redrawn 2nd District that year.

Like Sharp's old district, the new one will have an economy centered around the production of motor vehicles and automobile parts. Heavily dependent on the auto industry, Muncie will cast the district's largest concentration of votes. Other major manufacturing facilities are centered in Richmond and Columbus, the latter city being the home of the Cummins Engine Co. Although the addition of more rural territory in the southern part of the new 2nd District will partially dilute the United Auto Workers (UAW) strength that has helped Sharp in past elections, Sharp has been sympathetic to the carmakers' concerns and the GOP probably will share some of the blame for the slump the industry is in.

District 3

North central — South Bend

Incumbent: John Hiler (R)

John Hiler, a first-term Republican who defeated Democratic whip John Brademas in November 1980, should be strengthened by the modest changes made in his district.

Located at the northern end of the state and anchored by the industrial city of South Bend, the new 3rd District moves south to take in all of two predominantly rural counties (Starke and Marshall) and most of another (Kosciusko).

Hiler gives up industrial Michigan City to the expanding 1st District. Although Michigan City generally votes more Democratic than the rest of LaPorte County, Hiler was disappointed to lose it because LaPorte County is his home, and he wanted to include the entire county in his new district.

The new counties added from Democrat Floyd Fithian's old 2nd District will be strong Republican turf. Although Fithian ran well there, keeping his Republican opponent to just 45 percent of the vote in 1980, Reagan took 65 percent of the vote in the areas that will be transferred to Hiler. All three of the new counties are in the South Bend television market, where voters watched Hiler's commercials in 1980 even though they could not vote for him.

The district's identity will remain essentially intact. Approximately 80 percent of the population will come from the old 3rd District, most of it in South Bend and Elkhart, two economically hard-hit industrial cities with disturbingly high unemployment rates. Hiler narrowly lost St. Joseph County (South Bend) to Brademas in 1980, but he easily carried Elkhart County, traditionally a more Republican area.

South Bend, besides being the home of the University of Notre Dame, has several Bendix Corporation facilities and an American Motors assembly plant. Elkhart's economy is less closely tied to the auto industry; it is the headquarters for Miles Laboratories and is the band instrument capital of the United States. Elkhart's recreation vehicle industry, however, has been hit severely by rising gasoline prices.

District 4

Northeast — Fort Wayne

Incumbent: Dan Coats (R)

Nestled in the northeastern corner of the state, the new 4th District will be much like the one where Coats easily won a first term in November 1980. The only change will add territory from three rural counties on the district's southern border and remove Wabash County in the southwest.

Gaining the rest of Adams County along with all of Wells and Jay counties will place 75,000 new constituents in Coats' district. Although Adams often goes Democratic — it is influenced by a strongly partisan local newspaper, the *Decatur Daily Democrat* — Coats has little to worry about. Republican candidates for president, U. S. senator and governor have carried all three counties in nine of the last 10 elections.

The district is still dominated politically and economically by Fort Wayne, Coats' hometown. Allen County, which includes Fort Wayne, makes up 53 percent of the new district's population. Fort Wayne, Indiana's second largest city with 172,000, is a Republican-oriented manufacturing center with a large German ethnic population. Outside Fort Wayne the district is overwhelmingly rural. The second-largest city in the district, Huntington, has only 16,000 people.

District 5

North central, northwest — Kokomo

Incumbent: Elwood Hillis (R)

Hillis was surprised when he took a look at the new congressional map and discovered that his familiar district, centered on his hometown of Kokomo and stretching south into Indianapolis, had dramatically shifted directions.

The new 5th moves northwest from Kokomo up to the suburbs of Chicago, another political world and one in

Elwood Hillis

John T. Myers

Joel Deckard

Lee H. Hamilton

which Hillis will begin as a stranger. The only consolation for him is its continued Republican complexion.

The Legislature was determined to eliminate Democrat Fithian's old 2nd District and create a new Republican 6th near Indianapolis. They did both those things, but at Hillis' expense. He was given a radically redrawn 5th in which fewer than half of his old constituents will reside.

The new lines appear to pose no threat to the incumbent's career, but no member likes to lose more than half his voters, particularly when it means picking up areas where he is virtually unknown.

The district's population is split roughly in thirds. The segment friendliest to Hillis is around the Republican industrial cities of Kokomo and Marion in the southeast. Hillis usually runs well ahead of the winning Republican ticket in Howard County and even with it in Grant County.

Ninety miles to the northwest are the residents of southern Lake and Porter counties, fast-growing suburban areas that are attracting steel workers from the mills along Lake Michigan, plus former Chicago residents who want to escape the big-city life. Some townships in this area have more than doubled in population over the last decade.

Among the corn and soybean fields, live farmers who tend to vote a straight Republican ticket. Hillis will be gaining territory similar to areas he was forced to give up.

The biggest challenge will be in the northwest corner of the new 5th. Voters in Lake and Porter counties tend to watch Chicago television stations and read newspapers from Chicago and Gary.

This area turned sharply for Reagan in 1980, giving him 67 percent, but it is not safely Republican. A well-known Democrat from this region could cause Hillis trouble in the 1982 election.

District 6

Central — northern Indianapolis, Anderson

No Incumbent

As created in the spring of 1981, this district included the home of Democratic Rep. Andrew Jacobs Jr. But Jacobs will not be running here. As soon as the map was approved, he moved his official residence to an apartment in the neighboring 10th District, where he will have a far better chance to be re-elected.

The 6th was designed by GOP cartographers to be a guaranteed Republican seat. By the end of the summer, four candidates were running active campaigns. The leaders appear to be Bruce B. Melchert, former state GOP party chairman, and state Rep. Danny L. Burton, who has run twice before and plans to spend $200,000 on the primary.

A quarter of the new district's voters live in the northern part of Marion County (the boundaries of the county are identical with those of Indianapolis), in lightly populated parts of Pike and Lawrence townships and in suburban, affluent areas of Washington Township. All this territory is heavily Republican. In 1980, Carter received only 23 percent of the vote in the part of Marion County within the new 6th. Hamilton County, directly to the north, holds the honor of being the most Republican county in the state, as well as the fastest growing. Both Ronald Reagan and GOP Sen. Dan Quayle received 74 percent of the vote in Hamilton in 1980.

Anderson, with a population of 65,000, is the only city of any size in the new district other than Indianapolis. It and surrounding Madison County will contribute a quarter of the vote in the new district. Although two General Motors auto plants in Anderson give it a large UAW base and solid Democratic vote, surrounding Madison County has been going Republican in recent statewide elections. Since 1948, Madison has supported only one Democratic presidential candidate — Lyndon B. Johnson in 1964.

The remainder of the new district will be primarily rural. Speculation is that voters in the small towns east of Indianapolis might be reluctant to vote for a "city" candidate — who would just be another Indianapolis congressman — for fear that farm interests would not be protected.

District 7

West central — Terre Haute, Lafayette

Incumbent: John T. Myers (R)

The 7th District was shifted northward by redistricting, further from the Democratic traditions of the southern hill country and closer to the Republican-dominated Corn and Soybean Belt. Myers, who has had little difficulty at the polls since his first election in 1966, will be helped by the changes in his district.

The most significant shift involved trading one university community for another. The 7th District gives up Bloomington, the home of Indiana University, and obtains West Lafayette, the site of Purdue. Although both institutions have about 32,000 students, Purdue, with its stronger emphasis on agriculture and engineering, has a more conservative and Republican academic community. In 1980, Bayh carried Monroe County (Bloomington) with the help of a strong university vote, but lost West Lafayette and surrounding Tippecanoe County.

Terre Haute (Vigo County), an industrial and food processing center, is the district's largest city with 61,000

people. It is oriented toward southern Indiana and traditionally has been Democratic, but Myers has usually done well there.

Along with Tippecanoe County, the 7th District also gained rural Benton County and two booming counties adjoining Indianapolis — Hendricks and Morgan. Both are strongly Republican and becoming more so as conservative homeowners move out of Indianapolis to outlying suburbs and small towns.

District 8

Southwest — Evansville

Incumbent: Joel Deckard (R)

During the 1970s the 8th District was the most marginal district in the state. It elected four different people to Congress and switched political parties twice, in 1974 and again in 1978.

But Republican mapmakers carefully excised two key Democratic counties — Dubois and Perry — to make the district safer for Deckard. Dubois County came within 272 votes of going for George McGovern in 1972 — the closest McGovern came to winning any county in Indiana. Both times Deckard has run he has lost Dubois and Perry by substantial margins. Deckard won his last election with 55 percent of the vote, the highest mark for a Republican in the district since 1972 but the lowest *winning* GOP margin in the state.

The changes in the district, dictated to Indianapolis over the telephone by Deckard himself, kept his Evansville base firmly intact. In the last three elections, the GOP congressional plurality has increased in Vanderburgh County (Evansville) from 3,000 to 10,000 votes. About 30 percent of the new district's vote will come from Vanderburgh, and the political influence of the state's fourth largest city is even greater. More than one-half of the district's voters watch Evansville television stations, and the city's diversified economic base provides employment for a large area along the Ohio River.

The last two Democrats to run in the 8th District have not had an Evansville base, which many observers feel

David W. Evans   **Andrew Jacobs Jr.**

Indianapolis Districts

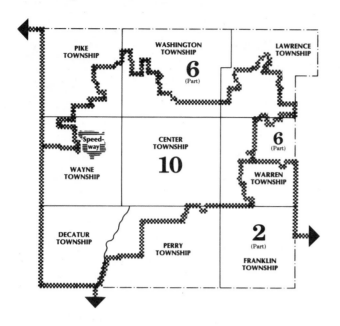

contributed to their defeat. Deckard's main Democratic challenger in 1982 is Bloomington Mayor Francix X. Mc-Closkey. McCloskey is popular enough in his home territory to permit him to concentrate much of his campaign on Evansville and his candidacy presents a serious threat to Deckard.

Over the last several decades the 8th District has gradually shifted its geography. Before 1966, the district stretched nearly the entire width of the state along the Ohio River. The Democratic heritage of the rural river counties, which dates back to the original settlement of the area 150 years ago, made the 8th a rural, Democratic district. In the four remaps that have taken place since 1966, the number of river counties has decreased from nine to just four. At the same time, the district has continued to move north into more prosperous, more Republican agricultural territory.

In 1982, the 8th will extend north all the way to Bloomington, taking in the southern part of the city. Deckard will have some of the Indiana University student and faculty population in his district, although most of this community will be in the new 9th District.

Once a rural Democratic district that stretched across the state along the Ohio River, the 8th District has gradually shifted to become a north-south district.

District 9

Southeast — Bloomington, New Albany

Incumbent: Lee H. Hamilton (D)

Democrat Lee H. Hamilton, who has represented most of this area since 1964, plans to move into the district from his hometown of Columbus.

Hamilton's relocation was an unintended consequence of the Republican strategy for this part of the state. Aware of Hamilton's tremendous popularity, Republicans made no effort to weaken him. They loaded him down with Democrats from the 7th and 8th Districts in order to help GOP incumbents Myers and Deckard. They took Republican areas out of Hamilton's old 9th and moved them into the new 2nd District, where they could vote against Sharp, the incumbent Democrat there.

Hamilton gains Dubois, Perry and part of Crawford counties from the old 8th District. In 1980 Carter nearly matched Reagan in this area, and Bayh took 55 percent of the vote. By contrast, the area Hamilton will be losing gave Bayh 40 percent and Carter 35 percent.

The addition of most of Bloomington will also increase the Democratic vote. The new district line runs along 3rd Street in Bloomington, putting the northern three-fifths of the city's 52,000 residents into the new 9th. Included in that area is all of Indiana University's campus as well as most of the off-student housing and faculty neighborhoods. In 1980 independent presidential candidate John B. Anderson won 13 percent of the vote in the two townships from Monroe County (Bloomington) included in the new 9th District. Anderson carried only 5 percent of the vote statewide.

The Indiana suburbs of Louisville, Ky., along the Ohio River, make up the district's largest concentration of voters. Centered on New Albany, the district's largest city with just 37,000 people, this area is experiencing a minor population boom. Most of the industrial activity in the new 9th District is just across from Louisville along the Ohio River.

District 10

Indianapolis

Incumbents: Andrew Jacobs Jr. (D)
David W. Evans (D)

Like Hamilton's 9th District, the 10th becomes a receptacle for Democrats removed from other constituencies. Democratic Rep. Andrew Jacobs Jr. currently represents most of this territory. He has had to move in order to run, because his home lies outside the new boundaries, but the move presents no political difficulties.

His only real problem is fellow-Democrat David W. Evans, whose 6th District was dismembered and who plans to fight Jacobs for the 10th. About 52 percent of the population in the new 10th District comes from Jacobs' old 11th District. Some 41 percent comes from Evans' old 6th. The rest comes from a portion of the old 5th that dipped into Washington Township in Indianapolis.

The Jacobs-Evans primary will feature candidates of markedly different political styles. David W. Evans is a consummate campaigner who uses every modern technique he can find, specializing in direct mail. He has already received an endorsement from the Indianapolis labor council. Andrew Jacobs Jr. is more of a loner who shuns the perquisites of office. He spends little money on his campaigns and has refused contributions from political action committees.

Whoever wins the primary should be elected in November 1982. This is the second most Democratic district in the state, after the 1st District along Lake Michigan. Compared to Jacobs' old district, which covered 58 percent of Marion County (Indianapolis), the new 11th is substantially more Democratic. In 1980, Carter lost the old 11th District, 41-53 percent. The 1980 presidential vote computed according to the new district boundaries gave Carter a 49-45 edge.

The new 10th District includes about 70 percent of Indianapolis' population, but excludes a heavily Republican section on the northern side and a largely suburban and rural area in Franklin and Perry townships on the southeast.

The major Democratic strength comes in Center Township, which is about 40 percent black. In the past, Evans and Jacobs shared this area. The new 10th District also picks up the black areas of Pike Township, which were in the old 6th District, and a middle-income, integrated neighborhood in southern Washington Township that was in the old 5th District. Fort Benjamin Harrison in Lawrence Township is also in the new district. The western side of the district, around Wayne Township, is a white-collar, middle income area that often votes Republican.

Iowa

It took most of the 1970s for the rest of the country to change its perception of Iowa. People had long thought of it as a rural conservative state, but that notion didn't square with Iowa's habit of electing liberal Democratic candidates to Congress.

Then, just as the lesson was being learned, the state reversed its course, turning out Democratic senators Dick Clark and John Culver in two successive elections and ending Democratic control of the House delegation.

Like most Midwestern states, Iowa is a more complicated place than Easterners usually imagine. It has always had a base of Democratic votes in its medium-sized cities and a volatile farm population capable of springing political surprises. Iowa elected a Democratic governor three times during the Depression and twice in the lean agricultural years of the 1950s.

So it was no shock when Harold Hughes launched the state's modern Democratic resurgence, winning three terms as governor in the 1960s and going to the Senate in 1968. Personally popular among voters of both parties, he laid the groundwork for the two later Democratic Senate victories, by Clark in 1972 and Culver in 1974.

A predominantly Yankee-settled state, Iowa began showing interest in "clean government" around the same time as did ethnically similar states such as Vermont and Oregon. This helped candidates such as Harold Hughes and Dick Clark. In addition, labor was gaining strength in Iowa in the 1970s, with the United Auto Workers union building an important base among farm implement manufacturing workers and the Amalgamated Meatcutters union playing an increasing role in Waterloo and other Iowa cities.

But Iowa never became a Democratic state, even though the party's registration reached a majority for a time at mid-decade. By 1978, voters reacted against what they perceived as Clark's excessive liberalism on foreign policy and his support for abortion. He was beaten by conservative Republican Roger Jepsen essentially because blue-collar Democrats, most of them Catholic, stayed home in surprising numbers. In 1980, Culver ran for re-election as an unapologetic liberal, choosing a stance different from most Senate Democrats in similar situations. He lost overwhelmingly to Republican Rep. Charles Grassley, a less articulate man who expressed the public sentiment that the government was simply wasting too much money.

Through all these political changes, Iowa has been governed by the same moderate Republican, Robert Ray, who replaced Hughes in 1969 and is now the senior governor in the United States. Ray does not evoke the militant support that a Clark or a Grassley does — nor the opposition either. He has won re-election four times, the last three by comfortable margins.

Des Moines and Central Iowa

Des Moines is Iowa's only major metropolitan area; it is looked to by the surrounding farm lands as a commercial, financial and governmental center. More than 50 insurance companies have their headquarters here, making it the nation's second largest insurance city.

Since Des Moines is the capital of Iowa, state government also contributes to the white-collar employment market. Industrial activity focuses on the manufacturing of farm machinery and tires.

Des Moines is home to two other institutions of Iowa life: one is the annual state fair; the other is the *Des Moines Register,* a newspaper of progressive reputation and statewide circulation that influences the tone and helps shape the agenda of state politics.

Democrats are strong in Des Moines and in areas north of the city in surrounding Polk County. Other suburban areas, such as West Des Moines, show a preference for Republicans.

The overall Polk County vote is generally Democratic, as seen in U. S. Senate races of the past decade. Polk County gave more than 58 percent to Democrats Clark and Culver in their winning Senate races of 1972 and 1974. In their unsuccessful re-election bids of 1978 and 1980, both Clark and Culver won approximately 56 percent of the Polk vote.

North of Des Moines in Story County is the town of Ames, home of Iowa State University. Since the voting age was lowered in 1971 to include college students, Story County has generally backed liberal Democrats for statewide office. But no Democratic candidate running for the presidency has carried the county since Lyndon B. Johnson in 1964. Carter might have topped Reagan there in 1980, except for the independent candidacy of John B. Anderson, whose 19 percent was his fifth-best county showing in the nation.

Eastern Iowa

This ought to be the most Democratic part of Iowa, because it contains several medium-sized cities with manufacturing-based economies and a significant number of blue-collar voters.

Culver represented northeast Iowa in the House from 1965 to 1975; he expanded his regional political base to win the 1974 Senate election. But today his district sends a Republican to Congress, as does the 1st District immediately below it, also briefly Democratic during the 1970s. Both Republican House members now serving from this part of the state, Jim Leach and Tom Tauke, have moderate records that allow them to do well in the manufacturing cities.

The largest city in eastern Iowa is Cedar Rapids (Linn County), the second largest in the state. Politically, Linn County is evenly divided. It gave Jepsen a slight edge in 1978 but narrowly favored Culver, a hometown product, in 1980.

The next largest city is Davenport (Scott County), which recently has gone Republican. Scott was the largest county in Iowa to vote for both Jepsen in 1978 and Grassley in 1980.

The Catholic vote is important in the Mississippi River city of Dubuque in northeast Iowa. Though Dubuque County almost always votes Democratic, the pro-abortion stands that Clark and Culver took in the Senate hurt them politically. Both won more than 66 percent there in their first Senate campaigns, but barely won Dubuque County when they sought re-election.

Burlington (Des Moines County) is another Mississippi River manufacturing city. It has consistently voted for Democratic statewide candidates in the past decade, but strongly supported Republican Leach in the past two elections.

The liberal bastion in this part of the state is Johnson County, influenced by the University of Iowa vote in Iowa City. Anderson received just under 19 percent of the vote in the county.

The Republican Party prevails in virtually all the other counties in the eastern part of the state, where the farmers depend largely on corn, livestock and poultry for their livelihood.

North Central Iowa.

The rich soil of the rolling prairie makes this section of the state one of the most agriculturally productive areas of the nation.

Advances in agricultural technology have boosted crop yields here in the past generation. But farming has also become a costlier, more complex business, and many small-scale farmers have sold their land to agribusiness operations. This has eliminated farm-oriented jobs and held down population growth in the region. The 6th Congressional District, home of the state's richest farm land, lost population in the 1970s — the only district in the state with a net decline.

The farmers and small-business executives in this part of the state generally vote Republican. But in some of the counties, the rural vote is balanced by blue-collar workers in farm-related manufacturing and meatpacking. Labor unions have demonstrated strength in Black Hawk County (Waterloo and Cedar Falls) and Cerro Gordo County (Mason City). Both of those counties voted for a liberal Democrat for the House in 1980.

Western Iowa

There are only three cities of any size in the vast expanse of rural farm land that is western Iowa. Two of them — Council Bluffs and Sioux City on the Missouri River — are predominantly Republican. The third is Democratic Fort Dodge in Webster County.

With few exceptions, the small towns and farms in this part of Iowa have voted for Republicans in Senate and presidential elections during the past decade. Reagan's best showing in the state came from this area as he won more than 55 percent in most western Iowa counties.

Yet the region's two representatives in the U. S. House are both Democrats. Tom Harkin and Berkley Bedell defeated incumbent Republicans in 1974 and have since developed personal followings among rural and small-town voters. These close ties have enabled them to withstand Iowa's drift to the right in recent elections.

The soil and terrain are not as favorable to farming in the southwest quarter of Iowa as they are in other parts of the state. Iowa's southern tier counties are often hilly and rocky, especially those that are located along the Iowa-Missouri border.

NEW MAP:
NO GERRYMANDERING

Republicans are in full control of Iowa state government, but they avoided the temptation to gerrymander and adopted a congressional redistricting plan that respects Iowa's tradition of competitive two-party politics. Gov. Robert Ray signed the new boundaries into law Aug. 20, 1981.

Under a law that Republicans pushed through the Legislature in 1980, the state's non-partisan Legislative Service Bureau was given the task of presenting proposals for new congressional and state legislative districts. The bureau's mandate was to follow "objective" criteria in drawing the boundaries — population equality, compactness, contiguity and preservation of local boundaries — but to ignore partisan concerns or the wishes of incumbents.

When the bureau's non-partisan map was presented in April, it caused a highly partisan uproar. "It looks like a Democratic computer wrote it," said an aide to GOP Gov. Robert Ray. Two of the state's three Republican representatives — Jim Leach and Tom Tauke — were placed in the same district.

On its second try, the bureau's computer gave Leach and Tauke separate districts, but took several GOP counties from Tauke and gave him Democratic Johnson County.

State law stipulated that the bureau's first two proposals could not be amended. But they could be rejected outright. The state Senate killed the first plan May 14 and the second one June 25, 1981.

In July 1981, the bureau offered another proposal. The law allowed the Legislature to make changes in this version, but none was made, and it was enacted verbatim. The person most upset by that action was Republican Rep. Cooper Evans, whose 3rd District gained Democratic Johnson County and lost several GOP counties under the proposal.

New
Iowa
Districts

U. S. Congress: 6 districts
Senate (2R)
House (3D, 3R)
Governor:
Robert Ray (R)
Population: 2,913,387
Area: 56,290 sq. miles
1980 Presidential Vote:
Carter (39%)
Reagan (51%)
Anderson (9%)

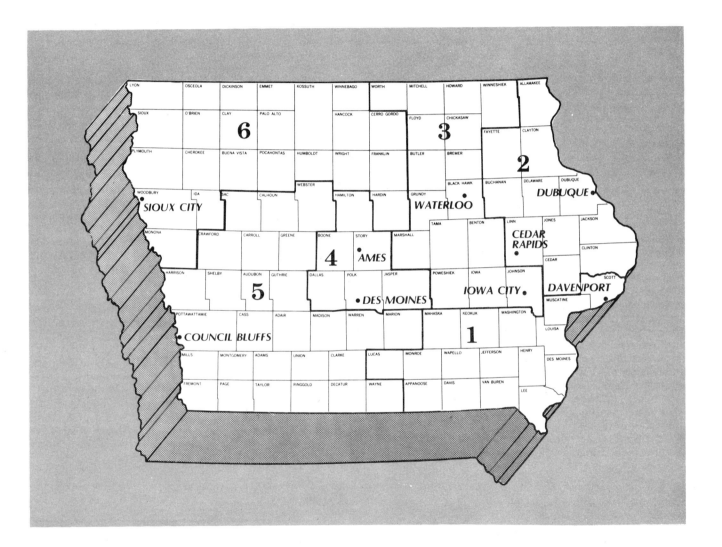

Republican leaders essentially ignored Evans' protests. They sensed that the public was becoming annoyed with the money and time consumed in the redistricting process and feared that changing the third plan to suit their partisan interests would be viewed as a violation of the "good government" principle embodied in the basic redistricting law.

The Senate considered and rejected a number of amendments to the third plan, including a totally redrafted version prepared by the Republican State Central Committee. The bill passed the Senate Aug. 12, 1981 by a 39-10 vote, and the next day the House approved the package 92-5. Ray signed it into law a week later.

Iowa's overall population growth in the 1970s was only 3.1 percent, and the population disparity among the old districts was not great: Leach's 1st was the largest, with 505,896 people, and Democrat Berkley Bedell's 6th the smallest, with 464,617 people.

Population deviations among the redrawn districts are virtually non-existent. The district farthest out of line is the 2nd, which is 144 people over the ideal population of 485,564, a deviation of .030 percent.

District 1

Southeast — Davenport

Incumbent: Jim Leach (R)

Redistricting should make life even easier for Jim Leach than it has been so far. His 1st District loses heavily Democratic Johnson County and gains several rural counties where the Republican Party plays a dominant role. Although the district will take in a total of 16 southeastern Iowa counties, 60 percent of the constituents will be in four Mississippi River counties located on the district's eastern fringe.

With a population of 160,000, Scott County (Davenport) is by far the largest population center of the district. It is a heavily industrialized area with a sizable blue-collar vote. Republicans gained ground in Scott County during the past decade; Leach lost it when he first ran for Congress in 1974, but in 1980, he took 68 percent of the county's vote. Scott was the largest county in Iowa to vote Republican in the hotly-contested U.S. Senate races of 1978 and 1980.

Davenport's factories produce cement, aluminum and heavy machinery, and the city is part of the Quad-Cities metropolitan area (with nearby Bettendorf, Iowa, and Rock Island and Moline, Ill.). Down-river from Davenport in the new 1st District are three other major shipping and manufacturing counties, each containing approximately 40,000 residents. Of the three, Muscatine County votes consistently Republican, but Democratic candidates running statewide often win Des Moines County (Burlington) and Lee County (Keokuk). By compiling a moderate congressional voting record and maintaining a high profile in the district, Jim Leach has put Lee and Des Moines counties in his column.

In addition to moving Democratic Johnson County from the 1st District to the 3rd, the redistricting proposal also took from Leach three Republican-dominated counties: Benton, Poweshiek and Iowa. But at the same time it gave him five Republican farming counties: Mahaska, Appanoose, Keokuk, Lucas and Davis.

Democrats have respectable strength in two other counties added in redistricting — Wapello and Monroe.

Ottumwa, a city with a population of 27,000 in Wapello County, produces farm machinery and is a trade center for area farm lands.

District 2

Northeast — Cedar Rapids

Incumbent: Tom Tauke (R)

This district will remain what it has been for decades: a triangle of interdependent industrial cities surrounded by corn, livestock and dairy farms.

All redistricting did was trade Winneshiek County to the 3rd in return for Buchanan County. Buchanan and Winnishiek cast less than 10,000 votes apiece in 1980 and gave GOP candidates 54 percent of the vote or better.

The population centers in the district are Cedar Rapids, Dubuque and Clinton. Cedar Rapids, the second largest city in Iowa, is a center for meatpacking, grain processing and manufacturing of farm hardware and radio equipment. Traditionally Republican, it swung to the Democratic side in statewide contests during the early 1970s but by 1980 seemed to be swinging back again.

Dubuque, with slightly more than 60,000 people, is largely Catholic and historically friendlier to Democrats. It is a processing point for the dairy industry; it also builds tractors and other farm implements. In 1980, Dubuque County was one of four Iowa counties carried by Jimmy Carter. Tauke did not carry the county in either 1978 or 1980, but is able to run competitively there.

The city of Clinton, about one-half the size of Dubuque, is another local manufacturing center located on the west bank of the Mississippi River. Democratic strength in Clinton County dropped dramatically during the past decade, and the area is only slightly less Republican than the district's eight rural counties, where Tauke and other Republican candidates often receive more than 55 percent of the total vote.

The only 2nd District county that lost population in the last decade was Fayette County. Every other Iowa congressional district contains at least two counties where population declined in the 1970s.

District 3

North Central — Waterloo, Iowa City

Incumbent: Cooper Evans (R)

Evans was so unhappy with his new district lines that he considered moving to his vacation home in the 6th District. However, he stayed in the 3rd where he likely will face Lynn Cutler, whom he narrowly defeated in 1980.

Johnson County, shifted into the 3rd from the 1st, is the primary source of Evans' discontent. It is a fast-growing county with a population of 81,717, and in 1980 it gave Ronald Reagan a meager 32 percent of the vote. John Anderson received nearly 19 percent of the county's presi-

Jim Leach   **Tom Tauke**

New Iowa Districts

New District	Incumbent*	Population	1980 Pres. Winner
1	Jim Leach (R)	485,601	Reagan
2	Tom Tauke (R)	485,708	Reagan
3	Cooper Evans (R)	485,529	Reagan
4	Neal Smith (D)	485,480	Reagan
	Tom Harkin (D)		
5	No incumbent	485,578	Reagan
6	Berkley Bedell (D)	485,491	Reagan

Incumbents' current districts: Leach, 1; Tauke, 2; Evans, 3; Smith, 4; Harkin, 5; Bedell 6.

dential vote. Johnson County has a strong liberal influence from the University of Iowa in Iowa City (population 50,508). The university has about 22,000 students.

Still, Johnson County's population amounts to less than one-fifth of the district's total. The largest bloc of 3rd District votes — nearly 30 percent — is cast in Black Hawk County, which will remain in Evans' constituency.

With the twin cities of Waterloo and Cedar Falls, Black Hawk County is Iowa's fourth-largest metropolitan area. Meatpacking and the farm implement industry are crucial, and labor unions have demonstrated political strength here. In 1980, Black Hawk County was the home base of Democratic House nominee Lynn Cutler, who lost to Evans by only 6,000 votes. But Black Hawk County also went for Ford in 1976 and Reagan in 1980.

Besides Johnson County, Evans will be gaining four counties in which he should be strong: Benton, Poweshiek and Iowa, all on the district's southern border, and Winneshiek, at its northeast corner. All four counties favor Republicans; none contains a major city.

But those four counties will only partially compensate for the Republican territory Evans is losing. He drops six counties on the western side of the 3rd District: Cerro Gordo, Hardin, Hamilton, Wright, Hancock and Franklin. All except Cerro Gordo County are solidly Republican, rural and small-town counties. On the eastern side of the 3rd District, Evans loses Republican Buchanan County to Tauke's 2nd District.

District 4

Central — Des Moines, Ames

Incumbents: Neal Smith (D),

Although Smith and Harkin both reside within the borders of the new 4th District, the solution is simple. Smith will run here; Harkin's territory will be the new 5th,

which is technically open but contains most of the constituency Harkin now represents.

More than 60 percent of the voters will be in Polk County, most of them in Des Moines, Iowa's big city. Surrounding farms and smaller industrial towns look to Des Moines as a commercial, financial and governmental center, and since Des Moines is the capital, state government contributes to the white-collar work force.

The city also depends on grain marketing, publishing and the manufacture of farm equipment. The United Auto Workers is a significant political presence. Des Moines is predominantly white, Protestant and middle-class, with less ethnic flavor than other Midwestern industrial cities.

Polk is the state's crucial Democratic county, but Democrats may be growing weaker here as the central city's population declines. Many fast-growing communities around Des Moines show a preference for Republicans. Areas such as suburban West Des Moines, where the population expanded 33 percent in the past decade, were largely responsible for Ronald Reagan's slim margin of victory in Polk County's 1980 presidential vote.

Redistricting took from Smith's district eight counties southeast of Des Moines: Marion, Mahaska, Appanoose, Keokuk, Lucas, Davis, Wapello and Monroe. Republicans hold the advantage in all but the last two.

The district gains four central Iowa counties: Story, Dallas, Boone and Hamilton. Story is the most important. It includes Ames (population 45,775), the home of Iowa State University's 23,000 students. With most of the college students eligible to vote, Story County has generally backed liberal Democrats for statewide office. But no Democrat running for president has carried the county since Lyndon B. Johnson in 1964.

District 5

Southwest — Council Bluffs, Fort Dodge

Incumbent: Tom Harkin (D)

Although Harkin's Story County residence is no longer in the 5th District and although the new 5th is even more

Cooper Evans   **Neal Smith**

Tom Harkin   **Berkley Bedell**

Republican than the old one, Harkin is expected to move his residence to the new 5th and win re-election. His original home, Cumming, in Warren County, remains part of the district.

By developing close personal ties with many voters, Harkin has defied Republican loyalties that run strong in many parts of southwest Iowa. Nonetheless, he is hurt by the transfer of Story, Dallas and Boone counties into the 4th District; Harkin won an average of 68 percent in those counties in 1980.

The 5th District expands north to take in Crawford, Sac and Calhoun counties, all of which are small-town, rural and Republican. Webster County, which delivers a generally reliable Democratic majority and makes up just under 10 percent of the 5th District's total population.

Fort Dodge (population 29,423), the Webster County seat, is an industrial center near large gypsum deposits. Factories manufacture gypsum products, chemical fertilizer and farm machinery.

Also new to the district is Marion County, with nearly 30,000 residents and a preference for the GOP. Marion County is actually southeast of Des Moines, testimony to the far-ranging nature of the 5th. Marion adjoins Warren County, which contains the outlying southern suburbs of Des Moines and leans Democratic. Warren, Iowa's fastest growing county in the past decade, experienced a population boom of 27 percent.

The district's most steadfastly Republican counties are Pottawattamie, Page, Montgomery, Mills and Fremont. Clustered in the extreme southwest corner of the district, they make up about 30 percent of the district's population.

Pottawattamie County contains the district's largest city: industrial Council Bluffs (population 56,449), which stands across the Missouri River from Omaha and is part of its metropolitan area.

The 5th District's sparsely-populated central counties are dependent on agriculture — livestock, poultry, feed grains and soybeans. The terrain in much of this area of the state is not as favorable for farming as in other parts of the state. Iowa's southwest tier of counties is largely hilly and rocky, especially those located along the Iowa-Missouri border.

The small towns and farms here almost always favor statewide Republican candidates by wide margins, but since 1974, Harkin's popularity has steadily increased in the agricultural areas.

District 6

Northwest — Sioux City

Incumbent: Berkley Bedell (D)

Redistricting could unsettle Bedell, who has enjoyed bipartisan support and three easy re-elections in a traditionally Republican area.

Bedell loses Webster County, where he received 71 percent of the vote in 1980, and picks up Cerro Gordo County, comparable in population to Webster but usually favorable to Republicans. Mason City (population 30,144), seat of Cerro Gordo County, is a major producer of cement and processor of meat and dairy products.

Also joining the 6th District are Hardin, Wright, Hancock and Franklin counties, formerly in the 3rd District. They cast fewer than 10,000 votes each and are Republican-dominated. Crawford, Sac and Calhoun counties, which vote GOP in statewide races, will be moving out of the 6th District into the 5th.

The rich soil of the rolling prairie makes northwestern Iowa one of the most agriculturally productive areas of the nation. But farming is becoming a costly, technologically complex business, and many small-scale farmers have sold their land to agribusiness operations. Large-scale farming has eliminated farm-oriented jobs and caused out-migration from the district. Of the 23 counties in the new 6th, all but seven lost population in the 1970s.

Sioux City, western Iowa's largest city, is the core of the 6th District. It is a manufacturing and food processing center on the Missouri River. The city and surrounding Woodbury County contain about one-fifth of the district's population and regularly vote the Republican line, although Bedell won 64 percent in the county in 1980.

Bedell should be able to overcome the hindrances imposed by redistricting, but he may face re-election problems from another quarter. Several officials of his multimillion-dollar fishing tackle business have been indicted for importing products from a Taiwan subsidiary at artificially low prices to avoid payment of customs duties. Bedell has not been charged, but his business is certain to be an issue for him in a 1982 campaign.

Missouri

The 1980 election offered Missouri Republicans some fresh hope that they might soon shake the state free of the traditional Democratic loyalties that often take precedence over any of the issues of the day.

Besides voting for Ronald Reagan for President, Missouri elected Christopher S. Bond as governor, reversing his 1976 defeat at the hands of Democrat Joseph Teasdale, and doubled its GOP representation in the U.S. House — to four of ten seats.

Reagan demonstrated broad appeal in many parts of rural Missouri, winning 99 of the state's 114 counties, even traditional Democratic ones in Little Dixie and the Bootheel. If Republicans have made a breakthrough there, future Democratic presidential nominees will be hard-pressed to win the state.

While other border states began going Republican in past years, Missouri showed few signs of breaking out of its Civil War voting patterns. Without substantial growth to disrupt its political habits or a major statewide racial crisis to turn white voters to the right, it kept most of its Democratic habits. For most of the 1970s, only one of its U.S. House members was a Republican. Several of its most conservative rural counties even backed George McGovern for president in 1972.

Democrats have needed rural votes because their urban constituency is shrinking. In 1948, St. Louis cast 22 percent of the statewide presidential vote. In 1980, St. Louis and Kansas City together cast only 15 percent. In early 1981, when a liberal Democratic bloc dominated by Kansas City legislators organized to control the Missouri Senate, they found themselves outvoted by a rival coalition including conservative Republicans (and some Democrats) from suburban St. Louis and Democrats from the Bootheel, Little Dixie and other rural regions.

The suburbs around St. Louis and Kansas City continue to grow and to show more affection for the GOP. In 1980, Reagan won not only in normally Republican St. Louis County, outside the city, but in suburban Kansas City (Jackson County), which Carter carried in 1976.

St. Louis

Much has been written about the decline of this once-great city, which has fewer residents today than it did at the turn of the century. Since 1950, nearly half of its people have fled, both black and white; the well-off to distant suburbia and the less affluent to neighborhoods just outside the city. Numerous factories and businesses have closed.

Auto and truck assembly and aerospace manufacturing, mostly outside the city limits, have come to play a more important role than traditional St. Louis industries such as shoe and apparel manufacturing and brewing. But the transportation industry has been an uneven performer in the past decade. Rising gasoline prices and Japanese imported cars hurt the domestic automakers. Demand for commercial jetliners fluctuated, and the NASA space program proceeded sluggishly.

With the exodus of people and jobs from the inner city has come a corresponding loss of political influence. St. Louis cast only 8 percent of the statewide presidential vote in 1980.

St. Louis today is composed of two distinct communities. The northern half is two-thirds black and has seen the most precipitous population decline in the city. Jimmy Carter won nearly 90 percent of the 1980 vote here. The southern part of St. Louis is an accumulation of older blue-collar, heavily German and Italian neighborhoods with few blacks and a slowly declining population. Reagan won 44 percent and Carter 52 percent of the vote in south St. Louis in the 1980 election.

About 60 percent of the St. Louis vote is cast in the southern part of the city, where there is still meaningful partisan competition. But the overwhelming Democratic majorities in north St. Louis have given presidential candidates John F. Kennedy, Hubert H. Humphrey and Jimmy Carter a steady 66 percent of the overall city vote in elections since 1960.

St. Louis Suburbs/Missouri River Valley

St. Louis County surrounds St. Louis on the north, west and south, but is a jurisdiction separate and independent from the city. The county has grown steadily in the postwar era, and Republicans have been the majority party for more than a decade.

In the 1960 presidential election, St. Louis County went narrowly for Kennedy, casting about 20,000 more votes than the city. In 1980, the county cast 314,000 more votes than the city, and it gave Reagan a victory margin of 14 percentage points. Nearly a quarter of Missouri's vote is now cast in this single county.

North and south St. Louis County have a significant blue-collar element, while the western part of the county is more affluent and white-collar.

The only parts of the county that Carter won in 1980 were the liberal academic community around Washington University and an area just outside north St. Louis where the neighborhoods are settled by poorer St. Louis emigrants. John B. Anderson drew a higher vote in the Washington University area than anywhere in the state except Boone County, home of the University of Missouri.

Reagan won St. Charles, Jefferson and Franklin counties, which contain outlying suburbs of St. Louis. Jefferson County gained the symbolic distinction in 1980 of being the geographic center of the nation's population — the first time that spot has been located west of the Mississippi River.

Proceeding beyond metropolitan St. Louis along the Missouri River, the southern river valley counties of Gasconade, Osage and Cole are as reliably Republican as the suburbs. Much of this area was settled in the early 19th century by pioneers of German ancestry. The immigrants lined up against the politically dominant Democratic planters and slaveholders north of the river and since then have seldom swerved from the GOP path.

In recent years, Republican dominance has crept north of the river into Warren and Montgomery counties, giving the GOP control over a swath of territory beginning in St. Louis County and stretching westward to the state capital, Jefferson City, in the center of the state.

Southwestern Missouri — The Ozarks

The Osage River flows into Missouri at Vernon County and meanders across the southwestern part of the state until it empties into the Missouri River just east of Jefferson City. Nearly every county south of the Osage is in the traditionally Republican-voting Ozark Mountain region.

Long a poor, isolated, Appalachian-like area, the scenic Ozarks have now been discovered by tourists, retirees and developers. The tourist presence is most obvious near Table Rock Reservoir in Taney County (near the Arkansas border) and along the Lake of the Ozarks in west-central Missouri.

But development has not altered the basic character of the Ozarks. Scots-Irish mountaineers from western Virginia, eastern Tennessee and Kentucky settled much of this region. As a rule, they kept to themselves, and there are still many small, isolated communities.

Ozarks residents had no use for slavery, were strongly pro-Union during the Civil War and voted Republican thereafter. That pattern shows no signs of abating: Reagan's 1980 margins in the Ozarks were higher than Ford's in 1976.

Springfield, becoming less Republican in recent years, and Joplin, an old lead and zinc mining town, are the largest cities in the area. The non-tourist economy these days revolves mostly around dairy and chicken farms, light industry and religious publishing by several fundamentalist denominations with headquarters in the region.

Metropolitan Kansas City (Jackson County)

Though it has not suffered a massive, St. Louis-like flight of people and businesses, Kansas City has many of the problems of older industrial cities.

After growing in population until 1970, the city shrank to less than 457,000 by 1980, fewer than lived in Kansas City 30 years earlier. The proportion of blacks in the 5th Congressional Disrict (Kansas City and a small part of Jackson County outside the city) grew from 24 to 31 percent in the past decade as whites moved outside the city limits.

Although the suburbs in Jackson County are growing as the city population shrinks, Kansas City still casts a solid majority (between 55 and 60 percent) of the overall county vote.

Kansas City is the financial and distribution point for a surrounding six-state agricultural region. The stockyards are less economically important than they were in the city's cowtown heyday, but meatpacking continues, along with auto assembly, steel manufacturing, and production of Hallmark greeting cards and electronic equipment.

In earlier days, Kansas City was known as a western-oriented, wide open town. Its jazz, gambling and the reknowned Democratic Pendergast machine gave it a much different image than it has today. There has always been a sizable GOP minority, but urban economic problems have kept the city in the Democratic camp. Jimmy Carter won 60 percent of the Kansas City vote in both 1976 and 1980.

Carter lost the suburbs in Jackson County by eight percentage points in 1980, but emerged with a 54 to 42 percent countywide win thanks to his urban strength. Overall, Jackson County cast 12 percent of the statewide presidential vote in 1980.

In addition to Jackson County, the Kansas City metropolitan area includes Platte, Clay and Ray counties to the north and Cass County to the south. Like most of the counties in west-central Missouri, these four have generally voted Democratic in the past. But in 1980, Republicans Reagan and Bond carried Platte, Clay and Cass and several other often-Democratic counties.

Little Dixie and the Iowa Border

Among the state's first settlers were westward-moving Tidewater and Piedmont Virginians and bluegrass Kentuckians who found the rich northeastern Missouri soil to their liking. They planted their Southern roots here, tried to pull Missouri into the Confederacy and have voted Democratic into the modern era.

Conservative Little Dixie's Democratic allegiance is a political anachronism, since the party has been tilting towards cities, labor and minorities since the New Deal. But there are relatively few blacks in Little Dixie, so natives have never been confronted with many of the social tensions that led to party shifts elsewhere in the country.

George McGovern scared nearly all of Missouri's conservative Democrats away from the party in 1972, but even then McGovern won Monroe County, in the heart of Little Dixie. Carter brought the rest of the region back to the party fold in 1976. But in 1980, Reagan took all but two Little Dixie counties, a hint that the area may finally be deciding that the conservatism it preaches is best-protected by the GOP.

Topographically and economically, parts of northern Missouri are similar to Iowa. The closest thing Missouri has to a Yankee influence is found in Putnam, Mercer and a few other counties on or near the Iowa border. Ohio and Iowa farmers moved into the area long ago, and for years it has rivaled the Ozarks for fidelity to the GOP.

Moving west toward the Kansas and Nebraska borders, partisan lines blur somewhat. Republicans are still preferred, but Democrat Eagleton won most northwest

New Missouri Districts

U. S. Congress: 9 districts
  Senate (1D, 1R)
  House (6D, 4R)
Governor:
  Christopher S. "Kit" Bond (R)
Population: 4,917,444
Area: 69,686 sq. miles
1980 Presidential Vote:
  Carter (44%)
  Reagan (51%)
  Anderson (4%)

Missouri counties in 1980. Buchanan County (St. Joseph) is the region's most populous and is politically marginal. Democrat Teasdale won the county by 66 votes in 1976, and Republican Bond took 50.9 percent there in 1980.

Southeast Missouri and The Bootheel

The southeast is philosophically very conservative, but partisan allegiances are in a state of flux. There have been recent Republican gains. Generally speaking, Republicans are a majority or a near-majority in the northernmost and westernmost counties of this region. There is a wedge of strongly Democratic counties in the central part of the area.

In the extreme southeast corner of the state lies the Bootheel, a cluster of Mississippi River counties that look and vote like the Old South. The Bootheel is today more entrenched in Democratic voting patterns than Little Dixie.

But Bootheel partisan traditions go back only to 1924, when cotton planters from the lower Mississippi moved into Missouri to escape the boll weevil blight that had ruined their crops further to the south. Black share-croppers arrived to work the fields, and in no time the Bootheel looked like typical post-plantation South.

George Wallace in 1968 won more than 20 percent of the vote in the Bootheel counties of New Madrid, Mississippi, Dunklin, Scott and Pemiscot. But Democratic traditions were so strong that Hubert Humphrey still won a plurality in all those counties except Pemiscot.

Reagan in 1980 gained 10 to 15 points over Ford's 1976 Bootheel showing, but he still fell short of defeating Carter. If Reagan could not win the Bootheel, it is hard to imagine what sort of Republican could win there.

TWO REPUBLICANS HURT BY MISSOURI REMAP

Missouri's new congressional map imposes a difficult burden on two freshman Republicans and takes care to preserve a district in which the state's only black House member has a chance for re-election.

Under the redistricting plan, announced Dec. 28, 1981, by a three-judge federal panel, GOP Reps. Wendell Bailey and Bill Emerson both must move in order to seek new terms. Bailey's 8th District is dismembered and Emerson's home is cut off from his southeast Missouri district.

Democratic Rep. William Clay, whose mostly black district based in St. Louis lost more than one-fourth of its population during the last decade, receives an expanded territory with a narrow black majority. With Missouri dropping from 10 House seats to nine in the 1980 reapportionment, Clay's underpopulated district was often suggested as a target for elimination. But the court chose to keep a district similar to Clay's current one and place the reapportionment burden on the state's rural areas, where significant growth took place.

Though the remap may save Clay and help defeat one or both of the Republican freshmen, it is not unqualified good news for the Democrats. A dozen counties now represented by Bailey are distributed among the 2nd, 4th, and 9th districts, making the Democratic incumbents in each of those constituencies less secure.

The federal judges acted after the state Legislature failed to produce a new district map in two attempts — once during the regular 1981 session, which ended June 15, 1981, and again in a special redistricting session, called by Republican Gov. Christopher S. "Kit" Bond, which adjourned Dec. 17, 1981.

Legislators could not agree on a way to drop one district as required by reapportionment. The suggestions included a plan to combine the 1st District and the 3rd District in St. Louis and a plan to establish a new northern Missouri district incorporating parts of the 6th and 9th districts. But a majority could not be found for either of those ideas.

District 1

North St. Louis, northeast St. Louis County

Incumbent: William Clay (D)

The inner-city 1st District lost more than one-quarter of its people during the 1970s. Black and white residents alike fled once-great St. Louis — the well-off moved to distant suburbia and the less affluent relocated in neighborhoods just outside the city limits. But most of the Democrats in the Legislature did not want to eliminate a black constituency, and the federal panel agreed with them.

To bring the 1st District up to the new ideal population standard, the redistricting map assigns it more than 200,000 additional people. The district moves south to take more St. Louis territory from Democrat Rep. Richard A. Gephardt's 3rd District; to the west and north it picks up territory located in suburban St. Louis County now represented by the 2nd District's Democratic Rep. Robert A. Young.

Though the 1st District remains Democratic, William Clay will have to struggle for renomination. The district he currently represents is two-thirds black; in the redrawn 1st, blacks compose just 52 percent of the total population. Most of Clay's new constituents will live not in St. Louis, where he has often won 85 percent of the vote, but in St. Louis County, where he has barely broken even in past elections.

Some of the new territory will be in neighborhoods whose residents used to be Clay constituents but left the inner city once they could afford it. Now the district is moving out to meet them. Among these blacks and some working-class whites, Clay's firm support for organized labor will win him votes.

But in the northern part of the redrawn 1st are white communities such as Ferguson, Bellefontaine Neighbors and Jennings, where the blue-collar voters are fiercely opposed to busing and abortion. The residents here are accustomed to Young's stand against both of these issues; Clay's opposite position seems likely to make him totally unsalable in many of these communities, even to loyal Democratic Party members.

In the extreme northern part of the county, suburbs such as Spanish Lake are transferred into the 1st District

New Missouri Districts

New District	Incumbent	Population	1980 Pres. Winner
1	William Clay (D)	546,208	Carter
2	Robert A. Young (D)	546,039	Reagan
3	Richard A. Gephardt (D) Bill Emerson (R) [1]	546,102	Reagan
4	Ike Skelton (D)	546,637	Reagan
5	Richard Bolling (D)	546,882	Carter
6	E. Thomas Coleman (R)	546,614	Reagan
7	Gene Taylor (R)	545,921	Reagan
8	Wendell Bailey (R) [2]	546,112	Reagan
9	Harold L. Volkmer (D)	546,171	Reagan

[1] *Emerson plans to run in the 8th District.*

[2] *Bailey plans to run in the 4th District.*

from the old 9th District. These suburban areas generally support conservative Democratic or Republican candidates.

District 2

Western St. Louis County, St. Charles

Incumbent: Robert A. Young (D)

The 2nd District contains the high- and middle-income suburbs of St. Louis, a significant blue-collar population and a few low-income neighborhoods. Net population change in the district during the 1970s was negligible; growth of outlying suburban areas in St. Louis County was negated by declines in areas closer to the city.

The district's vote tilts toward the Republican Party in statewide elections, although Democratic Rep. Robert A. Young has been able to increase his margins steadily since the 1976 election with his pro-labor, pro-defense and anti-abortion politics.

The new map reinforces the district's tendency to vote Republican, and it may improve the chances of a Republi-

can challenger to Young. Shifted out of the 2nd into the 1st are blue-collar areas currently in the northeast corner of Young's territory — communities such as Ferguson and St. Ferdinand, which identify closely with Young, who was a working member of the Pipefitters Union before coming to Congress.

From the 8th District, the 2nd takes in a large section of western St. Louis County, with about 58,000 residents who are for the most part affluent and Republican. From the 9th, north of the city, it picks up part of heavily Democratic Florissant, a city of 55,000, plus 65,185 residents of St. Charles and politically marginal St. Charles County.

McDonnell Douglas, the giant aircraft maker, is the most important employer in the 2nd District, and one that Young works consistently to protect. Other major employers are Chrysler, Emerson Electric, Ford and Monsanto Corporation.

District 3

South St. Louis, Southeast St. Louis County and Jefferson County

Incumbent: Richard Gephardt (D)
Bill Emerson (R)

When the remap placed Emerson's Jefferson County home in Gephardt's 3rd District, Emerson declared he would relocate to Cape Girardeau in the redrawn 8th District. His move reflected a consensus that Gephardt will be difficult to beat in the 3rd, even though the remap gives him more than 150,000 new constituents, many of whom tend to vote Republican. The new people are brought in to make up for the 3rd District's 13 percent population decline during the 1970s.

To accommodate southward expansion of the underpopulated 1st District, the 3rd also moves south, and all of it will now be located below Interstate 44 in St. Louis. That costs Gephardt some of his working-class ethnic communities in South St. Louis, but city residents will still make up more than one-third of the district's population.

William Clay   **Robert A. Young**

Richard A. Gephardt   **Bill Emerson**

South St. Louis voters were once firmly rooted in the New Deal coalition, but they have become increasingly concerned about taxes, government spending, abortion and busing. Nonetheless, Democratic ties persist — Jimmy Carter won 52 percent in 1980 in the city portions of the old 3rd — and Gephardt should continue to keep the city voters in his column.

But 40 percent of the voters in the new 3rd will be in St. Louis County, outside the city. The 3rd picks up from the 2nd part or all of several communities, among them Webster Groves, Crestwood and Sunset Hills. Some of the county voters grew up on St. Louis' South Side and moved out in the past decade; others are affluent, veteran suburbanites. Both groups are inclined to vote Republican in statewide elections; in 1980, Reagan won more than 60 percent in the county portion of the current 3rd. Like Young in the 2nd District, Gephardt has appealed to suburban voters with a philosophy blending conservative and progressive elements.

The residents of Jefferson County are the largest bloc of newcomers to Gephardt's territory; they make up more than a quarter of the redrawn 3rd District's population. Jefferson has come under the umbrella of metropolitan St. Louis in recent years, but much of the county is still rural and agricultural. Democrats can win Jefferson with a conservative pitch, but the GOP is always a threat. Carter won Jefferson in 1976, but Reagan took it four years later.

District 4

West — Kansas City suburbs, Jefferson City

Incumbent: Ike Skelton (D)

Redistricting enhances the rural character of the 4th District by removing some of its metropolitan Kansas City areas and extending the district's boundaries into the heart of south-central Missouri.

Taking on rural territory is no problem for Ike Skelton, who relied on support from farms and small towns to defeat two suburban opponents in his first House primary. But many of the rural counties he gains in redistricting are solidly Republican, and this could cause him trouble.

Republican Bailey, whose 8th District was dismembered by the remap, is moving into the 4th District to challenge Skelton in the 1982 election. Shifted into the 4th from Bailey's territory are seven counties: Cole, Moniteau, Miller, Maries, Camden, Pulaski and Texas. In 1980, Bailey carried six of those counties; all seven voted Republican in the presidential and Senate contests. Also moving into the 4th is Laclede County, a GOP bastion currently part of the 7th District.

In all, the new 4th will contain about one-third of Bailey's current constituency. But it will still have many of Skelton's best rural counties south and east of Kansas City, plus solidly Democratic areas of Jackson County east of the city. The incumbent has performed well in all three of his general elections so far; in 1980, he drew 67.8 percent of the vote.

The 4th gives up a slice of Jackson County to the 6th District, along with three rural counties in its northeastern corner. It loses most of Independence to the underpopulated 5th.

The district's farms raise corn, soybeans, wheat and some livestock. Outside Jackson County, the largest population center is Jefferson City (Cole County), the state capital. The redrawn 4th contains all the tourist territory around the Lake of the Ozarks and also Missouri's largest military facilities — the Whiteman and Richards-Gebaur Air Force bases, and Fort Leonard Wood. Skelton has made civil defense a central issue in his House career.

District 5

Kansas City and eastern suburbs

Incumbent: Richard Bolling (D)

Redistricting, combined with Bolling's retirement after 34 years in the House, should make Republicans a bit more competitive in a district that has seen little action in recent years.

Though Kansas City has not suffered the massive, St. Louis-like flight of people and businesses, its population shrank to less than 450,000 by 1980 — fewer than lived in the city 30 years earlier. The 5th, which currently includes most of Kansas City plus suburban Grandview and part of Raytown, will be expanded under the remap to take in 146,000 additional people, most of them in suburbs east of the city. This is sure to increase the Republican vote.

The eastern boundary of the redrawn district follows the route of Missouri 291, which cuts through the eastern sections of Independence and Lee's Summit, dividing those towns between the 4th and 5th districts. Partisan allegiances are much more closely divided in these suburbs than in Kansas City itself; Lee's Summit has leaned to Republicans lately, while Independence usually gives Democrats an edge.

Despite the remap, the 5th remains primarily Democratic in most elections. Carter won 60 percent of the Kansas City vote in 1980, offsetting Reagan's narrower advantage in suburban Jackson County.

Kansas City still depends to a great extent on grain; it is the marketing center for a surrounding six-state agricultural region. Meatpacking continues, though the stockyards are far less important economically today than they were in the city's cow-town heyday. Hallmark, a greeting card company, ranks as the second largest employer, with 7,000 workers. Blacks make up about one-fourth of the district's population.

District 6

Northwest — St. Joseph

Incumbent: E. Thomas Coleman (R)

Half the residents of this sprawling, 27-county district live in Clay, Platte and Buchanan counties, in the district's southwest corner. Clay and Platte send many workers to the industries and businesses of Kansas City, just to the south. The city of St. Joseph, a flour-milling and meat-packing center, is located in Buchanan County.

After voting for Carter in 1976, these three counties moved somewhat tentatively to the GOP column in 1980: Reagan carried each with about 54 percent of the vote. But the picture of partisan preferences is still blurry, for these counties also gave Democrat Thomas F. Eagleton solid support in his 1980 re-election to the Senate.

The rest of the counties in the 6th are rural and generally conservative. Coleman, who has won comfortably in three House races, is gradually leading the traditionally Democratic rural counties to the GOP. All but one of them went for Reagan in 1980, as he carried the district over Carter by nearly 19,000 votes.

The rolling prairies of northern Missouri are among the most fertile agricultural areas in the state, with parts of the 6th resembling the Iowa breadbasket. The closest thing Missouri has to a Yankee influence is found in Putnam, Mercer and a few other 6th District counties on or near the Iowa border. Ohio and Iowa farmers moved into that area long ago, and for years it has rivaled the Ozarks for fidelity to the GOP.

Though population in suburban Platte County expanded rapidly during the 1970s, most counties in the 6th either saw modest growth or slight decline. Redistricting gives Coleman five new rural counties and part of another: Saline, Cooper and Howard in the central part of the state,

Ike Skelton   **Richard Bolling**

E. Thomas Coleman   **Gene Taylor**

Putnam and Schuyler on the Iowa border, and a small slice of northeast Jackson County. Of those areas, only steadfastly Democratic Howard County, with 10,000 people, is likely to be an electoral nuisance to Coleman.

Transferred from the 6th to the 9th under the remap is Adair County.

District 7

Southwest — Springfield, Joplin

Incumbent: Gene Taylor (R)

Long a poor, isolated area resembling Appalachia, the scenic Ozark highlands have been discovered by tourists, retirees and new industry. Newcomers streamed into the 7th during the 1970s, boosting the population 22.2 percent, the fastest growth rate in any Missouri district. But there is little change in the district's Republican character.

The tourist and retiree presence is most obvious in the south-central part of the district, around Table Rock Reservoir and Bull Shoals Lake. Stone and Taney counties there each grew 57 percent in the last decade.

More than a third of Taylor's constituents live in Springfield and surrounding Greene County, the region's industrial and commercial center. Kraft, Litton, 3M, Rockwell and Zenith are major employers. The other population center in the district is Joplin, an old lead- and zinc-mining town now also engaged in manufacturing.

However, the rural and agricultural character of the Ozarks has not yielded completely to development and modernization. There are still many small, isolated communities, the legacy of the Ozarks' original settlers — Scots-Irish mountaineers who relocated from eastern Tennessee, western Virginia and Kentucky and who generally kept to themselves and coaxed their crops from the rocky soil. The international headquarters of the Assemblies of God are in Springfield, reflecting the traditional importance of fundamentalism in the Ozarks.

Political attitudes here have changed little in the past century. The Ozarks had no use for slavery on their small, hilly farms; most were pro-Union in the Civil War and have voted Republican ever since. GOP candidates regularly take more than 60 percent of the vote in southwest Missouri; Reagan swept every county in the 7th in the 1980 presidential contest.

Taylor, serving his fifth House term, has been held below 60 percent only once, in 1974, when Watergate burdened GOP candidates nationwide. Redistricting barely alters the 7th, shifting only one county, Laclede, into the 4th District.

District 8

Southeast — Cape Girardeau

Incumbent: Wendell Bailey (R)

The redrawn 8th merges 18 counties from Emerson's old 10th District with seven counties from Bailey's old 8th. The decision by Bailey to run elsewhere clears the way for Emerson to move here from his Jefferson County home, which the remap placed in the 3rd.

But without Jefferson County and its 146,814 people, the new 8th will be a challenge for Emerson or any Republican to win. In 1980, the county gave Emerson 55 percent of its vote, negating Democratic margins in the rural, traditionally Democratic counties of southeast Missouri's Bootheel.

Under the remap, the largest block of GOP votes in the district will come from Cape Girardeau County, which has just under 59,000 people. That county and neighboring Perry County both voted Republican in the last two presidential contests.

At the opposite end of the partisan spectrum are the Bootheel counties in the extreme southeast corner of the district. This area still looks and votes like the old South. Although Reagan's philosophy appealed to conservative Democrats throughout Missouri, four Bootheel counties with a total population of nearly 100,000 — Dunklin, Pemiscot, New Madrid and Mississippi — voted for Carter and the rest of the statewide Democratic ticket in November 1980.

In other traditionally Democratic counties elsewhere in the 8th, Republicans have gained ground in recent elec-

tions. Iron County, for example, voted only narrowly for Carter in 1980, and Emerson won it.

On the western border of the redrawn 8th are seven counties with 131,363 people currently represented by Bailey. Those counties are Phelps, Howell, Crawford, Washington, Dent, Oregon and Shannon.

The most populous of those is Phelps County (population 33,633); it is the only one of the seven that Bailey did not carry in his 1980 House race. The Democratic Party is strongest in Oregon and Shannon counties, but those two together contain fewer than 19,000 people. Overall, Republican candidates in the new 8th District should come out ahead in the seven counties brought in from Bailey's current territory.

District 9

Northeast — Columbia

Incumbent: Harold L. Volkmer (D)

Pushed north by the underpopulated St. Louis districts reaching outward for people, the 9th District draws away from metropolitan St. Louis and nearby St. Charles, taking on more of a small-town identity.

The loss of part of St. Louis County will not be entirely pleasant to Volkmer, who won the county portion of his current district by 7,000 votes in 1980. But the departure of St. Charles County may make up for any inconvenience. He lost that county in 1980, running poorly among suburbanites living in and around the city of St. Charles. The remap transfers out of the 9th about 65,000 people in those GOP-leaning areas. Volkmer retains 79,000 St. Charles residents, but most are in rural portions of the county and are likely to vote Democratic.

Having shed population in the St. Louis area, the redrawn 9th annexes the northern section of Bailey's old 8th District, beginning with Boone County (Columbia), whose 100,376 people make it the largest voting bloc in the new 9th.

The moderate-to-liberal University of Missouri community in Columbia lends an element of uncertainty to Boone County elections. Republicans have carried Boone in the last two gubernatorial contests, but Jimmy Carter won the county's presidential vote in both the 1976 and 1980 elections. Independent candidate John Anderson received 9 percent there in 1980, his best showing in the state.

The 9th crosses the Missouri River to take in Franklin, Osage and Gasconade counties. In a transfer with the 6th District, Volkmer gives up Putnam and Schuyler counties and takes in Adair County.

The remap enhances Republican strength in the 9th District, but surviving intact is the heart of Volkmer's constituency — northwest Missouri's "Little Dixie," a traditionally Democratic corn-and-cattle-raising area first settled by pro-slavery planters from Virginia and Kentucky. Though Ronald Reagan's conservative themes helped him carry all but two counties in this region in the 1980 election, Little Dixie is still a reliable supporter of Volkmer and most Democrats.

Wendell Bailey

Harold L. Volkmer

Nebraska

Nebraska knows what it likes in politics — stubborn, independent, common sense conservatives — and lately it has not worried about which party they belong to.

In national elections, Nebraska has been the most consistent Republican stronghold of modern times. Only one Democrat has carried it for president in the last 44 years. And for most of the postwar years, Nebraska behaved pretty much the same way in voting for Congress. From 1934 to 1976, it did not elect a single Democrat to the Senate.

Some would say it did not elect one in 1976 either. The Democratic nominee that year was Edward J. Zorinsky, the mayor of Omaha and a lifelong Republican. Zorinsky filed for the Democratic nomination only because Omaha congressman John Y. McCollister had the Republican primary sewed up. But once on the general election ballot, Zorinsky was an easy winner, and he serves in the Senate today as a Democrat.

In 1978, the other Senate seat switched parties for J. James Exon, a legitimate Democrat but one nearly as conservative as Zorinsky. That meant two Nebraska Democrats in the Senate for the first time in the state's history.

As Zorinsky proved, party loyalty is not very strong these days in Nebraska, the only state with a non-partisan Legislature. He and Exon both spoke for the low tax, low deficit philosophy of the state's farmers and ranchers, and of the increasingly conservative Omaha middle class. Both express their irritation at big government with a crankiness that goes over well all over the state. Candidates who carry that message can win on any ticket.

It was different in the early part of this century, when the two best-known Nebraska politicians were the populist William Jennings Bryan and the progressive George Norris. Bryan and Norris depended on struggling family farmers who sought to make a living on marginal land and usually found themselves dependent on the federal government for help. By World War II, most of this constituency had simply left the state. Nebraska suffered a net loss of more than 50,000 people between 1930 and 1950, while most other states were gaining, and the people remaining tended to be the more prosperous and conservative residents.

Nebraska is gaining population again now, although its 5.7 percent increase during the 1970s was smaller than the average gain nationwide. But it remains an overwhelmingly agricultural state. Agriculture provides employment, di-

rectly or indirectly, for over 80 percent of its 1,570,000 residents. Nebraska is one of the national leaders in beef cattle, corn, wheat and hogs. Its leading industries, meatpacking and food processing, are farm-related.

Omaha

Omaha is Nebraska's dominant city. Located across the Missouri River from Council Bluffs, Iowa, the city itself has 312,000 residents. More than 30 percent of the state's population, almost half a million people, live in the Nebraska portion of the Omaha metropolitan area, which includes Douglas and Sarpy counties.

Omaha is famous for stockyards that serve the cattle, hog and sheep growers of Nebraska. Although meatpacking, dairy products and food processing are the major industries, the economy is diversified. Omaha is an insurance center and the headquarters of the Union Pacific Railroad.

Although Omaha is an ethnic industrial city and nominal Democratic territory, it votes for conservatives. The blue-collar population, heavily Irish and Slavic, resembles that of ethnic areas in other Midwestern cities but has weaker Democratic Party ties. Omaha does have a substantial black community, which boosts the Democratic vote.

In gubernatorial contests, Democrats usually do well in Omaha. They have carried it and surrounding Douglas County in seven of the last eight elections. But the county has gone Republican for president every time but once in the post-Roosevelt era, and has had Republican representation in the House for all but four of the past 30 years. It elected Democrat John J. Cavanaugh to the House in 1976 and 1978, but when he retired in 1980, the Omaha-based 2nd District reverted to Republican control.

Lincoln

Lincoln is Nebraska's capital and second largest city, with 172,000 residents in the city and another 25,000 in the surrounding Lancaster County metropolitan area.

Republicans hold a majority in Lincoln, but there is a significant Democratic vote based around the university and the state government. Democrats here tend to be white-collar workers and more liberal than those in Omaha.

With the help of a strong showing in Lincoln, George McGovern beat Hubert Humphrey in the 1972 Nebraska Democratic primary. But in 1980, Lincoln stayed with

Jimmy Carter rather than taking the liberal alternative provided by Sen. Edward M. Kennedy.

In recent years Lancaster County has been slightly more Republican than Omaha in statewide elections, although Democrats have carried it in 6 of the last 10 gubernatorial contests. Republican Gov. Charles Thone, who comes from Lincoln, won it with 60 percent in 1978.

In presidential elections, Lincoln remains staunchly Republican. Republicans have won 10 of the last 11 presidential races here, losing only with Barry Goldwater in 1964. Since World War II, GOP presidential candidates have averaged almost 60 percent in Lancaster County.

Rural Nebraska

Nebraska's farmers raise corn, hogs and dairy cattle in the east and feed beef cattle in the the arid north-central "Sand Hills." Wheat is grown in the west and south, in fields irrigated by the Platte and Niobrara rivers.

Rural Nebraska has just over one-half of the state's population, about 800,000 people. Nebraska's small country towns sprang up along the Platte River system or along the rail lines that spread across the state. With the further mechanization of farming, rural residents have been leaving their farms and moving into these towns.

The largest city outside Omaha and Lincoln is Grand Island. Located 90 miles west of Lincoln, Grand Island is an industrial city and trading center of 33,000 people. Most of the other cities of any size are enlarged market towns that service the surrounding farmland.

Of the 90 counties in rural Nebraska, 58 have fewer than 10,000 residents. Four counties in the Sand Hills ranching region have fewer than 1,000 people.

Republicans normally carry the whole of rural Nebraska comfortably. GOP candidates do well in the small cities and even better on the farms.

The most Republican county in the state is Hooker County (population 990) in the Sand Hills. Richard Nixon took 88 percent of the Hooker County vote in 1968 and 1972. Barry Goldwater won 71 percent in 1964. No postwar Democrat has carried the county in a major statewide race.

Rural Nebraska was once a major breeding ground of populism, but that was long ago. However, the farmers still occasionally express their anger at the ballot box. In the 1980 Democratic primary, Kennedy ran best in the farming counties, largely because of the farmers' anger over President Carter's Soviet grain embargo rather than for any endorsement of Kennedy's liberal views.

There are a few pockets of regular Democratic votes in rural Nebraska. The largest is Saline County, southwest of Lincoln, with a population of 13,000. Others are Butler County, adjoining Lancaster County on the northwest, and a lightly populated tri-county area in central Nebraska — Greeley, Sherman and Howard counties.

RELUCTANT GOP
MAKES MINOR CHANGES

If Nebraska Republicans had had their way, the state's three congressional districts would have remained unchanged in the 1980s.

But under the threat of a Democratic lawsuit charging that the 2.4 percent population variance between the districts was too great, the GOP reluctantly made two minor changes that brought the variance to 0.23 percent.

The political impact of the revisions will be minimal. Fewer than 8,000 of the state's 856,000 registered voters will be affected by the changes, which will move six townships in Cass County from the 2nd District to the 1st and all of rural Thayer County from the 1st to the 3rd.

Democrats in Nebraska's unicameral Legislature introduced a more elaborate plan this year that featured a population variance of just 0.01 percent (57 people). It was designed to strengthen the party's chances in the 1st, which has elected a Democrat only once in its 20-year history.

The Democratic plan, proposed in late April, would have dropped three heavily Republican counties from the 1st (Knox, Pierce and Madison) and replaced them with three marginal counties currently in the 3rd. Republicans called this a "drastic and unnecessary change" and a blatant effort at political gerrymandering.

Although the single-chamber Legislature is officially non-partisan, senators registered in the Republican Party outnumber registered Democrats by about a two-to-one margin. So Democrats knew their plan had no chance of winning on a roll call. But they thought a federal court might approve it because its population variance was so much lower than that of the original GOP status-quo idea.

Republicans asked the state attorney general if keeping the old map would stand up in court, and were told it might be vulnerable to challenge. So they reluctantly drew their own plan altering the boundaries slightly to equalize population. The map drafted by the redistricting committee was finally approved May 27, 1981 on a 37-6 vote, and Republican Gov. Charles Thone signed it May 28, 1981.

District 1

East central — Lincoln

Incumbent: Douglas K. Bereuter (R)

The state capital, Lincoln, gives the 1st District a modest urban flavor, but the city does not dominate the district the way Omaha influences the neighboring 2nd.

Douglas K. Bereuter

Hal Daub

U. S. Congress: 3 districts
  Senate (2D)
  House (3R)
Governor:
  Charles Thone (R)
Population: 1,570,006
Area: 77,227 sq. miles
1980 Presidential Vote:
  Carter (26%)
  Reagan (66%)
  Anderson (7%)

New
Nebraska
Districts

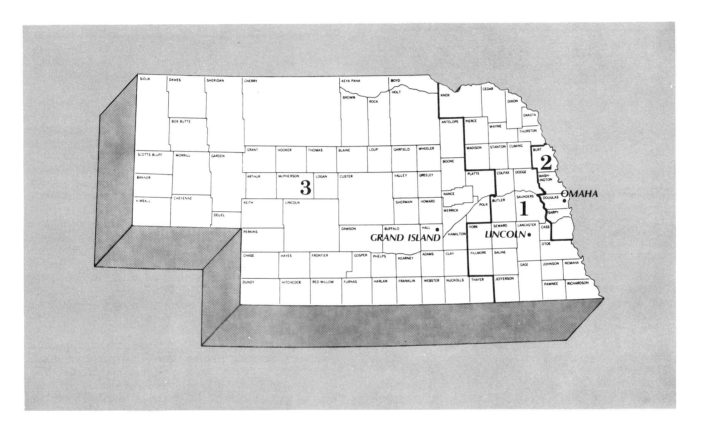

Lancaster County, which includes Lincoln and its few surrounding suburbs, makes up 37 percent of the new 1st District's population. Essentially a white-collar town, Lincoln is dominated by the state government and the University of Nebraska located there. Partisan registration in the county is nearly evenly split between the two major parties and Lancaster County can go either way in a close statewide election.

The rest of the district is largely made up of prosperous, predominantly Republican farming areas where corn is the major crop. The few small cities, such as Fremont, Norfolk and Beatrice, are market centers closely tied to farming.

The counties located along the Platte River (Colfax, Dodge, Butler and Saunders) provide some Democratic votes, along with Saline County, southwest of Lincoln, and Dakota County, a meatpacking area situated along the Missouri River that is becoming a suburb of Sioux City, Iowa.

The rest of the 1st District's 27 counties, particularly those located toward the northern border, vote with overwhelmingly Republican majorities. Ronald Reagan, who took 62 percent of the vote districtwide in November 1980, won 73 percent of the vote in the northern 10 counties of the 1st District. Bereuter won 83 percent in those same counties.

Douglas K. Bereuter should hardly be affected by the slight changes made in his constituency by the redistricting proposal. He loses rural Thayer County, where he has been running strong, while gaining six townships on the western side of Cass County. These counties are geographically located midway between Lincoln and Omaha but are politically closer to Lincoln. Two of the six townships have Democratic registration advantages, but all six have been voting as Republican as the rest of the district that they are joining.

There was some discussion of moving Knox County, located on the South Dakota border, from the 1st District

New Nebraska Districts

New District	Incumbent	Population	1980 Pres. Winner
1	Douglas Bereuter (R)	522,556	Reagan
2	Hal Daub (R)	523,765	Reagan
3	Virginia Smith (R)	523,685	Reagan

to the 3rd. But Bereuter has been active on behalf of the Santee Indians, who have a reservation in that county. He did not want to lose it, and the Legislature accommodated him.

District 2

East — Omaha

Incumbent: Hal Daub (R)

The 2nd is dominated by the old railroad and meat-packing center of Omaha, whose metropolitan area holds 60 percent of its population and whose newspapers and television stations provide nearly all of its information.

While Omaha is nominally a Democratic city, with large Irish and East European ethnic communities, it has voted conservatively for more than a generation, and its representation has nearly always been Republican. Still, the 2nd was the only district in the state that elected a Democrat during the 1970s. In 1976 and 1978, Democrat John J. Cavanaugh managed to win narrow victories on the strength of large majorities in the city, which in 1970 accounted for nearly 90 percent of the county population.

But with the suburbs doubling in size over the last decade and Omaha losing more than 10 percent of its population, Douglas County has gradually become more Republican. Many of the Irish and East European ethnics have left the city, which is now 12 percent black, and have moved into nearby suburbs in Douglas and Sarpy counties. When Cavanaugh chose to retire in 1980, the district quickly went back to its Republican tradition, electing Daub, who had come within 7,000 votes of defeating Cavanaugh in 1978.

While Democrats have maintained roughly a 50-40 registration advantage in the district's three southern counties over the last decade, voters there have been splitting their tickets for nearly a generation. The two smaller

counties to the north of Omaha are part of the Nebraska corn belt and solidly Republican.

The only change made in redistricting was the transfer of six townships in western Cass County to Bereuter's 1st. In 1980, Daub ran slightly behind most of the Republican ticket in the part of Cass County that remains in his district; he ran about even with it in the area he is giving up. But he carried even the areas where he ran behind the ticket, so the loss of 3,000 friendly voters should not hurt him.

District 3

Central and West — Grand Island

Incumbent: Virginia Smith (R)

Covering three-quarters of the state's land area, this is a rural district that runs from the corn belt at its eastern end to the wheat and ranching highlands west of the 100th meridian.

The 3rd is the most Republican district in the state. It gave more than 70 percent of its vote to Reagan in 1980, and 84 percent to Smith, now serving her fourth term. In strong Democratic years, Republicans are occasionally vulnerable in this area. A Democrat nearly defeated Smith in 1974. But the huge GOP registration advantage — exceeding 70 percent in some smaller counties — is usually more than enough to keep Republican incumbents in office.

The only city with more than 25,000 people in the district is Grand Island, largely a service center for the surrounding farm areas. Smaller population clusters such as Kearney, North Platte and Scottsbluff are strung along the Platte River west of Grand Island.

North of Grand Island are three heavily Democratic counties: Sherman, Greeley and Howard. Two others (Nance and Platte) have slimmer Democratic registration edges. During the 1970s Democratic Senate and gubernatorial candidates usually won these counties. But in recent years Smith has been able to carry them easily.

Virginia Smith

In the past decade more than one-half of the 61 counties in the 3rd District lost population. Most were in cattle lands just beyond the Platte River, or in the western panhandle. As a result, the 3rd was the only district in Nebraska that needed to gain people in redistricting. The addition of Republican Thayer County should make Smith's life even easier.

IV

The West

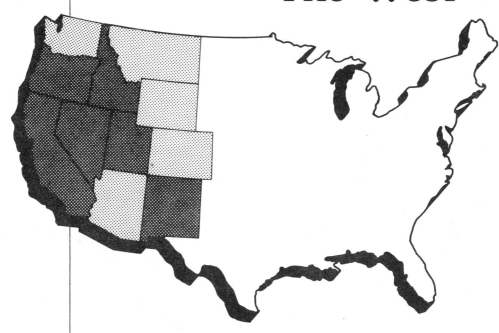

California

California is not embarrassed about being unusual. It thrives on its reputation for setting trends in American culture and politics. From tax rebellion to the skateboard, and from electing celebrities to establishing communes, California is often months, sometimes years, ahead of the rest of the nation.

California is seen from the outside as different; likewise, it also sees itself as different. "We like to be viewed as a land of fruits and nuts," says Ed Salzman, its veteran political writer and editor of the *California Journal*. "We enjoy our status as the breeding ground for weirdo politicians."

One does not have to describe any current office holder as a weirdo to document the state's penchant for entrusting public office to people with unorthodox backgrounds. In the last two decades California has elected to office two movie actors (Ronald Reagan and former Republican Sen. George Murphy), a 70-year-old Japanese-American semanticist (GOP Sen. S.I. Hayakawa), and a record promoter (Lt. Gov. Mike Curb). Its current governor, Edmund G. Brown Jr., came from a background in Jesuit study, social activism and part-time Zen contemplation to succeed almost overnight in state politics.

These men have been successful largely because of the weak party system that has existed in the state for most of the 20th century. Reacting against the railroad barons' domination of state politics in the late 19th century, political reformers eviscerated the political parties, introduced widespread use of referendum and set the stage for generations of politics dominated by personality rather than party.

The boom of the post-World War II years, when the population was increasing by a thousand people per day, turned the state into a quasi-nation. On its own, California's gross national product would be topped by only five nations in the world.

Massive waves of immigrants from the East, Midwest and South also have given a unique flavor to California politics. Nearly half of the state's current congressional delegation was born outside California. Whether seeking a fortune in real gold, green gold (lettuce), black gold (oil), or pure tinsel (motion pictures), millions have come to California in an attempt to assimilate their local values and political beliefs into the so-called California culture.

Throughout the 1930s and 1940s, the newcomers' political beliefs were predominantly Democratic. Registered Democrats have outnumbered Republicans in every general election since 1934, when Socialist Upton Sinclair was nearly elected governor on a tide of Depression discontent.

But the early wave of newcomers has grown conservative with prosperity, probably changing more than most generations elsewhere in the United States. It no longer makes much sense to talk about parts of the state being Democratic by registration; the people do not vote that way any more.

By any measure, the latest group of newcomers is overwhelmingly Democratic. The Hispanic population has moved across the Mexican border and from other parts of Latin America into the state, forming a potentially crucial force in state politics. The Hispanic population rose over the 1970s from 15 percent to 19 percent. But it has not realized its potential so far. A large but impossible-to-estimate number of these Hispanics are illegal aliens and cannot vote; others simply do not vote. No Hispanic has held major statewide office in recent years.

California's congressional delegation is almost evenly divided between Democrats and Republicans. Democrats control the state Legislature, although by decreasing margins. But in presidential voting over the last 30 years, none of the ten largest states have supported Republican candidates more often than California. Since 1948, only Lyndon B. Johnson among Democratic presidential candidates has carried the state.

The Rural North and Sierra Nevadas

Covering the distance from the Oregon border down to Death Valley, this area is the most scenic and least populated part of the state. Although partisan labels are largely ignored, voters in most of the region usually back conservatives. Six of the seven counties that Republican Paul Gann carried in his devastating loss to liberal Democratic Sen. Alan Cranston in 1980 were in this area. They included such lightly populated counties as Modoc, Sutter, Mono and Inyo, which usually give the Republican right its highest percentages in the state.

The only Democratic strength in the region is along the Pacific Coast north of the San Francisco Bay. Environmentalist voters have become highly organized in local fights with the area's developers and lumber interests, and are beginning to make their presence felt in elections for state and federal office as well.

The light population density dictates spacious congressional and state legislative districts in which challengers find it difficult to develop enough name recognition to unseat an incumbent. In contests without incumbents, however, virtually any district in the region can go to either party.

The forests, including the majestic redwood stands, are a major part of the economic base in northern California, along with the grape vineyards from California's wine region in the Napa Valley. North of Sacramento, between the Coastal Range and the southern part of the Cascades, lies the fertile Sacramento River plain, forming the northern part of the Central Valley. The rice and barley farmers around Yuba City tend to be more Republican than the fruit and vegetable farmers of the San Joaquin Valley directly to the south. Further east and south in the Sierra Nevadas, ski resorts and other recreational pursuits provide a large percentage of the local income, as well as controversy between local vendors and Sierra Club activists bent on keeping development to a minimum.

The Central Valley

From Sacramento on the north to the foothills of the Tehachapi Mountains on the south, the Central Valley forms a figurative fruit basket for the nation. The valley's rich soil, sun and extensive irrigation provide a suitable growing climate for virtually every species of fruit, vegetable and field crop found in the Temperate Zone.

Naturally, agricultural issues play a paramount role in the region's politics, with irrigation and farm labor causing the thorniest problems in recent decades. Agribusiness interests have tried to cut costs by keeping wages low for farm workers and taking advantage of federally subsidized irrigation. Mexican-American migrant workers — few of whom vote — have fought for unionization and better working conditions, while others have sought to break up the land holdings of the farming conglomerates by reimposing an acreage limit on federally subsidized water.

Many of the farm managers and small farm owners migrated to California from southern states. They retain a pro forma allegiance to the Democratic Party, but often find Republicans more sympathetic to their interests.

Alternating bands of Democratic and Republican strength work their way down the valley from north to south.

The most Democratic part of the region is at its northern end in Sacramento and Yolo counties. Sacramento has thousands of state government professionals and a large minority population — two groups which tend to favor greater government involvement in social problems. Yolo County is dominated by the University of California's Davis campus, the third largest branch of the massive state system. As with nearly all the state campuses in California, there is a strong liberal tilt. Yolo County gave George McGovern his second highest percentage in the state and was one of only three counties that opposed tax-cutting Proposition 13 in 1978. It rejected Ronald Reagan in the 1980 general election.

The farming areas around Stockton and Modesto, just south of the Sacramento area, tend to be more Republican. The farms are not as large as in other parts of the valley and are often devoted to dairy farming, fruits and vegetables.

One band further south is the Fresno area — the unofficial capital of the Central Valley. Fresno is the largest and most economically diverse city in central California. It is more Democratic than the surrounding area.

The southernmost portion of the Central Valley, around Bakersfield, tends to be the most Republican area. Oil wells and cotton produce a political environment akin to parts of Texas, from which some of the older residents of the area originally came.

The San Francisco Bay Area

Most Democrats run better here than anywhere else in the state, but it is not highly partisan territory. Only parts of San Francisco and a few of its nearby communities are true Democratic strongholds. The bulk of the area — much of it middle-class suburban — exhibits a high degree of independence in its voting behavior. While Cranston had no trouble winning 69 percent of the Bay area vote in 1980, Reagan still carried the region, despite losing San Francisco and Alameda counties. Nearly a third of the state legislators from the Bay area are Republicans.

San Francisco is the most liberal — some would say radical — part of the area. It was the only county in the state to vote against the death penalty in 1978. Homosexuals take an active role in San Francisco politics and are easily accepted by the city's liberal power structure, notwithstanding the assassination of a homosexual member of the city's board of supervisors by a former board member in 1978. The large Chinese and Japanese communities and the strong labor movement add to the city's Democratic tendency.

But San Francisco itself accounts for only 14 percent of the Bay Area population. Ringing the San Pablo and San Francisco bays are six counties which cover a wide spectrum of political values and life styles.

Moving in a clockwise direction from the Golden Gate Bridge, one first encounters the "mellow" affluent voters of Marin County, liberal but independent in their politics. Then come the blue-collar workers who labor in the shipyards and refineries of Vallejo and Richmond, and after that the student community in Berkeley and the poor black neighborhoods of Oakland. These provide Democratic majorities equal to those found in San Francisco. But further south, along the eastern shore of San Francisco Bay, are new suburbs and pockets of older ethnic neighborhoods, where the population is solidly middle-class and increasingly conservative.

At the southern end of the bay is the Democratic city of San Jose, once a quiet farm center that has seen rapid expansion and soon will have more people than San Francisco.

Turning north and moving up the western shore of the bay, one comes to the "Silicon Valley" — a center of modern electronic technology spurred on by its proximity to Stanford University — followed by some exclusive, wealthy Republican areas, and finally, blue-collar suburbs, such as Daly City, just south of San Francisco.

Central Coast

As in the Central Valley, the political cast of the Pacific Coast region becomes increasingly Republican the further south one travels. Beginning in Santa Cruz, on the northern shore of Monterey Bay, the region extends south along the coast for 335 miles to the Los Angeles County border.

Most of the region's population resides in coastal urban areas where the mountains have receded enough to

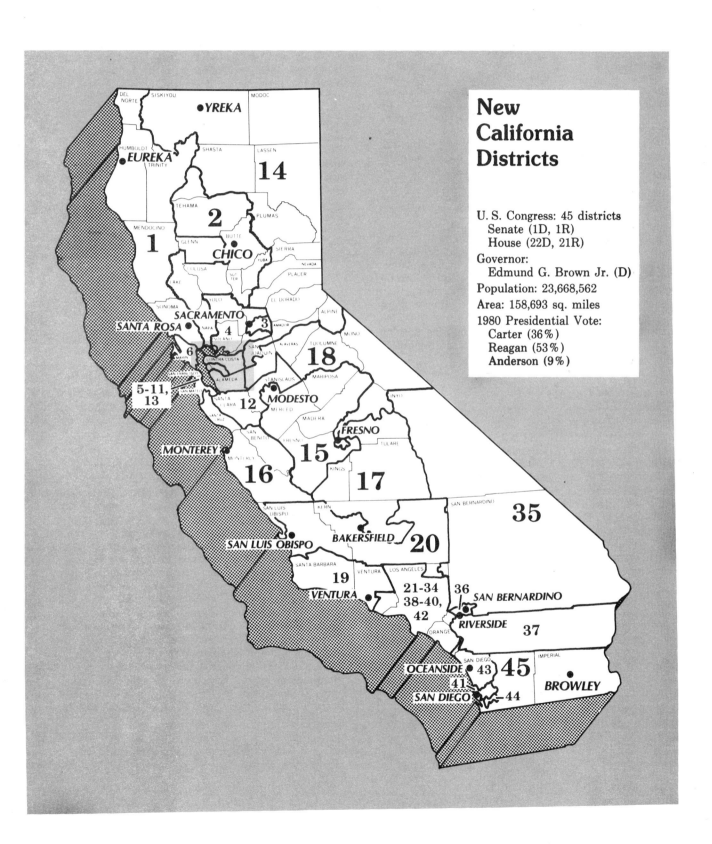

New
California
Districts

U. S. Congress: 45 districts
  Senate (1D, 1R)
  House (22D, 21R)
Governor:
  Edmund G. Brown Jr. (D)
Population: 23,668,562
Area: 158,693 sq. miles
1980 Presidential Vote:
  Carter (36%)
  Reagan (53%)
  Anderson (9%)

allow communities to develop. But while most of the region's voters are urban, agriculture is a vital part of the area's livelihood, particularly around the Salinas Valley in the north and in the citrus groves around Oxnard and Ventura in the south.

Once a predictably Republican area, the central coast has become marginal in the last decade, in part because of the 18-year-old vote and the large student concentrations in Santa Cruz and Santa Barbara, where state universities are located.

Santa Cruz students and others who have been drawn to the area for its scenery and relaxed pace make Santa Cruz County the most liberal area along the coast. It is also the only county in the region where the Democratic registration percentage has increased during the last decade.

Around the rest of the Monterey Bay and in the Salinas Valley exists a strange admixture of beach communities, exclusive Monterey Peninsula estates, military enclaves around Fort Ord and agricultural centers, such as Castroville, which bills itself as the "Artichoke Capital of the World."

As the farm land gives way to ranch land farther south, the population becomes more Republican, with the one exception of Santa Barbara. Over the last two decades, the expansion of exurban Los Angeles has gradually consumed Ventura County. Although few actually commute into Los Angeles from as far away as Ventura, it marks the northern edge of the urban conglomeration that continues almost uninterrupted to the Mexican border, nearly 200 miles south. The voters who live in the new housing developments of this area usually support statewide Republican candidates.

Los Angeles County

It has become almost axiomatic that a statewide candidate has to carry Los Angeles County in order to win. In the 26 statewide contests held over the last 14 years, only two have won without it — Republicans Gerald R. Ford for president and S. I. Hayakawa for the Senate, both in 1976.

Few places in the country can boast of having such great social, economic and ethnic diversity in such a compact space. In less than an hour, one can drive from the middle-class San Fernando Valley to the palatial homes on the Palos Verdes bluffs and pass through a demographic potpourri that includes the extravagant homes of Beverly Hills liberals, the West Side apartments of the elderly, ocean-front condominiums and yacht clubs, an Oriental community and a black ghetto.

Most of the city itself, which accounts for 3 million of the county's population of 7.5 million people, sits in a smog-enshrouded basin, surrounded by water or mountains. Living in relatively close proximity are the affluent liberal Jews of west Los Angeles, the burgeoning Hispanic community in east Los Angeles, and the black Watts neighborhood to the south of the central business district. Not surprisingly, the eight congressional districts from Long Beach north to the Santa Monica Mountains are all in Democratic hands. Since 1973, the city has elected a black Democrat, Tom Bradley, to the mayor's job.

But conservative suburban voters of all occupations and social classes surround this area, living in and over the various mountain ranges and along the Pacific Coast. Except for areas where the Hispanic vote has drifted to the east and the black vote moved southward, Republicans are dominant in suburban Los Angeles.

This diversity has resulted in a number of very close elections in the county over the last decade. With the political spectrum swinging back and forth, particularly in the marginal areas such as the San Fernando Valley and Long Beach, Los Angeles County has gone for both liberals and conservatives, often in the same election.

Orange County

This county, located between Los Angeles and San Diego, was once synonymous with the militant right. Democrats had little chance of winning, and membership in the John Birch Society was considered an advantage. For 17 years, voters in Orange County returned to Congress Republican James B. Utt, who likened government to a "child molester who offers candy before his evil act."

Orange County's conservative image has often been attributed to the homogeneity of its population. White, middle-class engineers and technicians who work in the area's aerospace firms have long been committed to a less-government-is-better philosophy, although that attitude was tested by recession in the aerospace industry in the early 1970s.

While Orange County still is predominantly Republican, working-class Democrats have begun to fill in the spaces Republicans left open. In 1978, Edmund G. Brown Jr. became the first Democratic gubernatorial candidate to carry the county since its orange groves were plowed under to make way for suburban annexation in the years after World War II. The Santa Ana-Garden Grove area regularly elects Democrats now to the state Legislature and U.S. Congress.

The southern and coastal areas of Orange County, however, remain overwhelmingly Republican. San Clemente, the location of Richard M. Nixon's Western White House, gave more than 70 percent of its votes to Ronald Reagan in 1980.

San Diego County

With one of the best natural harbors on the West Coast, San Diego is the home base of the Navy's Pacific fleet. That fact plays a vital role in the area's political leanings. Ranked with Norfolk, Va., as one of the two predominant Navy cities in the U.S., San Diego owes much of its economic prosperity to the military — the city's major employer. Not only is the military payroll enormous, but there are also thousands of civilian jobs dependent on Naval contracts, and the city has become a haven for retired Naval officers.

Overall, the state's second largest city tends to follow a pro-military Republican line. The last Democratic presidential candidate to carry San Diego County was Franklin D. Roosevelt in 1944. (In 1964 Republican Barry Goldwater edged out Lyndon B. Johnson in the county by less than 3,000 votes.) The Republican trend is likely to continue as thousands of retirees and skilled professional workers are drawn to the area by its warm climate and strong economy. In the last decade, San Diego was one of the fastest growing parts of the state.

Low-income black and Mexican voters, however, keep the GOP percentages lower in San Diego County than in neighboring Orange County. Concentrated in the city and close to the Mexican border, these blue-collar workers from the shipyards provide the core of Democratic support in San Diego. But to win, a Democrat must attract many Republican voters.

New California Districts

New District	Incumbent	Population	1980 Pres. Winner	New District	Incumbent	Population	1980 Pres. Winner
1	Don H. Clausen (R)	526,014	Reagan	23	Anthony C. Beilenson (D)	522,004	Reagan
2	Gene Chappie (R)	526,015	Reagan	24	Henry A. Waxman (D)	519,851	Reagan
3	Robert T. Matsui (D)	525,784	Reagan	25	Edward R. Roybal (D)	526,848	Carter
4	Vic Fazio (D)	527,549	Reagan	26	No Incumbent	532,941	Reagan
5	Phillip Burton (D)	527,053	Carter	27	Robert K. Dornan (R)	522,555	Reagan
6	John L. Burton (D)	523,174	Reagan	28	Julian C. Dixon (D)	525,838	Carter
7	George Miller (D)	526,226	Reagan	29	Augustus F. Hawkins (D)	525,830	Carter
8	Ronald V. Dellums (D)	525,907	Carter	30	John H. Rousselot (R)	519,869	Reagan
9	Fortney H. "Pete" Stark (D)	524,649	Reagan	31	Mervyn M. Dymally (D)	526,074	Carter
10	Don Edwards (D)	527,278	Carter	32	Glenn M. Anderson (D)	524,667	Reagan
11	Tom Lantos (D)	529,986	Reagan	33	Wayne Grisham (R) David Dreier (R)	520,215	Reagan
12	Paul N. McCloskey Jr. (R)	517,154	Reagan	34	No Incumbent	532,041	Reagan
13	Norman Y. Mineta (D)	532,717	Reagan	35	Jerry Lewis (R)	520,729	Reagan
14	Norman D. Shumway (R)	525,916	Reagan	36	George E. Brown Jr. (D)	531,619	Reagan
15	Tony Coelho (D)	524,419	Reagan	37	No Incumbent	525,870	Reagan
16	Leon E. Panetta (D)	524,535	Reagan	38	Jerry M. Patterson (D)	523,761	Reagan
17	Charles Pashayan Jr. (R)	529,134	Reagan	39	William E. Dannemeyer (R)	527,868	Reagan
18	No Incumbent	522,519	Reagan	40	Robert E. Badham (R)	525,298	Reagan
19	Robert J. Lagomarsino (R)	525,708	Reagan	41	Bill Lowry (R)	523,068	Reagan
20	William M. Thomas (R)	526,723	Reagan	42	Dan Lungren (R)	531,872	Reagan
21	Barry M. Goldwater Jr. (R) Bobbi Fiedler (R)	528,229	Reagan	43	Clair W. Burgener (R)	528,978	Reagan
				44	No Incumbent	525,886	Reagan
22	Carlos J. Moorhead (R)	532,285	Reagan	45	Duncan L. Hunter (R)	525,905	Reagan

The Imperial Valley

Irrigation in the Imperial Valley in the early 20th century turned desert into some of the most productive farm land in the nation, specializing in melons and winter vegetables. The politics of this self-proclaimed "Inland Empire," center around the booming twin cities of San Bernardino and Riverside, both centers for packing and shipping of the region's enormous citrus crop.

Once solidly Republican territory, the area east and south of Los Angeles has gradually turned into a competitive two-party area within the last decade. In Imperial and Riverside counties the increase in Democratic registration has clearly outdistanced GOP growth. But the farmers in the Imperial Valley tend to be conservative and often abandon their stated party preference at election time.

The industrial character of Riverside, along with a large steel mill at nearby Fontana, provides a base of Democratic votes on the edge of the desert. But it is sometimes offset by the voters in San Bernardino, a nearby metropolis devoted more to agriculture and the many military establishments in the immediate vicinity.

CALIFORNIA GOP MUST ACCEPT BURTON MAP

Nearly 200 years after Massachusetts Gov. Elbridge Gerry created the first "gerrymander," U.S. Rep. Phillip Burton has made a strong bid to have the entire practice renamed in his honor.

Burton alone is responsible for the new California congressional map that carves 43 current districts into 45 new ones and draws the lines expressly for the purpose of strengthening Democratic control.

The state was guaranteed two additional House seats by its population growth during the 1970s. But while most of the 18 percent increase occurred in Republican-minded suburban areas, Burton carved the district lines so that the Democrats' 22-21 margin in the state's House delegation would jump to 27-18, with a chance for a 28th Democratic district.

The redrawn map has resulted in the creation of two brand-new Democratic districts; three districts currently held by Republicans have been carved up beyond recognition. In almost every case, the lines of the open districts were formed with particular Democrats in mind, usually friends from the California Legislature.

One of the two new Democratic districts is in the Central Valley around Fresno; the other is in inner-city San Diego. Both of the new districts have been drawn to guarantee a Democratic registration advantage of more than 2-to-1. The damage to the Republicans is concentrated in Los Angeles County. Redistricting placed Republican Reps. Barry M. Goldwater Jr. and Bobbi Fiedler in the same district so that an open Democratic seat could be created in the San Fernando Valley. Goldwater averted a Republican primary duel by opting to run for the U.S. Senate seat held by S. I. "Sam" Hayakawa, who is retiring.

GOP Rep. Robert K. Dornan also chose the Senate option after most of the Republican areas in his old 27th District were removed, creating another Democratic seat in the western part of Los Angeles County. In the eastern part of Los Angeles County, Burton rearranged the districts represented by Republicans Carlos J. Moorhead, John H. Rousselot, Wayne Grisham and David Dreier. Grisham and Dreier ended up in the same district and will meet each other in the June 8, 1982, primary. Although most of Rousselot's old district was joined with Moorhead's district, Rousselot decided to avoid a primary battle with Moorhead. He is trying to get back to Washington the hard way, running in the largely Hispanic, heavily Democratic 30th District, vacated in March 1982 by Rep. George E. Danielson.

It is up to the California voters to decide how long the new district lines will remain in effect. Republicans were so outraged by the partisan nature of Burton's plan that they gathered enough signatures to qualify for a ballot referendum June 8, 1982. The Republican Party hoped to keep the new district map from taking effect this year. But in a 4-3 ruling handed down on Jan. 28, 1982, the state Supreme Court decided that the district lines as drawn by Burton would apply for the 1982 election regardless of the outcome of the referendum.

If voters reject the plan in June 1982, the Legislature will be required to come up with a new map for 1984. If the referendum is rejected and Burton's plan survives all court challenges, his map will stay in effect until after the 1990 census.

Providing only population figures of the 45 districts and a list of census tracts arranged by district, Burton convinced the Democratic majorities in both the state Senate and state Assembly to pass the new plan Sept. 15, 1981, without ever seeing a map. The plan evoked some dissension in the state Senate. Opponents claimed that Burton had tampered too much with some of the Democratic districts, notably the area represented by Anthony C. Beilenson, one of Burton's least-favorite colleagues. But those objections evaporated after Democratic National Committee Chairman Charles Manatt told the legislators that Burton's plan made up for losses Democrats had suf-

fered at the hands of Republicans in other states. Democratic Gov. Edmund G. Brown Jr. signed the bill on Sept. 16, 1981.

District 1

Northern Coast — Santa Rosa, Eureka

Incumbent: Don H. Clausen (R)

Covering more than 300 miles of Pacific coastline and including majestic stands of redwood trees, this district has a picturesque quality that masks the political tension growing within it.

For many years this area was the exclusive province of commercial fishermen and lumberjacks, some of whom made a few extra dollars every summer from the tourist trade. But in the past decade the northern coast has drawn a new class of immigrants — urban refugees from outside California who bring with them strongly held beliefs about protecting the environment at all costs. They are well organized politically, and their influence exceeds their actual numbers.

Various campaigns to block construction of dams and to expand the size of Redwoods National Park have pitted the district's two demographic factions against each other. These arguments have spilled over into congressional politics. Clausen, a veteran of nearly two decades in the House, generally sides with the developers, ranchers and lumbermen in the district who have been hurt by the economic downturn. The recession has pushed the unemployment rate in Del Norte County to nearly 28 percent. Economic well-being, Clausen thinks, is more important than making it easy for tourists to "view the redwoods from the side of the highway," as he once put it.

But this attitude has lost him support in Humboldt and Mendocino counties, which are now the Democratic center of the district. In 1978 Clausen lost Humboldt and narrowly retained Mendocino. Two years later, he won in Humboldt but lost Mendocino.

Redistricting gives this constituency a new number (it was the 2nd District in the past decade) and removes from it Napa County, with its grape vineyards, wineries and Republican voters. Smaller Lake County was also taken out in exchange for Glenn County, which is slightly more Republican.

The net effect of the change will be to give Mendocino and Humboldt county voters a larger voice in the district. This hurts any Republican running here, and Clausen more than most. Under the old lines, the combined population of Humboldt and Mendocino was about a quarter of the district's total. In the new 1st District, the two counties make up a third of the district's population.

Sonoma County at the southern end of the district holds the key to winning in the 1st. With nearly 300,000 residents, it is the fastest-growing part of the district and shows little party loyalty. In 1980, when Democratic Sen. Alan Cranston won Sonoma with 61 percent, independent presidential candidate John B. Anderson scored a significant 11.2 percent, taking votes from both Ronald Reagan and Jimmy Carter. Meanwhile, Clausen was carrying the county by a 55-41 margin. He will probably need to do that again to win in 1982.

District 2

North central — Napa, Redding

Incumbent: Gene Chappie (R)

At first glance, the cartography here looks unfavorable for Chappie and the Republicans. The GOP incumbent loses his home base in the foothills east of Sacramento, along with most of the land area of the old district.

But there is little for Republicans to worry about. In political coloration, the district is virtually identical to the one in which Chappie ousted a Democratic incumbent. Most of the land it loses is in sparsely populated mountain counties; nearly two-thirds of the constituents remain.

The new 2nd District, which replaces the old 1st, is settled neatly in the Sacramento Valley north of the state capital. The area is almost exclusively devoted to ranching and farming, which is fine with Chappie, a rancher who headed for the Agriculture Committee in his first term.

The four new counties added to the district — Napa, Sutter, Lake and Colusa — are largely agricultural. They are more Republican than the area Chappie currently represents. The peach and tomato farmers of Sutter County are the most conservative of the new constituents. Sutter County gave Reagan 64 percent in 1980 and even backed Paul Gann, the inarticulate candidate put up by the GOP against Cranston in 1980.

Across the low Vaca Mountains from Sutter and Colusa are the grape vineyards that cling to terraced hillsides in Napa and Lake counties. Napa County, the second most populous in the district, is known around the world for its wineries. Its politics has a Republican bouquet.

Barley and rice are the main crops of the Sacramento River basin. The 2nd District farmers who grow these crops tend to be conservative. At the northern end of the new 2nd District, near the headwaters of the Sacramento at Shasta Lake, the land is higher in elevation. This area, oriented toward ranching, often votes for Democrats.

All of the four counties that Chappie will continue to represent have supported recent Democratic candidates for president, for governor and for the U.S. Senate. But in his 1980 upset, Chappie beat Democratic incumbent Rep. Harold T. "Bizz" Johnson in each of these counties — Shasta, Tehema, Butte and Yuba.

Don H. Clausen   **Gene Chappie**

District 3

Most of Sacramento; eastern suburbs

Incumbent: Robert T. Matsui (D)

With some 275,000 inhabitants, Sacramento is the largest city in California's Central Valley. It is an agricultural center and major inland shipping port, but it draws its political identity from government — it is the capital of the nation's most populous state.

Close to 50,000 state employees live and work in Sacramento, providing the city with a strong pro-government, Democratic political base. The flagship newspaper of the McClatchy chain, the *Sacramento Bee*, takes a liberal editorial line that has been known to influence the outcome of elections in the area. Blacks and Hispanics — many of them state employees — make up more than a fourth of the city's population, which is another reason Democrats can usually count on carrying Sacramento.

The 3rd District includes all of the city except the primarily white, middle-to-upper-class area north of the American River. Also included in the 3rd are the suburban areas to the east, including Carmichael, which votes more Republican than the city. Because the old district was slightly overpopulated, the line was redrawn to exclude Folsom in the northeast corner of Sacramento County. The home of the large state prison, Folsom has the most conservative and Republican electorate in the county.

Since 1966, the 3rd District has been wholly contained within Sacramento County, and during that time it has never elected a Republican. John E. Moss represented Sacramento for 26 years until he retired in 1978. Although GOP presidential candidates Reagan and Gerald R. Ford and Republican Sen. Hayakawa have all carried the new 3rd District, Republicans appear to have given up hope of ousting Matsui. They made a strong effort to capture the seat when Moss retired in 1978, but Matsui edged by the GOP candidate, 53 to 47 percent, and won a second term easily two years later. The slight change in the district lines only makes Matsui stronger.

District 4

Suburban Sacramento to Bay Area — Fairfield, Davis

Incumbent: Vic Fazio (D)

Looking like a large jaw about to clamp down upon the state capital, the new 4th District surrounds Sacramento on three sides, and takes in the northern part of the city as well. Nearly half the population of the new 4th lives in the suburban part of Sacramento County, although the outskirts of the district spread west for more than 50 miles to San Pablo Bay.

Redistricting has given the 4th some additional areas around Sacramento, enhancing its suburban character. Most of this new territory, including the Folsom area and southern portions of Sacramento County, will make life

Robert T. Matsui

Vic Fazio

more difficult for Democratic candidates. None of the new areas are as friendly to Fazio as the northern Sacramento suburbs he currently represents.

Outside the Sacramento area, the district has only three cities of any size. The largest is Fairfield, in Solano County, with 58,000 residents. Located adjacent to Travis Air Force Base, Fairfield usually votes Republican, as does Woodland, 35 miles to the north in Yolo County. But between the two is Davis, a liberal, college community that gave Anderson a full 20 percent of the vote in his 1980 independent presidential campaign. For Davis voters, the more liberal and anti-establishment a candidate is, the better. Although the turnout in Davis tends to be high, the town accounts for only about one-tenth of the district vote, so Fazio will have to keep up his strength in the northern Sacramento suburbs to overcome the GOP vote elsewhere in the district.

In the old 4th, Democratic candidates could count on large pluralities in Vallejo, which has been removed in redistricting. The loss of Vallejo's blue-collar voters, who work in the city's shipyards and warehouses, will be a setback to any Democrat running in the district. Vallejo was the only city in Solano County that Carter carried in the 1980 election.

To offset the impact of losing Vallejo, the Democratic map makers also took out two agricultural counties to the north — Colusa and Sutter. These two, the only counties Fazio lost when he won his first term in 1978, consistently vote more Republican than any other part of the district.

District 5

Most of San Francisco

Incumbent: Phillip Burton (D)

To create a safe Democratic district for his brother John (who later decided to retire from the House), Phillip Burton made his own consituency a little less secure. But while its number changes from the 6th to the 5th, it remains Democratic territory. Contained completely within the city limits of San Francisco, the new 5th occupies all of the city except the eastern edge and the Haight-Ashbury and Hayes Valley sections in the center of the peninsula.

The major changes are the addition of Richmond and Pacific Heights in the north and the loss of the Bayshore and Hunters Point sections in the southeast. The parts of San Francisco most often seen by tourists — Chinatown, Nob Hill, North Beach and Telegraph Hill — are split between the two San Francisco districts along a line that roughly follows the Powell Street cable car.

Phillip Burton may be annoyed at having cost himself votes to make a safe district in which his brother is not bothering to run, but it remains to be seen whether Republicans can be competitive in the new 5th. A majority of the district's voters are the same people who have been returning Phillip Burton to the House for nine elections without giving him less than two-thirds of the vote. Among the districts in the state without a large Hispanic or black population, the new 5th has the highest percentage of registered Democrats — just under 60 percent.

The district is an ethnic, racial and sexual pastiche. A fifth of its residents are Asian, mostly Japanese and Chinese, members of the largest Oriental community on this side of the Pacific Ocean. Mexican-Americans live in the Mission District. A large and expanding homosexual community is centered around Castro and Market streets. There are white, middle-class neighborhoods of single-family homes on the western side of the city. And affluent professionals populate the neighborhoods around the Presidio, by the Golden Gate Bridge. The one thing these voters seem to have in common is an affinity for the Democratic Party.

District 6

Eastern San Francisco; Marin County; Daly City; Vallejo

Incumbent: John L. Burton (D)

Of all the oddly shaped districts on the new California map this one is the most bizarre. It was drawn this way so that John Burton might have enough Democratic constituents to win a fifth full term.

Three days before the filing deadline, however, John Burton decided he had no future in politics — not because

Phillip Burton

John L. Burton

George Miller   **Ronald V. Dellums**

of the shape of his new district, but because he wanted to go home and, as he said, "walk out in the fog."

John Burton's old district — numbered as the 5th — included the northwest section of San Francisco plus Marin County, across the Golden Gate Bridge. Because most of the Marin County residents worked or formerly lived in San Francisco, the district had a certain degree of social cohesion. Such is not the case in the new 6th District.

The new 6th has four distinct and detached parts. Two are connected only by water, the other two by a narrow piece of land used for railroad yards.

In land area and population, the largest of the four segments is Marin County, which will still cast more than 40 percent of the district's vote. Marin has been stereotyped in fiction and journalism as the home of "mellow" — a uniquely California lifestyle enjoyed by the rich and characterized by a social and cultural permissiveness that stops just short of intruding on another person's "space."

Politically, however, Marin County is not quite as liberal as its social image might suggest. It supported Reagan in 1980 and Ford in 1976. It favored tax-cutting Proposition 13 in the 1978 primary and the death penalty proposition in the 1978 general election. In 1980, John Burton lost Marin County to his GOP challenger.

About a third of the residents of the new 6th live in San Francisco, along the waterfront on the bay side and up into the hills as far as Haight-Ashbury. Much of the city's large and politically active gay community is located in the 6th District, as well as many counterculture people busy reliving the 1960s. For the most part, the wealthier homes built in the hills are in the 5th District, as is most of Chinatown.

The two sections of the new district farthest from downtown are Daly City and Vallejo. Vallejo, a city of 80,000 on the northeast side of the San Pedro Bay, is socially, politically and geographically separate from the rest of the district. It is easier for Vallejo residents to get to Sacramento than to Haight-Ashbury.

Vallejo, formerly in the 4th District, is a blue-collar, Democratic city that heavily relies on the defense industry for its economic support. Carter carried Vallejo in 1980, although with less than a majority.

Daly City, slightly smaller than Vallejo, is an industrial suburb immediately south of San Francisco. It is not quite as heavily Democratic by registration as Vallejo and not as dependent on the defense industry. Both Daly City and Vallejo were added to the 6th to give John Burton a reli-

able Democratic base to go with his natural constituency in San Francisco.

With Burton no longer running, the political future of the 6th is questionable. In statewide elections, no Republican has won in its territory in the last eight years. However, the Democratic vote consistently has been about four percentage points less than in the neighboring San Francisco district. A locally popular Republican, especially one who appealed to moderates, might run well here. Before John Burton came to Washington, Marin County and part of San Francisco had been represented for 21 years by a Republican, William S. Mailliard.

District 7

Most of Contra Costa County; Richmond

Incumbent: George Miller (D)

The 7th and Contra Costa County are split almost evenly between the urbanized, industrial areas along the east side of the San Pablo Bay and the new suburban tracts that have grown like crab grass behind the San Pablo mountain ridge.

In forty years of largely unchecked expansion, the county's population has exploded from 100,000 to more than 650,000. The shoreline property from Richmond to Pittsburg is given over primarily to commerce, particularly shipping and oil and sugar refining. The Contra Costa shoreline looks more like northern New Jersey than Marin County, only five miles distant across the bay. The blue-collar workers of Richmond and the crowded industrialized towns nearby are strongly Democratic. Richmond, nearly 50 percent black, voted for Carter in 1980 by an overwhelming margin.

The climate — both political and meteorological — is considerably different on the other side of the mountains that separate the coast from inland Contra Costa County. Once a fertile agricultural area, these inland areas are now largely occupied by housing developments.

Leaving the fog and the liberal politics on the other side of the hills, white-collar professionals have moved into communities such as Concord and Walnut Creek in mas-

Fortney H. 'Pete' Stark   **Don Edwards**

sive numbers. More of these commuters still register as Democrats than Republicans, but they tend to vote Republican. Thanks to a large Republican turnout on this inland side of mountains, Carter lost the new 7th District in 1980. Other statewide Democrats have been able to carry the district, but not by big margins.

A third-generation "Contra Costan," Miller usually runs well ahead of the Democratic ticket. He should be helped by the minor changes made in the district lines in 1981. To reduce the district's population by about 30,000, the mapmakers removed part of the San Ramon Valley in the inland section. This gave the Republican bedroom communities of San Ramon, Danville and Alamo to the new 8th District.

District 8

Northern Alameda County — Oakland, Berkeley

Incumbent: Ronald V. Dellums (D)

The Black Panther Party, the "free-speech movement" and the Symbionese Liberation Army all were born within this constituency, an intriguing mixture of poverty and intellectual ferment. The East Bay cities of Oakland and Berkeley make up about 60 percent of the district's voters and form its economic, philosophical and political base. To many of the left-wing activists who live and work in this area the term "liberal" has long been considered a pejorative.

The enormous University of California campus in Berkeley has provided an active political force in the area for decades, although in recent years it has been far less vocal than in the 1960s and early 1970s. It has been augmented by thousands of loyally Democratic black voters in Oakland, Berkeley's larger neighbor to the south. Oakland, 47 percent black, is one of the poorest cities in the state. Overall, the district is just over a quarter black.

The new 8th expands south to include some of the poorest black and Hispanic sections of Oakland, near the Alameda County Coliseum and the Oakland International Airport. The only part of the city not now included in the 8th District is an integrated middle-class area placed in the 9th.

Dellums's district also was forced to expand slightly farther into the upper-class, conservative areas of Contra Costa County that adjoin Alameda County. The Lafayette-Moraga section of Contra Costa County has never given Dellums more than 40 percent of the vote; the San Ramon Valley communities newly added will not support the black incumbent with any greater enthusiasm.

Dellums, like all Democrats in the area, relies on Berkeley and Oakland voters for his victories. They make the district as a whole solidly Democratic. Even Carter, who was swamped by Edward M. Kennedy in the 1980 presidential primary, was able to carry the new 8th in the fall. In fact, this was the only one of the redrawn East Bay districts he carried. Third party candidates John B. Anderson and Barry Commoner took more than 15 percent of the vote in the district — the highest in the Bay Area outside of San Francisco. In Berkeley, Anderson and Commoner combined to outpoll Reagan by 10,400 to 7,900 votes.

District 9

Suburban Alameda County — Hayward

Incumbent: Fortney H. 'Pete' Stark (D)

The new 9th is Democratic, but not nearly as liberal as Stark, its five-term incumbent, who has survived on his party label, his personal wealth and his usually weak opposition.

The fastest-growing portions of this constituency have shown increasing willingness to vote Republican at the statewide level. Despite a Democratic registration advantage of 60 to 28, Reagan managed to carry the newly drawn 9th District in 1980, thanks to his following on the eastern side of the San Leandro Hills.

Like most of the East Bay districts, the 9th has two divergent parts. Working-class Democratic areas lie along the bay; a high-tech, suburban growth area is firmly established on the other side of the hills that form the eastern wall of the San Francisco basin.

The more densely populated bay-side area is dominated by warehouses and older factories that make motor vehicle parts and office machines. This area includes San Leandro, once largely a Portuguese enclave that still has a strong blue-collar voting bloc. San Leandro has gone for every recent Democratic presidential nominee except Carter in 1980. Reagan's appeal to the economic interests of the voters here gave him a 48-41 margin.

To the north of San Leandro is Oakland. The transfer of black and Hispanic sections of the city to the 8th District left only a thin wedge of middle-class black and white communities in Stark's 9th.

To the south, the 9th District expands to include all of Hayward, now the largest city in the district, with 94,000 residents. Previously Stark represented less than 10 percent of the city, but now he picks up the entire student population around Hayward's California State University campus, which should be a political benefit. Statewide Democratic candidates have consistently run several percentage points better in Hayward than in the rest of the district.

The area of greatest concern for Stark will be the section of the district on the other side of the San Leandro Hills, where high-tech research industries centered around Livermore have drawn thousands of affluent suburbanites. In the last two decades Livermore has tripled in size; Pleasanton has increased its population eightfold. In 1980, both communities supported Stark's opponent with more than 55 percent and gave Reagan a 2-to-1 advantage over Carter.

District 10

Southeast Bay Area — San Jose, Fremont

Incumbent: Don Edwards (D)

Sitting at the southeastern end of the San Francisco Bay area, the 10th is split between Alameda and Santa

Clara counties. Of the four East Bay districts it is the most solidly blue-collar. Unlike the 7th and 9th, it does not reach eastward into the hills, where Republican voting strength is growing. As a result, the new 10th is a few degrees more Democratic than the others. Its voters backed Reagan in 1980 by a slim margin, but they have shown few other signs of Republican flirtation.

The Alameda County part of the district is centered on Fremont, a city of some 132,000 people that is known as the Detroit of the West Coast. General Motors has a large assembly plant in Fremont, and Ford and Peterbilt trucks are made in nearby Milpitas and Newark.

About one-third of San Jose is included in the 10th. Although the new district line between the 10th and 13th districts has been moved slightly, Edwards keeps about the same proportion of his hometown that he has had since 1974. San Jose is the fourth largest city in the state. With a growing influx of Hispanic-Americans into San Jose, more than one-quarter of the new district's population is of Hispanic origin.

Although registered Democrats overwhelm Republicans in both the Alameda County and Santa Clara County portions of the district, there are differences in outlook. The Fremont voters are considerably more conservative than those living in San Jose. Reagan's slim victory in the district was a result of his 54-33 percent edge over Carter in Fremont. Carter's 1980 Fremont vote was a full 10 points below George McGovern's 1972 showing there, a marked demonstration of the shifting political values of the blue-collar voters of this area.

Apart from the adjustment in the district line through San Jose, the only other change took Hayward out of the 10th and put it into the 9th District. Neither shift is expected to have much political impact on Edwards, who rarely has any difficulty winning re-election.

District 11

Most of San Mateo County; Palo Alto

Incumbent: Tom Lantos (D)

The new 11th District carefully skirts the most Republican areas of San Mateo County, drawing its population from the more Democratic territory between them.

The district's shape should help protect Lantos, a freshman Democrat who narrowly ousted Republican Bill Royer in 1980. Lantos' unexpected victory created problems for the Democratic map drawers because they had intended to simply use the Democratic portions of the old 11th to fill out the two underpopulated San Francisco districts. But with Lantos representing the area south of San Francisco, they had to find enough Democrats in the peninsula for three districts.

The eventual map forces Lantos to give up the solidly Democratic blue-collar community of Daly City, one of his strongest areas in 1980. But he also sheds Hillsborough, the most Republican part of his old district, and gains Palo Alto, a liberal bastion at the foot of the new district's eastern leg. Palo Alto, with 55,000 residents, is ideally suited to Lantos, who is a former economics professor. The home of Stanford University, it gave Anderson more than a

Tom Lantos **Paul N. McCloskey Jr.**

fifth of its vote in 1980 and still had enough Democratic strength for Carter to eke out a plurality over Reagan. Palo Alto voters were among the few in the state who opposed increasing the types of crimes punishable by the death penalty in a 1978 referendum.

Such liberal sentiment is not as evident elsewhere in the district. Both Reagan and Ford carried the area within the new 11th, even though registered Democrats — affluent liberals as well as working-class voters — outnumber Republicans by a 54-33 margin. But in contests for governor or U.S. senator, Democrats generally win by wide margins.

The eastern leg of this divided district has most of the voters; the western leg is primarily mist, fog and a smattering of small communities tucked into the mountains or perched on bluffs overlooking the sea.

Running 30 miles along the Bayshore Freeway through the eastern portion is a string of modest-sized suburbs ranging in population from Millbrae at 20,000 to San Mateo at 77,600. Two working-class enclaves, South San Francisco and San Bruno, occupy the northern end of this corridor. From Millbrae south to San Carlos are upper- and middle-class communities, all of which gave Reagan a majority in 1980 and supported Hayakawa in 1976. Atherton and Menlo Park, two exclusive Republican strongholds that separate Redwood City and Palo Alto, were carefully placed in the neighboring 12th District.

District 12

Parts of San Mateo, Santa Clara and Stanislaus Counties

Incumbent: Paul N. McCloskey Jr. (R)

With McCloskey running for the U.S. Senate, his compact district in the heart of San Mateo's "Silicon Valley" became a candidate for wholesale reworking.

Used primarily by the Democratic cartographers as a "dumping ground" for GOP votes, the new 12th District takes in several areas with little in common except Republican inclinations.

Although Sen. Cranston and Gov. Brown, both Democrats, carried the new 12th with 56 and 53 percent, respec-

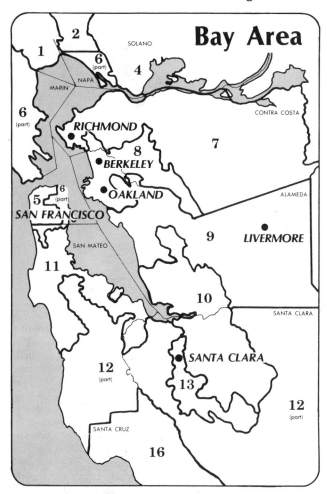

Bay Area

county's conservative Democratic farming areas were added to the 12th, a move that does not threaten Republican control.

District 13

Santa Clara County — San Jose, Santa Clara

Incumbent: Norman Y. Mineta (D)

In three decades of post-World War II growth, suburbanization has crept down both sides of the San Francisco Bay and come together at San Jose in Santa Clara County, 50 miles south of San Francisco and 42 miles south of Oakland.

The prune, cherry and apricot orchards that once made Santa Clara County a restful spot for Bay Area daytrippers have been replaced by electronics and aerospace plants and miles of tract homes occupied by young families.

The new 13th is a relatively compact suburban district contained entirely within Santa Clara County. It includes just under two-thirds of San Jose, although not the downtown area, and takes in the adjoining communities of Santa Clara, Campbell and Los Gatos.

Santa Clara, with 88,000 residents, is a new addition to Mineta's district and should strengthen the district's already solid Democratic tendencies. The younger, more working-class residents of Santa Clara replace affluent Republicans in Saratoga, Cupertino and the eastern part of Santa Clara County, all transferred to the new 12th District. Santa Clara went for Reagan in 1980 — like the new district as a whole — but did not give the margins he collected in the areas that have been removed.

Mineta, who served as mayor of San Jose for three years before coming to Washington in 1975, has always managed to run ahead of the rest of the Democratic ticket in his constituency. But the continuing migration of new residents prevents him from being able to coast to victory as a familiar face.

tively, in their last campaigns, the area went Republican in the 1980 and 1976 presidential elections. It is one of only two new districts in the state where Democrats do not have a majority in party registration.

Starting at San Francisco Bay and moving east, the district takes in the swank Hillsborough and Woodside sections of San Mateo County, where some of the residents commute to San Francisco by limousine. Hillsborough was high on the list of areas that Democrat Lantos wanted removed from his 11th District. Some 65 percent of the Hillsborough voters are registered Republicans — the highest figure for any place in the Bay Area. In 1980, Carter won a paltry 13 percent in Hillsborough.

In Santa Clara County, the 12th includes Mountain View and Sunnyvale at the southern end of the electronics and computer corridor known as the Silicon Valley. It has additional Republican turf taken from Democrat Norman Y. Mineta's 13th District — notably Saratoga and Cupertino.

Then the district crosses the Diablo Mountains and enters Stanislaus County, in the heart of the agricultural Central Valley. It comes to an end in the shape of a large arrow pointing towards Yosemite National Park, 30 miles further east.

In Stanislaus County, the lines carefully skirt the wine-making capital of Modesto, a city of more than 100,000, but take in smaller communities such as Turlock and Oakdale that often vote Republican. Several of the

District 14

Northeastern California; part of San Joaquin County

Incumbent: Norman D. Shumway (R)

After two terms representing a predominantly agricultural district focused on the canning center of Stockton, Shumway has been thrown into some unfamiliar territory.

Some 54 percent of the electorate — voters from the old 1st District — will be new to Shumway. San Joaquin County, which includes Stockton and formerly accounted for more than half the district's vote, will play a minor role in the new constituency. Only a quarter of the vote will come from San Joaquin County, and very little of that from the city of Stockton.

Norman Y. Mineta

Norman D. Shumway

In the new 14th, agriculture is far less important than lumbering, ranching and recreation. The entire eastern flank of the long district is taken up by the Cascade and Sierra Nevada ranges, and much of the land is in the national forest system. Lake Tahoe and nearby Squaw Valley attract most of the tourist dollars.

Politically, this is a marginal district. Although Democrats have a 51-38 percent registration edge, it means very little here. The 14th District voters have an individualistic streak and resist party labels. Some of them refuse to state a party preference at all — 17 percent, for example, in Alpine County, the highest such figure in the state.

Both the old and new parts of the 14th District have traditionally sent Democrats to the House. But Shumway and his Republican colleague Gene Chappie put an end to that in recent years, convincing voters that the Democratic incumbents had been around for too long.

In 1978, Shumway ousted 22-year veteran Democrat John J. McFall with strong support from the mountain counties that remain in the new 14th District — El Dorado, Amador and Alpine. In 1980, in what was then the 1st District, Chappie demolished Democrat Harold T. "Bizz" Johnson, who also had been around for 22 years. Chappie topped the incumbent in all but two counties in the district on the Nevada border, mountainous Sierra and Lassen.

In the last two elections for president, governor and U.S. senator, the voters of the new 14th District have usually gone with the GOP choice. The only decisive vote, however, was in 1980 for Reagan, who won all 12 counties and 58 percent districtwide. In 1976, Ford took just 50 percent and Hayakawa 54 percent. Brown lost the district in the 1974 gubernatorial race, but came back to win it in 1978. Cranston carried it against Gann in 1980, but with only 48 percent, his poorest showing north of Los Angeles.

District 15

Mid-San Joaquin Valley — Modesto

Incumbent: Tony Coelho (D)

State Highway 99 slices nearly 100 miles through the level, fertile fields of the 15th District, connecting two major farm centers of the San Joaquin Valley — Modesto in the north and Fresno in the south.

In the 1970s, the district included the western half of the city of Fresno and was the most Democratic of the San Joaquin Valley districts. Having lost that area in the 1981 redistricting, it is now only the second most Democratic. But for Coelho, that should be good enough.

The Democratic farmers of the Central Valley are not very loyal to their party these days, but given a choice and knowing little about either candidate, they will usually back the Democrat. That habit harks back to their political heritage in the Oklahoma dust bowl, brought with them to California more than a generation ago.

Coelho, who was exceptionally visible as an aide to former Rep. B. F. Sisk, stepped into Sisk's shoes when the 24-year veteran retired in 1978. He obliterated a strong GOP challenger that year and has continued to run far ahead of the rest of the Democratic ticket. In 1980, when agribusiness interests in the district turned against the Democratic president, giving him only 40 percent in the new district, Coelho's vote was above 70 percent.

Although Fresno now will be entirely outside his constituency, Coelho will still need to maintain a presence there. The new 15th curves around the city from the south and takes in its outskirts on three sides. The district line around Modesto also has been altered, leaving Coelho with that entire city of 106,000, plus a long, thin corridor connecting Modesto to the rest of the district further south. Modesto most often is remembered for its restless teenagers in the movie "American Graffiti" and for its large winery run by the Gallo Brothers.

Except for the population clusters at the northwest and southeast ends, the district is sparsely settled. Coelho's hometown of Merced, with 36,000 people, is the only other major city. The rest of the population is scattered throughout the irrigated farm land.

The eastern side of the district rises into the Sierra Nevada, with Yosemite National Park providing some tourist-related employment.

District 16

Central Coast — Salinas, Monterey

Incumbent: Leon E. Panetta (D)

The new 16th hugs the California coast for 150 miles, living off agriculture and tourism and providing a secure political base for Panetta, who is solidly entrenched after three terms.

The only change for 1982 — removal of San Luis Obispo and some of the surrounding area on the south — should make Panetta stronger. By taking more than 67,000 residents of San Luis Obispo County out of the 16th District, the mapmakers centered the constituency even more on Monterey and Santa Cruz counties, Panetta's home area, which now account for more than 90 percent of the population. Only the Morro Bay section of San Luis Obispo County remains in the new 16th District.

Although Panetta has gradually increased his majorities to more than 100,000 in 1980, the district is marginal in other contests. Reagan carried the area of the new 16th in 1980 with just under 49 percent of the vote; in 1976, Carter drew just over 50 percent.

The Monterey Bay, at the northern end of the district, is one of Northern California's favorite playgrounds, with a wide variety of the state's lifestyles visible along its shores. A vibrant counterculture has emerged in Santa Cruz on the northern side of the bay. Young residents have been drawn to the area by the permissive atmosphere at the University of California campus nestled among the trees north of the city.

Further south along the bay are Castroville — the artichoke capital of the world — and Fort Ord, a major military installation that employs a large civilian work force.

Liberal Democrats and upper-income Republicans live just south of the bay on the luxuriant and exclusive Monterey Peninsula. A little further south is Big Sur, another gathering place for the mellow.

But the areas contained in the 16th District are not all fun and games, as John Steinbeck and William Saroyan have illustrated in their novels and plays. The fishing industry, popularized in Steinbeck's *Cannery Row*, provides many of the jobs along the coast. Inland, agriculture is king, particularly around Salinas, which, with more than 80,000 inhabitants, is the largest city in the district. Although Democrats have the registration advantage in Salinas, the city has favored Republican presidential candidates in the last four elections.

District 17

Southern San Joaquin Valley

Incumbent: Charles Pashayan Jr. (R)

The 17th District is the food basket of the nation's most agriculturally productive state. Driving the length of the district from Fresno in the north to Bakersfield in the south, a traveler encounters virtually every kind of fruit and vegetable grown in the Temperate Zone.

Although parts of both Fresno and Bakersfield are in the new district, the majority of the population resides in smaller communities — dusty crossroads towns such as

Tony Coelho

Leon E. Panetta

Pixley and Terra Bella, or small-scale farm centers such as Tulare and Visalia — all with fewer than 50,000 people.

The irrigated farm land stretches almost to the eastern border of the district, where the Sierra Nevada Mountains climb steeply into Sequoia National Park. The mountains attract some recreational dollars to the district, but in minuscule amounts compared to the valley's farm income.

The farmers and those whose livelihoods depend on the farm economy register as Democrats. More often than not, however, they vote Republican. Of all the new California districts currently represented by Republicans in the House, the 17th has the highest Democratic registration — 54 percent. Reagan and Ford both carried it, and so did Hayakawa in 1976. The only major statewide Democrat to carry this district in recent years has been Gov. Brown.

Pashayan should not be hurt by the modest changes made in the district. Overpopulated by nearly 80,000, the 17th loses some densely settled parts of Fresno County (it retains the wealthier northeastern side of Fresno), and gains some lightly populated areas in Tulare County and the northern sector of Kern County, as far south as Bakersfield. To pose a serious threat to the two-term Republican incumbent, a challenger would need enough money to compete in two television markets and be able to attract support in the district's agribusiness community.

District 18

Central Valley and Sierra Nevada Mountains; most of Fresno and Stockton

No Incumbent

Like most of the districts drawn by Burton with particular candidates in mind, the new 18th has a very strange shape. If it were placed on its side, with the California-Nevada border as its base, it would look like a dragon. But to the state assemblyman from Fresno, Democrat Richard Lehman, it looks like an easy ticket to Washington.

The body of the dragon is found in three whole counties — Mono, Tuolumne and Calaveras. These counties often vote Republican, but they have little impact on the political outcome of the district. Located high in the Sierra Nevadas, they have no population centers and account for less than one-eighth of the vote.

The political purpose of the dragon's body is to connect two Democratic farming centers. The larger of the two, Fresno, is found at the end of the dragon's long, thin southern neck. Fresno has been Lehman's political base since he won his first Assembly term in 1976 at age 28. The other city, Stockton, is located in the dragon's tail. By joining these two distant sections of the Central Valley, Burton was able to come up with a wholly new Democratic district. The registration advantage is more than 2-to-1.

With a population of 218,000, Fresno is one of the most important agribusiness centers in the nation and accounts for nearly half of the new district's vote. Although it supported Reagan in 1980, it backs Democrats in most elections. Carter defeated Ford there in 1976, and McGovern carried it over Richard Nixon in 1972. The only part of the city not included in the new 18th District is the more Republican northeast corner, which is in the 17th.

Charles Pashayan Jr.   **Robert J. Lagomarsino**

There are strong political, economic and social divisions within the new 19th. The affluent Santa Barbara voters whose hillside homes overlook offshore oil rigs tend to place environmental issues at the top of their priority lists.

The oil workers of Oxnard, the ranchers in the foothills of the Coastal Range and the military families near Vandenberg Air Force Base are more interested in economic growth. A ballot proposition in 1980 authorizing the state of California to buy land around Lake Tahoe in order to preserve its scenic beauty was supported by 60 percent of the voters in Santa Barbara and rejected by 60 percent in Oxnard.

Stockton, in San Joaquin County, is split between the 18th and 14th districts, although the 18th has by far the larger portion. This city, too, is Democratic, but slightly less so than Fresno. McGovern did not win in Stockton, but Brown has run up healthy majorities there in his two successful gubernatorial bids. The major farm areas in the district are in the southern and eastern parts of San Joaquin County near Stockton.

Stockton and Fresno are 115 miles apart and are served by different media markets. Most of the land in between is in the 15th District, not the 18th. This will not be an easy district to run in and farm issues will be important at either end.

District 19

South central coast — Santa Barbara

Incumbent: Robert J. Lagomarsino (R)

Lagomarsino's coastal district, lying just beyond the northern fringe of metropolitan Los Angeles, has been changed little by the Democratic redistricting plan. As long as the popular five-term Republican remains on the ballot, Democrats are not expected to make much of an effort in the district. Running far ahead of the rest of the GOP ticket, Lagomarsino has won his last two terms with more than 70 percent of the vote.

However, in an open contest Democrats might have a chance in the 19th District. Cranston and Brown both have carried it, thanks to liberal votes from Santa Barbara (which has a large University of California campus) and support in the Mexican-American community in Oxnard. A quarter of the district's inhabitants are Hispanic.

For 1982, the 19th District will be contained in just two counties — Santa Barbara County, which will account for slightly less than 60 percent of the vote, and the northern and western parts of Ventura County. The lightly populated southern portion of San Luis Obispo County, which had been in the district since 1974, was removed with little anticipated political impact. The district line cutting through Oxnard has been altered slightly, but the differences there will be inconsequential.

District 20

Bakersfield; San Luis Obispo

Incumbent: William M. Thomas (R)

Crossing the new 20th District from east to west is like riding a roller coaster across half of Southern California. Beginning in the mountains at the southern end of the Sierra Nevada range, the district dips down to Bakersfield in the central valley and then lifts up again across the Coastal Range before plunging to the Pacific Ocean around Pismo Beach in San Luis Obispo County.

Politically, however, there is nothing rocky about this area. It is uniformly conservative. Although registered Democrats outnumber Republicans by 48 percent to 41 percent, most of the district's voters, whether Republican or Democrat, share the conservative views of Rep. William M. Thomas, who has been serving in the old 18th District since 1979.

The new 20th is less agricultural than the old 18th. It loses the Central Valley portion of Tulare County and much of the farm land in Kern County, including Delano, the one-time center of Cesar Chavez's United Farm Workers organization. In exchange, Thomas picks up most of hilly San Luis Obispo County to the west, an area which has little in common with the Central Valley. The new western orientation is not expected to cause Thomas much trouble, however, because the new turf has an even higher percentage of registered Republican voters than his old base.

Bakersfield, Thomas' hometown, remains the political core of the district. But the booming city of 106,000 has been split between two districts — the new 20th and the new 17th. The 17th District was given the small eastern portion of the city, which is predominantly Democratic and has a large minority population. The neighborhoods that remain are ones friendly to Thomas.

The most conservative — and most Republican — section of Thomas' constituency remains that part in the remote northern end of Los Angeles County in the Antelope Valley. The communities of Lancaster and Palmdale are closer in spirit to Bakersfield than to the city of Los Angeles, and almost as close in miles. Separated from Los Angeles by the San Gabriel Mountains, the Antelope Valley relies economically on the aerospace industry that has developed around nearby Edwards Air Force Base.

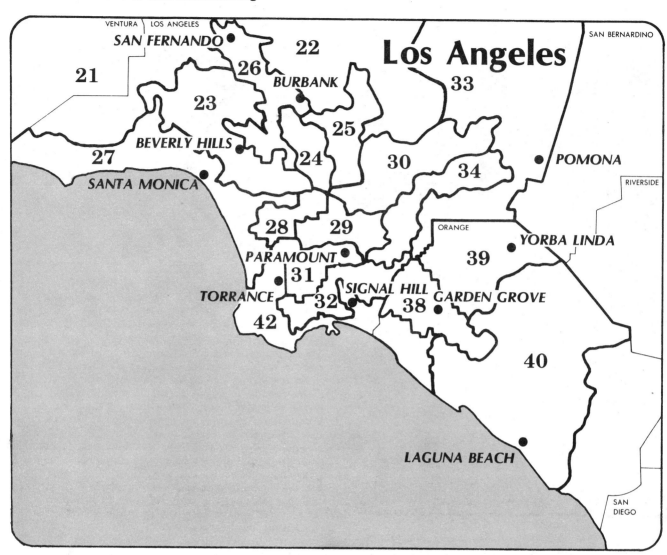

District 21

Part of Ventura County; western San Fernando Valley

*Incumbents: Barry M. Goldwater Jr. (R)
                     Bobbi Fiedler (R)*

No other part of the state embraced the 1978 property tax revolt — Proposition 13 — with as much fervor as the territory in the new 21st. Fully 82 percent of the voters in this collection of far-removed Los Angeles suburbs supported Howard Jarvis' plan to slash property taxes in half.

People in the Ventura County suburbs of Thousand Oaks and Simi Valley and the affluent Los Angeles County suburbs of Chatsworth and Hidden Valley were ripe for Jarvis' brand of government reform. For the most part they make a comfortable living, own well-landscaped homes and do not need the kinds of government services that have started to disappear as a result of the passage of Proposition 13.

The camel-shaped 21st District rides over the heart of the hot, flat San Fernando Valley, with the hump sitting in the foothills of the San Gabriel Mountains. The new 21st was drawn that way to incorporate staunch GOP areas at both ends of the valley while leaving out enough Democrats to populate two Democratic districts in between.

The result was to place two Republican incumbents in the same district. Goldwater's old 20th District covered the majority of the new 21st, including the entire Ventura County portion. But Fiedler's home base of Northridge is also included in the new district.

Luckily for Fiedler, Goldwater is running for the Senate, and she has the merged constituency to herself. Her main problem will be getting to know her constituents. While Van Nuys, Lakeview Terrace, Granada Hills and Selmar all carry over from her old 21st, most of the electorate will be new to her.

A candidate with a solid base in Ventura County could have given Fiedler a strong challenge in the GOP primary, but none appeared. As a result, Fiedler is likely to establish herself in the new territory in 1982 with little trouble.

This is the kind of district where the Republican candidate with the strongest conservative credentials normally

William M. Thomas   **Barry M. Goldwater Jr.**

wins. In 1978, the area favored the bombastic law-and-order candidate, Ed Davis, over several more moderate contenders in the Republican gubernatorial primary.

Once nominated here, any Republican candidate is a likely winner. The area within the new 21st gave Carter only 25 percent of the vote in 1980 and supported the weak GOP Senate candidate, Paul Gann. This is one of only six districts in the state where registered Republicans outnumber registered Democrats.

District 22

Glendale; part of Burbank; part of Pasadena

Incumbent: Carlos J. Moorhead (R)

By almost any standard of measurement, this is the most Republican district in California. It has the highest percentage of registered Republicans — 54 percent, compared to 38 percent registered Democrats. It is the only district that gave GOP gubernatorial candidate Evelle Younger a majority against Brown in 1978. Even the lackluster Gann picked up 54 percent of the vote here against Cranston in 1980.

As redrawn by the state Legislature for 1982, the 22nd included the homes of two of the state's most conservative Republican representatives — Moorhead and John H. Rousselot of San Marino.

Moorhead was given the advantage. The new 22nd retains his political base in Glendale and about 275,000 of the half-million residents of his old district. While the town of San Marino and other Rousselot territory also are included, Rousselot realized that Moorhead had a stronger claim on the district and decided to run in the vacant 30th District instead.

In combining the old 22nd and 26th districts, Democrats shaved off the blue-collar communities at the far ends of each district and left the most luxurious and affluent parts. The result is a safe Republican district Democrats may as well ignore.

Burbank and Pasadena both have been divided between two districts. The more Republican parts of both communities are in the 22nd. The middle-class black and Mexican-American areas of Pasadena have been pushed

into the heavily Hispanic 25th; the infamous "beautiful downtown Burbank" is in the new 26th District.

The quiet bedroom community of Glendale has been voting overwhelmingly for Moorhead since he began his political career in the state Assembly in 1966. He is likely to receive a similarly enthusiastic welcome from the voters in San Marino, an exclusive community named for the tiny European republic whose main industry is postage stamps. Today the luxurious homes still stand in San Marino and four out of five voters are registered Republicans.

Arcadia and South Pasadena are only a rung or two down on the socio-economic ladder. Another step lower are Temple City, Sierra Madre and Monrovia — comfortable middle-to-upper-middle-class bedroom communities.

District 23

Beverly Hills; part of San Fernando Valley

Incumbent: Anthony C. Beilenson (D)

The 23rd District is divided geographically and culturally by the Santa Monica Mountains.

On the southern slope of one of the world's few urban mountain ranges are the lush, well-tended neighborhoods of Bel Air and Westwood, the home of the sprawling U.C.L.A. campus. To the east, at the foot of the mountains is Beverly Hills, and to the south, Century City, Rancho Park and West Los Angeles. These are, for the most part, the provinces of wealthy, liberal families — many of them Jewish — that live in large single-family homes. Older residents and younger people living in small two-story apartment buildings are scattered through some of the area. They also vote Democratic.

On the other side of the Santa Monicas, where the ocean breezes seldom blow, is a different world. Here are the middle-class San Fernando Valley communities of Reseda, Tarzana, Canoga Park and Woodland Hills — flat, anonymous suburbs linked together by shopping centers and commercial strips. Although many of the voters in this area register as Democrats, most of them vote Republican.

Beilenson, who never received less than 60 percent of the vote in the old 23rd District, was not pleased with the changes in his district lines. Some of his stronger areas on

Bobbi Fiedler   **Carlos J. Moorhead**

Anthony C. Beilenson   **Henry A. Waxman**

both sides of the mountains were removed to help make the new 26th District safely Democratic. In exchange, the district was pushed further west in the San Fernando Valley, into territory that for the last decade has voted overwhelmingly for Goldwater.

The Democratic registration has dropped from 63 to 57 percent, and a majority of the district's voters now live on the valley side. These changes will hurt Beilenson, who has a consistent liberal record that goes back to his first days in the state Assembly nearly two decades ago. His environmentalist stance has always played well among the gentry in the hills; the workers in the valley may find it less attractive. But Beilenson still goes into the fall campaign a clear favorite.

District 24

Hollywood; part of San Fernando Valley

Incumbent: Henry A. Waxman (D)

More than any other district in the nation, the 24th depends on the entertainment industry for its economic well-being. It includes the symbolic center of the industry — the corner of Hollywood and Vine — as well as Universal Studios, Paramount Pictures, Samuel Goldwyn Studios and the West Coast headquarters of ABC and CBS.

Many of the heavily Jewish "bagel boroughs" of Los Angeles are also within the 24th District. Centered around the Wilshire Country Club, this area provides a solid core of votes for virtually any Democratic candidate. The new 24th was the only Los Angeles-area district without a large minority population that supported Jimmy Carter over Ronald Reagan in 1980.

Waxman, who has always won with ease, will notice very little difference in the shape of his new district. Like the 23rd and 26th districts, this one straddles the Santa Monica Mountains. Although it was pushed slightly further into the San Fernando Valley to include the Valley Plaza section, its new territory is not as Republican as other portions of the valley.

The new 24th has the largest concentration of Asian-American voters in the state outside San Francisco. Many of them are Koreans, concentrated at the southern end of

the district. There is a sizable homosexual community in Hollywood and West Hollywood.

District 25

Central and East Los Angeles

Incumbent: Edward R. Roybal (D)

This is the most heavily Hispanic district in the state of California. Nearly two-thirds of its residents identified themselves as being of Spanish ancestry in the 1980 census.

The district includes the shining glass-and-steel towers of downtown corporate Los Angeles. It has 10 expressways named for the places its professional people go home to each afternoon; for example, Pasadena, Pomona, Ventura, Glendale and Santa Ana.

But the real flavor of the 25th District is in the Hispanic barrios of Boyle Heights and East Los Angeles. It is there that Democratic loyalty is strong and loyalty to Roybal, the elder political statesman of the area, even stronger.

Although Roybal was not substantially damaged in redistricting, he will have a larger Anglo constituency after 1982. The western side of the district, nearly all Hispanic, was sheared off and replaced by middle-class neighborhoods in western and northern Pasadena. Even with the changes, blacks will account for less than 10 percent of the district's population.

But any group that votes in significant numbers can exert some influence here, because voting participation in the district is the lowest in the state. The new 25th is the only constituency in California where fewer than 100,000 people voted for president in 1980 — less than half the statewide average. Some 5,000 more people voted in the new 25th District in 1980 than in the same area in 1976.

District 26

Santa Monica Mountains; central San Fernando Valley

No Incumbent

This brand-new constituency was drawn by Burton to the specifications of Democratic Assemblyman Howard Berman, who passed up a chance to run in the 23rd District in 1976 and left that seat for Beilenson. To make the new 26th safe for Berman, Burton took care to include in it solid liberal territory that Beilenson depended on for victory throughout the 1970s.

Many of the voters reside in the fashionable Mulholland Drive area north of Beverly Hills. Further west, the district takes in Sherman Oaks and Studio City, at the base of the mountains in the San Fernando Valley. Berman has represented this entire area for a decade in the Assembly, always winning re-election with ease. Beilenson has done equally well in it.

Edward R. Roybal   **Robert K. Dornan**

The part of the district new to Berman is in the heart of the San Fernando Valley — communities such as Van Nuys, Panorama City and Sepulveda. The ranch-style houses that line the endless straight streets here are home to some professionals and some blue-collar workers, few wealthy and few poor. The aviation and electronics industries, brought to the valley in 1948 with the arrival of the Lockheed airplane factory, are still major employers.

Nearly all of the new 26th has been under Democratic representation for years in the state Legislature. But the 2-to-1 Democratic registration advantage belies its conservatism on many social and economic issues. The area warmly embraced tax-slashing Proposition 13 in 1978, and portions of it added from the old 21st District backed Republican Fiedler in her 1980 victory there over veteran Democratic Rep. James C. Corman.

The northernmost end of the district is the most industrialized part of the valley; it has attracted increasing numbers of blacks and Mexican-Americans. This area remained loyal to Corman in 1980.

In national and statewide contests this new district is competitive. Carter carried it in 1976 with 50.3 percent of the vote. Four years later, Reagan beat him with 50.9 percent. But it should be safe for Berman.

District 27

Pacific Coast — Santa Monica

Incumbent: Robert K. Dornan (R)

Dornan was one of the prime targets for the Democratic map drawers in 1981, who drew a district so unattractive for him that his decision to run for the Senate was relatively easy to make.

The old 27th, which the flamboyant conservative had narrowly won three times, was eviscerated. The most Democratic parts were retained, but the exclusive Palos Verdes Hills section at the southern end of the long coastal constituency was thrown into the new 42nd District. With the exception of a long thin finger poking its way into the heart of Los Angeles, the new 27th is a coastal district. The removal of the Palos Verdes Hills has narrowed its political

spectrum somewhat, but a wide variety of political and social styles still can be found along the Pacific Coast from Malibu to Redondo Beach at the southern border.

Santa Monica is the political and geographic hub of the district. A city of 88,000 people, it is a mixture of elderly middle-class residents and young families that like being close to both the city and the ocean. Political activism runs high in Santa Monica, the home base for actress Jane Fonda and her husband, Tom Hayden, the founder of the Campaign for Economic Democracy. Thanks in part to the activities of Hayden and Fonda, Santa Monica has received a reputation as a liberal community. But this image is not always reflected at the polls. Santa Monica has the second-highest Democratic registration of any community in the district, but it split its vote almost evenly between Reagan and Carter in 1980.

Life is more "laid back" on either side of Santa Monica. The Pacific Palisades and Malibu Beach sections to the north provide the district's most interesting architecture and a strong upper-class voting element. The voters are polarized between the far left and the far right. To the south of Santa Monica is Venice, an artists' community that has been overrun by young beach-oriented people with roller skates, surfboards and blaring radios. The hot tub and Jaccuzi set is found a few blocks further south in the plush Marina Del Rey condominiums, and just beyond is the giant Los Angeles International Airport, known to the local residents by its three-letter code, LAX.

The communities south of the airport — upper-middle-class suburbs inhabited mostly by professional people — show little loyalty to either party, but tended to back Dornan in recent elections, largely because of his strong pro-defense stands. Many of the workers here are employed by nearby aerospace and defense industries.

Manhattan Beach, Hermosa Beach and Redondo Beach all have Democratic registration advantages, but all voted for Reagan in 1980 by margins of nearly 2-to-1 — about the same as El Segundo, the new Republican stronghold in the district. All of them except El Segundo voted for Cranston, however. The lines here were drawn for Democratic Assemblyman Mel Levine, who has represented the Santa Monica area in Sacramento for five years. Levine will draw strong support from the district's large Jewish community, found in Santa Monica and in the inland part of the district that juts into the heart of Los Angeles.

District 28

Southern Los Angeles, Inglewood

Incumbent: Julian C. Dixon (D)

Directly south of Beverly Hills and Hollywood and stretching to the edge of downtown Los Angeles, the new 28th is a racially mixed, middle-class Democratic stronghold.

Some 43 percent of its residents are black, giving it a black population second only to that of the poorer 29th District to the east. The drop in the black population from 50 percent, brought about by slight changes in the district lines, is not expected to cause Dixon much concern. The support of the Los Angeles political machine run by Rep. Waxman and Assemblyman Berman helped Dixon win a substantial number of white votes in 1978, and he since has had no problem retaining his support among both whites and blacks.

Over the last two decades, middle-class blacks have been moving into the southern and western parts of the district in and around Inglewood. Except for the mostly black Coliseum area in the northeastern corner, the district is exceptionally well integrated, with whites, blacks, Asians and Hispanics living next to each other in well-built single-family homes.

Three-fourths of the district's residents live in the city of Los Angeles or the unincorporated Windsor Hills area. The only noticeable change made to the district in 1981 was to remove the Mar Vista part of Los Angeles, near Santa Monica, and replace it with the more fashionable Playa Del Rey section just north of the Los Angeles International Airport.

Inglewood, a city of nearly 100,000, has seen a remarkable shift in its racial mix during the last generation. In 1960, it had a black population of less than 1 percent. By 1970, as the migration of blacks began, the percentage rose to 11 percent. The 1980 census revealed that 57 percent of Inglewood's residents were black and another 20 percent Hispanic.

This racial change has been reflected in Inglewood's politics as well. Nixon carried the city in 1968 and 1972. But Carter defeated Ford there by a 2-to-1 margin in 1976 and won it over Reagan in 1980 by nearly 3-to-1.

Culver City, the home of the MGM studios, is the only loyal Republican area left in the district. While the new 28th as a whole gave Carter his second highest percentage in the state in 1980 — 67.5 percent — Culver City went for Reagan. A growing Hispanic influence there, however, is also keeping the Republican vote lower than it once was.

District 29

South-central Los Angeles; Watts; Downey

Incumbent: Augustus F. Hawkins (D)

The 29th changes significantly with the addition of Downey, a mostly white, Republican suburb of 80,000. But Hawkins or any other black candidate should be able to find enough support in the overwhelmingly black Los Angeles part of the district to win easily.

Blacks do not actually comprise a majority in the district. But the 47 percent black population, combined with the large Hispanic element in Huntington Park and South Gate — two modest-sized suburbs sandwiched between Los Angeles and Downey — make the 29th a minority enclave. Four-fifths of the electorate is either black or Hispanic. However, the Hispanic communities do not always mirror the Democratic voting patterns of the district's black voters. Huntington Park and South Gate both supported Reagan in 1980.

The riot-scarred Watts community makes up about 60 percent of the new district. The conditions in Watts, characterized by poverty, high unemployment and housing shortages, have changed little since the 1965 riots, although

Julian C. Dixon   **Augustus F. Hawkins**

the disturbances provoked an increased flow of state and federal funds to the community. Hawkins, the first black member of Congress from any Western state, has been winning comfortably in that area for two decades, never drawing less than 83 percent of the vote.

Downey, which gave Reagan 65 percent of its vote in the 1980 presidential contest and preferred Gann to Cranston in the Senate race, has been brought into the 29th District from the old 33rd District. It is unlikely that Downey will provide much support to Hawkins, but it will not be able to do him much damage. The new district as a whole remains at the top of the Democratic list. It has the highest percentage of registered Democrats in the state — 78 percent — and Carter's 68 percent here in 1980 was his highest mark anywhere in California.

District 30

San Gabriel Valley — El Monte, Alhambra

Incumbent: John H. Rousselot (R)

As California's Hispanic population grew over the last decade to 2 million, the Hispanic community moved beyond the inner-city barrios to nearby suburbs such as the ones included in the new 30th District.

Some 54 percent of the residents in the new 30th are of Spanish origin, a figure second only to that in the 25th District, just to the west. Democrat George E. Danielson represented most of this area during the 1970s, often turning back challenges from Hispanic primary opponents. Republican candidates showed little strength in the area.

Danielson departed the House in March of this year to accept an appointment on the state Court of Appeal. A special election to fill the empty seat in the old 30th is scheduled to coincide with the June 8 primary for the new 30th. Meanwhile, Rousselot, thrown together with fellow conservative Carlos J. Moorhead in the new 22nd District, chose to pass up a probably futile contest against Moorhead and moved into the new 30th.

He faces a difficult task. The new 30th includes a small portion of Rousselot's old 26th, in Alhambra and San Gabriel, but his political base around San Marino and

South Pasadena is outside the lines. While Alhambra and San Gabriel generally give Republicans modest pluralities, this support is not likely to be enough to counteract the overall 63-to-28 percent Democratic registration edge in the district. Reagan carried the district with 49 percent of the vote in 1980, but in a local contest against a Democrat with a Spanish surname, any Republican as conservative as Rousselot is at a pronounced disadvantage.

Once a paradise of orange, lemon and walnut groves, the area covered by the new 30th District is now heavily industrialized. Small tract houses and rows of palm trees sit alongside acres of land devoted to building rocket motors, automobile parts and electronic components.

The district cuts a diagonal swath across the western end of the San Gabriel Valley. The areas with the heaviest Hispanic vote — as much as 85 percent in some places — are in the southwestern end abutting East Los Angeles. Suburbs such as Maywood, Cudahy and Montebello all have substantial Hispanic majorities. In the far eastern end of the district, around Azusa, there is a greater ethnic mix, although the neighborhoods are all blue-collar.

Joining the eastern and western parts of the district is El Monte, which, with nearly 80,000 people, is the largest of the 14 independent municipalities in the district. For years El Monte was a major hog-ranching center, providing bacon for most of the Los Angeles area.

District 31

Southern Los Angeles County — Compton, Carson

Incumbent: Mervyn M. Dymally (D)

This is a working-class suburban district with more ethnic and racial diversity than can be found in almost any district in the state. More than a third of the residents are black, a quarter are of Spanish origin and nearly a tenth are Orientals. One thing most of them have in common is that they vote Democratic.

Only two other districts — the 28th and 29th, both with higher black populations — gave Jimmy Carter a higher percentage in 1980. The 31st is second only to the 29th in its Democratic registration percentage.

John H. Rousselot

Mervyn M. Dymally

Dymally, who had been the state's first black lieutenant governor, won this seat easily in 1980 after losing his statewide office two years earlier. Although the district lines have been altered slightly — the 31st will now take in all of racially mixed Carson and mostly white Bellflower — Dymally is not thought to be in any trouble.

The addition of Bellflower on the eastern end of the district adds 38,000 more white voters to the district. But their impact will be largely offset by the move further south into Carson, where Dymally picks up groups of roughly 10,000 each of blacks, Hispanics and Orientals — all strong Democratic blocs.

Bellflower and Paramount, each with about 90,000 people on the eastern side of the district, will give Dymally the most trouble. They supported Reagan in 1980, as did Hawthorne, another mostly white suburb of about 56,000 people on the western end of the district. The four suburbs between the two ends — Carson, Compton, Gardena and Lynwood — all backed Carter. Compton is poor and nearly all black. With 81,000 people — the same number as Carson — it gave Carter 19 votes for every one to Reagan.

The Asian vote in the district is located primarily in Gardena, a tidy suburb just off the Harbor Freeway, which bisects the district. Japanese-Americans have been a major part of Gardena's life and politics for several decades. On occasion the Japanese-American community will support Republicans, as it did for eight years when Paul T. Bannai, who came out of that community, represented the area in the state Assembly.

Perhaps the district's most famous resident is the Goodyear blimp *Columbia*, whose permanent mooring is clearly visible from the intersection of the Harbor and San Diego freeways. Those two highways are important to the economy of the 31st District. Twice each day they are filled with commuters from the 31st going to their jobs in the defense or electronics industries. Throughout the rest of the day the highways are clogged with trucks hauling the goods the district produces: aircraft engines, semi-conductors, Max Factor cosmetics and Mattel toys.

District 32

San Pedro, Long Beach and nearby suburbs

Incumbent: Glenn M. Anderson (D)

Anderson was one of the few Democrats not deliberately protected in the Democratic-controlled redistricting process. Although the 32nd remains Democratic on paper, Anderson has gained a lot of unfamiliar territory and lost some of his strongest areas.

The new turf is on the eastern end of his old district, around Lakewood and the comfortable Republican community of Cerritos, where Reagan won twice as many votes as Carter in 1980. Lakewood is slightly more Democratic than Cerritos, but it contains 75,000 new constituents who have never voted for Anderson. The district also dips down to take in part of Long Beach on the eastern side, around the California State University branch campus.

To the west and north, the district lost Carson, with its strongly Democratic minority vote, and the poor neighborhoods of Torrance, which also voted Democratic. To con-

Glenn M. Anderson   **Wayne Grisham**

nect two distant parts of a neighboring district, the map makers also trimmed off a small waterfront piece of Anderson's old constituency. Although Anderson no longer will have the San Pedro and Long Beach harbors in his district, their interests will still be of prime concern. Many of his constituents — old and new — are involved in the transportation and shipping industries.

Driving along the freeways that crisscross the 32nd District, one can see aerospace and automobile plants extending along the flat brown land, sharing space with fuel tanks, oil wells, and closer to the water, shipyards and loading docks. Behind this industrial landscape lie the older homes of Long Beach and San Pedro, where fishermen and sailors of many European nationalities provide a strong ethnic flavor not found in many places in the Los Angeles area.

Registered Democrats outnumber Republicans in the district by more than 2-to-1, but many split their tickets. Democrats usually prevail in statewide contests, but not by the margins they enjoy in other districts where the registration advantage leans so heavily in their favor.

District 33

Eastern Los Angeles — Pomona, Whittier

Incumbents: Wayne Grisham (R)
David Dreier (R)

Most of the land in this sprawling outer suburban district is given over to largely uninhabitable mountains and hills. The northern end is dominated by the Angeles National Forest. In the southern end of the district, two modest-sized ranges divide the valley-dwelling population. A mountain named after cornflake king W. K. Kellogg separates working-class Covina from the white-collar communities of Pomona and Claremont, home of the several Claremont Colleges. And the La Puente Hills isolate Whittier and La Mirada from the rest of the district.

Slightly less than half the population of the new district belonged to the old 35th, where Dreier defeated Democrat Jim Lloyd in 1980. This territory includes Pomona, with 92,000 residents, the largest city in the new

constituency. Living more than 30 miles from downtown Los Angeles, Pomona residents are more likely to commute to San Bernardino and Riverside counties to the east, or work in the Pomona-Claremont area, than make the daily trip into Los Angeles.

Dreier's old district straddled the Los Angeles-San Bernardino county line, but his political base was on the Los Angeles County side, around Claremont and LaVerne. When the Legislature's redistricting plan split up his old constituency, the 29-year-old first-term Republican decided to stay on the Los Angeles side and wage a Republican primary challenge against Grisham, a man 30 years older. Grisham's casual, unhurried approach to politics is quite unlike Dreier's sophisticated, energetic style.

Grisham's old 33rd District was decimated. Before redistricting, the bulk of its population was located south of the La Puente Hills, just beyond the Hispanic and black suburbs of the old 29th and 31st districts. The cities of Norwalk, Downey, Cerritos and Whittier made up more than half the district's population. Of these, the new 33rd retains only Richard Nixon's boyhood home of Whittier. It has fewer than 70,000 inhabitants.

Grisham and Dreier typify the different parts of the new district they represent. Those voters south of the La Puente hills, like Grisham, tend to be middle-aged homeowners with grown children. Those to the north, like Dreier, are more likely to be young people who have come to California in the last 10 years.

Whoever wins the Republican primary will be favored in the fall. Though far from unified geographically or culturally, the district is united in its Republican leanings. There are only a few more registered Democrats than Republicans, which in California means a Republican advantage in most elections. In the last several years most Republican statewide candidates have carried the district.

The only major GOP candidate to lose here recently was Evelle Younger, running against Gov. Brown in 1978. Brown carried the district by a slim margin, thanks to his popularity among the younger, ticket-splitting professionals and university residents in the Pomona-Claremont area. But Reagan carried both cities on route to an easy win in the new district in 1980.

District 34

Los Angeles suburbs — Norwalk

No Incumbent

This elongated slice of suburbia twists and slithers through parts of Los Angeles County tourists never see — unless they are racing by on one of four expressways that keep the area fragmented. The district more or less follows the San Gabriel River — a channelized concrete trough — through blue-collar communities that have little interaction with each other.

At the two ends of the district are two very different cities of about 80,000 residents each. In the south is Norwalk, an older working-class suburb with a declining population but a growing Hispanic community, now at 40 percent. On the northern border is West Covina, a newer, still-growing and significantly more affluent town on the Los Angeles-San Bernardino axis.

In between are the district's most heavily Hispanic areas, around Pico Rivera and South El Monte. Three-fourths of the residents there are of Hispanic origin. Nearly every community in the district except West Covina has at least a one-third Hispanic population, making the new 34th 47 percent Hispanic altogether.

Thrown together from parts of five old congressional districts — the 26th, 30th, 33rd, 34th and 35th — this is an unpredictable area politically. Artesia and Norwalk in the south and Baldwin Park and West Covina in the north are most likely to vote Republican, as they all did in 1980 for Reagan. But the center of the district is solidly Democratic. The districtwide registration is 64-27 in favor of the Democrats, although the Hispanic Democrats do not turn out in large numbers.

If the Hispanic community is mobilized politically, it has the strength to elect one of its own. But former Democratic Rep. Jim Lloyd of West Covina, who was defeated for re-election in the old 35th in 1980, is running here this year. On the old map, Lloyd was at the western end of a district that stretched into affluent Republican areas and on into the desert. Now he finds himself at the far eastern end of a district that meanders through lower- and middle-class suburbia, where Democrats are usually welcome.

District 35

San Bernardino and Inyo counties

Incumbent: Jerry Lewis (R)

The newly drawn 35th covers a vast and sparsely populated desert area between Los Angeles and the Nevada border. The Mojave Desert, Death Valley and the nation's hottest town, Needles, are the best known parts of the district. But the voters who make this a reliably Republican constituency are elsewhere — squeezed into the southwestern corner of the district, surrounding the city of San Bernardino on three sides.

Lewis, elected twice from the old 37th District, saw his district divided between the new 35th (primarily San Bernardino County) and the new 37th (Riverside County). Although Lewis never had any trouble carrying either county, he has run five to seven percentage points better in San Bernardino, his home base. So he chose to run in the new 35th, where he should have little difficulty winning re-election.

Lewis' constituency remains largely suburban, although he also has to stay attuned to the concerns of voters living in desert towns such as Barstow, China Lake and Victorville, where water is the main political issue.

In order to strengthen Democrat George E. Brown Jr. in the urban San Bernardino district (the 36th), a few changes were made in the boundary lines around that city of 118,000. These alterations made the new 35th even more Republican than Lewis' former district.

Lewis gives up the northeastern part of the city, including the Harlem Springs and Highland sections near Norton Air Force Base, and the California State College campus at San Bernardino. In return he gains part of western San Bernardino County, which was in Dreier's 35th District. This western territory includes communities such as Chino and Upland, on the border with Los Angeles County, that have been experiencing tremendous exurban growth in recent years. Most of the voters there tend to side with the GOP. The more Democratic city of Ontario, which was in the old 35th, has been placed in Brown's 36th.

Lewis retains the cities of Redlands and Loma Linda, both small university towns east of San Bernardino. This part of the district was once a citrus-packing area at the edge of the nation's southern citrus belt. Today it primarily packs a huge Republican vote, although some orange groves still occupy small parcels of the region's red soil.

The 35th District also gains Inyo County, where Death Valley is located. A small and strongly conservative county, it is the only one in the state that gave a majority of its vote to Gann, the hapless GOP Senate challenger of 1980.

The 35th supported the 1978 ballot issue expanding the categories of crimes punishable by the death penalty with a higher percentage than any other new district in the state — 84 percent.

District 36

San Bernardino, Riverside

Incumbent: George E. Brown Jr. (D)

Of the three districts covering the San Bernardino-Riverside metropolitan area, this is the only one a Democrat can win. Since his 1972 comeback, following a defeat for the U.S. Senate two years earlier, Brown has held the seat by combining the votes of the blue-collar residents of Riverside and San Bernardino and those of the growing Mexican-American population in San Bernardino.

But the burgeoning Republican suburban vote, particularly in the suburbs of Norco and Corona, began to have an effect in 1980 when Brown was held to 53 percent. To strengthen him, Burton removed Norco and Corona from the 36th District, along with a large part of the city of Riverside. Only the Democratic north side of Riverside remains in the new 36th District.

On the San Bernardino side, where Brown always has had the support of at least 55 percent of the voters, his territory was expanded. The district now extends westward

David Dreier   **Jerry Lewis**

to Ontario, once a shady residential town of a few thousand that has grown into a booming, industrial city of 88,000, supporting a major commercial airport and large Lockheed and General Electric plants. Although Ontario voters supported Reagan in 1980, they generally back Democrats and Brown should be able to satisfy them.

Because the district borders move north and east, the new 36th takes in all of San Bernardino's 118,000 inhabitants. More than 50 miles from Los Angeles, the city once marked the eastern terminus for the big, red trolley cars of Los Angeles' Pacific Electric interurban rail system.

Today, San Bernardino residents have little contact with the Los Angeles area. A fruit-packing center in the 1930s, San Bernardino now forces its citrus industry to share space with the many electronics and aerospace firms in the area, as well as the Kaiser Steel Corporation's blast furnace in nearby Fontana. These industries, along with the large Atchinson, Topeka and Santa Fe railroad yards in San Bernardino, give the city and nearby Rialto and Colton distinctly Democratic voting habits.

District 37

Riverside County

No Incumbent

A chain reaction created this new Republican district without a resident incumbent — the only such district in the state.

When Dreier chose to challenge fellow Republican Grisham in the new 33rd District, rather than run in the new 35th, Lewis was left with a choice between the 35th or 37th. He chose the 35th, leaving the 37th open for any GOP candidate skillful enough to win the June primary.

With or without an incumbent, the suburban and desert areas of Riverside County in the 37th District are simply not very lucrative places for Democrats to look for votes. The fast-growing western end of the county, around Norco and Corona, supported Reagan by more than a 2-to-1 margin in 1980. Further east in the desert are the oasis resorts of Rancho Mirage and Palm Springs, where the

leisure economy pumps thousands of dollars into the hands of local businessmen. The returns from that area are every bit as Republican as the ones from the suburbs.

Agriculture also plays a major role in the district's economy and politics, as irrigation ditches from the Colorado River Aqueduct spread across the non-mountainous areas. Recently farmers have been voting for Republican House candidates, although in the 1950s and 1960s it was a different story. Democrat Dalip Singh Saund served three terms from Riverside and Imperial counties between 1957 and 1963. A native of Amritsar, India, Saund came to the Imperial Valley in 1920 and became a successful lettuce farmer. Democrat John V. Tunney also represented the district for three terms, but when he left in 1970 to run for the U.S. Senate, Riverside County turned to the GOP and has been represented in the House by a string of Republicans since.

During the time Saund and Tunney represented the district, it included all of the city of Riverside, which usually votes more Democratic than the rest of the county. But Riverside was removed completely from the 37th District in 1974, and while the current redistricting plan placed some of its voters back in the district, they are primarily Republicans in the southern part of the city. The Democratic precincts of Riverside are in the new 36th District.

District 38

Northwestern Orange County; Santa Ana, Garden Grove

Incumbent: Jerry M. Patterson (D)

This segment of heavily Republican Orange County is no liberal bastion, but it has a marked weakness for Democrats if they do not veer to the left of center. For most of the last decade, it has been safe for Patterson and his Democratic House predecessor. It elects Democrats to the state Senate and the Assembly.

But Republicans running for state and national office can count on doing well in this district. In 1980, even though Patterson won twice as many votes as Carter in the district, Cranston edged his weak Republican Senate challenger by fewer than 2,000, and Reagan won by a 63-29 margin.

Garden Grove and Santa Ana, occupying the southern half of the district, make up more than half of the vote. Like most of the other communities in the district, they have a large working-class population. The Hispanic community in Santa Ana, the Orange County seat, is nearing 50 percent, which is one reason that city tends to vote more Democratic than Garden Grove. Hispanics make up between 10 and 20 percent of the population in the district outside Santa Ana.

Only minor changes made in the district's lines should strengthen Patterson slightly. By removing a Republican part of Santa Ana near the city of Orange and by shaving a few blocks off on the Huntington Beach side, the map makers probably added about 3,000 Democratic votes and cut the Republican vote by 10,000.

George E. Brown Jr.   **Jerry M. Patterson**

District 39

William E. Dannemeyer   **Robert E. Badham**

Northeastern Orange County — Anaheim, Fullerton

Incumbent: William E. Dannemeyer (R)

The changes made in Dannemeyer's district are almost undetectable. The new 39th is so Republican that the mapmakers knew they were wasting Democratic votes by including them in it. A few neighborhoods around the edges — most notably those between Orange and Tustin — were removed to bring the district's population down some 65,000. But the net political effect will be minimal. The new 39th, covering the heartland of Orange County, gave Reagan 69 percent of the vote, a margin he exceeded only in the new 43rd.

The 39th receives more visitors than most of the suburban Los Angeles districts, thanks to the presence of Disneyland and Anaheim Stadium, home of the California Angels. But it is the middle-to-upper-class families living around these sites in Anaheim and in the other Orange County suburbs that give the district its strong Republican flavor. These voters rarely even think about splitting their tickets. The new 39th was one of only two districts in the state that gave a majority to Gann against Cranston. Brown in 1978 was the only major Democratic candidate in any of the last four elections to carry the district.

The growth in the western part of the district — Anaheim and Fullerton — has slowed down somewhat in the last decade. The fast-growing communities now are ones such as Yorba Linda, Richard Nixon's birthplace, which more than doubled in size between 1970 and 1980. But Anaheim, Fullerton and Orange, the three anchors of the district, hold more than three-fourths of the electorate. In the three combined, Reagan received three votes in 1980 for every one of Carter's.

Thirty years ago — before Disneyland and scores of electronics firms arrived in the area — Anaheim was a sleepy community in the middle of the orange groves that gave the county its name. Fewer than 15,000 people lived there. Today, with 222,000 residents, Anaheim is the eighth largest city in California. It would be the largest city in 19 states.

District 40

Coastal Orange County

Incumbent: Robert E. Badham (R)

It is difficult for candidates to be too conservative for the voters in this region of Orange County. To win his seat in the House of Representatives in 1976 over eight other Republicans, Robert E. Badham campaigned as the most conservative of the group and repeatedly invoked the name of Sen. Barry Goldwater. John G. Schmitz, who was removed from the council of the John Birch Society this year for extremism, comes from this area and represented it for a term in the House. The society has its largest California chapter here.

The Republican registration of the new 40th District, 51.5 percent, is second only to the new 22nd. By moving the far southern portion of the old 40th into the new 43rd, the mapmakers gave Badham an even higher GOP vote.

Newport Beach, Badham's hometown and political base, remains the center of the district. A community of 63,000 people, Newport Beach regularly provides Republican candidates with tremendous margins at the polls. In 1980, Reagan topped Carter by 74 to 16 percent there.

Many of the residents of the district either commute to jobs in Los Angeles or are employed by high-tech concerns that are scattered throughout the district. The University of California Irvine Campus is located in the district. But any liberal influence from this academic center is hardly noticed in the 40th District.

The only two incorporated areas in the district where registered Democrats outnumber Republicans are Costa Mesa and Laguna Beach, two quite different areas. Trendy Laguna Beach, which saw an influx of counterculture types in the 1960s and 1970s, today is home for many single adults and couples without children who live in comfortable condominium complexes. It is reported to be California's "grooviest beach resort."

Costa Mesa, whose airport is named after actor John Wayne, is not so groovy. Just north of Newport Beach, it is home for young suburban families living in modest suburban homes that sprouted in the 1950s and 1960s. Although both communities supported Reagan by smaller margins than the rest of the district, they split on two policy questions in 1980. Costa Mesa voters joined those in Newport Beach in their opposition to requiring non-smoking areas in public places. They also objected to having the state purchase Lake Tahoe land to preserve it from development. Laguna Beach voters supported both ideas.

District 41

North San Diego and suburbs

Incumbent: Bill Lowery (R)

When Republican Bob Wilson retired in 1980, Lowery had to fight hard to keep the old 41st District in Republican hands. However, small changes in the district lines will make his job much easier in 1982. The 41st, like the nearby 45th, was made more Republican in order to create a Democratic district in between the two — the 44th.

The new 41st completely surrounds the huge Miramar Naval Air Station, which some would like to turn into the major commercial airport for San Diego. The presence of Mirimar and other naval installations gives the district a large military constituency. Aerospace and electronics firms associated with the military are also in the area.

The further north one travels in San Diego County, toward the Orange County border, the more Republican the area becomes. The new 41st loses some of its southern territory and extends northward as far as Poway in the mountains and along the coast beyond Del Mar to Leucadia. All of the exclusive La Jolla section of San Diego is now in the district. The 41st also retains the Mission Bay and Pacific Beach sections, as well as the Republican suburb of La Mesa, on the eastern flank of the city.

Voters here have shown a marked willingness to split their tickets. In 1980, Cranston ran a full 30 points ahead of Jimmy Carter — the biggest difference between the two candidates in any district in the state. Reagan carried the district with 60 percent and Cranston was not far behind with 56 percent.

District 42

Coastal Los Angeles and Orange Counties

Incumbent: Dan Lungren (R)

The oddly shaped and heavily Republican 42nd District is another one of the side effects of Burton's efforts to create new Democratic seats in Los Angeles County.

The new 42nd is a combination of the most Republican portions of two old districts — the 27th, represented since 1976 by GOP Rep. Dornan, and Lungren's old 34th. A strip of land only a few hundred feet wide runs along the Los Angeles Harbor waterfront, joining the two segments. The Long Beach Naval Shipyard, the *Queen Mary* and Howard Hughes' "Spruce Goose" are all in this isthmus, but there are very few voters.

Bill Lowery   **Dan Lungren**

The northern and western end of the new 42nd, which Dornan represented, includes the heavily Republican suburb of Torrance, with 131,000 people, and the lush, upper-income Palos Verdes Hills area. The Hills, forming a bluff overlooking the Pacific Ocean, include four exclusive communities — Palos Verdes Estates, Rancho Palos Verdes, Rolling Hills and Rolling Hills Estates. The voters who live there are overwhelmingly Republican and rarely split their tickets. Even Gov. Brown, who in 1978 carried such Republican areas in the district as Torrance and Huntington Beach, was trounced in the Palos Verdes Hills. These communities were vital in Dornan's narrow victories in 1978 and 1980.

Lungren, the incumbent who takes over Dornan's best Republican turf, will have to spend some time becoming acquainted with the voters from this area, which contributes slightly less than half of the new district's population. In the part of the district that he has represented since 1979, however, the young Republican should have no problems.

Since his first bid for office in 1976, Lungren has had the strong support of the district's Orange County residents, who account for 25 percent of the new district's vote. The part of Orange County in the new 42nd closely resembles the area formerly in Lungren's old 34th. It includes Seal Beach, Rossmoor, part of Westminster and all but the southeast side of Huntington Beach. Huntington Beach, with 170,000 people, is the district's southern anchor. Known as a haven for surfers who congregate around the city's pier, it is also a haven for Republican candidates, who can count on a large vote from the white-collar professionals who live in the area's cul de sacs.

A largely Democratic portion of the old 34th District, in Los Angeles County, was taken out of Lungren's new 42nd. The communities of Lakewood, Bellflower, Artesia and Hawaiian Gardens have been scattered among several other districts, along with the eastern part of Long Beach.

District 43

North San Diego County, South Orange County

Incumbent: Clair W. Burgener (R)

After having won more votes in 1980 than any congressional candidate in American history, Burgener is retiring at the end of his fifth term. Only one thing seems sure about his successor: He or she will be a Republican.

The 18 Republicans vying for the new 43rd District seat will have an even more favorable district to campaign in than Burgener did. It is more compact, shedding the vast Imperial Valley and eastern San Diego County portions. And it is more Republican. The registration, which was split evenly between Democrats and Republicans in the old district, is now weighted toward the GOP by a 51-35 margin. Such a margin translates into enormous majorities for most GOP candidates. In 1980, based on the new district lines, Reagan took 71 percent of the vote to Carter's 19 — Reagan's highest percentage in the state.

The new district runs along the Pacific coast from Carlsbad north to San Juan Capistrano, and inland about 30 miles into the mountains. About two-thirds of the voters

Clair W. Burgener   **Duncan L. Hunter**

live in the San Diego County portion of the district, which is similar in makeup to the smaller Orange County section. Both are upper-middle-class residential areas. There is little industry and the major incorporated cities, such as Oceanside and Escondido, are essentially aggregations of suburban housing developments.

The communities in the new 43rd were among the fastest-growing places in both Orange and San Diego counties in the 1970s. San Marcos, in the San Diego County hills near Escondido, grew by nearly 350 percent between 1970 and 1980. And the swallows of San Juan Capistrano find their community more crowded each March when they return to their historic mission. The population of that community quadrupled during the 1970s.

Because of its phenomenal growth in the last decade, the 43rd District had to lose more people in redistricting than any other in the state — more than 300,000. By removing the entire eastern end of the district, the booming western side of Riverside County, and the northern edge of the city of San Diego, the map makers took out enough population to allow them to add a heavily Republican slice of Orange County as well as Oceanside, in San Diego County. With 76,000 people, Oceanside is the largest city in the district and the only one with more registered Democrats than Republicans. However, Reagan carried this residential, beach resort community in 1980 by nearly a 3-to-1 margin.

District 44

Central San Diego

No Incumbent

Although San Diego County has not voted for a Democratic presidential candidate in nearly four decades, the county has always contained enough Democrats for one safe Democratic district. For most of the 1970s that district was the old 42nd, held for 18 years by Lionel Van Deerlin. But when he was unexpectedly turned out of office by Republican Duncan L. Hunter in 1980, it was clear some changes had to be made.

Renumbered and reincarnated as the new 44th, Van Deerlin's old constituency looks much safer for the Demo-

crats. The party's registration advantage within the new lines is even better than the 2-to-1 margin the old district enjoyed, and the map has been carefully drawn to exclude some heavily Republican precincts. By removing Coronado, sitting on a peninusla to the west of the San Diego Bay, map makers eliminated one of the most staunchly Republican areas in the old 42nd District.

The areas left are white, working-class residential neighborhoods near the center of the city and on toward the east; the blue-collar suburb of National City, further south; and all of San Diego's black and Mexican-American neighborhoods, including the San Ysidro ghetto, less than a mile from the Mexican border.

Many civilian government employees who are part of San Diego's vast naval operations live in the district. For local economic reasons, they tend to be supportive of a strong defense policy, which helps explain why Reagan carried the district by a 48-to-40-percent margin over Carter in 1980. But in nearly every other contest for state and local office, Republican candidates find little support from the registered Democrats of the area.

District 45

Imperial Valley and part of San Diego

Incumbent: Duncan L. Hunter (R)

Crossing the entire southern border of the state from the Colorado River to San Diego's Sunset Cliffs, the new 45th is sparsely populated and overwhelmingly Republican.

The district was created to give freshman Republican Hunter a secure place to run in. Democrats did not want him to interfere with their plans to elect a Democrat in the 44th, which includes much of Hunter's old constituency.

The lines of the new 45th should keep Hunter happy and keep him out of downtown San Diego. Although the 45th is not the most Republican of the San Diego area's three GOP districts, it supported Reagan with 62 percent in 1980. Hunter is confident he will have little trouble, even though he gains a substantial amount of new real estate.

The district has two distinct parts. Hunter already represents the suburban areas near San Diego. They include most of the eastern suburbs, such as Chula Vista and El Cajon, as well as the spit of land — Coronado — that separates the Pacific Ocean from the San Diego Bay. Coronado is the home of many retired Navy officers. They give the area a decidedly pro-military, Republican flavor.

The area that will be new to Hunter is the Imperial Valley. Below the level of both the Colorado River and the Pacific Ocean, the Imperial Valley was relatively easy to irrigate at the turn of the century and has since become one of the most productive farm areas in the country.

As transient farmers and others are moving in with their house trailers, the valley is experiencing its first substantial population growth in several decades. Just under 100,000 people now live there. Although registered Democrats outnumber Republicans by 56 to 34 percent, the electorate here is conservative. In 1980, Reagan nearly reversed the registration figures and defeated Carter, 56 to 37 percent. Imperial County has not voted for a Democratic presidential candidate since 1964.

Idaho

A competitive two-party state for much of the postwar period, Idaho has been moving gradually to the Republican right in recent years, an evolution symbolized by the defeat in 1980 of Sen. Frank Church, the symbol of its remaining ties to the national Democratic Party.

In many ways, the fact that Church came within 5,000 votes of winning in the Reagan presidential year seems more remarkable than his defeat. There had been warning signals in other elections for nearly 20 years. In 1964, Barry Goldwater drew 49.1 percent of the vote in Idaho, his best showing outside Arizona and the South. By 1966, the last Democratic congressman was gone, and there has not been another one since. In 1974, moderate Republican Rep. Orval Hansen lost his House seat to George Hansen, a militant conservative.

Much of this represented the same anti-Washington sentiment prevalent in other Mountain states, expressed against liberal Democrats and environmentalists. What is interesting is that the attitude has not really hurt Democrats running at the state level. Cecil Andrus took the governorship for the Democrats in 1970, and by 1974 he was popular enough to win a second term by 115,000 votes, the largest margin in Idaho history. Republicans felt certain they would take the statehouse back when Andrus left in 1977 to become President Carter's secretary of the interior. But John V. Evans took advantage of Republican bickering to keep the governorship in Democratic hands.

So Idaho has had a decade of moderate Democratic leadership at home and, except for Church, militant conservative representation in Washington. The current congressional delegation is solidly anti-government and pro-development. Sen. Steven Symms, the conqueror of Church in 1980, has been allied with the John Birch Society. Senior Sen. James McClure, chairman of the Senate Energy Committee, was an early leader in the "Sagebrush Rebellion" against federal land control. George Hansen is a strident voice of the right on foreign policy.

This lineup does not seem likely to change in the near future. The state's population grew by 32 percent in the 1970s, and many of the new residents were "refugees" from high taxes and urban problems in major metropolitan areas. Others were attracted by corporate jobs at the large number of businesses headquartered in Boise or by the high technology jobs becoming available as the electronics industry grows.

Idaho's natural beauty has consistently attracted environmentalists, and they are certain to remain a vocal and influential voice in the Democratic Party. But winning congressional elections may be another matter.

Southeast Idaho

In the mid-1800s, Mormons wandered north from Utah and founded the first settlements in what would become the state of Idaho. Today, southeastern Idaho is still Mormon. While only about a quarter of the state's residents are Mormons, almost two-thirds of the people in southeast Idaho are of the Mormon faith.

The early Mormon settlers quickly discovered that the desert-like soils of southeast Idaho, assisted by the waters of the Snake River, were perfect for growing potatoes. Today, potatoes are the leading source of income, not only for southeast Idaho, but for the entire state.

The Mormons of southeast Idaho are generally Republicans, although Gov. Evans is a Mormon and a Democrat. GOP candidates can usually depend on comfortable margins in southeast Idaho. In Bonneville County (Idaho Falls), the region's largest, Republican presidential candidates since 1952 have averaged well over 60 percent of the vote; Ronald Reagan won 78 percent in 1980.

Idaho Falls is the state's third largest city. It is near the nuclear plant test site that pioneered commercial nuclear power in the 1950s. There is limited local opposition, but most residents are amenable to nuclear power. McClure has pressed for federal approval of a nuclear breeder reactor for Idaho Falls.

There are a few pockets of regular Democratic votes in southeastern Idaho, the greatest being Pocatello (Bannock County). Pocatello is the region's largest city with more than 40,000 people. It is a chemical industry center, specializing in phosphate fertilizers. With a heavy Democratic labor vote and a sizable student vote from Idaho State University, Bannock County gave Church a solid margin in his 1980 defeat.

But Pocatello does not cast enough votes to swing the region to Democratic candidates. Only the most popular Democrats, such as Andrus and Church in his better days, manage to carry southeast Idaho. There are few other major cities in southeast Idaho.

Twin Falls, in the "magic valley," is the third major city in this part of the state. It is in the center of a prosperous farming area that raises sugar beets and other cash crops, and it contributes to the Republican vote.

Southwest Idaho—Boise

The Snake River rolls on into the southwest part of the state, watering potato and sugar beet fields. The agricultural area here is almost as fertile for Republicans as it is for crops.

The hub of southwest Idaho is Boise, the state's capital and its largest city, with a population of slightly more than 100,000. The entire metropolitan area has close to a quarter million people and has been growing at a faster rate than the rest of the state.

The main reason for Boise's remarkable growth is its unusual capacity for retaining corporate headquarters. Boise inaugurated a thorough urban renewal program in the late 1960s and early 1970s to replace an aging downtown. This convinced a number of major corporations to locate or remain there.

Boise is home to Boise Cascade (the lumber and paper conglomerate), Ore-Ida (a food processing company best known for frozen french fries), J. R. Simplot Co. (a food processing and mineral development company founded and run by Idaho's "Potato King"), Albertson's (a major supermarket chain) and Morrison Knudsen (a construction firm that began a $40 million expansion of its Boise headquarters in 1980).

Although the recent influx of out-of-staters has changed Boise politics somewhat, the city is still essentially conservative and Republican. Ada County (Boise) makes up one-fifth of the state vote and has given at least 56 percent to every Republican presidential candidate in the last 10 elections. The same is true of neighboring Canyon County, the state's second largest, which includes the growing cities of Caldwell and Nampa.

The rest of southwestern Idaho is made up mostly of lightly populated, Republican-voting farm counties. The Democrats in the area are mainly miners, lumbermen and Basque sheepherders, whose ancestors were among the early settlers of Idaho. This is where George Wallace scored his highest percentages in the state in 1968, winning from 15 to 23 percent in the non-urbanized counties in the region.

The Northern Panhandle

Idaho is divided into a clearly defined north and south by the Rocky Mountains. The south is mainly irrigated farm land, with some reasonably flat terrain and many wide-open spaces. The northern panhandle, by contrast, is mainly mountains, forests, lakes and mines. Much of it remains in wilderness. Unlike southern Idaho, the panhandle has little Mormon population.

The difference between the north and south extends into politics as well. The north has a much stronger traditional Democratic base than the south. There was considerable labor unrest in the panhandle during the late 19th and early 20th centuries, as underpaid lumbermen and miners sought to organize. Support for "free silver" also helped to establish Democrats as the party of northern Idaho.

To this day, Democratic candidates do best in the major silver mining and logging areas, although Republicans often prevail in the panhandle on the presidential level. While Church carried the panhandle by a substantial margin in 1980, Carter lost all 10 panhandle counties to Reagan.

Democrats generally do best in Shoshone County (home of the world's largest silver mine), Clearwater County and Nez Perce County. The latter contains Lewiston, the panhandle's biggest city and a major lumber center on the Snake River. The University of Idaho is also in the panhandle, at Moscow in Latah County.

The overall impact of the panhandle vote in statewide elections is limited by its relatively sparse population. Only 20 to 25 percent of Idaho's vote comes from the north.

The political complexion of the panhandle may be changing somewhat. Refugees from urban life have been settling near Coeur D'Alene, the region's second biggest city and one that is in the sphere of Spokane, Wash. Many of the new arrivals are fleeing from high taxes and city pressure; their voting habits appear to be Republican and conservative.

MINOR SHIFT SOLVES IDAHO'S PROBLEMS

Republicans, who dominate both chambers of the Idaho Legislature, have passed a redistricting plan that barely alters the state's congressional map.

The Democratic leader in the state Senate wanted to unite Ada County (Boise) in a single district, but the GOP rejected that concept because uniting Republican Boise in one district might have improved Democrats' chances of winning Idaho's other district.

So the redistricting bill drafted by the GOP equalized population in the two districts simply by shifting 15 Boise precincts containing 20,633 people from the 1st District to the 2nd. That measure passed the Legislature July 16, 1981. Democratic Gov. John V. Evans, who had shown some interest in uniting Boise, finally signed the Republican remap into law July 30, 1981.

Democrats hold a slight edge in most of the 15 shifted precincts, but the partisan balance in the precincts is so close that the political impact of their transfer should be minimal. The population variance between the two new districts is 175.

District 1

North and West — Lewiston, Boise

Incumbent: Larry E. Craig (R)

Although the 1st is traditionally the more Democratic of Idaho's two districts, conservative Republicans are firmly in control and may continue to gain ground.

Democratic strength in the 1st stems from labor influence in the mountainous northern panhandle, where underpaid lumbermen and miners fought to organize unions early in this century. Adding to Democratic strength is a community of relatively liberal voters linked to the University of Idaho, at Moscow in Latah County.

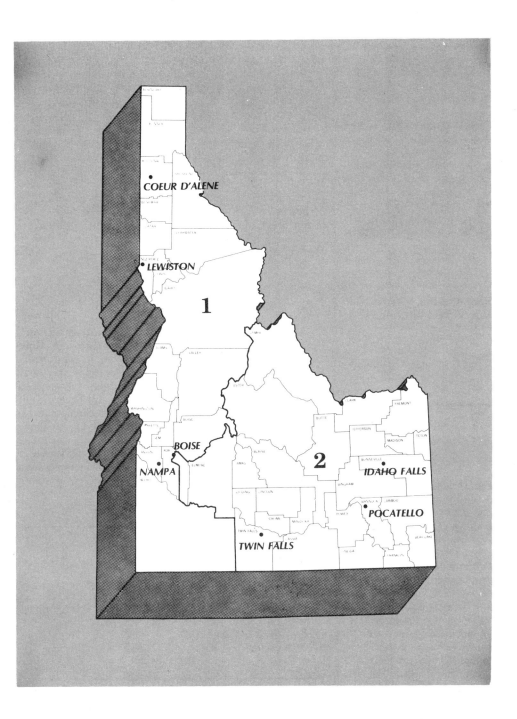

New Idaho Districts

U. S. Congress: 2 districts
    Senate (2R)
    House (2R)
Governor:
    John V. Evans (D)
Population: 943,935
Area: 56,400 sq. miles
1980 Presidential Vote:
    Carter (25%)
    Reagan (66%)
    Anderson (6%)

In the 1980 Senate contest, the nine northernmost counties in the state sided with Democrat Frank Church in his loss to Republican Steven D. Symms; several of those counties gave Jimmy Carter about 40 percent of the vote. Independent John Anderson's highest statewide tally (17 percent) and Reagan's lowest (47 percent) came in Latah County.

But the vote in the nine panhandle counties is more than offset by two heavily Republican urbanized areas at the southern end of the district — Canyon County and western Ada County — which have more than 40 percent of the district's residents.

The state capital of Boise is located in Ada County. It is Idaho's only city with more than 100,000 residents, and its Republican tendencies stem from the numerous lumber,

paper, food processing and construction corporations who have their headquarters there. Canyon County contains the growing cities of Nampa and Caldwell — agricultural processing centers that usually vote a solidly Republican ticket.

In 1980, Canyon County and the 1st District portion of Ada County each gave 68 percent of their vote to Reagan. Craig, running for a vacant seat in 1980, carried only four of the 15 Boise precincts that he will be giving up to the 2nd District, so the change may make him slightly stronger. Districtwide, Craig won 54 percent of the vote last year.

Demographic trends in Idaho's northern panhandle do not bode well for the Democratic Party. Shoshone and Clearwater counties were the only two counties in Idaho to lose population during the 1970s, and Nez Perce County

Larry E. Craig

George Hansen

grew by a total of less than 10 percent. Jimmy Carter's highest 1980 percentages in Idaho came from those three counties.

District 2

East — Pocatello, Idaho Falls

Incumbent: George Hansen (R)

Mormons migrating north from Utah first settled southeastern Idaho in the mid-1800s, and today their influence is pervasive in the area. Almost two-thirds of the people in southeast Idaho are of the Mormon faith, and like their religious brethren elsewhere, the Mormons here support conservative candidates and causes. In the 1978 gubernatorial election, a conservative Mormon Republican received majorities in many of the southeastern counties of the 2nd District while losing badly in the 1st District, where the Mormon influence is much less significant.

In Bonneville County (Idaho Falls), the region's largest county, GOP presidential candidates since 1952 have averaged well more than 60 percent of the vote; Reagan won 78 percent here in 1980. The city of Idaho Falls processes potatoes grown in the surrounding upper Snake River Val-

ley. It is located 30 miles from the nuclear plant test site that pioneered commercial nuclear power in the 1950s.

The other populous and reliably Republican county in southeast Idaho is Twin Falls County. It is in the center of the Magic Valley farming area, so named because the sandy soils in this region, when irrigated with Snake River water, produce remarkable yields of potatoes, sugar beets and other cash crops. Twin Falls County gave Reagan 74 percent in 1980.

The most significant pocket of Democratic strength in the 2nd District is in Bannock County, which has 14 percent of the district's population and gave Church nearly 60 percent of the vote in 1980. Located in Bannock County is southeast Idaho's largest city, Pocatello, a railroad and chemical center, specializing in phosphate fertilizers. Democratic strength springs from a heavy labor vote and a sizable student vote from Idaho State University.

Two other centers of Democratic votes in the 2nd are in Blaine County, home of the Sun Valley resorts, and in the eastern section of Boise around Boise State University. Church won 69 percent of the Blaine County vote in 1980, his highest percentage in the state. The eastern section of Boise went Democratic in both the Senate and House elections in 1980, although Reagan won it comfortably. Hansen seldom runs well in the eastern Boise part of his district, but the addition of 15 marginally Democratic Boise precincts should not make much difference. Despite the Democratic strength in Bannock and Blaine counties and in Boise, those areas together amount to less than a third of the total 2nd District vote. That is not nearly enough to offset overwhelming Republican majorities in Bonneville and Twin Falls counties and in the farm, ranch and wilderness region around them.

New Idaho Districts

New District	Incumbent	Population	1980 Pres. Winner
1	Larry E. Craig (R)	472,055	Reagan
2	George Hansen (R)	471,880	Reagan

Nevada

The importance of gambling to Nevada is hard to overemphasize. The gambling industry accounts directly or indirectly for 65 percent of the jobs in Nevada. It brings approximately $2.5 billion into the state each year. When fire gutted the MGM Grand Hotel in Las Vegas in 1980, killing 84 people and laying off the hotel's workforce, the unemployment rate of the state jumped by 1.4 percentage points.

Nevada in 1931 consisted mainly of cattle ranches and abandoned silver mines, and was home to only 91,058 people. Today, 50 years after the legalization of gambling, Nevada is a thriving Sun Belt state with 800,000 residents and the second highest per capita income in the United States.

Until the 1950s, Nevada politics was dominated by Reno and the older communities in the northern part of the state. It was generally Democratic but more so because Democrats were the traditional party of silver interests than for any modern reason.

Both of those traditions began to change with gambling and prosperity. Clark County (Las Vegas) overtook Washoe County (Reno) in population in 1960, and by 1980, it had nearly three times as many people. In the 1980s, Nevada will have two congressional districts for the first time in its history; Clark County is populous enough now to support one district entirely within its borders.

Las Vegas came of age in Nevada politics in 1958, when Howard Cannon, running as a self-proclaimed liberal Democrat, became the city's first U. S. senator. Cannon has changed with Nevada over the years and now votes conservatively, the only way Democrats can vote and survive very long representing the state.

Cannon's first re-election in 1964 was by 48 votes over Republican Paul Laxalt, then the lieutenant governor. In the years since then, Laxalt has won the governorship and two U. S. Senate terms, symbolizing the newest and strongest strain in Nevada politics — opposition to the federal government. The government owns a vast majority of the state's land, and its policies have generated a "Sagebrush Rebellion" to which Laxalt and most Nevada politicians adhere.

The land resentment has erased what was left of Nevada's old Democratic tradition in national elections. Jimmy Carter drew an embarrassing 26.9 percent of the vote in November 1980.

Clark County — Las Vegas

In 40 years Las Vegas has developed from a sleepy town of 10,000 to a neon extravaganza with 165,000 full-time residents. Clark County, including Las Vegas and the surrounding area, has almost 60 percent of the state's population.

Clark County is more diverse demographically than many outsiders realize. It has a substantial Catholic population, more than 40,000 blacks and a large blue-collar community.

Clark County is still reliable territory for most Democrats. Jimmy Carter carried it by about 3,000 votes against Gerald R. Ford in 1976, although he lost it by a resounding margin to Ronald Reagan.

There is a large Mormon community in Clark County, and it provides Republican votes. There is also a strong Republican contingent near Nellis Air Force Base.

Reno and Vicinity

Though dwarfed now by Las Vegas, Reno still has over 100,000 people and is the heart of the northwestern part of the state that includes the state capital of Carson City and Lake Tahoe, a major resort center.

The northern cities of Reno and Sparks and the Lake Tahoe area provide Republicans with their greatest margins in Nevada. If the turnout in Clark County is low or if the contest is close there, the Republican vote in this populated part of the northwest is usually strong enough to swing a statewide election to the GOP.

The Cow Counties

The 15 percent of Nevada's people who do not live near Reno or Las Vegas live in the Cow Counties — a huge expanse of desert and sagebrush that occupies most of the state.

Cattle raising is the main economic interest there, but silver and gold mining have been making a comeback.

These are old populist Democratic areas, gradually turning Republican in frustration over land and water policies of Democratic administrations. Laxalt is very popular in the Cow Counties. He carried nearly all of them in his 1974 Senate comeback, and their vote, although light, enabled him to win the 624 vote statewide victory that launched his career in Washington.

LAS VEGAS DOMINATES NEW DISTRICT

Regional loyalties prevailed over partisanship as Nevada's Legislature debated where to put the state's newly acquired second House district.

Conservative Democrats from northern Nevada joined with Republicans to thwart a proposal by Las Vegas Democrats that would have split moderate-to-liberal Las Vegas (Clark County), enabling it to dominate both districts.

The bipartisan state coalition passed a remap that concentrates Clark County voting strength in a single district, leaving northern Nevada dominant in the state's other constituency. Because its population grew 63.5 percent during the 1970s, Nevada earned a second House seat in 1980 reapportionment. The state has been limited to one at-large seat since its admission to the Union in 1864.

The intervention of GOP Gov. Robert List was critical to passage of the coalition plan. Democrats have majorities in Nevada's Assembly and Senate, and both chambers initially approved the Las Vegas Democrats' plan.

But List vowed to veto their work and threatened to call lawmakers into a special session. Pressured because the regular legislative session was dragging on to record length, the Assembly reversed itself May 30, 1981, and adopted the coalition plan by a 21-19 vote. After more pressure from the governor, the Senate June 3, 1981, followed suit, by a vote of 11-8. Gov. List signed the bill into law that evening.

Jim Santini, the state's only current House member, will run for the Senate in 1982 against fellow-Democrat Howard W. Cannon, who will be seeking a fifth term. So Nevadans will elect two new House members in 1982. A Democrat is likely to take the 1st District; either a Republican or a conservative Democrat could win in the 2nd.

most of the people with service jobs in the gambling, entertainment and tourism industries usually vote Democratic, the 1st should be reasonably safe territory for Democratic candidates in House elections.

Population in Clark County grew by 69 percent during the past decade, and today more than 58 percent of all Nevadans live in the county. With a population of 461,816, Clark contains enough people to support one congressional district and still have more than 60,000 left over.

Jim Santini

The 60,000 excluded from the district under the remap live in the northern part of the county, where there is a substantial concentration of Democratic-voting blue-collar workers and blacks with service-oriented jobs linked to the tourist trade or to Nellis Air Force Base. Had these voters been placed in the 1st District, its Democratic future would have been unquestioned. As it is, Republicans feel a serious campaign might be worth the effort. But Democrats are confident that their 60-40 registration advantage will still assure them victory. Running for re-election to his at-large House seat in 1980, Democrat Santini won 70 percent in Clark County.

In statewide elections, however, many of the county's registered Democrats do cross party lines to support conservative Republicans, joining with the county's substantial Mormon population and its affluent white-collar communities. Both Ronald Reagan and GOP Sen. Paul Laxalt carried Clark County by comfortable margins in 1980.

District 1

South — Las Vegas

Incumbent: Jim Santini (D)

The casinos, nightclubs and hotels of Las Vegas are the economic focal point of the new 1st District, and since

District 2

North — Reno and the Cow Counties

No Incumbent

Although 15 percent of the people in the new 2nd live in North Las Vegas and northern Clark County, the 2nd is referred to as the "non-Las Vegas" district. It is dominated by northwestern Nevada's Washoe County (Reno), a Republican stronghold containing nearly one-half of the district's voters.

Gambling is an all-important component of the Washoe County economy, but Reno and Lake Tahoe take pains to differentiate themselves from Las Vegas. This is "old Nevada," the part of the state that was built on mining in the 19th century and dominated the state politically until Las Vegas overshadowed it in the 1950s. Republicans have a registration advantage in Washoe County and nearby Douglas County and Carson City. Those three areas each gave Reagan at least 64 percent of the vote in 1980.

About one-fourth of the district's residents are dispersed through the Cow Counties, a huge expanse of mountain and desert that occupies most of the state. Cattle- and sheep-raising are the main economic activities here, but

New Nevada Districts

New District	Incumbent	Population	1980 Pres. Winner
1	Jim Santini (D)	400,948	Reagan
2	No Incumbent	398,236	Reagan

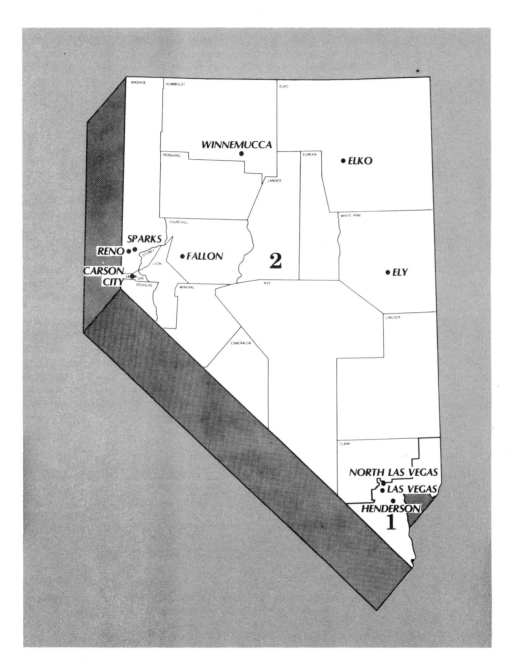

WASHOE HUMBOLDT ELKO

WINNEMUCCA

PERSHING

● ELKO

EUREKA

LANDER

CHURCHILL

WHITE PINE

SPARKS

RENO ●● STOREY ● FALLON **2**

CARSON LYON

CITY CARSON CITY

DOUGLAS

MINERAL

● ELY

NYE

LINCOLN

ESMERALDA

CLARK

NORTH LAS VEGAS
● LAS VEGAS

HENDERSON **1**

New
Nevada
Districts

U. S. Congress: 2 districts
  Senate (1D, 1R)
  House (1D)
Governor:
  Robert F. List (R)
Population: 799,184
Area: 110,540 sq. miles
1980 Presidential Vote:
  Carter (27%)
  Reagan (63%)
  Anderson (7%)

silver and gold mining are mounting a comeback as techno-logical improvements make it profitable to extract and process low-grade ore.

The Cow Counties were populist and Democratic for most of this century, but their voters are gradually turning Republican in frustration over national Democratic liberal-ism, especially the party's land and water policies. (Nearly all of the land in the 2nd District is federally owned.) Most residents thought President Carter's plan to place a mobile

MX missile system in this region would strain the meager water supply, and there was rejoicing when President Rea-gan decided to deploy the MX in existing silos outside Nevada.

Although Reagan won comfortably in all the Cow Counties in 1980, Santini has proven that a popular Demo-crat can still prevail there. In 1980, he carried every north-ern county, winning many with better than 70 percent of the vote.

New Mexico

Once the exclusive domain of Hispanics and Indians, New Mexico is being increasingly "Anglocized."

For most of this century, the "Anglos" — all non-Indians or Hispanics — came to ranch, to mine or to regain their health in the sunny, dry climate. But in the boom years since World War II, the attractions have been more diverse. Some Anglos have come to develop the oil and mineral resources in New Mexico or to work in the laboratories in Los Alamos and Albuquerque uncovering the secrets of nuclear power. Others have been drawn by the mountain scenery and relaxed pace of life in the "Land of Enchantment."

Between 1940 and 1960, the population of New Mexico nearly doubled. The boom ebbed in the 1960s with a decline in defense-related jobs but revived dramatically in the 1970s when the growth in private-sector jobs spurred a population increase of 28 percent. For the first time in its history, New Mexico will have three seats in the U.S. House after 1982.

The influx of newcomers has meant an increasingly dominant Anglo majority. Hispanics — many descendants of Spanish settlers who entered New Mexico more than 350 years ago — comprise 37 percent of the population. Indians — mostly members of the ancient Navajo or Pueblo tribes — make up 8 percent.

These groups remain the backbone of the once-dominant Democratic Party in New Mexico. With their help, the party ruled the state from the early days of the New Deal until the late 1960s.

But the defection of conservative Democrats in southeastern New Mexico ("Little Texas") and the influx of Anglos has spurred a Republican resurgence. Republicans now have both U.S. Senate and U.S. House seats. They do not hold the governor's chair or control either chamber of the state Legislature, but they were only two seats down in the state Senate after November of 1980. They lost both the 1974 and 1978 gubernatorial elections by fewer than 4,000 votes.

Because many of the Hispanics and Indians are poor, New Mexico ranks near the bottom tier of states in per capita income. But the economic picture will improve in the 1980s as the state's rich natural resources are developed. By the late 1970s, New Mexico was the leading state in the mining of uranium and among the top seven in the production of crude oil and natural gas.

Albuquerque

This is New Mexico's commercial hub and major population center. Including its Bernalillo County suburbs, the Albuquerque area is home for nearly one-third of New Mexico's 1.3 million residents.

In the post-World War II years, there has been an ebb and flow in defense contracts that has affected Albuquerque's growth. Originally a health spa and trade center along the Rio Grande, the city had fewer than 40,000 inhabitants in 1940. But 20 years later, with the coming of a lucrative military-aerospace connection, Albuquerque had grown to more than 200,000 residents. Growth slowed in the 1960s but with a more and more diversified economy, the city surged forward again during the 1970s.

Large clothing and office machine plants have located in Albuquerque. But the real boom in recent years has been provided by electronics firms. The influx of young engineers and scientists, as well as retirees — many of them formerly with the military — have helped push Bernalillo County increasingly into the GOP column. Although its population is 37 percent Hispanic, the county has voted Republican in all but one presidential election since 1952. It has been reliably Republican in recent races for major statewide offices, but has a Democratic mayor, David Rusk, the son of former Secretary of State Dean Rusk.

Santa Fe and the Hispanic North

The greatest concentration of Hispanics and Democratic votes in the state is in the mountainous north.

The region is the site of some of the earliest 17th century Spanish settlements in the state, including the state capital of Santa Fe. Today, six of the state's eight predominantly Hispanic counties are in the north, with the other two in the southwest corner of the state near the Mexican border. Except for Santa Fe County, the Hispanic north is an area of slow growth.

Santa Fe is the center of the region. Its strong Hispanic and Indian culture is seen in its adobe buildings, still the most prominent architectural style in use. With nearly 50,000 residents, Santa Fe is the state's largest city north of Albuquerque. The melding of the Spanish and Indian cultures has created an ambience attractive to young Anglos, who are migrating to Santa Fe in increasing numbers. The county grew by 38 percent in the past decade.

A colony of artists and writers has flourished in the cosmopolitan atmosphere. These residents join with the Hispanics and state government workers to provide Democratic candidates with comfortable margins in Santa Fe County.

Seven different Pueblo Indian tribes live in the Rio Grande Valley north of Santa Fe. Although they usually vote Democratic, the council for the Pueblo tribes endorsed Reagan in 1980.

The rest of the Hispanic north is primarily mountainous, semi-arid grazing land, with much poverty and subsistence farming. An exception is the prosperous Anglo community of Los Alamos, where the atomic bomb was secretly developed during World War II. After the war, the gates of Los Alamos were opened, and it became a separate county. During the last three decades, Los Alamos has remained a center for the research and development of atomic energy. Its scientifically skilled, well-educated electorate is largely Republican. But voters in Los Alamos also have an independent streak, shown in 1980 when John B. Anderson received 15 percent of the vote, his highest percentage in the state.

Little Texas

Economically, culturally and politically, the southeastern part of New Mexico is similar to the adjoining plains of Texas. That is no accident. The region was settled by Texans early this century and Anglo dominance has never been threatened. Hispanics comprise only about one-quarter of the population of Little Texas.

Most of the land is used for grazing cattle or sheep, with some suitable for dry farming crops such as wheat. Irrigated farm land along the Pecos River produces cotton, vegetables and fruit.

Conservative and heavily Protestant, Little Texas was overwhelmingly Democratic for most of the century. But as the national Democratic Party moved leftward, party loyalty began to crack. In 1968, votes from Little Texas helped to send conservative Republican Ed Foreman, a former Texas congressman, to the House. Foreman lasted only one term before being unseated by conservative Democrat Harold Runnels. But in statewide contests, the region has regularly turned in GOP majorities.

Although Little Texas is not a booming area like Albuquerque, it has remained stable with oil, mining and military activity. Oil deposits are concentrated in the southern portion of Little Texas around Carlsbad, Roswell and Hobbs.

Located near the famous caverns, the town of Carlsbad is also a tourist center. Located nearby are the nation's most productive potash mines where unionized miners occasionally give Democrats enough votes to carry Eddy County (Carlsbad).

Alamagordo, situated just across the Sacramento Mountains from Little Texas, is culturally in step with the region. Just outside Alamagordo is the White Sands Missile Range, where the first atomic bomb was exploded in 1945.

Mexican Highlands and Indian Country

The western third of New Mexico is really two distinct areas. The largely Hispanic southern portion is known as the Mexican Highlands. It is a semi-arid region of desert and mountains. A wide range of mineral deposits — copper, zinc, silver, gold and lead — are located in the heart of the mountains. In the Rio Grande Valley near Las Cruces, there is irrigated farm land, where cotton, vegetables and fruit are grown.

The semi-arid high plateau to the north is Indian country. A large Navajo reservation stretches from the town of Gallup about 100 miles north to the Four Corners — the point where New Mexico, Colorado, Utah and Arizona meet. Like the Mexican Highlands, the Indian country is rich in minerals — coal and uranium — as well as oil and natural gas. Many of the energy reserves were found on Indian land, enabling them to attain a level of prosperity unmatched by other Indian tribes in New Mexico.

With the exception of Grant and Socorro counties — major mining centers in the south — the Mexican Highlands usually vote Republican. By contrast, the Indian country is predominantly Democratic. The exception is San Juan County, where a conservative Anglo population has settled in the energy-rich Four Corners area near Farmington. San Juan gave Reagan a higher share of the vote than any New Mexico county outside Little Texas.

Valencia County, the center of uranium mining activity in the 1970s, grew by 50 percent. San Juan County, one of the state's leading oil, gas and coal producing areas, grew by 54 percent. Sandoval County, which abuts Bernalillo County and drew suburban spillover from Albuquerque, had a population growth of 99 percent.

NEW MEXICO DRAWS THIRD DISTRICT

Rejecting conservative appeals for a drastic revision of district lines, New Mexico legislators approved a remap that created a new seat in the Albuquerque area while leaving the two existing districts essentially intact. The plan was signed Jan. 19, 1982, by Democratic Gov. Bruce King.

New Mexico's 28 percent population growth during the 1970s entitled the state to a third congressional seat. That windfall gave rise to a year of squabbling among New Mexico politicians. Both parties quickly agreed that one district would be dominated by Bernalillo County (Albuquerque). But they were divided on how to redraw the rest of the state.

The ruling conservative coalition in the New Mexico House won House passage of a plan to scrap the existing northern and southern districts in favor of an eastern and western configuration that would have divided the Democratic Hispanic vote in northern New Mexico, possibly allowing conservatives to take three seats.

But the Democratic-controlled Senate and the state's two Republican congressional incumbents, Manuel Lujan Jr. and Joe Skeen, objected to the House plan. Lujan and Skeen argued that cultural and economic ties favored retention of northern and southern districts outside the Albuquerque area. They warned that an effort to change the district lines could produce a voter backlash.

Lujan and Skeen also were concerned that the House plan would disrupt their re-election efforts. Lujan had been gearing up to run in the new Albuquerque district, while Skeen wanted to retain his base in conservative southern New Mexico.

New
New Mexico
Districts

U. S. Congress: 3 districts
  Senate (2R)
  House (2R)

Governor:
  Bruce King (D)

Population: 1,299,968

Area: 121,666 sq. miles

1980 Presidential Vote:
  Carter (37%)
  Reagan (55%)
  Anderson (7%)

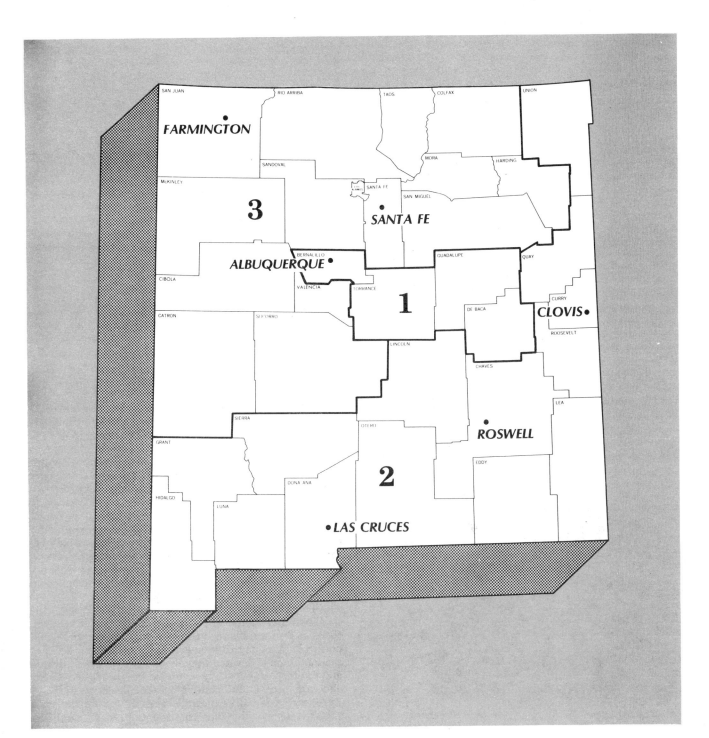

Thanks to active lobbying by both incumbents during the state Legislature's special January 1982 session, a north-south plan was approved by votes of 54-12 in the House and 32-9 in the Senate. Bernalillo County was joined with De Baca, Guadalupe and Torrance counties to form a new central district.

Although the candidate filing deadline passed March 2, 1982, there is a possibility that the new map could be voided. Under an amendment to the redistricting bill, a successful court challenge to the state legislative redistricting plans also would invalidate the congressional plan. While the legality of this linkage has been questioned, several lawsuits have been filed against the state redistricting map.

District 1

Central — Albuquerque

Incumbent: Manuel Lujan Jr. (R)

After a decade as the center of New Mexico's sprawling northern district, the fast-growing Albuquerque area will dominate a constituency of its own in the 1980s.

It should have a GOP flavor. Bernalillo County has voted Republican in all but one presidential election since 1952 and has provided a solid political base for Lujan, a seven-term House veteran. A resident of Albuquerque, Lujan needed his 9,000-vote majority in Bernalillo County to save his House seat in 1980. He lost the rest of the northern district by nearly 4,000 votes.

Originally a health resort and trade center, Albuquerque had fewer than 40,000 residents in 1940. Its postwar emergence as a Republican stronghold was fueled by the development of a prosperous military-aerospace industry. By 1960 the population exceeded 200,000. During the past two decades a diversified economy has sustained the boom. The city's population grew 36 percent in the 1970s, enhancing its position as New Mexico's commercial hub and major population center. Including the Bernalillo County suburbs, the Albuquerque area is home for nearly one-third of New Mexico's 1.3 million residents.

Electronics firms have provided the impetus for Albuquerque's latest round of population growth. Young engineers and scientists, attracted by jobs, and retirees, attracted by the weather, have helped in recent years to retain the county's Republican slant.

But Albuquerque is not as stridently conservative as many other Sun Belt population centers. Reagan's 53 percent share of the 1980 vote in Bernalillo County was 2 percentage points below his statewide figure and no better than Gerald R. Ford's showing in the Albuquerque area four years earlier.

The county's large minority population provides Democrats a potentially strong base. Hispanics alone comprise 37 percent of the county population. Indians, blacks and Asians make up another 6 percent. In addition, the newest generation of white-collar migrants exhibits some liberal tendencies. Independent John B. Anderson drew 10 percent of the county vote in 1980, well above his statewide mark of 6 percent.

Three sparsely populated counties east of Albuquerque are also included in the new 1st District. Together the three — De Baca, Guadalupe and Torrance counties — hold only 3 percent of the district population. Ranching is the mainstay of the economy in De Baca and Guadalupe counties, both of which lost population in the last decade.

District 2

South and East — Las Cruces, Roswell

Incumbent: Joe Skeen (R)

The redistricting plan has removed energy-rich northwestern New Mexico from the 2nd District, with its large Indian population, and added lightly populated Union and Quay counties in the northeast. But the sprawling district remains politically homogeneous. It is mostly rural and very conservative.

The boundary changes should strengthen Skeen, a conservative Republican who won as a write-in candidate in 1980. He lost the Indian country, but carried the rest of the district by nearly 8,500 votes.

Skeen's election was further evidence of crumbling party ties in southern New Mexico, territory that was once firmly Democratic. During the 1970s the district developed a strong habit of voting Republican in statewide contests, in part because ranchers and other Southern-style Democrats resented their party's liberal national program. The district kept its Democratic House representation only because incumbent Harold E. Runnels maintained a strictly conservative voting record. Runnels encountered little opposition during his decade in office, but Democrats could not hold on after his death in 1980.

The centerpiece of the 2nd is "Little Texas," the southeastern corner of the state. Settled by Texans early in the 20th century, the region is economically, culturally and politically similar to the adjoining Texas plains. Most of the land here is devoted to grazing cattle or sheep. But oil and military projects have increased the standard of living and reshaped voting habits in a Republican direction.

Nearly one-half of the vote in the 14-county district is concentrated in the four counties that make up Little

Manuel Lujan Jr.   **Joe Skeen**

New Districts in New Mexico

New District	Incumbent	Population	1980 Pres. Winner
1	Manuel Lujan Jr. (R)	434,141	Reagan
2	Joe Skeen (R)	436,261	Reagan
3	None	432,492	Reagan

Texas. The oil- and gas-producing centers of Chaves County (Roswell) and Lea County (Hobbs) are bastions of conservatism. Each gave Reagan more than 65 percent of the vote in 1980. So did Curry County (Clovis), which is the site of a large Air Force base.

Eddy County is less conservative. Near Carlsbad are the nation's most productive potash mines, and the area's unionized miners occasionally give Democrats enough votes to carry the county. Reagan won it in 1980 with 56 percent of the vote.

Located to the west are Otero County and Dona Ana County. Together they include nearly one-third of the 2nd District population. The city of Alamogordo, located in Otero County across the Sacramento Mountains from Little Texas, is culturally and politically in step with the region.

Dona Ana County is located further west in the Rio Grande Valley. Most of the county's population lives around Las Cruces, the largest city in New Mexico south of Albuquerque. Cotton, pecans and green chilies (the official state vegetable) are grown in profusion on the valley's irrigated farms. The county has a Hispanic majority, giving the Democrats a substantial base, but Republicans generally carry it. Reagan drew 54 percent of the Dona Ana vote in 1980.

The district's lone Democratic strongholds are in the Mexican Highlands, along the Arizona border, where copper and lead mines have attracted a unionized work force. But less than 10 percent of the district's voters live in this semi-arid region of desert and mountains.

District 3

North and West — Farmington, Santa Fe

Incumbent: None

Like the 2nd District, the revamped 3rd covers about half the land area of New Mexico. But with three out of every five residents either Hispanic or Indian, it is decidedly more liberal and Democratic than either of the state's other constituencies.

The population of the 3rd is almost equally divided between the predominantly Hispanic counties of northern New Mexico and the energy-rich Indian lands along the Arizona border.

Northern New Mexico was in Lujan's old 2nd District during the 1970s, while the Indian lands were represented by Skeen. But neither man showed any reluctance to part with his old constituents. In 1980 Lujan trailed Democratic challenger Bill Richardson by more than 5,000 votes in the Hispanic north and Skeen ran nearly 2,000 votes behind Democrat David King in the Indian country.

Of the two regions, the Hispanic north is the most loyally Democratic. It includes the only five New Mexico counties carried by Jimmy Carter in 1980. The capital city of Santa Fe is the center of the region. Its nearly 50,000 residents make it the second largest city in the state. A pleasant mixture of Spanish and Indian cultures in Santa Fe has attracted a steady influx of young Anglos. Santa Fe County comprises 17 percent of the district population, far more than any other county in the region.

The rest of the Hispanic north is primarily mountainous, semi-arid grazing land, with much poverty and subsistence farming. By the end of 1981 the unemployment rate had topped 10 percent in four rural counties, with a staggering 31 percent of the population unemployed in Mora County.

An economic oasis is the Anglo community of Los Alamos, where the atomic bomb was developed during World War II. Los Alamos, one of the most prosperous counties in the country, has had an unemployment rate of less than 2 percent. Los Alamos voters — well educated and scientifically inclined — largely vote the Republican ticket.

But Los Alamos County comprises only 4 percent of the district population. And its voters have an independent streak, exhibited in 1980 when Anderson drew 15 percent there, his highest vote in the state.

The Indian country divides more closely at the polls. The Indians, most of them Navaho, usually vote Democratic. But they turn out in small numbers and occasionally bolt to the Republicans. The council for the Pueblo tribes endorsed Reagan in 1980 and McKinley County — the only county in the state with an Indian majority — gave Reagan 57 percent of the vote. Republican beachheads have also been established in the towns of Gallup and Grants, which have growing Anglo populations.

The region's largest GOP stronghold, however, is San Juan County, where a conservative Anglo population has settled around Farmington to tap the vast supply of oil, gas and coal in the Four Corners area. San Juan gave Reagan 66 percent of the vote in 1980, his largest share in the state outside Little Texas.

San Juan was one of three New Mexico counties with a population growth of more than 50 percent in the 1970s. The other two counties, Sandoval and Valencia, are also in the new 3rd District. Valencia County was divided by the state Legislature in 1981. The more conservative western portion, centered in the one-time uranium boom town of Grants, became a new entity called Cibola County, taking its name from the Spanish word for female bison. The eastern portion, near Albuquerque, remained in Valencia County. Both it and Sandoval abut Bernalillo County and are a combination of Indian villages and growing suburban communities. Together, Sandoval, Valencia and the new Cibola County comprise 15 percent of the district population.

Oregon

Oregon has spent much of this century moving in an opposite political direction from other Western states. It used to be called the "Vermont of the West" because it was so consistently Republican in national elections. Even while the states around it were going Democratic during the Depression, Oregon, like Vermont, kept up most of its GOP ties at the state level, although it did vote for Roosevelt four times.

Then in postwar years, when the Mountain states began to turn conservative and Republican, Oregon — like Vermont — moved left. Today, both states are attracting a new electorate of young professionals seeking a greener and quieter way of life. Environmental concerns have become salient political issues, and both states have begun electing moderate Republicans and liberal Democrats.

The two controversial symbols of modern Oregon politics are Wayne Morse, who was elected to the Senate in 1944 as a progressive Republican and ended up in 1968 as an anti-war Democrat; and Tom McCall, a popular governor who urged people to visit Oregon for the scenery and then go home rather than place a permanent drain on its resources.

For most of the 1970s, Oregon sent two moderate Republicans to the U.S. Senate and four Democrats to the U.S. House. Jimmy Carter and Gerald Ford virtually tied in Oregon in 1976 — Ford ultimately won by 1,713 votes. Ronald Reagan took it in 1980, but John B. Anderson drew one of his strongest votes in the nation.

One reason Oregon does not vote much like the other Western states is that it does not have much in common with them. Settled before the Civil War, the state had a stronger Yankee strain than its neighbors. That group has been dominant for most of the state's history, although a minority group descended from Southern Democratic settlers has also had periods of power and influence.

The bulk of the state's population has always been west of the Cascade mountains, in Portland and a string of coastal and Willamette Valley towns similar in climate and temperament to San Francisco and Seattle rather than Denver and Reno.

Today, Oregon politics reflects environmental values that are distinctly in the minority in surrounding states. Most Oregonians have been jealously protective of their magnificent shorelines, valleys, mountains, rivers and forests and have sought to prevent rapid development. Although Oregon's population has grown by over 25 percent in the past 10 years, state environmental and zoning laws held down an even more explosive potential growth. Environmental pressures have been consistent despite the state's dependence on the timber industry, whose fortunes rose and fell periodically during the 1970s.

Portland

The green city of Portland dominates the state's economic activity as well as its politics. Sitting along the Willamette River, Oregon's largest city (population 366,000) has a reputation for being a pleasant, livable place. As the only major metropolitan area between San Francisco and Seattle, it has attracted large banks, law firms, headquarters of giant lumber firms and a large shipping trade. Electronics firms, specialty woolen mills and some heavy industry have also located in the area. There is a sizable blue-collar vote in Portland.

Bisected by the Willamette River, Portland is socially and politically two cities. On the west side, beyond the modern, high-rise towers of the thriving downtown area, are the affluent West Hills. Scenic parklands and quiet residential areas with magnificent views make this a favorite spot for the liberal professionals who can afford it. Politically, this is the more Republican side of town, although Jimmy Carter matched Ronald Reagan vote for vote in the area.

The majority of Portland's citizens live east of the Willamette River. Poor blacks in the Albina section join blue-collar whites in the North End and the East Side's many elderly residents to give Democrats comfortable margins. Carter easily defeated Reagan in the eastern part of the city, where the vote for independent John B. Anderson was lower than in the western hills.

With Mt. Hood and the Cascade mountains blocking expansion on the east, Portland's suburban growth has been pushed into Clackamas and Washington counties on the south and west. Both counties have been growing at twice the state rate, and each now has nearly a quarter-million people. Beaverton, with less than 6,000 people in 1960, had more than 30,000 residents by 1980.

The suburban vote is now nearly double that of Portland, and is predictably conservative, as white-collar management people have settled into an affluent life style. With the highest median income in the state, Washington County joined Clackamas and the part of Multnomah

County outside of Portland in giving Reagan a 37,000-vote plurality in 1980. Carter's plurality in Portland was less than 24,000.

The Willamette Valley

Stretching 180 miles south from Portland, this 60-mile-wide valley sits comfortably between the Cascades and the Coastal mountains. With mild temperatures and fertile land, it is the state's food-basket and claims to have the potential to feed up to 12 million people. Dairy products, poultry, wheat, barley, oats, hogs, fruit and vegetables are all found in the valley. But there is more to it than farmland.

Spaced unevenly down the valley, and connected by Interstate 5, are all of Oregon's significant urban areas. From Portland on the north to Eugene and Springfield on the south, the Willamette Valley is home to two out of three Oregonians. Also located in the valley are the state's two major universities — the University of Oregon at Eugene and Oregon State University at Corvallis — and enough of the state's vast timberlands to support several sawmill towns.

Willamette Valley voters register Democratic but often vote Republican. In 1980, Reagan carried every county in the valley, including Linn and Lane, the two Carter won in 1976.

Lane County, the most populous part of the Willamette Valley south of Portland, has a reputation for being the liberal heartland of Oregon. The reputation comes from Eugene, a growing city with a population of 105,000. Commonly thought of as a university town, Eugene also relies heavily on the nearby fir and cedar forests for much of its non-university employment. The university vote was important in helping to pass a 1971 city referendum calling for the withdrawal of all U.S. troops from Vietnam. But workers in the lumber mills and in other diversified timber industries were the ones responsible for the defeat of a homosexual rights law seven years later. John F. Kennedy, Hubert Humphrey and George McGovern all lost Lane County to Richard Nixon.

The Coast

Only 25 miles wide, the Oregon coast is wet, wooded, and more reliably Democratic than any other part of the state.

With close to 130 inches of rainfall each year, it is the part of the state that brought on Gov. McCall's quip about tourists rusting on the coast's plentiful beaches. Tourism and fishing are the two economic mainstays of the coastal area, which is not as prosperous as most of the rest of the state. The two counties in the northwest corner of the state — Clatsop and Columbia — also have some fruit orchards and logging activity.

Those two counties are the most Democratic in Oregon. Columbia has voted for every Democratic presidential candidate since 1932. Neighboring Clatsop was one of the few Oregon counties to back Adlai Stevenson in 1956. It has not left the Democratic column since.

In recent years, Republicans have made some inroads in the area, particularly in the southern coastal counties. Coos County, the region's largest county, has a Democratic tradition dating back to the New Deal era, but it went Republican for president in 1980 and supported Republican Senate and gubernatorial candidates in 1978.

Eastern and Southern Rural Oregon

Farms, forests, and cattle ranges make up the rest of Oregon. Covering more than 70 percent of the land, it has less than 25 percent of the voters, but they are the most conservative ones.

Directly south of the Willamette Valley, in the Klamath Mountains, are a few modest-sized cities scattered among the fruit orchards and forests. Medford is the largest city, with a population of 40,000 residents. Roseburg, Klamath Falls, Grants Pass and Ashland all have about 15,000 people.

Across the Cascade mountains to the east are only two towns with more than 10,000 people (Bend and Pendleton). The rest of the area's population live on farms in the irrigated Columbia River Valley to the north, or in the ranch land of the Great Basin in the wide-open, desert-like south end of the district.

This region is more typically "Western" than any other part of the state. Suspicion of "big government" and environmentalists has brought substantial Republican majorities in many elections. Mainstream Republicans such as Sen. Bob Packwood do well in the northernmost counties, along the Columbia, where the hilly wheat fields bring farmers a steady income.

Twenty years ago, support for public power development turned voters in the remote Wallowa Mountains toward the Democratic Party. But since then, an anti-government mood has taken over the area; Union County and Wallowa County, both of which supported Stevenson in 1956 and Kennedy in 1960, voted overwhelmingly against Carter and veteran Democratic Rep. Al Ullman in the 1980 election.

The most Republican county in the state is Malheur County, located in the southeastern corner. It is the only county in the state where the Republicans have a registration advantage.

OREGON AWARDED 5TH CONGRESSIONAL DISTRICT

More than a half-million people migrated to Oregon during the 1970s, earning the state its fifth seat in the House of Representatives, a distinction that barely eluded it a decade ago. In the 1971 reapportionment, Oregon fell just 235 shy of the number of people needed to jump from four to five representatives.

The Democratic-controlled state Legislature approved the new redistricting bill in late July 1981, keeping in mind the possibility that Republican Gov. Victor L. Atiyeh could veto any plan unfavorable to his party. The House voted 40-20 on July 27, 1981; the Senate concurred the following day, voting 19-10.

Instead of trying to undermine GOP strength through gerrymandering techniques, Democratic state legislators set the less ambitious but more practical goal of drawing a redistricting map to protect the state's three House Democrats.

To that end, the remap solidifies Republican Party control in the 2nd District in a way that aids 4th District Democrat James Weaver. The new 5th District in the Willamette Valley is taken mostly from the western part of the

New Oregon Districts

U. S. Congress: 5 districts
  Senate (2R)
  House (3D, 1R)
Governor:
  Victor L. Atiyeh (R)
Population: 2,632,663
Area: 96,981 sq. miles
1980 Presidential Vote:
  Carter (39%)
  Reagan (48%)
  Anderson (10%)

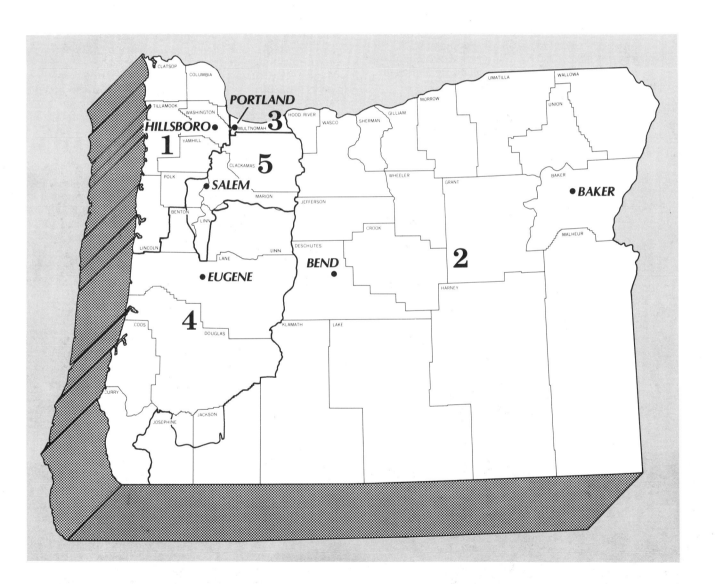

old 2nd, a technique that gives it a Republican tilt but minimizes tampering with neighboring Democratic districts.

The Democratic map was so kind to the Republican Party that it gave freshman Republican Denny Smith a good chance to win in either of two districts, his 2nd or the new 5th District. Smith has chosen to run in the 5th.

Atiyeh objected to the map because it divided Republican strength in Lake Oswego. But the governor signed the redistricting measure Aug. 22, 1981.

District 1

Western Portland and suburbs

Incumbent: Les AuCoin (D)

AuCoin's new district is much like the one that has elected him easily four times, but it has too many Republicans to allow him to feel very comfortable for very long. The new boundaries enhance the electoral influence of west Portland and adjoining Washington County suburbs, areas where the GOP gained strength in the last decade.

The Willamette River cuts through the city of Portland, separating the 1st and 3rd districts. Most of Portland's population lives east of the river, in the 3rd. West of the river, in AuCoin's territory, are the downtown business district and the city's ritzier residential sections.

Downtown Portland (Multnomah County) is the hub of a metropolitan area of more than 1.2 million people, the largest between Seattle and San Francisco. Decisions shaping Oregon and the Northwest are made by the banks, businesses and law firms headquartered here.

Many of the important decisionmakers live not far from their offices, in the fashionable West Hills area of the city. Much of this affluent professional community identifies with the Republican Party, but Democrats have considerable strength there and independent voters wield decisive influence. In 1980, independent presidential candidate John B. Anderson won nearly 14 percent of the vote in western Multnomah County, leaving Jimmy Carter and Ronald Reagan virtually tied.

As one moves west into Washington County, GOP power increases. Republicans outnumbered Democrats in the county last year for the first time. The county's population grew 55 percent during the 1970s as modest-sized bedroom communities such as Beaverton, Tigard and Hillsboro blossomed into economic satellites of Portland, with electronics and computer firms such as Hewlett-Packard, Intel and Tektronix providing jobs.

AuCoin fares considerably better in western Multnomah and Washington counties than do most other Democratic candidates. In 1980 he won 64 percent of the combined vote in those areas. AuCoin can be expected to pay even closer attention to Multnomah and Washington in the future; in his new, more compact district, nearly two of every three people live in one of those two counties.

Les AuCoin   **Ron Wyden**

Dropped from the 1st by redistricting are most of the people AuCoin has represented in Polk County and all his current territory in Benton County, including the city of Corvallis. Since both Polk and Benton gave AuCoin margins exceeding two-to-one in 1980, losing them in the remap hurts him somewhat.

The strongest Democratic areas of the district are along the Columbia River and Pacific coast in the fishing and logging counties of Columbia, Clatsop, Tillamook and Lincoln. Columbia has voted for every Democratic presidential candidate since 1932; Clatsop went for Adlai Stevenson in 1956 and has stayed Democratic since.

Astoria (Clatsop County), plagued by 20 percent unemployment, hopes to find economic salvation by improving its harbor facilities to handle large shipments of coal from Western states to new markets in Japan, Korea and Taiwan. With current economic conditions sharply curbing logging activities in the Siuslaw National Forest, the jobless rate in Tillamook County is above 20 percent.

The problems of the lumber industry in Tillamook are repeated throughout Oregon. High interest rates that discourage construction are lessening demand for lumber; nearly two-thirds of the 31,000 Oregonians in the lumber industry are unemployed or working curtailed hours.

Tourism props up the economy in some coastal areas, with towns such as Seaside, Cannon Beach, Lincoln City and Newport drawing visitors from Portland and other inland population centers.

Filling out the district are northern and western Polk County and Yamhill County, which are predominantly agricultural areas in the Willamette River Valley. Important crops grown and processed there are grass seed, hazelnuts and strawberries. AuCoin is popular in Yamhill and Polk, but voters prefer Republicans in other contests.

District 2

East and Southwest — Bend, Medford

No Incumbent

Eastern Oregon's "desert district" changed hands in 1980 for the first time in nearly a quarter-century, as Republican Denny Smith unseated veteran Democratic Rep. Al Ullman. But there will be no incumbent in the 2nd this election year, because Smith is running for re-election in the newly created 5th District. The 5th contains all the Willamette Valley areas in the western part of the old 2nd, including Smith's hometown of Salem.

After severing the Willamette Valley from the 2nd, the Legislature added Josephine and Jackson counties to the 2nd District's southwest corner. Because those two counties usually vote Republican, their addition to the 18 conservative counties of eastern Oregon gives the GOP an excellent chance to hold the 2nd despite Smith's departure.

There are more jackrabbits in the new 2nd than there are voters, so any congressional candidate has to focus his efforts on the few widely scattered population centers where the overwhelming majority of the district's people live.

In the southwest, Jackson County (Medford) and Josephine County (Grants Pass) together contain one-third of the people in the 2nd. Medford is surrounded by pear,

New Oregon Districts

New District	Incumbent	Population	1980 Pres. Winner
1	Les AuCoin (D)	526,840	Reagan
2	No Incumbent	526,968	Reagan
3	Ron Wyden (D)	526,715	Carter
4	James Weaver (D)	526,462	Reagan
5	Denny Smith (R)	526,120	Reagan

peach and apple orchards of the fruit-growing Rogue River Valley. The lumber industry also plays a prominent role in Medford, but the sawmills there are having as much difficulty surviving as those elsewhere in the state. With nearly 40,000 people, Medford is the district's largest city.

Lumbering is the main work in Grants Pass; also contributing to the economy are dairy cattle and visitors to the nearby Siskiyou National Forest. Reagan won Josephine County by a two-to-one margin in 1980.

A candidate working Jackson and Josephine counties would also schedule a stop in Klamath Falls, 75 miles east of Medford. Other than Medford and Grants Pass, it is the only sizable town in southwest Oregon. Though the lush forests become drier and thinner on the way east to Klamath Falls, lumbering is still important there. Fishermen are drawn to the Upper Klamath Lake, north of the town.

The fastest growing county in Oregon during the 1970s was Deschutes; the county's largest population center is Bend, a town of 17,263 in the west central part of the district. Population in Deschutes soared 104 percent during the decade as the majestic Three Sisters Wilderness Area and the Mount Bachelor Winter Sports Area lured people to build summer homes and vacation condominiums. Many of Deschutes' newcomers are young people.

Most of eastern Oregon is a sparsely populated plateau dusted with sagebrush and dry grasses. The only towns of any significance are Baker (Baker County), Burns (Harney County) and Ontario (Malheur County). All have fewer than 9,000 people.

Burns and Baker are isolated trading outposts for surrounding livestock rangelands, and are generally Republican. Some of the residents of Harney and Malheur counties are of Basque descent. Two-to-one GOP margins are typical there. Ontario has a transient population of fruit and vegetable pickers, many of them foreign born.

In the northern part of the 2nd, most people live along or near the irrigated Columbia River Valley, where wheat ripens on steep golden hillsides. The largest town in the area is Pendleton (Umatilla County), with nearly 15,000 people. Cattle and livestock are raised in the county, and Pendleton holds an annual rodeo. Like most of the counties in northern Oregon, Umatilla County is solidly Republican.

The population centers in the district's northwest corner are The Dalles and Hood River, both on the Colum-

bia River. Wheat and grass are grown around The Dalles; Hood River processes cherries and other fruits grown in the Hood River valley to the south. Carter won Wasco County (The Dalles) in 1976, but that was an aberration from the usual GOP allegiance.

District 3

Eastern Portland and suburbs

Incumbent: Ron Wyden (D)

Ninety percent of the people in the redrawn 3rd are residents of Multnomah County, Oregon's most populous county and a reliable provider of votes to Democratic candidates in congressional and most state elections.

The 3rd begins in Portland at the east bank of the Willamette River, the waterway that separates West Portland from the generally less elegant eastern part of the city.

Eastern Portland has a substantial population of working class people who labor in shipping trades. The city's freshwater port has been important since the mid-19th century, when it was the funnel through which pioneers poured south into the Willamette River Valley, the end of the Oregon Trail. Today Portland's port is a major departure point for Oregon's agricultural products. Other blue-collar workers in the 3rd are employed at factories producing chain saws, hoists and other logging equipment, fabricated metals and parts, clothing and wood products.

The communities of northern Portland, all part of the 3rd, have the strongest blue-collar presence. Three-fourths of Oregon's 37,059 blacks live in the city, many in the Albina section. Moving further east, away from the Willamette, light manufacturing operations give way to comfortable middle-income neighborhoods such as Parkrose, with a blend of business and professional people.

Portland's population declined nearly 4 percent in the last decade — a loss of more than 13,000 residents — but the overall population of Multnomah County was stabilized by rapid growth in suburbs east of the city, a few of which are as sumptuous as the in-town residential areas west of the Willamette. The largest of the suburban cities in the 3rd District is Gresham, which tripled in size during the 1970s, reaching a population of 33,005. Exceeding that growth rate was Troutdale, which lies north of Gresham.

Beyond suburbia, Multnomah's population quickly thins out. There are a few farms along the Columbia River, the northern boundary of the 3rd, but Mount Hood National Forest occupies most of the eastern part of the county.

The only changes made to the 3rd District by remapping are in the small Clackamas County portion of the district. The 3rd District loses some rural Clackamas territory and gains part of Lake Oswego, an upper-income bedroom community that tends to vote Republican. Remaining in the 3rd is Milwaukie, a Clackamas town east of Lake Oswego with a blue-collar population and warehousing facilities.

The political character of the 3rd will not be affected by the boundary changes in Clackamas, where only 10 percent of the district's people live. The Multnomah vote is still all-important, and Democrat Wyden shows no weakness there.

James Weaver   **Denny Smith**

District 4

Southwest — Eugene

Incumbent: James Weaver (D)

Redistricting does James Weaver an important favor by transferring most of Josephine and Jackson counties from the 4th District to the 2nd.

Those two counties gave the liberal Democrat cause for concern in the old 4th. He normally won Jackson County by a narrow margin — 52 percent in 1980, for example — but was fortunate to break even in conservative Josephine. His Republican opponent won 58 percent there in 1980, reducing Weaver's districtwide percentage to 55.

Under the remap, more than one-half of Weaver's constituents will live in Lane County (Eugene and Springfield). Lane has regularly given Weaver comfortable margins, although it is closely divided in local and presidential elections. The University of Oregon and the timber industry are the two most important factors in the economy of Eugene and Springfield, which lie on opposite banks of the Willamette River. Eugene has more than 105,000 people, Springfield less than half that.

The university, with 17,058 students and 1,509 faculty members, is located in Eugene and its influence there is easily noticed. Many of the young people who came to the school in the last 20 years stayed in Eugene after graduation, enthralled with the beauty of the Cascade Mountains to the east and the Coastal Range to the west. As those former students moved into workaday society, they learned how to influence local politics and coalesce to elect their own candidates. One of the 1982 Democratic gubernatorial candidates is a Lane County commissioner who won his seat with strong support from the Hoedads, a 500-member tree-planting cooperative.

The Hoedads and other liberal elements have had an interesting impact on Lane County elections. In Oregon's 1976 presidential primary, California Governor Edmund G. Brown Jr., D, won the county on a write-in vote. In 1980, Lane was the second-best county in the nation for Citizens Party presidential nominee Barry Commoner.

Matched against this environmentalist faction are the lumber industry, developers and some lumber millworkers who are concerned about growth and jobs. Unemployment is above 14 percent in Eugene and higher in timber-dominated Springfield, which is absorbing the shock of a Weyerhaeuser plant layoff that idled 1,400 workers.

This conflict prompts campaigns of remarkable intensity. Conservatives have been most effective in presidential elections: Richard M. Nixon carried Lane County in 1968 and 1972; Ronald Reagan won it in 1980. In contests for state and congressional offices, Democrats usually prevail.

Weaver's identification as a belligerent environmentalist and foe of nuclear power has not alienated enough Lane County residents to cause him any trouble there. In 1980, he won 62 percent of the Lane County vote.

Two other counties together make up nearly a third of the district's population — Douglas County (Roseburg) and Coos County (Coos Bay). With Josephine County out of the new 4th, Douglas County is Weaver's most significant conservative problem. It is a farming and sheep-raising area that gave him only 44 percent of its vote in 1980.

Coastal Coos County supports Weaver and occasionally other Democratic candidates; it went for Carter in 1976, but shifted to Reagan in 1980. Coos County has been crippled for two years with an unemployment rate exceeding 20 percent. The salmon fishermen of Coos Bay have been pummeled by high fuel costs and bad weather and are losing ground to huge corporate aquaculture facilities that produce higher salmon yields. The lumber situation is equally bad; in Coos Bay and other coastal towns alone, 32 mills have been closed, putting 5,000 workers out of work.

Redistricting makes some changes on the northern border of the 4th, but none is likely to affect election outcomes. All of western Benton County and part of northern Linn County are brought into the 4th, but the population centers in those counties are both in the new 5th.

District 5

Willamette Valley — Salem, Corvallis

Incumbent: Denny Smith (R)

The newly created 5th District is hardly the dream of a meticulous mapmaker. Created from parts of the 1st, 2nd and 4th districts, it does not contain an entire county, covering instead parts of five counties that lie on either side of the Willamette River as it runs south out of Portland.

Rep. Denny Smith pondered whether to seek re-election in the redrawn 2nd District, which is the most conservative Oregon district and contains much of the territory he currently represents, or to run in the 5th District, which does not match his views quite as closely but includes his home base of Salem and about half the people in his current constituency.

Several Republican politicians with bases in the Willamette Valley area waited to see which district Denny Smith would pick; when he decided on the 5th District, other Republican hopefuls dropped their ambitions for the 1982 election, and he is unopposed for his party's nomination.

Nearly all of Marion County (Salem) is included in the 5th. Against the veteran Ullman in 1980, Smith managed to win Marion County narrowly. Since Smith will not be fighting an entrenched incumbent this year, he expects to broaden his advantage in Marion, which contains 39 percent of the district's population.

Salem is the capital of the state, so a substantial number of the residents are on the state payroll. Another revenue producer is the processing and canning of fruits, berries and vegetables grown in Oregon's fertile river valley.

Clackamas County, with 36 percent of the new district's population, has nearly as much clout in the 5th as Marion does. Clackamas County grew at a rate of approximately 46 percent in the last decade, thanks partly to expansion of Portland suburbs into the northwest section of the county.

One of the most affluent of those suburbs is Lake Oswego, part of which is in the new 3rd District. Democrats have a considerable edge over Republicans among registered voters in Clackamas County, but some who label themselves Democrats frequently cross party lines to elect Republicans.

The other major city in the district is Corvallis (Benton County), home of Oregon State University (16,666 students). Although Benton County votes Republican in most races, Smith may have some trouble in Corvallis; that city was part of Democrat AuCoin's 1st District during the 1970s and AuCoin always ran well there.

The redrawn 5th District includes the western portion of Linn County as well as southeastern Polk County.

Utah

In Utah, church and state share the same symbol, which says a lot about Utah. The Church of Jesus Christ of Latter-Day Saints (LDS) founded the state and still imposes its values on everyday life.

The values are conservative ones. The church-state symbol is the beehive, a testament to the reverence Mormons have for the industriousness of the free enterprise system. The LDS influence prevents Utah bars and restaurants from serving liquor by the drink. When Rep. Allan T. Howe was convicted in 1976 of soliciting sex from a policewoman posing as a decoy, the voters decisively turned him out of office. As late as 1978, blacks were prohibited from the Mormon priesthood. Utah is the only state that still executes convicted murderers by firing squad — which was the way Gary Gilmore was put to death in 1977.

Like most of the Mountain States, Utah went through a period of flirtation with Democrats and the New Deal in the 1930s, and as late as 1948 it chose Harry S Truman in a closely contested presidential election. But Utah began its reaction against the national Democratic Party soon after that, and the reaction has been thorough. In 1980, Jimmy Carter drew an absurdly low 21 percent of the Utah vote — less than George McGovern had drawn eight years earlier. At this point, it is hard to imagine any Democratic candidate capable of winning the party's presidential nomination who would also have any chance to carry Utah in the fall of 1982.

Democrats, even one or two liberal ones, continued to win congressional elections in the state through the 1970s. But by 1980, Utah had thrown out the last one, Rep. Gunn McKay, who often voted with Republicans in Washington but was unable to persuade voters at home that he was sufficiently skeptical about the role of the federal government. Democratic Sen. Frank Moss worked hard to win a fourth term in 1976, waging well-publicized campaigns against smoking and alcohol, but he was swept out of office by a little-known, late-starting Republican, Orrin G. Hatch. Today, the all-Republican team of Sens. Hatch and Jake Garn, and Reps. Dan Marriott and James V. Hansen may constitute the most conservative delegation in Congress.

In state politics, however, it is a different story. Democrats have held the governorship for 16 years, first behind conservative Calvin L. Rampton, and since 1977 with Scott Matheson, who is more liberal but who has waged popular fights with Washington over nerve gas and the MX missile.

Utah's religious history inspires a distrust of the federal government that runs even deeper than the "Sagebrush Rebellion" taking root in all of the Mountain States.

From 1847 when the Mormons arrived in Utah, to 1896 when the state finally gained admittance to the Union, the federal government harassed the Mormon Church over its practice of polygamy, which had to be abandoned before statehood could be conferred. Even the state name was chosen by the federal government over "Deseret," the Mormon name.

Those experiences are not public issues anymore, but they are imbedded in Utah values. And while the church does not exercise any overt control of the political process, it remains a potent presence. Many office-holders are LDS officials as well.

Salt Lake County

Most of the people in the state live along a narrow fertile strip at the foot of the mountainous Wasatch Range. This strip, linked by Interstate 15, is centered on Salt Lake City to the east of the Great Salt Lake and stretches south to Provo and north to Ogden. The rest of the state consists of sparsely populated mountains and deserts.

Salt Lake City was where the great cross-land migration of the Mormons ended in 1847, after they had been driven out of the East by the persecution of non-believers. Mormon leader Brigham Young, the successor of founding prophet Joseph Smith, chose the site in part because its saline lake reminded him of the Dead Sea of Palestine. Over the years, the "Saints" irrigated the arid land, constructed a magnificent Temple and laid out boulevards wide enough to turn a span of oxen.

The capital of both church and state, Salt Lake City contains enough Democratic blue-collar workers and liberal young professionals to give the more dominant suburban Republicans an occasional challenge. For governor, Salt Lake County as a whole favored Matheson in both 1976 and 1980. Both those years, however, it went against Jimmy Carter.

The city itself leans Democratic. The working-class West Side, home of the area's copper miners, votes with the Democrats, as does the central city section. In the northern hills, called The Avenues, professionals in their 20's and 30's often vote Democratic, too. But in the wealthy

Wasatch foothills section called the East Bench, Republicans hold sway.

More people live in the Salt Lake suburbs than in the city itself. Voters in such suburban communities as Cottonwood and Murray habitually opt for the GOP. But there are exceptions such as Sandy City, which Democrats sometimes capture.

With 42 percent of the state's population, Salt Lake County dominates Utah politically.

The Ogden Orbit

The Democratic strong-hold in Utah is north of Salt Lake City in the railroad center of Ogden in Weber County. Originally a rough-and-ready trapping outpost in the early 19th century, Ogden was taken over by the Mormons in the middle part of the century. But the arrival of the railroad brought another influx of "Gentiles" — that is, non-Mormons. In 1869 at Promontory, north of Ogden, the Central and Union Pacific railroads were joined with the driving of a golden spike, and thus the nation's first transcontinental rail link was created.

Today, Ogden lives under the same strong Mormon influence seen elsewhere in the state. The clean-cut singing duo, Donny and Marie Osmond, were born there. Still, the city has a high number of "Jack Mormons" — those who have wandered from the church's teachings.

Weber's Democratic affiliation stems from its large blue-collar employment and union membership, a legacy of the railroad era. The county also has a sizable number of federal employees who work at Hill Air Force Base and other defense installations in the area. In both their losing efforts, Moss in 1976 and McKay in 1980 built up decent pluralities in Weber County. Carter, however, lost Weber both times he ran.

Rapidly developing Davis County sits in the corridor between Ogden and Salt Lake City. It is a politically polarized county. Its northern part, around Clearfield and Sunset, follows the lead of nearby Weber County and votes Democratic. In southern Davis County, towns such as Bountiful are part of suburban Salt Lake and vote Republican.

This partisan balance is reflected in the 1980 vote for governor. While Democrat Matheson won Weber County by more than 10,000 votes, he squeaked through in Davis County with a mere 242-vote edge.

Provo

If an undiluted bastion of Mormonism exists in the state, Provo and surrounding Utah County is it. That is in large part because Provo is the home of Brigham Young University (BYU), established in 1875 to prepare LDS youth for school teaching and religious proselytizing. Current-day Mormons still ready themselves for missionary work at the university and at a special church-run facility in Provo.

With few Jack Mormons and only a small blue-collar vote, the Brigham Young influence makes Utah County predictably Republican. Over the past two decades, its sole defection to the Democrats on the presidential level came when Barry Goldwater was the Republican Party nominee in 1964.

The northern section of the county contains Lehigh and American Forks — pockets of blue-collar workers employed at the Geneva Steelworks plant. Nevertheless, they tend to have strong Mormon beliefs and cannot be counted on as a solid Democratic bloc.

Desert and South

Only a quarter of the state's residents live outside the Ogden/Salt Lake/Provo strip. But the influence of the hinterlands may grow as the rugged desert and mountains of western and southern Utah experience an energy boom and accompanying growth.

The most consistent Democratic counties in the state are Carbon and Emery, where coal mining has taken off. They are the only Utah counties that Carter won in 1976. This is a mostly non-Mormon area, with many ethnic residents of Greek, Italian and Mexican extraction.

In Millard County, the Inter-Mountain Power Project is under construction. This huge coal-fired generating facility will furnish electricity to cities as distant as Los Angeles. Millard was the lone Utah county that Carter carried in 1980.

The GOP stronghold in the rural areas is verdant Washington County in the southwest corner, where Brigham Young once dispatched church members to grow cotton. Its population doubled in the 1970s as retirees and the wintering wealthy found its semitropical climate attractive.

Juab County, in the central-western section, has tar sands, and Uintah County, in the northeast, has oil shale. Both await expansion.

The biggest boom for the entire rural region could be touched off by the massive MX missile complex, which the Pentagon would like to build there. But this system would take up vast amounts of terrain, use large quantities of scarce water and bring in hordes of outsiders. The Mormon Church and most Utah politicians oppose the MX, despite their hard-line defense views.

NEW REPUBLICAN DISTRICT CREATED

Utah's population grew 37.9 percent over the last decade, giving the state a third House seat, and the GOP-dominated Legislature saw to it that Republicans have a strong chance of winning all three districts in 1982.

Democratic Gov. Scott M. Matheson decided not to veto the redistricting bill that was sent to him Oct. 30, 1981. He said he thought the measure would stand up to legal challenges, so he allowed it to become law Nov. 11, 1981, without his signature. Republicans had enough votes to override a veto anyway. The vote on passage was 50-21 in the state House and 20-8 in the state Senate.

Gov. Matheson had tried to prevent Republicans from drawing a partisan map by appointing a citizens' panel to devise an "objective" plan. The panel favored creating two solidly Republican districts but keeping a substantial Democratic vote in GOP Rep. Dan Marriott's Salt Lake City-based 2nd District.

The Legislature accepted the outlines of the commission proposal but helped Marriott by moving Democrats from his district into the new 3rd.

To create the 3rd, the Legislature attached the Democratic southwestern part of Salt Lake County to staunchly Republican Utah County (Provo). The 3rd was fleshed out with lightly populated counties in the eastern part of the state. Its Republican leanings seem secure.

New
Utah
Districts

U. S. Congress: 3 districts
  Senate (2R); House (2R)
Governor: Scott M. Matheson (D)
Population: 1,461,037
Area: 84,916 sq. miles
1980 Presidential Vote:
  Carter (21%)
  Reagan (73%)
  Anderson (5%)

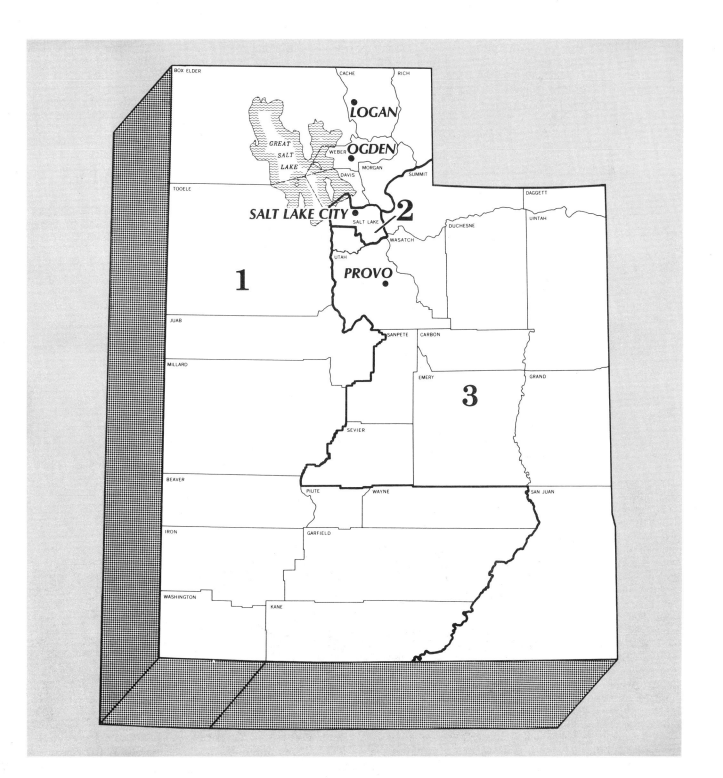

Freshman Republican Rep. James V. Hansen's 1st District will still be centered in Davis and Weber counties. But it now has Republican rural territory in the state's western half, which will help nullify Democratic strength in Weber County.

Republican legislators from rural southern Utah were distressed by the fact that the metropolitan areas along the Wasatch Range near Salt Lake City will dominate all the districts politically. Several of the rural Republicans joined the minority Democratic legislators in voting against the plan.

Conservative, Mormon Utah has become a bastion of Republicanism. The last time it went Democratic for president was in 1948. In 1980, Jimmy Carter scored an embarrassingly low 21 percent of the vote there. Democrats continued to win House elections into the 1970s, but the last Democratic congressman, Gunn McKay, was ousted in 1980.

District 1

Ogden and rural Utah

Incumbent: James V. Hansen (R)

The railroad center of Ogden and surrounding Weber County comprise Utah's Democratic core. It was at Promontory, just north of Ogden, that the golden spike was driven in 1869 that created the nation's first transcontinental rail link. The Church of Jesus Christ of Latter-Day Saints (Mormon Church) is an important influence in Weber County, as everywhere in Utah, but the railroads brought a higher number of non-Mormons than in other parts of the state.

Weber's Democrats are largely blue-collar workers and union members, a legacy of the railroad era. The county also has a sizable number of federal employees who work at Hill Air Force Base and nearby defense installations. In both their losing efforts, Democratic Sen. Frank Moss in 1976 and McKay in 1980 ran up good pluralities in Weber. But the county is no longer Democratic on the national level. It has not supported a Democratic candidate for president since 1964.

Rapidly developing Davis County, also in the 1st District, sits in the corridor between Ogden and Salt Lake City. It is a politically polarized county in which Republicans have the edge. Its northern part, around Clearfield and Sunset, follows the lead of adjacent Weber and votes Democratic in many contests. In southern Davis, towns such as Bountiful are part of suburban Salt Lake and vote Republican.

The 1980 vote for governor reflects the difference between Weber and Davis counties. Democrat Matheson won Weber by more than 10,000 votes, while edging his opponent in Davis by a mere 242 votes.

The rural remainder of the district has an almost uniformly Republican coloration. An exception is Millard County, which has an influx of blue-collar workers at the Inter-Mountain Power Project. But they are too few to make a difference.

A major issue in this part of the state has been the proposed mobile basing mode for the MX missile. Much of the project would have been built in the Great Salt Lake Desert in Tooele County. But opposition to the project — a concern that extended to other parts of Utah as well — has quieted down now that Reagan apparently has scrapped the original race track idea.

Washington County, in the southwest corner of Utah, has a devout Republican loyalty. Its population doubled during the 1970s as senior citizens and affluent outsiders looking for winter homes found its semitropical climate attractive. But it is not a major population center; Washington has one-sixth the population of Weber County.

In 1980, Hansen defeated McKay by using Davis County, Republican Utah County (Provo) and a tide of rural votes to offset the Democrat's strength in Weber. Hansen, who had been Speaker of the Utah House, comes from Davis, and that added to the Republican total there.

Redistricting removes Utah County from the 1st, denying Hansen an important source of strength and a counterbalance to the Weber County vote. His 1980 plurality of 13,000 votes in Utah County almost exactly matched his overall winning margin. But now that he is in office, Hansen is likely to find Davis and the combined rural vote sufficient for re-election. He gets a different set of rural counties, losing the ones in the eastern part of the state and gaining ones in the west. But both sets are Republican, so the partisan impact will be minor.

So far, no major Democratic opponents for Hansen have emerged. McKay likely will not seek a rematch. After his defeat, he accepted a three-year stint as the Mormon mission president in Scotland.

District 2

Salt Lake City

Incumbent: Dan Marriott (R)

In order to concentrate Marriott's district entirely within Salt Lake County, which contains more than 42 percent of the state's population, the state Legislature lopped off the 2nd District's rural counties and gave them to the 1st District. Those were dependable Republican votes for GOP Rep. Marriott, so the move threatened to weaken him politically. But it was neutralized by a

Dan Marriott   **James V. Hansen**

New Utah Districts

New District	Incumbent	Population	1980 Pres. Winner
1	James V. Hansen (R)	487,833	Reagan
2	Dan Marriott (R)	487,475	Reagan
3	No Incumbent	485,729	Reagan

second change, dropping the Democratic southwestern portion of Salt Lake County and sending it to the new 3rd District.

The 2nd District has had a variety of shapes over the last few decades, but its linchpin always has been Salt Lake City, the governmental, commercial, cultural and spiritual capital of the state. Salt Lake City is the world headquarters of the Church of the Latter Day Saints, and it exerts great political force there. Disapproving Mormon voters tossed out Democratic Rep. Allan T. Howe in 1976 after he was convicted of soliciting sex from a policewoman posing as a prostitute.

The city harbors enough Democratic blue-collar workers and liberal young professionals to lean Democratic in many elections and to give the dominant suburban Republicans an occasional challenge countywide. The portion of Salt Lake County in the new 2nd District, which includes all of the city proper, favored Democratic Gov. Scott M. Matheson in the 1976 and 1980 gubernatorial elections. But in both those election years, the same area went heavily against Democratic President Jimmy Carter and for GOP Rep. Dan Marriott.

Salt Lake City's working-class West Side, the traditional home for many of the people who work in the area copper mines, generally votes Democratic, as does the central city section. In the northern hills, called The Avenues, young professionals in their 20's and 30's often vote the Democratic ticket as well. But in the wealthy Wasatch foothills section, called the East Bench, the Republican Party is the dominant one. More people live in the Salt Lake suburbs than in the city itself. Voters in such suburban communities as Cottonwood and Murray habitually opt for the GOP.

Rep. Dan Marriott, who defeated Allan T. Howe in the 1976 election by 52-48 percent, has lifted his performance up to the safe level since then. He crushed the Democratic

Party candidate in 1980 by more than 2 to 1. The new redistricting map gives Marriott a less populous but equally favorable constituency.

District 3

Provo and rural Utah

No incumbent

Provo and surrounding Utah County are home to the most intense Mormon community in the state. That is in large part because Provo is the location of Brigham Young University, founded in 1875 to prepare Mormon youth for teaching and religious proselytizing.

This influence makes Utah County overwhelmingly Republican. Over the past two decades, its sole defection to the Democrats on the presidential level came when Barry Goldwater was the GOP nominee in 1964. Goldwater came within about 3,000 votes of taking the county.

The northern section of the county contains Lehigh and American Forks — towns whose blue-collar workers are employed at the Geneva Steelworks plant. Even in these communities, however, Mormon values are crucial and Democrats cannot count on a heavy vote.

Democrats do predominate in the southwest part of Salt Lake County, moved into this district from the 2nd to help Marriott. Howe, whom Marriott ousted in 1976, always ran well there. Many of the residents, living in towns such as South Jordan and West Valley City, work in the Kennecott copper pit in Kearns. But these voters differ little from those elsewhere in the district when it comes to national elections. The 3rd District part of Salt Lake County voted for Reagan by 2-1.

The rest of the 3rd is rural and sparsely populated. Much of it is mountains and desert. Cattle ranching and mining are leading industries and Republicans dominate.

Democrats, though, are strong in Carbon and Emery counties, where coal mining has taken off. Carter carried both counties in 1976, the only counties in the state he won. In 1980, as he was being humiliated statewide, he still came within three votes of carrying Carbon.

This is a mostly non-Mormon area, with many residents of Greek, Italian and Mexican descent who came to work in the mines. Uintah County harbors large deposits of oil shale, yet little growth has occurred there so far.

Name Index

DATE DUE